KU-101-449

Slaves and Highlanders
Silenced Histories of Scotland and the Caribbean

David Alston

EDINBURGH
University Press

This book is dedicated
to all those
from beyond our boundaries
whose voices give us the gift
'to see ourselves as others see us'

Edinburgh University Press is one of the leading university presses in the UK. We publish academic books and journals in our selected subject areas across the humanities and social sciences, combining cutting-edge scholarship with high editorial and production values to produce academic works of lasting importance. For more information visit our website: edinburghuniversitypress.com

© David Alston, 2021

Edinburgh University Press Ltd
The Tun – Holyrood Road
12 (2f) Jackson's Entry
Edinburgh EH8 8PJ

Typeset in 10.5/13pt Sabon by
Servis Filmsetting Ltd, Stockport, Cheshire
and printed and bound in Great Britain

A CIP record for this book is available from the British Library

ISBN 978 1 4744 2730 2 (hardback)
ISBN 978 1 4744 2731 9 (paperback)
ISBN 978 1 4744 2732 6 (webready PDF)
ISBN 978 1 4744 2733 3 (epub)

The right of David Alston to be identified as author of this work has been asserted in accordance with the Copyright, Designs and Patents Act 1988 and the Copyright and Related Rights Regulations 2003 (SI No. 2498).

Contents

Figures, Tables and Maps

To ensure an appropriate focus, all illustrations in this book include people of African descent.

FIGURES

TABLES

MAPS

Standard Abbreviations

BL	British Library
GROS	General Register Office for Scotland
HCA	Highland Council Archives
ICS	Institute of Commonwealth Studies
LRO	Liverpool Record Office
NAG	National Archives of Guyana
NLS	National Library of Scotland
NPG	National Portrait Gallery
NRAS	National Register of Archives of Scotland
ODNB	*Oxford Dictionary of National Biography*
SNPG	Scottish National Portrait Gallery
SOAS	School of African and Oriental Studies
TNA	The National Archives

Acknowledgements

More than twenty years of research on this topic has left me with debts of gratitude to more people than I can mention – and, indeed, to more than I can remember. Many of these are individuals who have freely shared their research with me – as I have done through my website 'Slaves & Highlanders'. The opportunities for such cooperation make this an exciting time in the study of history.

I am particularly thankful to those institutions which have digitised records and made them available free online. In this regard the National Archives of the Netherlands is outstanding, especially in their joint work with the National Archives of Guyana. I also acknowledge the assistance I have received from the staff of our own institutions across the UK, including the UK National Archives at Kew, the National Records of Scotland in Edinburgh and the Highland Archive Centre, among others. I believe it is a matter of justice that our nations in the UK do much more to make these records freely available in digitised form to the peoples of the Caribbean islands and Guyana, whose histories are in part recorded there.

I am also indebted to the holders of private archives who have made their records available, with a special thank you to Kathy and Malcolm Fraser at Reelig.

In February 2020 the companionship of my friend and colleague Michael Hopcroft made possible a trip to Suriname and Guyana, with Michael driving us from Paramaribo to Georgetown and back. It enabled me to visit the other Cromarty – in Berbice – and the many other villages in Guyana which share a name with this part of northern Scotland. To have stood on the ground of these plantations which I have studied for two decades was an important and emotional experience.

And, finally, thanks as ever to Caroline for her support.

David Alston, Cromarty
November 2020

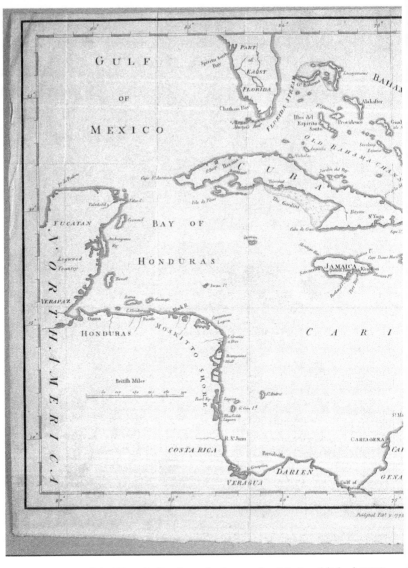

Map 1 'A map of the West Indies from the best authorities', published 1799.

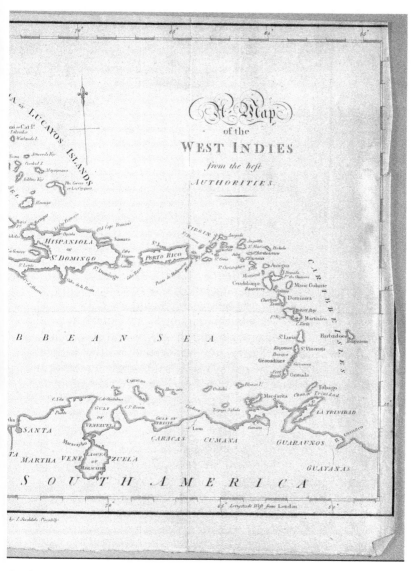

A Map of the
WEST INDIES
from the best
AUTHORITIES.

© John Carter Brown Library, Providence, RI.

Foreword

'Like a web / is spun the pattern / all are involved!'

Martin Carter

In March 2019, the Lord Provost of Aberdeen signed a twinning agreement between the cities of Aberdeen in Scotland and Georgetown in Guyana. It followed ongoing work between Aberdeen University, Edinburgh Heriot-Watt University and the University of Guyana to establish an oil and gas faculty in the latter country. From the perspective of the general public in Guyana, the twinning was a somewhat random but welcome development. Some may have, with further thought, reflected on commonplace Guyanese surnames like Ross, Fraser, MacPherson, Gordon, Munro and McWatt; the 'curiously' named St Andrew's Kirk in the capital, Georgetown, or on the plethora of Scottish-sounding place names like Kildonan, Cromarty, Dunrobin, Kiltearn, Inverness or Fyrish, all of which point to a connection of some significance to Scotland. It is the little-known and rarely acknowledged historical links between Scotland, Guyana and other Caribbean territories that form the core of David Alston's illuminating research into *Slaves and Highlanders*.

As the co-founders of Guyana SPEAKS, a monthly community initiative established in 2017 to 'educate, entertain and inspire' UK-based diasporans, we had hoped to find a speaker to address the theme: 'An Historical Glance at the British in Guiana'. On 16 April 2019 we coincidentally read Yvonne Singh's, 'How Scotland Erased Guyana from its Past' (*The Guardian*) and were struck by the words of a man she had met in Cromarty:

Guyana offered some the prospect of making a fortune, even for
those of limited means, if they were prepared to start work as clerks,
overseers and tradesmen. The key to success was to own slaves.

We contacted that man, David Alston, and immediately received
an enthusiastic response. On 28 April 2019 he shared his
research to a rapt Guyana SPEAKS audience. His presentation
was so inspiring we too decided to make a trip to the Highland
town of Cromarty. We stayed in a local hotel and were treated
by David to a guided historical tour of both Cromarty and
Inverness. Both of us have a keen interest in the history of the
Caribbean, Juanita having previously taught Caribbean Studies
at the London Metropolitan University, and Rod having set up
and conducted Black Legacy walks in the city of London and
Westminster. We had not anticipated how impactful it would be
to walk around an area that appeared connected, with virtually
every step, to Demerara and Berbice. Still standing were homes
of slave-holders like William Fraser and Aeneas Barkly, and a
factory building that had once employed over 250 people (and
over 600 outworkers) to produce hemp cloth for bagging cotton
in the West Indies. David's tour included tales of local fishermen
who had caught and processed salt herring as a much-needed
protein for Africans who had been forced into slavery.

At Cromarty harbour, David pointed to two standard-looking
mooring posts that, dating back to the 1830s, had been made
from Guyana's much-prized greenheart timber. As a metaphor
for the far-reaching extent of tangible and intangible intercon-
nectedness of Cromarty with the rich coastlands of Guyana,
nothing had been more powerful. The tired wood was totally
unremarkable and easily overlooked. Yet there it stood: profound evidence that while the gross brutalisation of an enslaved
workforce had taken place thousands of miles away and conveniently out of view, local Highlanders would nevertheless have
been fully aware of the importance of Demerara and Berbice to
their lives. It was not just a case of sugar, cotton, coffee or
tobacco: 'Guyana' had penetrated the Scottish Highlands in just
about every way imaginable.

We wondered why David had not written a book. Nobody else
had been able to demonstrate the extent to which the Northern
Scots had benefited from its long, historical connection to the
Americas. As the regular sharer of new and exciting research,

David became a great and valued friend of Guyana SPEAKS. His updates have led to the programming of other well-received events including one on Doll Thomas, the Queen of Demerara (31 May 2020) and another on the life and legacy of Andrew Watson, a man of Scots-Guyanese heritage, who is today recognised as the world's first black international footballer (8 March 2021). When David did eventually announce he was writing a book, we could not have been more delighted.

David's encyclopaedic knowledge of 'Demerara and Berbice' – the outcome of over twenty years of dedicated research, has long been shared with the general public and scholars via his 400-page website (also called Slaves and Highlanders). Scholars and historians like Douglas Hamilton, Gaiutra Bahadur, Tony Talburt, Kit Candlin and Cassandra Pybus, Bram Hoonhout and Llew Walker all acknowledge the importance of his invaluable research and its influence on their work. By anyone's estimation David's knowledge is unparalleled. Our only reservation about his plans to write *Slaves and Highlanders* was that he had never been to Guyana. We need not have worried. In early 2020 he emailed to say he was conscious of the need to experience the landscape of Demerara and Berbice for himself. He made the trip in February 2020, just over a month prior to the Covid-19 lockdown.

As David explains in Chapter 1, Scottish historiography has, with few notable exceptions, been characterised by a 'catalogue of silences' on the involvement of the Scottish in plantation slavery and so, too, on the profits that were made from it. The hitherto reluctance of the Scottish to face this uncomfortable aspect of their national history is, in some respects, understandable. Recent events, the Black Lives Matter campaigns, the toppling of the statue of the Bristol slave trader Edward Colston, as well as calls within universities to 'decolonise the academy', are nevertheless underscoring the need for Scotland to engage in a national conversation on its involvement in the trans-Atlantic slave trade and plantation slavery. *Slaves and Highlanders* could not be more crucial or timely.

David's revulsion for the many atrocities that took place in Guyana during slavery is more than apparent. He once asked us: 'Were you aware that as punishment for rebelling, the captured slaves had their heads sawn off with [sugar] cane knives, screwed onto sharpened poles and displayed for all to see?' His look of incredulity – but for evidence to the contrary – said all.

The discomfort, or rather horror, of recognising how central terror had been to the functioning of large plantations would, he later remarked, never leave him. His research objectives, however, are not about shaming Scotland. They are, to us, about creating an awareness of the role Scottish Highlanders played in the system of plantation slavery; of highlighting the extent to which profits made had permeated Highland society whilst also bringing to the fore previously hidden stories of enslaved (and free people) of both African and mixed Scottish-African descent where/whenever, possible. It is about hearing voices that have stood for too long in silence.

Slaves and Highlanders relates a complex, entangled and nuanced history in a fact-driven yet eminently readable and accessible way. The opening scene may lead off-guard readers to believe he is writing about an event taking place in modern-day Britain and cleverly prompts reflection in the reader's mind not only on how much has changed but also on how familiar the narrative feels. The 1818 setting paves the way for untold stories of a black presence in Scotland: stories of loyal black servants and of those who abscond; stories of the 'mixed-race' offspring of Scottish slave-owners and enslaved women who, on being born free or manumitted, were sent to Scotland for their education; stories of transience and disappearances.

David's approach is to zoom in on particular aspects of this entangled history and illustrate how, to quote the Guyanese poet, Martin Carter, 'all are involved'. His exploration of the slave trade, for instance, introduces us to a wide range of characters: James Fraser, a captain of slave ships; Evan Baillie of Dochfour, a slave trader; George Baillie, a slave factor; William Mackenzie & Co., slave auctioneers; Donald Mackay, a slave auctioneer's clerk; Thomas Staunton St Clair, a soldier garrisoned in Berbice and Demerara; and Inverness, an African whose repeated attempts at escape point to a man determined to reclaim his freedom. David exposes 'honourable gentlemen', like Evan Baillie, whose involvement in the slave trade remained, even in death, conveniently undisclosed. He also portrays various ways in which people from different strata of society (including those impacted by Highland clearances) became complicit in the slave trade and/or slavery.

But this is a book devoid of single one-direction narratives. We thus find, in the chapter on Jamaica, Zachary Macaulay, a plantation bookkeeper so disturbed by the horrors of slavery that he returns to Scotland. He later becomes an associate of William Wilberforce and a leading figure in the parliamentary campaign for the abolition of slavery. We hear too of the failure and misfortune of Scottish individuals, young chancers who faced the possibility of premature death at sea or in fever-ridden climates. Yet the magnitude of human suffering in the regimes of chattel slavery is never forgotten: nor, too, the stolen identities of enslaved Africans or the voices of its victims.

The impossibility of being proud of the achievements of past generations while failing to acknowledge or atone for the wrongs that continue to haunt the present, are openly pointed to by David. It is this awareness, his commitment to truth and keen sense of fairness that make him the respected, best-qualified author of this groundbreaking book.

Juanita Cox-Westmaas and Rod Westmaas
Co-Founders: Guyana SPEAKS
Twitter: JCWestmaas
Email: guyanaspeaks@gmail.com

1

Jumbies

Only a few minutes' walk from my home in the small community of Cromarty in the Scottish Highlands, a seventeen-year-old black student was stabbed during a brawl outside the local school. A recent immigrant from the Caribbean, he had been shunned by other students and often carried a knife, which he had previously brandished in confrontations with older boys. This time his opponent – who was younger and claimed to have been hit first – retaliated, drew his own knife, jinked to one side and stabbed the black teenager in the thigh.

Both boys were from troubled backgrounds. The black student was probably an illegitimate child sent to Scotland for education, with no close family around him in a strange country. His white assailant, at the age of five, had lost his father in an accident at sea, the family had struggled financially, his two sisters had died, and now he was reacting badly to his mother's recent remarriage. The school turned a blind eye to this incident but the white student was expelled shortly afterwards for an assault on a member of staff.

Although you will probably be aware of similar attacks in other parts of the UK, you may be surprised that this could happen in a small Highland community. I know you will not have seen it reported in the media. It happened two hundred years ago, in 1818.[1] The white student was sixteen-year-old Hugh Miller, who after being thrown out of school started work as an apprentice stonemason but went on to be a leading figure in Scottish public life as a journalist, geologist, writer and churchman. As editor of the *Witness* newspaper he was to the fore in the campaign for the right of congregations to

choose their own ministers, without interference from either
landowners or the state, a movement which led to the creation in 1843 of the breakaway Free Church of Scotland. By the
mid-1800s Miller had become something of a national hero as
a champion of the rights of 'the people in the pews' against the
dead hand of the authorities controlling the established church.

But who was the unnamed black student? Why was he in the
Highlands in 1818? Were there others like him? And what had
been the connections between the West Indies and Cromarty,
then a small, thriving Highland town of two thousand people?
These questions of local history, which I began to ask in the
late 1990s, led me to challenge the story that Scotland was
confidently telling itself about its involvement – or lack of
involvement – in the sordid business of slavery and the brutal
regimes of slave-worked plantations in the Caribbean.

I have never been able to name with certainty that young black
man who steps from the shadows of anonymity only through
the prejudicial words of the victorious Hugh Miller: 'There was
a mulatto lad, a native of the West Indies . . . older and stouter
than I . . . much dreaded by the other boys for a wild, savage
disposition which is, I believe, natural to most of his country-
folks.' But there were clues to the town's connections to the
Caribbean, clues which I will describe in some detail because I
want to illustrate how good local studies can inform and challenge the national narrative. They led me to the questions: Was
Cromarty's degree of involvement in the slave plantations of the
West Indies particular to this town? Or was it a wider aspect of
Highland, and Scottish, history?

By the late 1820s Miller's hand, which had held the knife,
wielded a stonemason's chisel – but he also held a pen. His lungs
had been damaged by stone dust and he had left off labouring
in quarries for the less demanding but skilled trade of carving
gravestones. Two of his elegant inscriptions referred to the West
Indies. One stone in Cromarty was erected by 'JOHN MUNRO
ESQ late of Demerara' to the memory of his father, who died in
1825; the other was a memorial to 'DANIEL ROSS of Berbice',
who died in 1827. I had heard of Demerara, on the north coast
of South America, but not of neighbouring Berbice, both now
part of Guyana. Daniel Ross, it turned out, was a relative of
Miller, an older, distant cousin by marriage who had entranced
the teenager with accounts of life in this colony.

[His] graphic descriptions of that part of South America made a strong impression on me when a boy, and still dwells in my memory. He was settled on a cotton plantation near the coast side; and so exceedingly flat was the surrounding country, that the house in which he dwelt, thought nearly two miles distant from the shore, stood little more than five feet above its level. The soil consisted of a dark gray consolidated mud; and in looking seawards from the land, there was nothing to be seen, when the tide fell, save dreary mud flats whole miles in extent, with the line of blue water beyond stretching along the distant horizon ... my cousin, a keen sportsman in his day, has told me that he used to steal upon them in his mud shoes, – flat boards attached to the soles, like the snow shoes of higher latitudes, – and enjoy rare sport in knocking down magnificent game, such as 'the roseate spoonbill' and 'gorgeous flamingo'.[2]

Later, when Miller as a geologist explored the Caithness flagstones, these Berbice mud flats provided his image of how the strata had been laid down. Daniel also told him of an adventure 'boarding ... under cover of a well sustained discharge of musketry, the vessel of an enemy that had been stranded on the shores of Berbice'. He was also, I guess, the butt of a practical joke played by 'a South American Indian, on the banks of the Demerara [who] dropped, unseen, into the pocket of my light nankeen jacket a piece of sun-baked alligator's dung' – which Daniel (if it was he) mistook for snuff.[3]

As for the other gravestone, I would later discover, thanks to new methods of research made possible by online searches of digitised material, that John Munro had gone to Demerara with his brother Alexander, and when Alexander died there in 1823 he left five children – Eliza, Jane, Sophy, Mary and Jessey – all daughters of Eve, an enslaved African woman. Since Alexander had not freed Eve, their daughters were also born slaves and all five were advertised for sale, along with their mother, by the executors of his estate. Someone, probably John, stepped in to buy them and then paid the hefty fee for their manumission, the formal process of granting freedom. When John died in 1833 he left his property to be divided three ways between his mother Jessy, his sister Sophia – both in Cromarty – and his five, free black nieces in Demerara.[4]

There were other ties to Berbice. A school fellow of Miller's, John Layfield, was 'dead in Berbice' before 1836. (Could he have been the 'mulatto lad'?) William Fraser, the son of a Cromarty house carpenter, had gone there in 1803, aged sixteen, and returned in the 1820s with, it was said, a considerable fortune and, certainly, four children born to two 'free coloured' women. One of his sons, John Fraser, was apprenticed to the surgeon in Cromarty in 1832 and must have been known to Miller. And on the coast of Berbice I found a mirror of the coast of the eastern Highlands – a looking-glass world of plantations named not only Cromarty but Borlum, Kingillie, Belladrum, Alness, Kiltearn, Edderton, Lemlair, Fyrish, Foulis, Culcairn, Brahan, Kintail, Kilcoy, Kilmorack, Tarlogie, Glastullich, Fearn, Geanies, Ankerville, Nigg, Tain, Ross, Golspie and Dunrobin. And there were more links, too, with neighbouring Demerara. John Hossack, the son of another Cromarty carpenter, had run a gang of slave carpenters in the colony and returned about 1810 to build his house near the shore – a building erected from, if not with, the labour of enslaved Africans.

Then there was the wider Caribbean. Cromarty's largest industry was its hemp works, a handloom factory employing hundreds of men, women and children in spinning and weaving hemp, imported from St Petersburg and Riga. They made bags for the cotton trade. There was a similar factory in Inverness and you could find the product of both advertised for sale in the Caribbean as 'Inverness bagging'. From Cromarty's harbour, salt herring and salt pork were being shipped as provisions for the plantations and in 1824 both Tain and Cromarty had, perhaps unsurprisingly, petitioned Parliament against the abolition of slavery and warned against exciting the slaves 'by delusive hopes'.[5]

In Jamaica, Miller's closest school friend, Alexander Findlay, had made good as proprietor of the *Twickenham Park* estate in Spanish Town. On the same plantation in 1817 Margaret Graham, from a Black Isle family, had married the colony's physician general, Michael Benignus Clare, later knighted for his services. In 1832 Sir Michael died at Cromarty House and his widow then bought the largest of the merchant houses in the town, renaming it Clare Lodge. Built in 1795, it had towered above Hugh Miller's childhood home. The Clares brought with them Nancy Graham, the illegitimate daughter of Francis Graham and Miss Jackson, a 'free coloured' woman in Jamaica. Francis Graham claimed to have controlled, as administrator or owner, almost fifty plantations and 13,000 slaves. Nancy arrived in Scotland as a young girl and had her portrait painted by the fashionable society artist, Henry Raeburn. This painting, now in the Louvre, hung in Clare Lodge, where she lived with her husband (yet another Graham) and their nine children until her death in 1883. Miller, as an adult, must have known the couple. And as a boy he had known Miss Elizabeth Bond who had rented the house and ran a boarding school for young ladies. When the school was inspected by the local gentry in 1816, one of her 'prettiest young ladies' had read out Miller's first attempt at verse 'before the assembled taste and fashion of Cromarty'. The next year the young ladies were joined by Jacobina Maria Nicholson (*c.* 1810–26), born in Goa, in the East Indies, the illegitimate daughter of an unknown Indian woman and a Scottish soldier.

I came to feel that Cromarty was haunted, not just by a black teenager, but by many ghosts of the Caribbean and beyond, half-glimpsed figures who flitted on the edges of the conventional view of the town's past. In many parts of the Caribbean they call these ghosts *jumbies*. Things have changed and, more than twenty years on, it is clear that Scotland as a whole, and not just my little town of Cromarty, had immersed itself in the exploitation of enslaved Africans and their descendants. In the words of Rosemary Goring, '. . . this little country was a big player in a hellish business'. But back then, in 2000, there was little or no acknowledgement from professional historians that Scotland, let alone the Highlands, had had any significant involvement with slavery.

A simple exercise in historiography – a technical term for the study of the writing of history – is revealing. Although one important book had come from an American, Alan Karras, whose *Sojourners in the Sun* (1992) dealt with 'Scots migrants to Jamaica and the Chesapeake', the indexes of the major works in Scottish history at the time were a catalogue of silence. Michael Lynch's *Scotland: A New History* (1991) had no entry relating to slavery; *Modern Scottish History* (1998) from the Open University and the University of Dundee had none; and although Thomas Devine's *The Scottish Nation: 1700-2000* (1999) had two references, these were only in relation to the role of the churches in the abolition movement. In a similar manner, twenty years earlier, the six-volume *New History of Scotland* (1981) had referred to slavery only in the context of the contribution of Scottish intellectuals to the debate on abolition. Works on Glasgow's *Tobacco Lords* (1975) and *Scottish Textile History* (1987) were silent on the plantations which produced tobacco and cotton – and there was no account of Scotland's enduring love affair with the other staple crop of the plantations, sugar.[6]

Chris Harvie, in *Scotland: A Short History* (2002), would acknowledge but not expand on the fact that the 'huge profits' made in cotton manufacturing 'were the dynamo of early indus-trialisation, kept going by slaves in the continuously expand-ing plantations'.[7] There was also some acknowledgement of the profits made from slavery by Michael Fry in an essay in *Eighteenth Century Scotland: New Perspectives* (1999) but he gave more space to his theory that, while Scots disliked slavery when they came into direct contact with it in the West Indies, they 'saw little need to do anything practical about it' despite the 'intellectual censure' at home which arose from the spirit of the Scottish Enlightenment. Fry's explanation was that Scots saw themselves only as 'transient actors' seeking self-improve-ment within a wider British Empire, whose vast scale left them 'overawed'. Only evangelical religion, he claimed, would later lead Scots to espouse abolition as a moral cause. This was the position he developed in *The Scottish Empire* (2001). As for the Highlands, Jim Hunter's *Last of the Free: A History of the Highlands and Islands of Scotland* (1999) was silent, and only Allan Macinnes in *Clanship, Commerce and the House of Stuart* (1996) noted the involvement of Highlanders in the plantations of the Caribbean and North America.[8]

Historiography is not simply a description of the writing of history – it is an attempt to understand why history is written in a particular way. In this case it must involve an attempt to answer the question: why did Scottish historians not give more attention to the evidence of Scotland's involvement with slavery? I believe that finding an answer requires enough humility to acknowledge that academics, including historians, are as prone as anyone else to the many biases inherent in human thought.

The study of Scottish history in the second half of the twen-tieth century was the creation, from almost nothing, of a sub-stantial body of academic work which, allowing for healthy debates within the academic community, nevertheless pre-sented an increasingly comprehensive and coherent account of Scotland's history, especially for the period after the Union of the Parliaments in 1707. While not all agreed on the answers, Scottish social and economic history focused on key issues of industrialisation, urbanisation, agricultural improvement and radical change in rural communities, internal migration, emigration, the role of women in Scottish society and, especially towards the end of the century, the place of Scotland within the United Kingdom. In the Highlands, mere romanticism for the Jacobites was replaced by hard-edged studies of clearances, emigration and military service. The daunting task which had been undertaken, the success of well-researched and widely read academic studies, and the general coherence of the resulting body of knowledge had the result – as it always does – of establishing an orthodoxy, resistant to the idea that something big and important might have been ignored. If we try to understand why this happened, then we are asking a question, not about history or the study of history, but about the systematic biases inherent in human thought. They are the same biases which led economists and financial experts to ignore the impending crash of 2008 and which created resistance in the medical community to the evidence that most stomach and duodenal ulcers were caused by bacteria rather than stress and lifestyle. Fortunately the intellectual tools which enable us to better recognise such systematic biases have been provided by the relatively new discipline of behavioural economics.

For now it will be helpful to consider in some detail one important example of unconscious bias in the presentation of Scottish history – the Museum of Scotland, which opened in 1998. I noticed, on my first visit, that there was not a single reference to slavery, the slave trade or slave plantations. While migration from Ireland to Scotland in the nineteenth and twentieth centuries was deemed to be important in the 'movement of peoples', the involvement of Scots in the trade which forced the migration of seven million Africans to the Caribbean and North America was not worth one word. An incisive critique by Dr Sheila Watson places this failing in the wider context of the institution's approach.[9]

> [The museum was] in effect the first nationalistic museum for Scotland in that it sets out to tell Scotland's story over the centuries and thus positions it as an independent nation within the Union ... Between 1986 and 1992 all non-Scottish components of the proposed museum ... were abandoned, leaving only material relating

to Scotland ... Originally, the curators had expected that the collections would lead the story. However, during its planning stage the curators were told to make the collections fit the narrative – the story of the Scots people over time. When collections did not do this then the story was told anyway.

What was wrong with the 'story' should have been apparent when one looked at the sections which dealt with the role of Scots in the British Empire. There was a reference to a 'profound influence' of Scots in East Africa that we were to assume from 'the tone of the text' and the reference to 'medical work and education' was entirely positive. At the time the Scottish journalist Ian Jack concluded that 'If a museum of England imitated the Edinburgh Museum's treatment of Empire ... there would be a lynch mob at the gates.'

Despite some minor changes implemented through a policy described as 'a careful adjustment of displays rather than root-and-branch revisionism', it is notable that when, in 2013, the museum hosted the exhibition 'Vikings!' with five hundred objects from the collections of the Swedish History Museum in Stockholm, there were still more references to slavery in the Viking world, in this visiting exhibition, than in the whole of the 'story of Scotland' in the rest of the museum.[10] The explanation sometimes offered is that few artefacts relating to slavery have survived to become part of museum collections. This is a poor excuse – even fewer artefacts survive from the Viking period. The true explanation is that slavery did not fit the story which the museum set out to tell.

Some Scottish novelists, perhaps being more subtle storytellers, appear to have had a greater awareness of slavery than the historians. In a review of Arthur Herman's overly enthusiastic *How the Scots Invented the Modern World*, Irvine Welsh commented:

> Herman almost seems to claim that the 'good' things in the empire – education, social reform and engineering – were solely the Scots' doing. The bad bits – racism, slavery, religious indoctrination – were down to others (the English). For example, it seems remiss to refer to Hutcheson, whose *A System of Moral Philosophy* inspired anti-slavery abolitionists in both Britain and America, while ignoring the compelling evidence of the Scots' darker role in the slave trade.

And Welsh also showed an awareness of the role of Highlanders in the 'bad bits' of Scottish imperial history.

> While it's refreshing to hear such an enthusiastic account of the Scottish ideas and practices that shaped the modern world, we need to offset them with harsher realities. Given the traditional role of Highlanders as mercenaries and soldiers, some cultures' first contact with Scottishness is more likely to have been on the receiving end of a broadsword, bullet, whip, stick, knife, boot or fist.[11]

Yet Herman's upbeat approach remained influential, still enthusiastically and repeatedly quoted in 2014 by Scotland's then First Minister, Alex Salmond, during the referendum campaign.

In 2003 James Robertson published *Joseph Knight*, a historical novel based on a Scottish court case of 1778 – 'Joseph Knight, a Negro of Africa v. John Wedderburn of Ballindean' – in which the former slave won his right to freedom. Ali Smith described it as 'a book which doesn't flinch from the ceremonies of torture, execution, slavery and power, all the foul things people are capable of inflicting on each other in the name of fashionable politics and economic prosperity'.[12]

So, had Scotland's historians flinched? Not all of them. In the late 1990s I had become aware that, at the University of Aberdeen, Douglas Hamilton was working on his doctoral thesis 'Patronage and Profit: Scottish Networks in the British West Indies, *c.* 1763–1807'. He was generous in sharing his research, in which he gave due attention to the networks based around Inverness and the Highlands, and when his thesis was developed into *Scotland, the Caribbean and the Atlantic World 1750–1820* (2005) we had the first book devoted to the links between Scotland and the Caribbean. There was, as Professor Kenneth Morgan noted, 'no comparable study' and it placed Highlanders clearly in the framework of an extensive Scottish involvement in these plantation economies. Devine's *Scotland's Empire: 1600–1815*, published in 2003, had similarly devoted a chapter to 'The Caribbean World' and had begun to raise questions as to the extent and impact of Scotland's involvement in the slave plantations, in marked contrast to Michael Fry's *The Scottish Empire* of two years before.[13]

The 2007 bicentenary of the abolition of the slave trade in the British colonies should have been the point at which Scotland woke up to its past. In 2006 Iain Whyte published

Scotland and the Abolition of Black Slavery, 1756–1838 which, although focused on Scotland's role in the abolitionist movement, also made clear the extent to which Scottish prosperity in the eighteenth century was based on slavery and the slave trade.[14] Yet the material prepared in the same year by Iain Whyte and Dr Eric Graham for a planned official publication – *Scotland's Involvement in the Transatlantic Slave Trade and its Abolition: A Historical Review* – was rejected by civil servants in the Scottish Executive as too sensitive.[15] At the same time the Heritage Lottery Fund made grants available for projects which marked the bicentenary but a decade later, in her thesis 'The end of amnesia?', Cait Gillespie observed that:

> Scotland took part in the bicentenary, but it displayed a lacklustre response. Only seven commemorative projects took place in Scotland, compared to hundreds throughout England and Wales, and to a lesser degree Northern Ireland. The National Museum of Scotland did nothing to mark the bicentenary.[16]

In the same year, Thomas Devine gave a lecture at the Edinburgh Book Festival called 'Did slavery make Scotland great?', which grew to become a chapter in his *To the Ends of the Earth: Scotland's Global Diaspora, 1750–2010* (2011). At the same time, a team of scholars at University College London, led by Nick Draper and Catherine Hall, had begun a systematic examination of the records of compensation paid to slave owners following emancipation in 1834. As this progressed it showed that the compensation received by Scots was, in proportion to the country's population, greater than that paid to people in England.[17]

It was not, however, until 2015 that there was a further publication to complement Douglas Hamilton's *Scotland, the Caribbean and the Atlantic World* and Iain Whyte's *Scotland and the Abolition of Black Slavery*. I am proud to have been a contributor to *Recovering Scotland's Slavery Past: The Caribbean Connection*, a collection of essays edited and introduced by Thomas Devine, which was hailed by Kevin McKenna in the *Observer* as 'one of the most important books to have been published in Scotland this century' and by Ian Bell in the *Herald* as 'an illuminating marvel'. There has been much more attention paid to this aspect of Scotland's past since then, including material directed to a wider audience such as the two-part BBC documentary *Slavery: Scotland's Hidden Shame* (2018) presented by David Hayman, who has continued to take an active interest in the subject. And in 2020 the Black Lives Matter movement extended the discussion to even more people.

If all that has happened is to mark a real turning point in the assessment of 'Scotland's slavery past' then it must open new areas of study, begin debate and, in the words of Professor Ewen Cameron, invite 'a long overdue national conversation'. Unfortunately there is a regressive strand in the discussion of Scottish identity which thrives on the false view that Scotland was a colony of England.

> Nor is the identification of Scotland as a downtrodden colony any longer confined to the margins of political debate ... The phenomenon is sufficiently widespread to have attracted the notice of outside observers. The distinguished historian Linda Colley – English-born but based at Princeton University in the USA – recently expressed her surprise at the number of Scots who believe Scotland's relationship with England to be a colonial one ... This is not only largely nonsensical as history, but offensive and insulting to many non-white, non-European peoples who did, in fact, find themselves oppressed or even dispossessed by the 'British' Empire.[18]

A consequence of this myth is that many Scots, once again, distance themselves from the reality of their country's involvement with slavery and some claim instead to be fellow victims with the enslaved of a colonial past. In a single week in August 2020 the *National* newspaper published contributions which included the historian Michael Fry's claim that 'Edinburgh's part in the Caribbean slave trade was minimal' and a reader's comment that 'the vast majority of Scots were in no position to have either profited or prospered from the slave trade as they were often little better than slaves themselves'.[19] A report by Iain MacKinnon and Andrew Mackillop on plantation slavery and landownership in the western Highlands and Islands, published in 2020, is a useful corrective to this, indicating as it does the extensive impact of wealth derived from slavery on the region and acknowledging that 'culpability and complicity in the benefits of enslaving other human beings spread throughout the region and down its social order'.[20] We might also remember Douglas Hamilton's observation that, as the Bill to abolish slavery passed through Parliament in 1833, '... the preponderance of [pro-slavery petitions] came from the north ... [and]

of the sixteen places named in the petitions, ten came from the Black Isle ... more than from the whole of England'.[21] I hope that the following chapters will encourage a continued reassessment of the connections between the Highlands of Scotland, the slave trade and the slave-worked plantations of the Caribbean and South America.

To end this chapter, I return to Cromarty in 1818. The ownership of the Cromarty estate was in dispute and subject to a long-running, and expensive, legal case which would not be settled until the 1840s. The successful claimant was Hugh Rose, the son of a minister of the Church of Scotland in Easter Ross. Hugh Rose had made his fortune in the West Indies through corrupt dealings in contracts for supplies to the Royal Navy, with the profits subsequently invested in plantations and slaves. His claim to the Cromarty estate was through his second wife, Catharine Munro – his first wife, Arabella Phipps, having died in 1806 at Bayfield House in Nigg, across the waters of the Cromarty Firth. At some point people began to tell the story that Arabella had been stabbed by Hugh's 'quadroon' mistress who had come back with him from the Caribbean and had been installed by him as a 'servant' in the attics. I cannot establish when this tale began to circulate – and it is obviously reminiscent of Bertha Antoinetta Mason, the 'first Mrs Rochester' in Charlotte Brontë's *Jane Eyre* (1847) – but I know that the story is still told and that 'the White Lady of Bayfield' is still said to haunt this Georgian house.

However, like the black student with which this chapter began, it appears to me that the 'black lady of Bayfield' – whether she is real or fictional – is the more significant character as we reassess the involvement of Highlanders in the slave plantations of the Caribbean. And it is long past time to bring her out of the attics.

PART 1

The African Slave Trade, the English 'Sugar Islands' and Scots in the Expanding Empire

I begin with an account of the involvement of Highland Scots in the trading of Africans into and within the colonies of the Caribbean and the Americas. Chapter 2 describes the slave trade in its full and proper sense – beginning with kidnap, continuing in the conversion of human beings into commodities, and extending to all parts of the plantation economies within, and beyond, British control. For wherever people were enslaved, they were traded. From the millions of personal histories, mostly lost, I have attempted to recover as much as I can of the life of one man – a slave called Inverness. His story ends Chapter 2.

The three following chapters describe the growing presence of Scots in what had been the English – but now British – 'sugar island' of Jamaica (see Chapter 3) and then the disproportionately high number of Scots who seized the opportunities opened to them after 1763 by the acquisition of the Ceded Islands – Grenada, Tobago, St Vincent and Dominica. Chapter 4 considers some northern Scots in Grenada and the tensions in the island between staunchly Presbyterian Scots and Catholic French planters – tensions which coexisted with growing militancy in the enslaved population and finally erupted in the Fédon Revolution of 1795. Chapter 4 then explores the fortunes of one extended family from a relatively modest background in Inverness, the Frasers of Boblainy. They became carpenters and slave owners in Grenada and Tobago – and also in St Vincent where they benefited, with other northern Scots, from the suppression and 'ethnic cleansing' of the indigenous Black Caribs.

2

The Slave Trade

The slave trade in the British Empire was more than the seizure of Africans for transportation to the Americas, where they would labour at the production of tobacco, sugar, cotton, coffee and other plantation crops. It was more than this because enslaved people were themselves reduced to commodities – goods which could be traded. There was therefore, first, a production process: the making of a slave. This began with physical capture and confinement. Some were then held in the dungeon of a 'slave castle' on the African Coast, others were sold directly to ship captains – all were dehumanised in the hold and on the deck of a slave ship. And the process continued in disciplining, training, renaming and the breaking, if possible, of whatever spirit of resistance remained. The final product was a 'seasoned' slave.[1] Through this process around seven million Africans were transported in the northern Atlantic trade, often known as the triangular trade because European ships carried goods to Africa, traded them for slaves, carried the enslaved to the Caribbean and North America, and finally returned to Europe with plantation produce. But there was also the southern Atlantic trade in the Spanish and Portuguese empires, in which about five and a half million Africans were transported.[2]

Perhaps the most enduring and potent images of the reduction of human beings to commodities were the various depictions of slave ships produced and circulated by abolitionists.

> Nearly identical human figures ... symbolise how slavery turns individuals into anonymous commodities ... Each detail makes the image more horrifying: men sorted out and ordered by size, shackled in pairs; women gathered ... adjacent to the relatively vast

Captain's cabin and wine lockers; the fierce microeconomic optimi-
sation in packing a cargo of 227 men and 120 women.[3]

As commodities, slaves were sold through a sophisticated
system which responded to changing demand throughout the
Americas. Capture and purchase in Africa, of which a first-
hand account is given in Chapter 4, was followed by shipment
across the Atlantic, a voyage referred to as the 'Middle Passage'
because, for British slave traders, it came between the shipment
to Africa of trade goods (with which slaves were purchased)
and the shipment of plantation produce from the West Indies
to Britain. But for enslaved Africans it was followed by many
further journeys on what Gregory O'Malley has called 'Final
Passages'.[4] As commodities, enslaved Africans were prepared
for sale, batched to suit local demand and sold into supply
chains, whose links, becoming smaller, extended into every
corner of the Americas where slavery was encouraged or tolerated. It is entirely appropriate to think of this in terms of
wholesalers, large retailers and a range of small traders, who,
like the importers, would prepare, sort, price and move their
goods to find the highest profit. This network extended beyond
British colonies both through legitimate inter-colonial free ports
and into black markets of trade with non-British colonies in the
entangled British, Dutch, French and Spanish Atlantics. And
because slaves were themselves trade goods, they were used
not only as bargaining chips to secure further contracts for the
purchase of plantation produce but also, in inter-colonial trade,
to secure supplies of silver mined in the Spanish Empire. Thus
a slave taken from Africa as part of a 'cargo' of five hundred
might pass through traders in a Caribbean island and finally be
sold alone, packed with other cargo, to a tobacco planter in the
woods of South Carolina or to a silver mine in Spanish Caracas.

The suppliers of slaves responded to a market which changed
over time. Not all British colonies in the Americas were plantation economies but, as Trevor Burnard writes, 'the plantation system [came to] encompass the southern parts of North
America, the Caribbean, and the northern parts of South
America as a coherent whole, with close connections and struc-
tural similarities over a sustained period of time'. The economic
success of these colonies as generators of fabulous wealth for
their small white populations – and for investors and owners

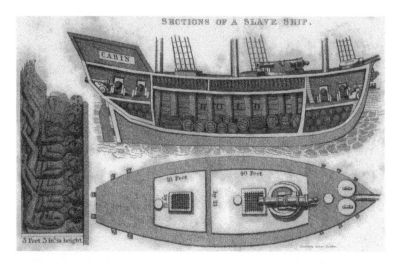

SECTIONS OF A SLAVE SHIP.

CABIN

HOLD

10 Feet

40 Feet

5 Feet 3 in. in height.

Figure 2.1 Section of a slave ship carrying cargo and slaves.
© John Carter Brown Library.

in Britain – came from the adoption of a system of agricultural production in large, integrated plantations, with a correspondingly large enslaved labour force. This was different from the use of enslaved labour on smaller units and this system did not come into existence with the slave trade itself. It developed over time, emerging first in the English colony of Barbados in the mid-1600s, and only slowly extending to Jamaica around 1700.[5] Thus the centre of the American plantation economies, where the greatest wealth was generated, changed and in the early 1800s that centre 'moved both northward and southward – to Louisiana in the United States and to British Guiana in the British Empire'.[6]

The spread of large plantations was linked to demand for sugar. Because sugar cane had to be processed immediately after it was cut, each planter usually erected his own mill and boiling house, creating an integrated system of production on one site. And since Caribbean sugar could be grown all year round, the most efficient use of the mill and boiling house was achieved when cane was planted so as to deliver a steady flow of cut cane. This required a plantation of a larger size, with hundreds of slaves, and by the mid-1700s there were almost no small-scale sugar plantations in the British Caribbean.

Divorced from the rhythm of natural seasons, or even the cycles of labor and rest incorporated within the church calendar, the experience of labor on a sugar plantation was monotonous and relentless, a continuous staged cycle of cutting, crushing, boiling, curing, cutting, crushing, boiling, curing. The sugar plantation realised the very modern drudgery of industrial efficiency. The plantation was a machine.[7]

Burnard argues that the spread of the large, integrated sugar plantation was slow because there was a key obstacle.

The shift from small-scale to large-scale plantations [only] came about once planters solved the problem of discipline through the application of terror. To terrify slaves, they needed people willing to inflict terror. These people were ordinary white men acting as overseers and bookkeepers on slave plantations.[8]

Where this obstacle was overcome, large plantations were established in greater numbers and the demand for enslaved Africans increased. Scots – including many northern Scots – played their part in developing the large, integrated plantations of the Caribbean and of both North and South America, inflicting terror as required. They also played their part in the African slave trade.

JAMES FRASER – A HIGHLAND SLAVER

The Society for Affecting the Abolition of the Slave Trade was formed in May 1787 by twelve men who gathered in a printing shop in London, their number being surely an indication of their sense of religious mission. Nine were Quakers and three Anglicans. Within eighteen months they had created three effective tools with which to spread their message. By the end of 1787 Josiah Wedgwood had produced the Society's pottery medallion, showing a kneeling slave in chains with the simple question: 'Am I not a man and a brother?'. Later there would be a companion piece: 'Am I not a woman and a sister?'. Then, in November 1788, the Plymouth branch of the Society published William Elford's engraving of a slave ship, showing Africans packed side by side between its decks. It would be reproduced in many different forms. And in December of the same year, the Society published Alexander Falconbridge's *Account of the Slave Trade on the Coast of Africa*. The medallion would soon be seen on objects ranging from plates to brooches, and the words became the campaign slogan of abolitionists in Britain and North America; the print of the slave ship hung in the houses of abolitionists through the country; and Falconbridge's work became what Simon Schama has called 'the most widely read and graphic account of the physical cruelties of the [slave] trade'.[9]

Falconbridge, before being converted to the abolitionist cause, had sailed as a ship's surgeon on four slaving voyages to Africa and described, among other abuses, the cramped, insanitary conditions between the decks; poor food and a shortage of water; Africans being burned with hot coals held to their lips if they refused to eat; rape of women; deaths from heat and suffocation; dead and living slaves shackled together; and suicides by hanging or drowning. He named no names in his *Account* but in 1790 he gave evidence to a Select Committee of the House of Commons. These sources can then be combined with information gathered in *Slave Voyages: Transatlantic Slave-trade Database* to identify his service as being on the ships *Tartar* (1782), *Emilia* (1783–4), *Alexander* (1785–6) and, again, *Emilia* (1786–7). John McTaggart was master of the *Alexander*, while both the *Tartar* and the *Emilia* were captained by James Fraser.[10] It is a strange quirk of history that three of these slaving voyages, which would have such a profound impact on public opinion, were under the command of a Highland sea captain.

James Fraser was a resident of Bristol but his family roots were in Glenconvinth, in the parish of Kiltarlity, near Inverness. He was a cousin of the prosperous merchant and slave trader Evan Baillie, the third of three brothers from Dochfour (Inverness-shire) who were all making money from the slave trade and from their plantations in the Caribbean. It was Evan, and another Bristol merchant, Walter Jacks, who in 1782 built the *Emilia*, one of the ships on which Falconbridge served. It was named after Evan's mother, Emilia Fraser of Reelig. By the time of his death in 1797 or 1798, James Fraser owned a share of a cotton plantation in Demerara and, in addition to this asset, was able to bequeath almost £8,000 to friends and relations, almost all in the Highlands or with Highland connections. The largest bequests were to his cousin, Edward Fraser of Reelig, and to Evan Baillie.[11]

Like Falconbridge, James Fraser gave evidence to the House

of Commons Select Committee in 1790 – but in support of the slave trade.[12] By this date he had twenty years' experience in the trade. After sailing as second mate and chief mate, he served as master of five different slave ships, which made ten voyages from Africa to the Americas between 1773 and 1789. An eleventh voyage failed when the *Tartar* was captured by the French before leaving the African coast. Between 1790 and his death in 1798 he made a further three voyages, two on the *Hector* and finally on the *Pilgrim*. These sixteen voyages were made at a time when most slaving captains made fewer than four and this placed him in the ranks of the senior captains in the trade.[13] As a captain, Fraser embarked a total of 5,513 enslaved Africans but disembarked only 4,973, since 540 African men, women and children died under his command, and he delivered these human cargoes to South Carolina, Jamaica, Dominica, Grenada, Tortola, St Thomas, St Kitts, St Vincent and Demerara.

Fraser's testimony was often contradicted by that of Falconbridge. Fraser claimed that Africans were enslaved according to the laws of their own country and then sold in a fair manner, by brokers on the coast, to captains such as himself; Falconbridge was clear that they were enslaved as a result of kidnapping and crime, and when questioned he observed that, 'Captain Fraser, or any other captain that goes for Slaves, seldom trouble themselves how they were caught or made Slaves'. Fraser told the Committee, 'It is the custom with the Africans to lay close together, in such a manner that one does not breath [sic] into the other's face – this is also a very common custom among the Slaves on board the ships.' Falconbridge described them as having less space than in a coffin.

When it came to the physical punishment of slaves, Fraser claimed that he had only punished slaves reluctantly and then only because of their 'peevishness, perverseness, and obstinacy' in refusing help. One example was his response to some enslaved Africans' refusal to eat. Falconbridge, in his *Account*, had written: 'I have seen coals of fire, glowing hot, placed on a shovel, and placed so near their lips, as to scorch and burn them. And this has been accompanied with threats, of forcing them to swallow the coals, if they any longer persisted in refusing to eat.' When examined, Fraser denied that he had ever 'held hot coals to a negro, threatening to force him to swallow them', but being pressed conceded:

Being sick in my cabin, the chief mate and surgeon, at different times informed me, that there was a man upon the main deck, that would neither eat, drink, or speak – I desired them to use every means in their power to persuade him to speak, and assign reasons for his silence – when I was informed he still remained obstinate, and not knowing whether it was sulkiness or insanity, I ordered the chief mate, or surgeon, or both, to present him with a piece of fire in one hand and a piece of yam in the other, and to let me know what effect it had on him – it was reported to me that he took the yam and eat [sic] it, and threw the fire overboard.

Thus was 'peevishness, perverseness, and obstinacy' overcome. Often Fraser's own matter-of-fact tone was enough to reveal the barbarity of the trade. On his voyage on the *Emilia* in 1784, he conceded that he had lost about fifty slaves 'by the ship getting on shore on the bar in coming out, which obliged us to shut the air ports' to prevent water coming into the ship. The slaves suffocated in the hot and airless hold.

One incident in particular illustrates the extent to which Africans were turned into commodities – the sale by 'scramble' on board the *Emilia* at Port Maria, Jamaica, in 1784.

The ship was darkened with sails, and covered round; the men Slaves were placed on the main deck, and the women on the quarter deck; the purchasers on shore were informed a gun would be fired when they were ready to open the sale; a great number of people came on board with tallies or cards in their hands, with their own name upon them, and rushed through the barricade door with the ferocity of brutes; some had three of four handkerchiefs tied together, to encircle as many as they thought fit for their purpose.

A scramble, with slaves sold at a fixed price and with no chance to examine them, was a way of shifting stock and passing off low-quality or sick slaves, prepared for the sale so as to mask their defects. Those suffering from dysentery would have their anuses plugged with oakum. Others would be oiled, blemishes dyed, and their heads shaved to remove grey hair. There could be no pretence in a scramble that there was any attempt to keep families together, a claim often made by defenders of the slave trade. Falconbridge said that 'the Slaves themselves used to cry and beg that such a man or woman (their friend or relation) might be bought and sent with them, wherever they were going'. And he knew of 'a person who would not purchase a man's wife, and the next day I was informed the man hanged himself'.

Fraser's career of almost thirty years in the slave trade is summarised in Table 2.1. Although Scottish captains like Fraser were uncommon on Bristol slave ships, perhaps a fifth of the Liverpool slavers were commanded by Scots, many from the Clyde.[14] However, the role of James Fraser, Master of the *Emilia*, in the history of the slave trade is eclipsed by that of his cousin, Evan Baillie, the joint owner of the ship.

SLAVE TRADER: EVAN BAILLIE OF DOCHFOUR

When he died in 1835 aged ninety-five at Dochfour House, by Loch Ness, Evan Baillie was regarded as 'one of the richest commoners in Britain'. His obituary in the *Inverness Courier* went on to claim that this was 'a distinction which he obtained from honourable commercial enterprise, and unsullied integrity'. This was despite the fact that he had been a slave trader and that his sons would be among the largest recipients of compensation following emancipation. He was soon commemorated by a tall, grey granite obelisk, erected in a private burial ground near Dochfour House, now largely hidden by trees but then visible to all passing through the Great Glen, by road or on the Caledonian Canal.[15] It remains one of the most substantial monuments in Britain to a leading figure in the slave trade.

Evan remembered watching, as a five-year-old boy, the defeat of the Jacobite army at Culloden, from the hill above Dochfour, and one of his older brothers, either Alexander or James, was said to have fought there. He could also remember a visit from Lord Lovat, a prominent Jacobite, to his mother, Emilia Fraser – in whose honour he would later name his slaving ship – urging her to persuade the Baillies to join the cause. There is, however, no evidence to support the statement that 'as a result of the Baillies' support of the Jacobite cause, Dochfour House was burnt and the estate forfeited'.[16] The Baillies had not been persuaded by Lord Lovat and remained loyal to the Hanoverian state.

While his older brothers Alexander and James had attended university, after schooling in Inverness, fifteen-year-old Evan joined the army and served with distinction in the West Indies before retiring in 1763 and joining his brothers in business. Alexander had been the first to go to the Caribbean, arriving in Nevis in 1752, followed in 1755 by James, who joined

Table 2.1 Slaving voyages of Captain James Fraser

Year	Vessel	Rank	Region	Notes from Voyages database and Fraser's evidence to Parliament	Enslaved embarked, disembarked & died.		
					Emb.	D-emb.	Died
1769	Amelia	2nd mate	Angola	To Virginia.			
1772	Polly	Chief mate	Angola	To St Kitts.			
1772	Catharine	Master	Angola	Three months on shore at Melimba Hill (Africa). Slaves sold at Charlestown, Carolina.	260	237	23
1775	Catharine	Master	Angola	Seven months on shore at Melimba Hill (Africa). Not allowed to land at Carolina so returned to St Kitts, nearly foundered at sea. Mortality 'trifling,' until ship foundered.	350	300	50
1776	Alexander	Master	Calabar	To Jamaica. 'Very moderate mortality.'	355	325	30
1777	Valiant	Master	Bight of Biafra	To Jamaica. 'Considerable mortality due to measles.'	500	399	101
1781	Tartar	Master	Windward and Gold Coast	To Jamaica.	250	229	21
1782	Tartar	Master. Surgeon: Falconbridge	Captured by French				
1783-4	Emilia	Master. Surgeon: Falconbridge	Angola and Windward Coast	140 or 150 from each location. On coast for eight or nine months after purchase of first group. Then to Jamaica. Ship damaged by shot from French.	380	340	40
1784	Emilia	Master	Bonny	To Dominica.	490	450	40
1785	Emilia	Master	Bonny	To Jamaica. A further 60 died after arrival at Kingston.	393	360	33
1786	Emilia	Master	Bonny	To Grenada.	414	379	35
1787	Emilia	Master. Surgeon: Falconbridge	Bonny	To St Kitts. The number embarked may have been higher, with about 150 sent by tender to St Thomas.	359	328	31
1789	Ten months in France						
1791	Hector	Master	Bonny	To Jamaica.	764	700	64
1793	Hector	Master	Bonny	To St Vincent.	596	558	38
1798	Pilgrim	Master	Gold Coast	To Demerara.	402	368	34
					5,513	4,973	540

Alexander in St Kitts – both St Kitts and Nevis being established English 'sugar islands'. By the early 1760s they had built up connections with the neighbouring Dutch island of St Eustatia, and had formed a partnership in St Kitts – Smith & Baillies – with Alexander's former employer, James Smith. The partnership was probably established in 1762 when Alexander married Smith's daughter, Sara. Then, like many other Scots, they seized the opportunity to buy land in Grenada after it was ceded by the French, acquiring plantations *Hermitage* and *Mount St Bernard* in 1765, and then expanded their network into St Vincent, one of the other Ceded Islands. At *Hermitage* a grim 'slave pen' – a basement prison – survives under the decaying ruins of the plantation's great house.[17]

On his arrival in Nevis in 1752, Alexander Baillie had observed the 'great numbers' who flocked to the colony 'from a very mistaken Notion indeed the Gold may be got for the gathering of it'. None were 'more deceived in this respect than the Scots'.[18] But Alexander was one of those who prospered, as did his brothers. Evan married in St Vincent, to a Mary Gurley through whom he acquired a number of other estates, and only James married in Britain.[19] When a new firm of Alexander, James & Evan Baillie was formed in St Kitts in 1770, the Baillies were establishing themselves as merchants in a British Empire encompassing North American and Caribbean colonies. One of their most important connections was to Henry Laurens of Charleston (South Carolina), who sold them the stores they needed, bought plantation produce and used them as a supplier of slaves. Sometimes Smith & Baillies 'supplemented a cargo with a few Negroes that were unable to sell in St Kitts; sometimes they dispatched large consignments' and often there were complaints from Laurens about the condition of the 'cargo'. Laurens wanted 'healthy new Negroes to be pretty well clothed and have a blanket each' rather than the fifty who in 1764 'came in all alive but extremely meagre and thin', and he urged that further shipments 'be sent under a humane master who will take care of them'. The enslaved Africans supplied by Smith & Baillies often sold for £4 or £5 less than those supplied by other merchants in St Kitts and this, along with Laurens' repeated complaints, suggests that they habitually employed harsher captains and scrimped on the costs involved in sending slaves north into a colder climate.[20]

Christine Eickelmann's research on the *Mountravers* plantation on the neighbouring island of Nevis is a groundbreaking longitudinal study of an entire plantation population which identifies 850 named enslaved individuals who have through this study 'emerged from obscurity and now can take their place in history'. Thirty of these enslaved people on *Mountravers* were purchased from Smith & Baillies in 1766. Eickelmann details what can be gleaned of their lives. They included twelve-year-old Judy, earmarked as a mistress for a friend of the plantation owner; Daniel, a 'refuse boy' – that is, a slave so ill and debilitated he was unlikely to survive and therefore sold at a reduced price; Cuffee, a young man who soon hanged himself; Dorchester and Cordelia, a boy and a girl who died from 'eating dirt'; and others, like the longest survivors, York and Caroline, who died in their late sixties in 1822 and 1823, having lived the remainder of their lives in slavery. It is in these details that the horror of the slave trade is brought home – in stark contrast to the 'honourable commercial enterprise' referred to in Evan Baillie's obituary and the description of him as a gentleman 'of the most punctilious honour and correctness in all his transactions and intercourse with society'.

As the opportunities presented themselves, the Baillie brothers each returned to Britain to pursue their commercial and social interests – Alexander before 1769 to Inverness, where he had inherited the Dochfour estate; James in 1771 to London; and Evan about 1774 to Bristol. Giving evidence to the House of Commons in 1790, James Baillie said that during his time in the West Indies he had been 'in the habits of selling considerable numbers of Slaves each year, but never imported any on my own account' – that is, he was engaged in the 'Final Passages' of the trade rather than the African trade.[21] Evan, however, became directly involved in the African slave trade with the building of the *Emilia* in 1784 and in 1787 he also owned a share in the *Daniel*. The family network was extensive. On one of the *Daniel*'s later voyages in 1790, credit was provided by James Baillie Esq & Co. (Evan's brother in London) and slaves were sold in Grenada by James Baillie jr & Co. (Evan's cousin).[22] James Baillie junior also worked with Edmund Thornton and Thomas Campbell in Grenada, trading as Baillie, Thornton & Campbell, later described as the 'first [that is, most important] mercantile house in the island'.[23]

SLAVE FACTOR: GEORGE BAILLIE

Unlike his cousin Evan, George Baillie (1755–1807) never owned a slave ship but like him he was a slave factor in the Caribbean and later a financier of the slave trade in England.[24] The slave trade relied on an extensive network of credit. Slave factors, who bought enslaved Africans from ship captains, paid for them by a 'bill of exchange', that is, a promise to pay a specified sum of money at a defined future date, guaranteed by a British-based financier. Planters who then bought these slaves were also given credit in the form of a second bill, drawn on (payable by) the planter at a defined future date. Planters shipped their produce to British markets to pay off their debts, often consigning them to the merchant house which had provided their credit.

It was 'Guinea factors' such as George Baillie who created the 'migratory pathways along which millions of enslaved Africans were forcibly transported' – the 'Final Passages' of the slave trade. It was common by the later 1700s to find Scots in this role. Nicholas Radburn's study of the merchant John Taylor, from Montrose, shows that in 1793/4 Tailyour, Ballatine & Fairlie of Jamaica were 'briefly the largest Guinea factoring firm in the Caribbean, if not the entire Atlantic World'.[25] Between 1785 and 1796 at least 23 per cent of enslaved Africans sold in Jamaica were traded through Scottish slave factors: John Tailyour (17,295 enslaved: 11 per cent), James Wedderburn (7,802: 5 per cent), Alexander Shaw (5,551: 4 per cent) and Francis Grant (3,906: 3 per cent). Radburn explains how factors build up their customer base.

> Aspiring factors such as Tailyour obtained a 'country interest' of planter customers by trading first as town factors, enabling them to learn the creditworthiness of potential slave buyers. Guinea factors then forged connections with well-capitalized West India houses, which provided credit for slave sales, and selected British merchants who steered their human cargoes to their American correspondents.[26]

George Baillie, the son of William Baillie of Rosehall in Sutherland, followed a similar path. He left Scotland for St Kitts in 1770, at the age of fourteen or fifteen, and then moved between St Vincent and Grenada, settling in St Vincent in 1773 to work for Evan Baillie and his partner. George returned to

England in 1783 in poor health but was back in St Vincent later the same year and was then in partnership with a Charles Hamilton from 1784 to *c.* 1787. It was in St Vincent in 1787 that George Baillie & Co. sold the cargo of the slave ship *Juba* – a vessel now notorious through being one of the four ships used by the modern City of Bristol to highlight the nature of the African slave trade.[27] The *Juba* sailed from Bristol for Old Calabar (Nigeria), where it loaded 230 enslaved Africans along with ivory, palm oil and redwood (used to make a dye). The Middle Passage lasted thirteen weeks rather than the usual six and twenty-nine slaves died during the voyage. The ship's surgeon later accused the captain, John Kennedy, of raping and beating some the women:

> [Surgeon] Neely, whose reputation for honesty was later backed up by other members of the ship's crew, made another, more telling revelation, namely about Kennedy's treatment of another enslaved woman 'the sister of the girl he [the captain] did commonly sleep with . . . He beat her unmercifully on account she would not submit to sleep with him tho a Savage, yet at last was forced to comply . . . even in the middle of the day and on deck his actions were more like a Beast than a man.'[28]

Losses, at 12 per cent of the slaves, had been higher than usual and the *Juba* sank off the coast of Ireland on its return voyage to Bristol. Yet the owners, and no doubt George Baillie & Co., still made a profit. And, despite these complaints, the owners re-engaged the captain.

Although George had initially aligned himself with Evan Baillie, he came to see James as the more dynamic of the Dochfour brothers and transferred his interests to him, and on James Baillie's death in 1793, George returned to England. This was during a period of rapid wealth creation in the slave economies, particularly in Grenada and St Vincent, which came to an abrupt end with the Fédon Revolution in Grenada in 1795. As rapidly as they had been created, fortunes were lost – threatening networks of credit within Britain. George Baillie, now in London, was a leading figure in securing Government loans to prevent the collapse of major merchant houses. In his own words, 'after great perseverance, and being three times refused, I succeeded in my application to Government for a loan, to the extent of one million and a half, for all the sufferers'.[29] In fact, sixty-two loans amounting to £1.367 million were granted by the Exchequer following legislation in 1795, the bulk going to merchants rather than resident planters. In his study of these loans Nicholas Draper concludes that 'proximity to the metropolitan government appears to have been critical'.[30]

Baillie's success in working with others to secure these loans is an indication of his connections to leading figures in London. The extent of his network is further revealed in a series of pamphlets he published following the acrimonious dissolution of his first merchant house in London in 1800 and the financial instability and bankruptcy of his second house in 1806.[31] Baillie was also sued for defamation by Mr Kaye (the solicitor to the Commissioners for the Government loan), whose counsel denounced Baillie as 'a malignant, malevolent, and black-blooded libeller'. Kaye was awarded damages of £1,000.[32]

There was a significant Highland dimension to George Baillie's network. His sister Elizabeth had married Colonel James Sutherland of Uppat and their son Robert Sutherland (1776–1828) was for many years the manager of George Baillie's estates in St Vincent;[33] George Inglis (1764–1847), brother of the provost of Inverness, had been his partner as a slave factor on the island, as had the brothers Alexander and William Alves, also of Inverness; and Eric Mackay (1773–1847, later 7th Lord Reay), his father's cousin by marriage, was a partner in London in the firm Baillie founded in the early 1790s. There were, however, bitter family disputes. George accused Evan Baillie of having sold an estate in St Vincent at a high price to a naive newcomer to the island in 1771. This was John Fraser of Achnagairn (d. 1785), the son of Provost James Fraser of Inverness (d. 1777), who had come out with extensive credit from his relation George Ross, an army agent in London and from 1767 owner of the Cromarty estate near Inverness. Fraser's failure in St Vincent brought down the London house of his brother, John Fraser & Co., and forced George Ross to mortgage his estates in Scotland.[34] George Baillie was also in dispute with Colina Campbell, the widow of James Baillie of Dochfour, over an annuity of £3,500 due to her under her husband's will. Although she was a relative of George Baillie, she was also related to his partner Eric Mackay (Lord Reay) and used this connection to pursue her interests.

Baillie's next company was formed in partnership with

John Jaffray (d. 1832), who had gone to North America as a young man, fought as a British Loyalist in the American War of Independence and then entered Government service. He was an agent in Montreal (1780–4), then in the Leeward Islands, and commissary general for the West Indies (1793–5). In his own words, he 'acquired by practice and observation more knowledge of the business of an army than most men' – and army contracting was a lucrative business.[35] He no doubt brought valuable experience to the partnership and by 1801 one plantation manager in Guyana observed that George Baillie's new house had 'effected a very extensive and complete system of business in the West Indies . . . likely to command the cream of the African trade in Guiana and the Leeward Islands'.[36] They also began importing cotton to Britain from Guyana, poaching trade by means of their contacts with planters and merchants. Then they acquired their own property in Berbice.

SLAVE AUCTIONEERS: WILLIAM MACKENZIE & CO.

In the early 1800s the colonies of Essequibo, Demerara and Berbice were the fastest growing in the Caribbean, generating what seemed an insatiable demand for slaves, and to supply this market Baillie and Jaffray joined with James Craufurd MacLeod (1775–1821) of Geanies (Ross-shire) and William Mackenzie, who traded in Demerara as William Mackenzie & Co. In 1802 they took over the slave-selling of another business, Fraser, Littledale & Co., in which MacLeod had been a partner along with two other Highlanders – Simon Fraser (of either Belladrum or Kilmorack) and William Robertson (of Inverness).[37] Their other partner, Alfred Littledale (d. 1805), was the brother-in-law of the Liverpool cotton merchant and slave trader John Bolton (1756–1837). Enslaved Africans would pass from Bolton's captains into the hands of George Baillie & Co. in St Vincent and the other Leeward Islands, and then be shipped on to be sold at auction in Stabroek, the only town in Demerara. In neighbouring Berbice there was another Scots partnership which sold slaves, trading as Ross & Sinclair and consisting of John Ross (1776–1806) and James Fraser (d. 1801), both from Nigg (Ross-shire), and John Sinclair (d. 1805) from Halkirk (Caithness).

There were, however, tensions within Mackenzie & Co. from as early as 1802, with complaints being made to George Baillie that MacLeod was 'too long absent in the islands and of his uncivil usage of a shipmaster'. In 1805 Mackenzie had 'gone home to keep Baillie in order'.[38] Nevertheless the partnership continued until 1806, shortly before the abolition of the African slave trade in 1807.

CLERK: DONALD MACKAY

The success of firms such as Mackenzie & Co. depended on men like Donald Mackay (1776–1851) who, from a relatively modest background in Inverness, rose to become a landed gentleman in Hertfordshire.[39] He was sufficiently well off to have had good education and to have the patronage of yet another provost of Inverness, James Grant, but he had no capital and his relations, including his sister, teetered on the brink of poverty. A letter of recommendation from Provost Grant gained him employment as an overseer with a Mr Gordon in Demerara but he soon left this for a position as a clerk with William Mackenzie & Co., principally because of the higher salary of £300 rather than £100.

He then bought two slaves, for £200 on twelve months' credit, from Simon Fraser of Belladrum, and hired them out for £50 to another young man from Inverness, Patrick Grant. Grant, who had 'knowledge of Negroes beyond what one can hardly believe for so young a Planter', was bound for Essequibo with 'his ten Negroes and mine' to enter into a partnership in a wood-cutting business. By September 1802 Mackenzie & Co. had provided Mackay with credit for the purchase of a further '10 Negroes at a very moderate price', which he added to those he had already hired out. By the time Mackenzie & Co. wound up their business in 1806, Mackay's income of £400 from hiring out his slaves was greater than his salary – and, as his board and lodgings were provided, he had probably paid off the cost of buying them. But he saw the abolition of the African slave trade as putting an end to opportunities for men like him.

> To another class of people, overseers, clerks & tradesmen, it is a check on their industry; for their only encouragement to live in so baneful a climate was the benefit derived from owning some Negroes, their wages being barely sufficient for the necessities of existence.[40]

In May 1811 Mackay purchased a sugar estate, *Reliance* in Essequibo, with a George Mackenzie from Fodderty (Ross-shire), who had already been his partner in running a task gang. The estate had 114 slaves and was bought on credit for £25,000. They were to pay for this by shipping 250,000 lb of sugar each year to Robert & William Pulseford of London, until the capital and interest were paid off, but Mackay estimated that they would, in fact, produce 500,000 lb annually.

Mackay returned to England in 1815, married, and sent his nephew, Donald Mackintosh, to manage his plantation. However, in 1833, when it was clear that slaves would be freed, Mackay embarked once more for Demerara.

> We are driven to this necessity by the unprecedented spoliation of West India property by the British Government; an act of so villainous a character as could only be expected from the most lawless and despotic Government that ever cursed any Age or Country. It is different with me now than when 33 years ago I went to seek my fortune in Demerary, I was single & a young man and it was of little consequence whether I succeeded or not; I now go in my 59th year with my wife and three of my children torn away from 4 who we are obliged to leave in England for their education, in order to rescue as much of the property as I have acquired by my good conduct, industry & talents for so many years as I possibly can for their benefit. I trust you will pardon this egotism, and the severity of my remarks concerning the government of my country, for times and occasions do arise when a conscientious man may give expression to his feelings, and his just indignation, without being ashamed.[41]

He subsequently claimed compensation of over £24,000 for 467 slaves and died at Callipers Hall, Hertfordshire, in 1852. Mackay stands as an example of how the opportunity to buy slaves could benefit those from a modest background but of 'good conduct, industry & talents'.

SOLDIER: THOMAS STAUNTON ST CLAIR AND THE LAST SLAVE SHIP

Armed forces were essential to any slave economy but especially to Guyana with its extraordinarily small white population in relation to the number of enslaved – in Berbice a population of about 500 whites to 20,000 slaves. These forces consisted of the colony militias and troops sent from Britain. Thomas Staunton

St Clair (1785–1847) served as an ensign in the Royal Scots, who garrisoned Berbice and Demerara for part of the first decade of the 1800s. He arrived there in 1806 and was present at the last large slave auction held in the colony after a schooner, sailing under the American flag, entered the River Berbice in the spring of 1806. A party from the garrison at Fort St Andrew, including St Clair, boarded her. He later described how on deck there were more than 250 emaciated individuals, who, if they moved at all, were like 'animated automata'. More lay listlessly below decks and a few were confined in the ship's five punishment cells or 'black holes', including one man who had tried to end his life by jumping overboard. In the cabin at the stern of the vessel were half a dozen naked young girls – better fed than the others on board – who had been sexually abused by the captain and mate for the duration of the voyage. The smell, throughout the ship, was appalling and St Clair was horror-struck by the conditions on board. He saw what they had been fed for the last five weeks of the voyage – a little cornmeal boiled in sea water, mixed with a few drops of fish oil. There is no reason to doubt St Clair's revulsion at what he saw but he was soon mentally distancing himself from the hoard of 'ignorant and miserable' creatures who 'jabbered like monkeys with unpleasant voices and in an unintelligible language'.

St Clair published his account in 1834. He was then a distinguished major general, later to become a Companion of the Order of the Bath, and he was able to claim credit for his country's abolition both of the African slave trade and of slavery with the British Empire. This coloured his account of the conditions of slaves in Guyana. He was, for example, at pains to point out that their treatment had been better than under Dutch control of the colonies. But there is no reason to doubt the accuracy of his account of conditions on that last slave ship, bringing Africans to a colony in which simply surviving slavery was an achievement – and which, as we will see in Chapter 6, can on some measures be regarded as the most Highland of the British colonies in the Caribbean.

A SLAVE CALLED INVERNESS

Tens of thousands of enslaved Africans lived and died in Berbice. What follows is an attempt to create a biography of one of them, who enters the surviving historical record on 18 July 1803 when Peter Fairbairn, manager of Lord Seaforth's plantations in Berbice, bought twenty newly arrived enslaved Africans from William Mackenzie & Co. of Stabroek, Demerara. The ten men and ten women had been offered to him on particularly attractive terms – a full twenty-four months' credit. Fairbairn gave the men the names Brahan, Britain, Kintail, Lewis, Gordon, Crawfurd, Ross, Sutherland, Dingwall and Inverness.

They were set to work on plantation *Brahan*, under the supervision of Hector Mackenzie of plantation *Dunrobin*, creating new cotton grounds by draining the coastal land to create polders. These were works of engineering on a colossal scale which created the coastal plantations of Guyana, initially for the production of cotton. It was not long before Inverness escaped from this back-breaking labour and by the end of the year Fairbairn was aware of 'a settlement of about 50 discovered on the Demerara side of the Abery [Abary river] about a days journey away – with plantains, rice, tobacco, cassava etc in abundance'. Planters used the terms 'runaway' or 'bush negro' to refer to people like Inverness. They are more appropriately called Maroons.

By mid-January 1804 there had been an 'expedition to the bush in search of runaways' and Fairbairn heard that 'one of ours has been taken'. Soon there was confirmation that this was Inverness, although two other Africans, Peter and Dingwall, had not been captured. Some time after this, on one of Seaforth's other plantations, an enslaved man called Favourite was found practising *obeah*, a catch-all term used to refer to a variety of spiritual, healing and cursing rituals of African origin, all seen as nefarious by the white population but in reality part of the continuing spiritual life of the enslaved. It was believed that Favourite had also formed a plan to 'carry off a number of the women to the Woods'. He was punished by confinement in the colony barracks and then returned to plantation *Seawell*, where he was again found practising *obeah*. Fairbairn handed him over to the Governor of the colony, van Batenburg, and he was set to work 'in irons'. Yet Favourite escaped again and the following May he was caught at *Brahan* as he attempted to 'carry off' one of the slaves. On this occasion he had been assisted by Inverness, 'who had been long absent but who it seems knows the way back and holds correspondence with the

Figure 2.2 The enslaved man Sampson punished as a runaway, Demerara *c.* 1806. Drawn by Thomas Staunton St Clair, *A Residence in the West Indies* (London, 1834).

coast'. Clearly Inverness had once more escaped and remained free, perhaps for a number of years. Favourite was once more imprisoned in the barracks.

This coincided with mounting concern in Berbice about the growth of a Maroon camp where there were now about a hundred 'runaways' and the Governor came under increased pressure to mount an expedition against them. These expeditions were led by Charles Edmonstone, a Scot from Cardross (Dunbartonshire) who had been in the colony since 1780 and whose Demerara-born wife was part Amerindian. He worked a timber plantation up the Demerara River and his 'bush-expedition' launched from there in 1809/10 destroyed the Maroon camp, captured about seventy runaway slaves and killed about thirty. The bounty for those slaves who were killed was paid on production of a severed right hand. A list of the seventy slaves from Berbice who had been captured, re-enslaved and finally auctioned in June 1812 was later published in the *Berbice Gazette*.[42] There were seven slaves belonging to Peter Fairbairn but Inverness was not among them – and so he may have been among the thirty who were murdered, his right hand cut off to claim the bounty.

Whatever his fate, Inverness was kidnapped in Africa, made into a commodity called a slave, suffered the horrors of the 'Middle Passage', was sold, renamed, set to back-breaking work on the fever-ridden coast of Guyana, escaped more than once, lived free again, was captured and finally died or was killed – almost entirely by Scots, many of them from the Highlands.

3

Jamaica – 'As much gold as will fill a flagon'

In the north of Sutherland, sometime in the 1750s or 1760s, the Gaelic bard Robert Mackay (1714–78) – who was known, perhaps from the colour of his hair, as Robb *Donn* (brown) – looked for the homecoming of the 'man who is in Jamaica'. He imagined him 'coming to shore' and hoped that he would 'bring gold with him / As much as will fill a flagon'.[1]

> Tha 'm fear a tha 'n Seumeuca
> A tigh 'nn gu cladach,
> S bheir e leis a dh' òr,
> Uiread 's a lioness flagan.

Many others thought of Jamaica in the same way – as a dream of a pot of gold.

Although he never learnt to read or write, Robb Donn had been strongly influenced by a Gaelic translation of the verse of Alexander Pope and he composed songs and verse which were, like Pope's, both insightful and critical of the society in which he lived. He left a body of work which 'might arguably be as important to poetry in the Gaelic language as Robert Burns is to poetry in Scots'.[2] While a number of Gaelic poets of the eighteenth century mention Jamaica – perhaps sometimes using it as a generic term for the West Indies as a whole – it is Robb Donn who refers most frequently to the Caribbean island more than four thousand miles from his home in Sutherland.

In 1789, eleven years after Robb Donn's death, Donald Sage (1789–1869) was born in the manse of Kildonan, where his father Alexander Sage had become the parish minister two years before. Donald was brought up speaking Gaelic and English, knew Robb Donn's songs and, like the bard, became an acute observer of the society around him. He left a richly textured account of his own life in *Memorabilia Domestica: memories of parish life in the North of Scotland*, largely written in the 1840s but not published until 1889, twenty years after his death. He was brought up in Kildonan but through his father's second marriage he had many relations on the *Machair Chatt*, the east coast of Sutherland, many of them in the parish of Loth, on which he made the following comment:

> The circle of society of the better classes in Loth at this period was, perhaps, as respectable as any of the same kind in all Scotland. They were the tenants or tacksmen, to be sure, of the Marchioness of Stafford, but they were more on a footing of proprietors than of tenants. They were all, without exception gentlemen who had been abroad, or had been in the army, and had made money. They had each of them, too . . . their long leases or wadsets, in virtue of which they each had a vote in the county. Such, indeed, was the state of society throughout the whole county, more especially on the coast side of Sutherland, then and long previously, particularly so in the parish of Loth, which might not unjustly be regarded as an 'urbs in rure' [a city in the country].[3]

They had 'without exception . . . been abroad or had been in the army . . . and had made money'. And when one looks at the detail of their lives, that generally meant the East or West Indies, particularly Jamaica.

Together Robb Donn and Donald Sage give us deep insight into the nature of society in the north and the east of Sutherland before, during and after the notorious Sutherland Clearances, of which Sage was a trenchant critic, commenting on the fate of the people of Strathnaver in these words:

> This high-souled gentry and this noble and this far-descended peasantry, 'their county's pride,' were set at naught and ultimately obliterated for a set of greedy, secular adventurers, by the then representatives of the ancient Earls of Sutherland.

Both Mackay and Sage recognised the significance of Jamaica to the society in which they lived and, while emigration to North America was a consequence of the clearances, the West Indies shaped ideas and minds in Sutherland society in the period before clearance began. The West Indies also shaped Sage's own childhood.

JOSEPH GORDON'S PARROT

Donald was five years old at the time of his father's second marriage in 1794. A few years later, Donald and his older brother Aeneas were taken by their father from the manse of Kildonan to visit some of their new relations – their stepmother's family. The new Mrs Sage had six sisters, three of whom lived on the *Machair Chatt*. They were Williamina, Elizabeth and Roberta Sutherland. As they approached Helmsdale, Donald, now seven or eight, saw the sea for the first time and, at the house where they lodged for the night, sat by his first coal fire. The next day they went south to Midgarty, where they met Williamina and her husband, Robert Baigrie. Captain Baigrie, born near Peterhead, had gone to sea as a cabin boy and rose to become a captain in the London/West India trade. This sailor turned farmer could tell tales of life at sea, including a voyage into the Arctic, and Donald felt he was 'in fairyland'. After a few weeks they went four miles north to Navidale, to the house of Elizabeth Sutherland and her husband, Joseph Gordon. This was also the home of the third Sutherland sister, Roberta. Gordon, from the neighbouring parish of Clyne, had made a few thousand pounds as a coppersmith in Jamaica – an essential trade on a sugar plantation – and on his return in the 1770s had taken the lease of Navidale Farm. He had carried out such significant improvements to the farm that when Andrew Wight visited in 1780, as part of his survey of the 'State of Agriculture in Scotland', he remarked that Navidale gave 'a filip to my spirits'.

> The state of this farm has more the air of an expert Improver than of an ailing gentleman from Jamaica, settling there to spend the remainder of his life in his native country among his friends.[4]

Young Donald would become 'enthusiastically fond' of Joseph Gordon. His most vivid memory of this visit was when Joseph brought out his parrot, which was kept in a wooden cage by the window at the head of the stairs. Its appearance was striking enough but when Joseph spoke to it and the parrot replied, 'No dinner, no dinner for pretty Poll!', Donald fled in terror. For a young boy, this was the exotic world of the Caribbean come alive in the Highlands.

As he grew older, Donald would slowly become aware of the

extent of his new relations' involvements in the Caribbean. His stepmother's brother James had died in the West Indies and her sister Charlotte had gone out to Jamaica in 1780 to marry a doctor in the island, where they lived and where their children were born. Tragically, their young son was lost overboard as they returned to Britain. And Mrs Sage's oldest sister Janet had married William Gray, who made money in Jamaica and acquired the estate of Skibo in Sutherland. This was an unhappy relationship – there were no children – and the couple separated well before Gray's death in 1788.

Soon after Donald's first visit to the *Machair Chatt*, the youngest sister, Roberta Sutherland, was courted by a Robert Pope, who had also returned to the parish from Jamaica with a few thousand pounds. She was teased so much by her acquaintances that she retreated from Navidale to the manse at Kildonan, where her suitor pursued her and where they were privately married in July 1799. Donald, who would soon be ten years old, became aware of this when he saw 'Bertie's little shoes placed side by side with Mr Pope's boots at his bedroom door' and one of the housemaids said, "S cinnteach gu bheil iad posda' (Surely they are married).

The next year the Baigries' son Robert, who Donald had met at Midgarty, was in trouble. Although only about sixteen, he had lost money playing cards 'at the tables of the great' and had then broken into a shop and stolen twenty pounds in order to pay his debts. When this was discovered, his parents repaid the money and Robert was sent to the West Indies, where he died of fever a few months after his arrival. The West Indies was a place of danger as well as of wealth and opportunity.

From 1801 Donald and his brother Aeneas were sent to school in Dornoch. Their fellow pupils included Hugh Bethune, the son of the Alness minister, and they may have heard how Hugh's older brother John was entering into a partnership with two other men from Easter Ross – Hugh Rose of Glastullich and John Crauford MacLeod of Geanies – in establishing plantation *Geanies* on the Corentyne coast of Berbice (Guyana). They also met Fergus, John and Sandy Hay, all born in the Caribbean to a Scotsman and a black woman, possibly a slave. Donald and Aeneas went home each 'harvest vacation' and one autumn John and Sandy came with them and spent the week at Kildonan. We do not know which Caribbean island the Hay brothers came from but there were a number of that name in Jamaica at the time of emancipation.

There was another black child in the area. Donald's step-mother had a younger half-sister, Janet, and a half-brother, Robert Sutherland. Robert had also gone to Jamaica, where he had a 'natural [illegitimate] son' who was brought up by his sister Janet and her husband, Captain Kenneth Mackay, at Torboll, west of Dornoch. Robert had prospered in Jamaica and at one point he was rumoured to be buying the whole of the parish of Loth. However, 'the sale being postponed, Mr Sutherland extended his speculations, and, sustaining great losses in business, he soon found his whole fortune dissipated'.[5] Donald may also have been aware of – although he does not mention – a 'mulatto boy' at Wester Helmsdale, who Robert Pope, his aunt Bertie's husband, provided for in his will and who lived with Pope's sister and her husband. The boy's name was Hector Roberts, probably because he was, indeed, Robert's.[6]

Young Aeneas Sage had a poor relationship with their step-mother and when the boys left the Dornoch school in 1803 there was an 'open rupture' with her. Aeneas was determined to leave home and go to sea. Through Captain Baigrie a place was secured for him on a West India trading ship owned by William Forbes of Echt in Aberdeenshire. Forbes was in partnership with the Hogarth family in a company which leased the salmon fishings on rivers in the Moray Firth, including the Helmsdale. This allowed Aeneas to board their smack at Helmsdale in the autumn of 1804 and sail to Aberdeen and then on to London. He wrote home from London but the family received only one further letter, from Philadelphia, after he had served for a short time on a British man-of-war. He was not heard of again.[7]

Donald would have been seven or eight when he encountered Joseph Gordon's parrot and fifteen when he broke down in tears as he saw his brother leave the quayside at Helmsdale, setting off to join 'a West-India-man on a voyage to the West Indies'. The influence of the Caribbean was all around him in these years – in the prosperity of his stepmother's relations, in the death of others, in the shadowy presence of illegitimate children, in his friendship with the Hay brothers, and in the absence and ultimate loss of his brother Aeneas.

ROBB DONN

As a young boy almost a century before, in the 1720s, Robb Donn was taken into the household of a distant relative, Iain mac Eachainn (John Mackay) of Musal, a prosperous cattle drover and tacksman (principal tenant) on the estates of Lord Reay, the Chief of Mackay.[8] Iain mac Eachainn's son Hugh left for Jamaica about 1740 and Robb Donn composed two love songs in the voices of Hugh and his sweetheart, Christine Brodie, daughter of the parish minister in neighbouring Edrachilles. Christine is given words which express her fears that Hugh will not return to her:

Tha mi 'g athchuing' ort bhi tigh'nn,	I am praying that you will come back
Mu 'n dean a' ghrian milleadh ort,	Before the sun harms you,
Mu 'm faigh thu biadh ni tinneas duit,	Before you take food that makes you ill
'S mu 'm faic thu òigh nì mire riut.	And before you see a girl who flirts with you.[9]

Her fears were well founded for Hugh had a daughter, Isobel, with a Frances de Larue in Jamaica. At some point after Iain mac Eachainn's death in 1757, Hugh returned from Jamaica with the rank of colonel from the colonial militia and in 1770 took a lease of Balnakeil, living in its mansion house where he employed Robb Donn and his wife. Robb Donn's description of the unnamed man coming from Jamaica with enough gold to 'fill a flagon', with which this chapter began, could well have been a reference to the bard's childhood friend and employer, Colonel Hugh Mackay.

Colonel Hugh lived 'in sin' at Balnakeil with his Scottish housekeeper, who he eventually married – having tolerated Robb Donn's criticism of them in one of his songs.[10] A sexual relationship with an enslaved or 'free coloured' housekeeper was common in Jamaica and one wonders if Frances de Larue, the mother of his Jamaican-born daughter, was a woman of colour who had served him in a similar way. Their daughter Isabella married another Hugh Mackay, who had gone to Jamaica from Sutherland as a doctor, and Robb Donn had earlier composed an emigration song when Dr Hugh's brother Rupert left for Jamaica:

Na robh feartan aig fuachd ort,	May the forces of cold spare you,
Na toir teas dhuit a chuartaich,	May fever not envelop you,
Na bu treise luchd t' fhuath	May those who hate you not be stronger
na luchd t' fhàbhoir.	than your supporters.[11]

Although Robb Donn showed himself to be a sharp satirist and a moralist, there is no direct or implied criticism of those who made their fortunes on the slave plantations. Instead, Jamaica and the West Indies in general were symbols of potential wealth, of independence and of security.

THE CARIBBEAN COLONIES AND THE SUTHERLAND CLEARANCES

James Hunter in *A Dance Called America* describes the kirkyard beside the parish church of Kildonan with its 'fallen over, invariably less legible, slabs of rock . . . [with] some small trace of the Gunns, Mackays, Sutherlands and Bannermans who . . . had been inhabiting this place for as long as it made sense for anyone to remember'.[12] Donald Sage's fierce denunciation of the Sutherland Clearances adds an awareness that the leading families in these communities, many of whom would lose their long-held tenancies, were often headed by men with international experience and connections. They had served in the Scots Brigade of the Dutch army, in the armies of the Honourable East India Company, and in the regiments of the British army. And they had been owners, managers and overseers of cotton and sugar plantations. Some were men like Colonel Hugh Mackay at Balnakeil who had returned with enough gold 'to fill a flagon'.

The 'actors in the clearance drama' – to use Hunter's term from *Set Adrift upon the World: The Sutherland Clearances* – included both 'improvers' who implemented policies of clearance and those who opposed them. Examples of both drew their wealth from the slave plantations. The 'improver' William Clunes of Crakaig was the brother of a prosperous planter in St Vincent, while Joseph Gordon of Carrol, who opposed the clearances, was from a family with extensive involvements in Berbice. His brother William was a doctor and slave owner there and their brother-in-law James Crauford MacLeod was a merchant, slave holder and slave factor in the same colony. And some of those 'set adrift upon the world' by the clearances found their way to the Caribbean. For example, George Mackay (d. 1840) of the Aberach Mackay family tenanted the farm of Arichliney in Kildonan until he was evicted in 1813. He and his wife, Catherine (Kitty) Mackay, had seven sons and three daughters. Of these children, Hugh died in Jamaica in 1815, James and Robert both died in Demerara in 1829, and William, a planter in Demerara, was lost at sea in 1841 on the *India*, burnt off the coast of Brazil.[13] The Mackays of Carnachy, also in Strathnaver, were cleared and established themselves in Pickering, Ontario – but only after some time in Guyana. Their third son, John, died in Demerara in 1831 and three years later, on the eve of emancipation, Donald Mackay (probably another son) left the colony, sailed to New York and travelled to Ontario where he bought a 98-acre farm and later built a house which he called 'Charnachy'.[14]

Other responses to the clearances involved families with links to the Caribbean. Adam Gordon of Griamachary, after service in the army, returned to Kildonan in 1817 and proposed to lead an emigration of evicted tenants to settle on the South African veldt. Although be claimed in April 1818 that 'more than one half of the inhabitants of [the Strath of] Kildonan [had] expressed their determination to accompany him', the plan came to nothing.[15] At the same time, Adam's older brother, Major John Gordon, was in Demerara, where his relationship with a 'free coloured' woman would come to define the law of marriage in Scotland. I will return to them in Chapter 8.

There was a further connection to prospective migration to South Africa. In 1819 George Laing, then living in Brixton, applied without success for a Government post superintending a hundred families from the counties of Sutherland and Ross-shire, who it was proposed should be settled there to grow sugar cane. Laing already had some connection to the north of Scotland and in 1798 he subscribed ten guineas (£10.50) from Demerara towards the establishment of the Northern Infirmary in Inverness. In his application for the post in South Africa he was described as 'having been from 1797 to 1812 a Settler & Sugar & Cotton Planter in the Colonies of Demerera &

Essequibo and during that period in the constant habit of following up and superintending the labour of Negroes in the cultivation and planting of new lands &C'.[16] It is not clear if this was the same or a new scheme.

A final example of these links to the Caribbean is the parliamentary election of 1790, in which there was an unexpected challenge to the influence of Lady Sutherland and her husband, Lord Gower. They had had their candidate returned unopposed as MP in 1787 and the influence of the Sutherland family was regarded as 'almost insurmountable'. Nevertheless, Robert Home Gordon (1765–1826) stood against them. Donald Sage gave an account of the contest:

> Mr Gordon lost his election, yet by a narrow majority. He was supported by the most respectable barons of the county. Dempster of Skibo, Gordon of Carrol, Gordon of Navidale, Captain Clunes of Cracaig, and Captain Baigrie of Midgarty; and most of those gentlemen, being tacksmen and wadsetters on the Sutherland estate, gave by their opposition to the candidate of the Sutherland family, almost unpardonable offence.

Robert Gordon was the Jamaican-born son of Dr John Gordon (1728–74) who had gone to the colony from Sutherland in the 1750s and had become a plantation owner and slave holder. Sage was wrong. Gordon received only three of the seventeen votes cast but his account may reflect a memory of the underlying sympathy towards Gordon from these families. Even to pursue an election to a vote involved vast expense and the challenge was only possible because Robert Gordon's wealth derived from Jamaica. It was believed that Gordon had built the magnificent mansion house at Embo solely for the purpose of entertaining the electors during his campaign.

In summary, the slave plantations of the Caribbean with their real, imagined and dreamt of wealth shaped the world of the inhabitants of Sutherland at the time of the clearances. Many of the main actors had made their money there, migration to these colonies was one option for the better off among those cleared, and – as we will see in later chapters – there were important connections between the skills necessary to run the complex business of a sugar plantation and the ideas of 'improvement' which motivated the transformation of the Sutherland estates. By the time of the Sutherland Clearances the most common links were to the new colonies of Berbice and Demerara, but this had begun with the lure of Jamaica.

SCOTS IN JAMAICA

Although Scots had full access to Jamaica and the other English 'sugar islands' only after the parliamentary union with England in 1707, their presence in Jamaica by the end of the century was remarkable. In 1774 the island's first white historian, Edward Long, reckoned that a third of Jamaica's white inhabitants were of Scottish descent, at a time when Scots were about a sixth of the combined population of Scotland, England and Wales.[17] Long's estimate would make the number of Scots in Jamaica in the 1770s about 6,000.

The networks which these Scots formed have been described by Douglas Hamilton, Allan Karras, Eric Graham and others. Karras' *Sojourners in the Sun* (1992) described settlement from 1740 and provided a detailed account of the web of patronage and personal relationships centred on Francis Grant (1745–1818), who was connected to the Grants of Castle Grant in Strathspey and who arrived in the colony in the 1770s. He had close dealings with other northern Scots, including the Gordons of Buthlaw and Cairness in Aberdeenshire. Karras shows that Scottish settlement increased from the 1740s and, as a result of their late arrival relative to their English counterparts, most of these Scottish planters purchased land in the frontier regions on the west and north coasts, where a quarter of the estates were Scottish-owned by the end of the century.

Hamilton, in *Scotland, the Caribbean and the Atlantic World*, although dealing with the period after 1750, rightly draws attention to the earlier Barclays of Cairness (near Fraserburgh) who arrived in the colony in the 1720s and to the extensive network of Campbells originating with Colonel John Campbell, who arrived in Jamaica in 1700 and settled in the south-west of the island. In 2015 a petition presented to the Scottish Parliament calling for 'Scotland to recognise our responsibility to do all we can to improve the lives of ordinary Jamaicans' began by citing the history of this Colonel John Campbell, as an example of one of the many Scottish slave holders and overseers engaged in the exploitation of enslaved Africans in Jamaica.[18]

During the period of almost 140 years between the arrival of

Colonel John Campbell in 1700 and the full emancipation of slaves in 1838, Jamaica's plantation economy changed significantly and these changes are key to understanding the roles which Scots played in the colony. We have already seen in Chapter 2 how the large, integrated plantation spread only slowly to colonies beyond Barbados, where the system had developed in the mid-1600s. It is worth repeating Trevor Burnard's observation:

> The main reason Jamaica ... [was] so slow in developing the large integrated plantation was that the logistics of managing large numbers of slaves constrained planters from increasing their slave forces past a certain size ... The shift from small-scale to large-scale plantations came about once planters solved the problem of discipline through the application of terror. To terrify slaves, they needed people willing to inflict terror.[19]

Among those most suited to inflicting terror were, as Burnard further notes, men who had themselves experienced brutality as soldiers and as non-commissioned officers, and by the 1690s a group of such men was emerging as part of society in Jamaica. However, the transition from small-scale slave holdings to large integrated plantations in Jamaica did not gather momentum for another ten years or so. It was from 1707 that demand in Jamaica for enslaved Africans increased, with a consequent rise in the price of slaves. Jamaican planters began to have to pay more than planters in Barbados.[20] Demand was driven by that growth of large, integrated plantations. This was, of course, the point at which the 'English sugar islands' opened up to settlement by Scots, following the parliamentary union of the two kingdoms in 1707. And the settlers led by Colonel John Campbell match Burnard's profile of those hardened by military service and civil war, who were able and willing 'to inflict terror'.

Campbell's tomb still stands at Hodge's Pen in the parish of St Elizabeth, Jamaica, bearing the following extensive inscription:

> Here lies the Hon. John Campbell, born at Inverary [sic], Argyllshire, North Britain, and descended of the Ancient family of Auchenbrock, when a youth he served several campaigns in Flanders. He went as Captain of the Troops sent to Darien and on his return to this Island, in 1700, he married the daughter of Col. Claiborne by whom he had several children. In 1718 he married Elizabeth (now

alive) relict of Col. Cames. He was for many years Member of the Assembly, Colonel and Custos of St Elizabeth. In 1722 he was made one of the Privy Council. He was the first Campbell who settled in this Island, and thro' his extream generosity and assistance, many are now possessed of opulent fortunes. His temperance and great humanity have always been very remarkable. He died January 29, 1740. Aged 66 years. Universally lamented.[21]

John Campbell is significant because he had been part of the failed attempt to establish a Scottish colony at Darien between 1698 and 1700, serving there under Colonel Alexander Campbell of Fonab. This national endeavour to create a Scottish Atlantic colony having ended in disaster, John Campbell settled at Black River in Jamaica, an English colony, working first as an overseer and then, through marriage, rising to become a plantation owner and merchant.[22] Eric Graham has summarised the way in which John Campbell's early presence in Jamaica and his continuing connections to Argyll allowed 'a veritable empire of Campbells [to become] entrenched in the western half of the island by the mid-century':

> Five cousins alone owned 21,000 acres across three parishes ... collectively they constituted the third largest family holdings on the island, with each cousin in possession of an 'opulent fortune'.[23]

John Campbell's service in Flanders was probably, like that of Alexander Campbell of Fonab, in the Argyllshire Highlanders. This regiment, raised in 1689 and disbanded in 1697, was created by the Earl of Argyll on his return from exile in the Netherlands, explicitly to support the new British joint monarchs, William of Orange and his wife Mary Stuart, and to oppose Jacobite supporters of the deposed King James. It is sometimes described as the first Highland regiment and although it was said to contain some with Jacobite sympathies, it demonstrated its loyalty in the field to the House of Orange.[24] The many Campbells who had served under Fonab in Flanders and had gone with him to Darien had expected their loyalty to the Dutch monarchy to bring them support, or at least an absence of opposition, from the powerful Dutch East India Company. It was not to be. But such proven loyalty to the Protestant succession in Britain would have aided John Campbell in establishing himself in Jamaica, and it was to be a characteristic of many successful Scots throughout the British West Indies. However, we might also wonder if those who had both served in Flanders and experienced the trauma of the failed Darien experiment were also characterised by that aptitude for brutality which would be much in demand in Jamaica.

Alongside the growth of large integrated plantations, there came another change. In the early years of the eighteenth century there was no sense of a British Empire as an integrated whole. Scotland and England were joined in an incorporating union the effects of which were yet to be seen, the American and West Indian colonies each enjoyed a degree of autonomy, and Ireland's status sat somewhere between the two. Yet by the mid-1700s a unifying vision had emerged of an empire which was 'Protestant, commercial, maritime and free'.[25] This new vision was a 'reimagining of the empire ... forged in the colonies' and drew on the collective British identity that had only 'coalesced a full generation after the Anglo-Scottish Union of 1707'. Elite Jamaican planters, made fabulously wealthy by their integrated sugar plantations, both exercised influence in London and 'actively worked to shed the identity of "colonial," preferring instead the identity of Briton in Jamaica, a subtle but to them important distinction'.[26]

All this changed again in the decades between the 1760s and the late 1790s. An uprising of at least 1,500 enslaved Africans in 1760 – known as Tacky's Rebellion – began to undermine the planters' sense of security. The promises of freedom (for white colonists) implicit in the new vision of the British Empire did not deliver constitutional equality with Britons at home and the declaration of independence by the thirteen North American colonies in 1776 led to economic isolation of Jamaica and other Caribbean colonies. A major hurricane in 1780 devastated the island and the abolitionist movement in Britain grew, putting greater pressure on the whites in the island. One remarkable legacy of the increasing sense of insecurity among planters, especially in the north of Jamaica where there was also a threat from privateers, was the building of fortified houses. At least two of these, Stuart Castle and Edinburgh Castle, are in the form of sixteenth-century tower houses from the Scottish Borders – but they were constructed in the 1760s by Scots who saw this as the most effective means of combining comfort with defence.[27] During these decades the planters who could afford to do so left for Britain and the opportunities increased for 'sojourners', men able and willing to act as attorneys, managers, bookkeepers, overseers and doctors.[28] One Highland planter in Jamaica who lived through this change in Jamaica was John MacLeod of Colbeck.

'MANSIONS OF PLEASURE': MACLEOD AND COLBECK CASTLE

In the early 1760s John MacLeod (*c.* 1722–75), from the island of Lewis, spent £70,000 building Colbeck Castle in the south of Jamaica. At over £7 million in today's purchasing power, it was something much more than the temporary residence of a sojourner and appears to have been part of an attempt by MacLeod to rise into the society of the island's wealthiest men. These were the super-rich of the West Indies – men like Dawkins, Price, Long, Pinnock and Blagrove. But if he had hoped to join their ranks, MacLeod was unsuccessful and never held any senior office in the colony.

MacLeod's father and grandfather were tacksmen in Lewis and on his mother's side he was descended from a family of similar status on the island of Raasay. It was his uncle, John MacLeod of Raasay, who in September 1773 entertained Samuel Johnson and James Boswell during their tour of the western islands of Scotland. On that occasion there was music and dancing, they sat down to dinner with thirty-six people, and Boswell in his *Journal* remarked that 'more gentleness of manners, or a more pleasing appearance of domestick society, is not found in the most polished countries'. For Johnson this was the more surprising and delightful because they were 'so far remote from all those regions which the mind has been used to contemplate as the mansions of pleasure'. Meanwhile, in Jamaica, Raasay's nephew had created his own 'mansion of pleasure'. This younger John MacLeod bought *Colbeck* plantation on 12 November 1749 and is probably the same John MacLeod who was an overseer there in 1743 under the previous owner.[29] His mansion house, later known as Colbeck Castle, was built in the early 1760s.

We can appreciate the significance of Colbeck Castle through the work of Louis P. Nelson, professor of architectural history at the University of Virginia, who led field studies of Jamaican buildings and in 2016 published *Architecture and Empire in*

Jamaica. Nelson demonstrates that it was MacLeod, rather than an earlier owner, who built the mansion and argues that he did so in a bid to enter the ranks of the island's elite planters, who by this point both exerted political influence in London and were determined to present themselves not merely as colonists on the margin of empire but as 'Britons in Jamaica'.

> Elite Jamaicans worked to demonstrate themselves as worthy Britons by . . . building 'gentlemen's seats' worthy of their station, and translating the wild, dense growth of Jamaica's mountains and bush into an Anglo-tropical 'picturesque' landscape . . . Colbeck's form was adapted directly from plans, elevations, and sections published in the Italian architect Sebastio Serlio's early sixteenth-century treatise, *I settee libra dell'architetura* or *The Seven Books of Architecture*, first published in English in 1611 . . . In doing so John MacLeod participated in an important marker of eighteenth-century elite English identity, the adaptation from the ancients or from Renaissance authorities in the making of modern country houses.[30]

While in Britain adaptations of Renaissance Italian architecture had to take into account the colder climate, in Jamaica the provision of shade and cooling breezes were essential and the Italian model could be used with little modification. The inventory of MacLeod's Jamaican property at his death in 1775 reveals a spectacular degree of wealth and conspicuous consumption. In the storerooms of the house were 772 bottles of wine and a range of fine cloth, including chintz, damask, printed linen, yellow and blue fabrics for servants' livery, and red-check to cover furniture. The wood-panelled rooms with plastered ceilings were adorned by ten paintings and more than seventy-five framed prints, there was a billiard table and a small pipe organ, and a 'very sophisticated eighteenth-century kitchen' with specialist equipment. One wing had a sunken bath for cold-water bathing, with a changing room and flushing privies – in contrast to Raasay, where two years before Johnson and Boswell had 'sought in vain at the Laird's new-built mansion' for 'a certain accommodation [that is, an indoor toilet]'.[31] All in all, John MacLeod's house 'signalled an incredible degree of elite cultural currency . . . at the very fringe of empire'.[32]

At the same time, MacLeod was enhancing his status by seeking a grant of arms as the representative of the MacLeods of Lewis, a claim based on a spurious genealogy but successful nonetheless. At his death in 1775 his property was inherited by his brother Donald, in trust, and then by his nephew, also John MacLeod (1758–1822), who married his father's cousin, one of the MacLeods of Raasay. He thereafter used his Jamaican wealth to combine a military career and pride in his Highland ancestry with life in fashionable society in Cheltenham. I will return to the family in Chapter 11.

The MacLeods of Colbeck – John MacLeod I (*c.* 1722–75) and John MacLeod II (1758–1822) – thus transitioned from being 'Britons in Jamaica' to being absentee plantation owners and subsequently provided opportunities in Jamaica for their friends, relations and acquaintances in the Highlands. Alexander MacLeod (1753–1830), a cousin by marriage of John MacLeod I, was resident attorney for the *Colbeck* plantation in the 1790s and Malcolm MacLeod (1765–1842), a cousin by marriage of John MacLeod II, had become resident attorney for Colbeck and its 247 enslaved people by 1817.[33] Malcolm died as the owner of his own estate on the island and his obituary described him as 'an old and respectable planting attorney, [who died] in the 77th year of his age, 56 of which he spent in Jamaica'.[34]

In 1824 Alexander Innes, from Ruthven (Banffshire), spent three months on *Colbeck*, where he was to learn the business of running a sugar plantation. He noted that 'the majority of the Planters here are Scotchmen' but added that they were 'chiefly Scotchmen of the lower orders' and 'too much wedded to prejudice and old customs'. In addition to the 'empire of Campbells' in this part of Jamaica, there was a clear network of northern Scots and one evening at *Colbeck* there was gathered 'a large party at Dinner of Gentlemen from the counties of Aberdeen & Banff'. Three days before, they had found shelter in a thunderstorm at 'a Plantation belonging to a Mr Fraser from Inverness who entertained us in true West India style' and the next day they 'dined at Cherry Garden with a Mr Smith from Huntly'.[35]

There were also mixed-race children of the MacLeods. In 1817 the Colbeck slaves included the 'sambos' Joseph MacLeod (1761–?) and John MacLeod (1762–?) and the 'mulattos' Bessie MacKenzie (1768–*c.* 1820), Bessie Gordon (1792–?), Anne MacKenzie (1805–?), Jane Morrison (1805–?) and Margaret Roy (1815–?). They were among the few slaves to have surnames. The term 'sambo' – the plantation owners used these words with a precise meaning – indicates that the two slaves named MacLeod were children of a mulatto mother and a black father. Was their mother a daughter of John MacLeod I, born when he was an overseer at *Colbeck* under its previous owner?

There was one further legacy of the regime at *Colbeck*. Between 1784 and 1789 a young bookkeeper from Inveraray was employed there. He was only sixteen years old when he arrived in Jamaica. His name was Zachary Macaulay.[36] The 'accounting revolution of the Scottish Enlightenment' was important in the effective management of large sugar planta-tions and Zachary, although largely self-taught, would have had a grounding in these methods through the Glasgow merchant house where he was employed from the age of fourteen.[37] In Jamaica, Zachary was shocked by 'the cruelties practised at the will of a thousand petty despots' on fellow human beings who were 'bred and raised like a stock of cattle' and at the 'shameless licentiousness' of their white masters. For four years he tried 'to alleviate the hardships of a considerable number of my fellow-creatures, and to render the bitter cup of servitude as palatable as possible' until, against the wishes of his father, he 'threw up his position' and returned to Scotland.[38] Macaulay went on to become a member of the Society for the Abolition of the Slave Trade, an associate of William Wilberforce and a leading figure in the parliamentary campaign against the African slave trade and, later, slavery itself. His major contribution was to work on the collection and collation of a mass of evidence, a role to which he was suited as a skilled statistician with a meticulous approach and a head for figures. The skills he had taken to Jamaica as a bookkeeper at *Colbeck* were now applied to the cause of abolition.

4

The Ceded Islands – Grenada

Ottobah Cugoano was born in 1757 in the Fante town of Ajumako in present-day Ghana.[1] His father was a companion and perhaps an advisor to his chief – the Ajumako-hene – and Ottobah lived in the chief's household. When he was about ten years old he was sent for by the Ajumako-hene's successor and brought up at the court with the new chief's children, enjoying 'peace and tranquility for about twenty moons'. Ottobah's uncle then took him to live at Assini, closer to the coast, where he 'got well acquainted with some of the children of my uncle's hundreds of relations'. It was a carefree childhood which many might envy, playing in the woods, picking fruit and catching birds. Thirty years later, when Cugoano looked back on this society with its proud traditions of military service, loyalty to the chief and love of liberty, he compared it to the traditional society of the Scottish Highlands.

In both societies courage was valued and one day, as a boy, Ottobah was taunted because he seemed reluctant to join in.

> '[It is] because you belong to the great men, you are afraid to venture your carcass.'

On that day in 1770, aged thirteen and enraged at the slight on his bravery, Ottobah made the fatal decision to go into the woods with his friends.

> I was snatched away ... with about eighteen or twenty more boys and girls, as we were playing.

With a combination of threats and deceit by a band of men he called ruffians, who spoke the same language as the children, they were led along the coast. A little more than a week later, now separated from his companions, Ottobah was handed over to white men at a slave castle. The slave traders paid for him with a piece of cloth, a gun and some lead. He lay with others in the prison of the fort for three days and nights until a boat arrived.

> There was nothing to be heard but the rattling of chains, smacking of whips, and the groans and cries of our fellow men. Some would not stir from the ground, when they were lashed and beat in the most horrible manner.

The boat took them to Cape Coast Castle, owned by the Company of Merchants Trading to Africa, a not-for-profit corporation established by the British Government in 1750 to maintain a series of trading – that is, slaving – forts on the African coast. The Company, run by a committee of merchants from London, Bristol and Liverpool, had reconstructed and enlarged Cape Coast Castle so that its dungeons could now contain upwards of 2,000 people in five chambers.[2] Here Ottobah was confined and then, with many others, transferred to a slave ship, which sat offshore for several days before sailing.

> When we found ourselves at last taken away, death was more preferable than life, and a plan was concerted amongst us, that we might burn and blow up the ship, and perish altogether in the flames.

It was the women and boys who were to set fire to the vessel, with the agreement of the men who were 'chained and pent up in holes', but the plan was revealed 'by one of our own countrywomen, who slept with some of the head men of the ship'. The discovery of the plot led to 'a cruel bloody scene'.

Cugoano survived the voyage to the Caribbean, where he was sold by a slave factor to a plantation in Grenada – in the 'brutish, base, but fashionable way of traffic'. The cruelties continued. He saw men have their teeth knocked out for eating a piece of sugar cane and lashed by 'hard-hearted overseers [who had] neither regard to the laws of God, nor the life of their fellow-men'. He was treated better than many and after nine or ten months he was taken into the household of a gentleman. This man was Alexander Campbell. It is not clear whether or not Campbell was already his owner but something about Cugoano must have made him feel that the fourteen-year-old was a suitable personal slave for a prosperous white planter.

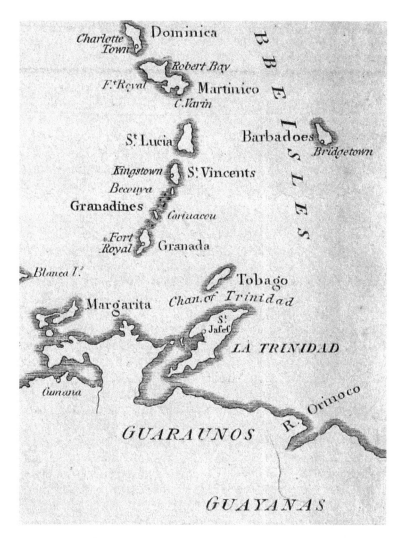

Map 2 Detail from 'A map of the West Indies from the best authorities' (London, 1799) © John Carter Brown Library. Showing the Ceded Islands of Tobago, Grenada and the Grenadines, St Vincent, St Lucia and Dominica.

Alexander Campbell (1739–95) was the youngest son of John Campbell of Lossit on the island of Islay.[3] He was almost forty years younger than his oldest half-brother and it was with the support of his older half-siblings, especially Archibald Campbell (*c.* 1715–99), that he gained his early experience of plantations through the tobacco trade in Virginia. Then in 1763, at the age of twenty-four, he borrowed £40,000 to buy two plantations and three hundred slaves in Grenada. By 1790 he was both a successful West Indian planter – 'lord of a petty fiefdom containing well over 1,000 ... slaves divided among a dozen estates' – and 'a leading crusader in the battle against the abolition of slavery'.[4]

Campbell travelled a number of times between the West Indian colonies and to London. In late 1772 he sailed for England accompanied by Cugoano, who had been given the slave name 'Stewart' or 'Stuart'. (If it was Campbell who chose this name it must have been with a sense of irony, the Protestant Campbells being the arch-enemies of the deposed Catholic Stuart kings.) They arrived in London at a crucial time for those like Cugoano, shortly after Lord Mansfield, the Lord Chief Justice, had declared that James Somerset, a slave brought to England by his master the previous year, could not be forced back to the colonies. Although Mansfield had not declared slavery to be in itself illegal in England, the 'Somerset judgement' was commonly interpreted in that way and after the decision advertisements for the sale of slaves or the apprehension of runaway slaves in Britain disappeared from the newspapers. Cugoano could glimpse freedom. There was also a common belief that a slave who had become a Christian enjoyed fuller protection under the law and so in 1773 on the advice of 'some good people' Cugoano was baptised, thinking that this would prevent him being 'carried away and sold again'. He added the Christian name John to his slave name. The entry in the register for the Church of St James, Westminster, for 20 August 1773 reads: 'John Stuart – a Black, aged 16 years.'

Cugoano may have remained in the service of Campbell until 1778, when Alexander returned to Grenada. He tells us that with the help of others he had learned to read and write, which soon became his 'recreation, pleasure, and delight', and that his master then sent him 'to a proper school for that purpose'. But knowing that to return to Grenada was to return to a state of slavery, he must have left Campbell's service. We know nothing of Campbell's reaction to the baptism but some of the other black servants in London who had helped Cugoano were dismissed.

Cugoano next became a servant in the household of the fashionable painters Richard and Maria Cosway, in their house on Pall Mall, and through them he met campaigners for abolition such as Granville Sharp and the Afro-Briton Olaudah Equiano (c. 1745–97).[5] Cugoano was one of the first Afro-Britons to fight against slavery and he was the most radical of those who campaigned in Britain in the eighteenth century. In 1787, under his true name and probably with the support of some of those he had made contact with through the Cosways, he published *Thoughts and Sentiments on the Evil and Wicked Traffic of the Slavery and Commerce of the Human Species*. The book was one of the first accounts in English written by an African of the experience of being enslaved.[6] But it went unreviewed and largely unnoticed because of his uncompromising stance. Two years later he helped Equiano by subscribing in advance to the publications of his friend's more influential book, *The Interesting Narrative of the Life of Olaudah Equiano*.

Cugoano's book was a powerful, fiercely argued and eloquent work in which he called for the immediate abolition of slavery and argued that slaves had not only a right, but a duty, to rebel against their masters – 'the enslavers of men [who] are the servants of the devil'. In the words of Brycchan Carey, a leading scholar of Cugoano's works, the 'predominant tone is anger and Cugoano rarely makes use of what the eighteenth-century reader would have understood by "sentiment"'.[7] Cugoano's words still challenge us. He held 'every man in Great Britain responsible, in some degree, for the shocking and inhuman murders and oppressions of the Africans', even if 'kings and great men' were 'more particularly guilty'. And he condemned those Africans who participated in the trade, for 'if a man is bad, it makes no difference whether he be a black or a white devil'. We may be able to see Cugoano as well as read his words, for he could be the figure who appears in a portrait of the Cosways.[8]

Less than ten years after he published his book, Cugoano's old master, Alexander Campbell, was dead – executed in Grenada on 8 April 1795, along with forty-seven other prisoners. They were shot on the orders of Julien Fédon, the nominal leader of

Figure 4.1 Probably Ottobah Cugoano, with Richard and Maria Cosway, 1784. © National Portrait Gallery, London.

a rising of French-speaking 'free coloured' people, supported by thousands of the island's enslaved people. This uprising – known as the Fédon Rebellion or sometimes as the Fédon Revolution – has received surprisingly little attention from historians. Yet it was an 'incendiary moment in colonial Caribbean history' and, for British plantation owners and slave holders, it was 'far more destructive . . . than the better-known slave revolts in Barbados (1816) and Demerara (1823) and far more costly in terms of lives than the Jamaican Baptist War of 1831'.[9]

What, then, had been the role of Alexander Campbell in the island and in the events which led to the uprising – and to his death?

NEW PROSPECTS IN THE CARIBBEAN

In acquiring land in Grenada in the 1760s, Alexander Campbell was responding to the opportunities opening up in the British colonies. The first conflict which can justifiably be described as a 'world war' had ended in 1763 after seven years of conflict, with over a million war dead across Europe, India, the Philippines, West Africa, North America and the Caribbean. It is known to British historians as the 'Seven Years War', to Americans as the 'French and Indian Wars' and to others by other names. Notwithstanding the different names and the various peoples caught up in it, it was driven by a single struggle across continents between Britain and France, both having their colonies and allies, and it ended with British victory and significant territorial gains. The peace treaty of 1763, known as the Treaty of Paris, gave Britain new colonies in the south-east Caribbean, with France handing over (ceding) the islands of Dominica, Tobago, St Vincent and, most importantly, Grenada, with the scatter of small islands to the east called the Grenadines – afterwards all known as the Ceded Islands. To be more accurate, France ceded control of its former colony Grenada and of the formerly neutral islands of Tobago, St Vincent and Dominica, in which there were a number of French settlers. The Seven Years War thus resulted in an extension – and not simply a change – in colonial control in the Caribbean, to the detriment of the indigenous Carib populations.[10]

Eyes were now on the prospects victory had brought. There were twenty-six British colonies in the Americas and although the thirteen colonies in North America would later declare their independence, this was not something foreseen in the early 1760s. Instead the developing British Empire appeared to be strong and united, offering opportunities to adventurous investors both from the home countries and from within the network of colonies – and the greatest wealth, or potential wealth, lay in the colonies of the Caribbean.[11] Developments in the plantation system, with the large integrated units needed to realise economies of scale in sugar production, meant that 'the big players in eighteenth-century colonial commerce disproportionately focussed their attentions on new lands opened up to settlement rather than upon the lands of established settlers'.[12] The task of promoting and overseeing the sale of these lands was given to a commission presided over by William Young (1724/5–88), the son of a Dr Young who had fled from Scotland to Antigua following the failure of the Jacobite Rising of 1715. Young, an experienced planter, was to spend nine years away from home, enthusiastically pursuing this mission as well as acquiring estates himself, and he also served as Lieutenant Governor (1768) and then Governor (1770) of Dominica. Young and the commission were under instructions to create model colonies, which could learn from the success of others but which would also avoid their problems of depleted fertility and environmental degradation. To this end they harnessed contemporary scientific expertise and, in an early environmental policy, insisted on preserving adequate woodland in the islands.[13] Young proved to be a skilled publicist, writing his own promotional book and employing the Anglo-Italian artist Agostino Brunias to provide British patrons with an idealised view of the life of slaves in the Ceded Islands.[14] Brunias' paintings soothed the consciences of investors, suggesting that better treatment of slaves could create a tropical Garden of Eden characterised by abundance and the contented harmony of its diverse inhabitants – enslaved Africans, native Caribs, free people of colour and white French and British planters and their employees. Again and again, Brunias displayed the charms of the islands' free women of colour, at this date mostly French-speaking:

> Brunias's mulâtresses provoke the fantasy of possessing a body that both is and is not white, bearing the marks of refined whiteness and the promise of savage sexual pleasure so closely associated with blackness.[15]

Yet Brunias' paintings, whatever Young's intentions, allowed other interpretations. In the 1790s the revolutionary leader in Haiti, Toussaint Louverture, disseminated prints of his works as a celebration of a possible and desired multicultural society and Louverture himself wore a waistcoat with eighteen buttons decorated with reproductions of the paintings.[16]

But at the time they served Young's purposes. Money poured into the Ceded Islands from both Barbados and Britain, especially to Grenada which had eighty-two plantations, mostly large and fertile, which were thought by the British to be underdeveloped because the French planters had too few enslaved people to cultivate them.[17] There was also much uncultivated

Figure 4.2 Buttons attributed to Agostino Brunias. © Smithsonian Institution, Washington, DC.

land and all this offered opportunities in both sugar production and slave-trading. In 1764 the advertisement of the sale of land in the Ceded Islands caused immense excitement in Britain and particularly in Scotland. Douglas Hamilton estimates that ambitious Scots purchased at least 30 per cent of all land made available in the Ceded Islands.[18]

This was the beginning of a period in which we can increasingly see Scottish families with children spread over a number of colonies. The related Harvie (or Harvey) and Farquhar families from Midmar (Aberdeenshire) are but one example of such involvement and of the increasing wealth and status of those who succeeded. The local schoolmaster, John Harvie senior (1690–1767), and his wife Elizabeth Mackay (1691–1776) had three sons who went to the English 'sugar island' of Antigua, where the eldest, Alexander Harvey (1719–74), was settled by 1749. In 1764 the second son, John Harvey (1721–71), also described as a planter in Antigua, was 'intending shortly to embark for . . . Grenada and to Settle as a Planter'. The third son, Robert Harvey (1732–91), then inherited both the Antiguan and Grenadian plantations. Meanwhile, the schoolmaster's daughter Elizabeth Harvey (1724–1807) had married first a William Rae and then Alexander Farquhar (1725–1807), a bailie of the burgh of Kintore (Aberdeenshire). Elizabeth's five sons became a second generation of adventurers from Aberdeenshire to the Caribbean. The Farquhar boys were Robert (1755–1836), who died in London as the absentee owner of plantations in Antigua and Grenada; Alexander (1761–92), who died of a fever in Antigua; Charles (1769–98), who also took ill and died in the Caribbean; and James (1765–95), who became aide-de-camp to the Governor of Grenada, Ninian Home, and was another of the forty-eight prisoners executed during the Fédon Revolution. From her first marriage, Elizabeth's other son, John Rae (d. 1820), inherited estates in Grenada from his uncle Robert and took the surname Harvey. He has been described as 'a key figure in the transmission of Grenada slave-property' and the family's rising status can be seen in the marriage of his daughter, Elizabeth, to the Earl of Buchan in 1830. Caribbean wealth thus enabled the family's notable 'upward mobility' – from schoolmaster to countess in four generations.

At the same time there were the usual, barely acknowledged offspring in the Caribbean. When John Harvey died in 1771 he left, by way of a codicil to his will added in 1769 while he was in Bath, instructions that 'a mulatto boy named David and two mulatto girls named Sally and Rachel' should be bought from the estate of Josiah Marten and made free. David was to learn a trade and Sally and Rachel were to become seamstresses and milliners. The girls were to be taught to read and write – and were left substantial legacies – but only if they too were 'upwardly mobile' and married free white or 'free mulatto' men.[19]

A 'RANCOROUS HATRED OF THE CATHOLIC RELIGION'

While unoccupied land in Grenada was offered exclusively to British investors, the French plantation owners were offered the option of selling their lands to British planters within eighteen months or of swearing allegiance to the British Crown and leasing back their lands for a period of forty years. The official policy of the British Government was to allow Catholic French planters, including the substantial population of Catholic 'free coloureds', both freedom to practise their religion and civil rights, including the right to vote in elections to the local Assembly. These French-speaking subjects of the British Crown were thus to enjoy greater freedoms than Roman Catholics within the British Isles. The guarantees of religious and civil liberties persuaded most to remain. But twelve years later, in 1776, the new Governor, Lord Macartney, found the free community in Grenada riven by feuds, in particular between the French and the 'Scotch party'. The Scots exhibited a 'rancorous hatred of the Catholic religion' and were the more violent and difficult to placate.

As early as 1765, a group of Scottish Protestants resident in Grenada had 'made it their personal objective to ensure that . . . any liberalisation for Catholic dissenters in Britain would not occur in Grenada'.[20] The Grenadian historian Beverley Steele concludes that this was 'by far the greatest problem in Grenadian society at the time'.[21] It was also a more general question for the expanding British Empire, now with a substantial number of Catholic subjects in Canada. Thus Aaron Willis comments:

> Contemporaries agreed that Grenada stood at the centre of a broader imperial and constitutional debate. In an increasingly heterogeneous empire where the formation of loyal and stable colonies was a fundamental goal of the British state, the case for a more

flexible ideal of empire and the constitution gained traction in the dispute over Grenada.[22]

The tensions were mirrored in Britain and in 1778, when Parliament passed the Papist Act to mitigate some of the effects of official discrimination, this was met with opposition which sparked the week-long 'Gordon riots' of June 1780, in which hundreds of people were killed. In Grenada the fact that a number of the Catholics were 'free coloureds' simply added another layer of prejudice. Over the next twenty years the position of French-speaking Catholic planters, both white and 'free coloured', would be further undermined and this was one of the spurs to the Fédon Revolution of 1795, in which Alexander Campbell died. For Campbell, and many others like him, the pressing questions of freedoms and liberty had not been about enslaved Africans but about French subjects of the British Crown.

ALEXANDER CAMPBELL AS PLANTER, LOBBYIST AND ANTI-ABOLITIONIST

Mark Quintanilla has published two studies of the Campbell network in the Ceded Islands.[23] He divides Alexander Campbell's career into three phases: between 1763 and 1773 Campbell adopted and developed the system of sugar cultivation; between 1774 and 1788 he diverged from traditional practices and diversified crop production, to guard against the risks of monoculture and the impact of political instability on markets; and from 1788 he 'became part of a cadre of large landowners who emerged as a colonial oligarchy ... [which] dominated the political, social and economic life of the Ceded Islands'. Campbell's interests extended into the colonies of Tobago, St Vincent, the Grenadines and Dominica, and this may have helped him to prosper despite French reoccupation of Grenada between 1779 and 1783. His own *Tivoli* plantation in Grenada, which he operated in partnership with fellow Scot Jonathon Aitcheson, became one of the most profitable on the island:

> [They had also purchased] large numbers of African slaves to clear remaining wooded acreage and cultivate minor cash crops, [and] they continued to grow coffee, cotton, cocoa, and indigo, which required smaller labor forces and limited capital, but they intensified sugar production.

Campbell's evidence to Parliament in 1790 included his description of 'the general character of managers and overseers' in the West Indies:

[They are] men of some education and ability ... and are very often sons of gentlemen from this country [England], Scotland and Ireland who go out from this country as overseers, and by their good conduct, after having experienced the management of Slaves, and manufacturing the produce of the grounds, they become managers.[24]

There was no mention of the ability to inflict terror. Yet in this drive to intensify sugar production, Cugoano had seen such overseers – possibly on Campbell's estate – knock out men's teeth for eating a piece of sugar cane and whip them for being seen at church on Sunday.

To protect his profits and that of the 'tight-knit community of British (mostly Scottish) planters who looked after their mutual interests', Campbell became a lobbyist in London for West Indian interests. This is why he travelled there in late 1772, with Cugoano as his servant. There in 1774 he won his case in *Campbell v. Hall*, in which he had challenged the Crown's right to impose a 4½ per cent sugar duty in the Ceded Islands. This was highly important to the planters and it was probably through this success that Campbell emerged as a spokesman and leader of the West India interests during the debates on abolition in 1790, when he gave evidence to the House of Commons Committee.

Caitlin Rosenthal has recently argued that absenteeism among plantation owners was not necessarily a sign of decline but an early example of the separation of ownership and management:

Indeed, as the challenges to slavery became increasingly political, being located in England could even be a strategic advantage. Planters promoted their interests in and around British Parliament, seeking advantageous trade arrangements ... which safeguarded their existing sugar markets, and more open trade to the new independent and growing North American markets. Eventually their focus shifted from trade policies to defending against abolitionism.[25]

Alexander Campbell is a clear case of this shift in focus.

Quintinilla – understandably, given the plethora of Campbells in the Caribbean – misidentifies Alexander's family. While he had a brother James (1736–1805) who became President of the Council in Tobago, he had no brother Duncan; there is no evidence that he was a cousin of Mungo, Thomas and John Campbell (of the merchant house John Campbell senior & Co.); and he was neither an uncle of George Campbell (of Alexander Bartlet & George Campbell in Tobago) nor of Colin Campbell. But he did operate as part of a Scottish network and Quintanilla's conclusions on Campbell's career stand. Contrary to stereotypes, Campbell's success did not lead him to become a perpetually absentee owner, although his long periods of absence from the island annoyed Governor Macartney.[26] Rather he divided his time between London and the Caribbean colonies in response to where he saw the greatest need for his presence. And it was this which led him back to his death in the Fédon Revolution.

The seeds of that whirlwind had been sown from the moment Britain gained control of the Ceded Islands. Grenada after 1763 was a society founded on brutal violence towards enslaved Africans and characterised by feuds between British planters, distrust and hatred of French planters, petty squabbles over honour and precedence, and a fear of runaway slaves – the Maroons. The rest of this chapter is a 'deep dive' into that society, so dominated by those Scots who brought with them the bigotry and prejudices of their homeland.

ROBERT MELVILL'S 'LITTLE EMPIRE'

When he became Governor of the Ceded Islands in 1763, General Robert Melvill (1723–1809), eldest son of the parish minister of Monimail in Fife, was already a veteran of the battle of Fontenoy in Flanders where, in 1745, a third of his regiment had been killed; of Culloden in 1746; and of seven years of conflict in the West Indies. But he was more than a battle-hardened soldier. He had studied at Glasgow and Edinburgh universities, would establish a botanical garden in St Vincent, and was later elected a Fellow of the Society of Antiquaries and of the Royal Societies of London and Edinburgh. For the latter fellowship he was proposed by both James Hutton and Melvill's contemporary at Glasgow University, Adam Smith. He was also credited with the invention of a highly successful, mass-produced cannon – the carronade, manufactured at the Carron Iron Works in Falkirk. Yet this scholar-soldier was a disastrous and venal Governor, whose acquisition of land 'approached illegality'; who, according to his enemies, had a 'well known taste' for women, including young enslaved girls; who colluded in the torture of slaves; and who engendered and presided over bitter internal political conflicts in the newly acquired colonies.[27] Despite having been appointed with the directive to repair relationships with the French community, his legacy was the feud-riven society which Macartney described in 1776.[28]

How had this come about? In April 1764 eighteen of the most prominent British subjects in the Ceded Islands were appointed to a 'Colonial Council for the Southern Caribbee Islands', which sat in Grenada under the authority of Melvill. Following pressure from other interested parties, a lower house in the form of an elected Assembly was established in February 1766. This Assembly was initially established only for Grenada and the Grenadines, it being argued that there was not yet a sufficient number of freeholders in the other islands to form an electorate. In time each colony had both a Council, appointed by the Governor, and an Assembly, elected by the white inhabitants. Douglas Hamilton's account of Scots in West Indian politics – Chapter 6 of *Scotland, the Caribbean and the Atlantic World* – remains the most comprehensive study of Scots in the political institutions of the eighteenth-century Caribbean. More recently it has been supplemented by Tessa Murphy's doctoral thesis 'The Creole Archipelago'.[29] Hamilton's analysis demonstrates the dominance by Scots of the legislatures of the four ceded islands: Dominica, Grenada, St Vincent and Tobago. Scots were 'an extremely significant minority in three of the island legislatures [Dominica, Grenada and St Vincent] and an overwhelming majority in the fourth [Tobago]', figures which point to 'the size and status of the Scottish populations'. But Hamilton also observes that 'these were not stable electoral blocs [and] disputes could often arise between Scots' – as was the case in Grenada, where local animosities grew into a campaign against Melvill, pursued in London by a complaint to the Privy Council and through a pamphlet war between his influential supporters and his opponents.

The core issue in Grenada, which had been an established French colony rather than a neutral island with some French settlers, was the right of the French-speaking, Catholic planters – referred to as 'new subjects' of the British Crown – to vote in elections and sit as members of the elected Assembly. In advance of the first meeting of the Assembly in April 1766, a number of French planters petitioned for the right to vote in the forthcoming election, having asserted their loyalty to the British Crown by swearing the oaths of 'allegiance and supremacy' – oaths which were required of all French planters who had remained in the island. Governor Melvill agreed to their request, perhaps influenced by the situation in the British colony of Monserrat where Roman Catholics of Irish descent had been given a vote. There was no question of French Catholics being allowed to sit in the Assembly, since any candidate for public office had to be a land-owning male and a 'Protestant Natural Born, or Naturalized Subject, who hath attained the Age of Twenty-One Years'. Yet even the prospect of French inhabitants voting in the election sparked a fire of controversy, which began with a Memorial to the Governor signed by eighteen British planters opposing Catholic votes. A counter Memorial followed from twenty-six British planters supporting the extension of rights to French planters, and then came a third Memorial from over thirty French planters. Melvill sought to contain the situation by allowing the election to go ahead and then immediately suspending the Assembly.

Although Melvill had a tendency to sway with the wind, he was by upbringing and conviction anti-Catholic. In 1751 he had joined Edinburgh's Old Revolution Club, which celebrated the overthrow of 'popery' in Britain in 1688, and he supported the hardline position of those who saw Protestant faith as essential to identity as a Briton, whether at home or in the colonies. The allegiance of Roman Catholics, it was argued, was to the Pope and this was incompatible with allegiance to the Crown. New elections in November 1767 returned a split Assembly and thereafter Melvill aligned himself with the anti-French faction, maintaining their support by means of his considerable power of patronage. The first outright confrontation over the rights of French planters occurred in this election when a justice of the peace, Walter Robertson, refused to accept the vote of a Frenchman. It was later said of Robertson that:

> The Governor's caprice raised him . . . from the station of an undone and creditless shopkeeper, to the offices of Member of the Assembly, Treasurer, Judge of the Court of Common Pleas, Curator of vacant Successions, Trustee of the Colony Hospital, &. and all without any

apparent merit or abilities, than those of flattering, and implicitly following in *all things*, the will and direction of his Patron.[30]

Robertson ended his career as Chief Justice of Tobago, having bought an estate there in partnership with Melvill's private secretary, Alexander Symson. Without irony, he named it *Bon Accord* – 'Good Fellowship' – the motto of his home town of Aberdeen.

Robertson was a useful tool in Melvill's hands but the Governor's power relied on bigger players. These included Alexander Campbell, the brothers Ninian Home (d. 1795) and George Home (d. 1820) and the Baillies of Dochfour (see Chapter 2). Ninian Home, who had been a member of the same Masonic Lodge in Edinburgh as Melvill, was rewarded for his support with the presidency of the island's Council and in 1790, with Campbell's help, he was appointed Lieutenant Governor.[31] In that year, when Campbell returned in triumph from London, the two men had their portraits painted at their estate, *Paraclete*. These paintings have been described as being of men who had 'secured their fortunes by taming the West Indian frontier'.[32] But as the Fédon Revolution was to show, it was not as tame as they had thought.

While Melvill, Home, Campbell and others saw themselves as having key roles in 'the moral guardianship of Britishness' – and were supported at home by letters published in the *Scots Magazine* – not all Scots planters were united and another group on the island deplored what they saw as the intolerance of Melvill's supporters.[33] Melvill was, they argued, stirring up 'those ignoble distinctions of new and old subjects, Protestants and Catholics, which ought to have been buried in oblivion'.[34] One of his staunchest critics was Alexander Johnstone (1727–83), one of eleven children (four sisters and seven brothers) in the Johnstone family of Westerhall (Dumfries-shire), whose lives are detailed in Emma Rothschild's *Inner Life of Empires*.[35] Alexander Johnstone – a shy, discontented and odd young man – served in the army in North America before being promoted to the rank of colonel and placed in charge of fortifications on Grenada where, in late 1764, he bought plantation *Baccaye* and its 178 enslaved people. Following a dispute with his superior officers, he was convicted of mutiny and dismissed from his command, being described at the time by an acquaintance as

'more disordered in Mind than in Body'. However, his plantation, which he renamed *Westerhall*, prospered with financial
support from two of this brothers.

Johnstone became a member of the Assembly elected in
1767 which became increasingly dissatisfied with the colony's
London agent and determined that Alexander, who was by
then in London, should represent their views. In this role he
pursued a complaint to the Privy Council against Governor
Melvill. Since Melvill had presided over Johnstone's dismissal
from his command, there was also a personal score to be settled.
Johnstone's views were also expressed through two anonymous
pamphlets, one of them almost certainly written along with his
fellow Scot, and Grenadian planter, William Macintosh. These
pamphlets, in contrast to the views of most Scottish planters,
supported the civil rights of French Catholics on the island.

WILLIAM MACINTOSH

William Macintosh (1738–1806), one of the strongest voices in
support of the rights of the French inhabitants, was probably
born at Achinduich in the parish of Creich (Sutherland).[36] He
was one of at least four sons and at least one daughter of Lachlan
Macintosh, a stonemason who became factor for the estate of
Newmore (near Alness, Ross-shire) and later held the tack of
a number of farms in Sutherland. The family is remembered in
histories of the Highlands through the role of William's younger
brother, George Macintosh (1739–1807), who became a merchant in Glasgow and later, in partnership with David Dale and
George Dempster, managed the pioneering, although ultimately
unsuccessful, cotton mill at Spinningdale on the Dornoch Firth.[37]

William became an overseer in the Caribbean at an early age
and, after the ceding of Grenada in 1763, became Comptroller
of Customs for the port of Grenville, where he bought an estate
for £27,000.[38] It is possible that James Macintosh, a Scot born
in 1733 and also a plantation owner in Grenada, was William's
older brother. William was also one of the original purchasers of
plantations in both Dominica and Tobago, where he was in partnership with William Pulteney (a brother of Colonel Alexander
Johnstone in Grenada, who had taken the name Pulteney on
his marriage). Macintosh was elected to the second Grenada
Assembly in November 1767 and, along with Johnstone, con-

sistently opposed the Governor and his faction. Macintosh had been elected for St Andrew's Parish on the basis of forty-six votes from 'new adopted subjects' – that is, French planters – and just four from the twenty-one 'old' British subjects eligible to vote in the parish.[39]

Macintosh was aware that many of the Catholics in Grenada were members of the Gallican Church who 'universally deny the supremacy of the Pope and acknowledge that of their own sovereign'. He argued that when Gallican Catholics became British subjects they were in a different position to 'our own natural born Catholics' and should suffer no political disadvantage. There was a depth in Macintosh's understanding of these matters lacking in many others engaged in these debates.[40] This may be something he had come to understand in Grenada but it is interesting that an almost exact contemporary from the Highlands was Inverness-born Seignelay Cuthbert (1735–1811) who, with his surname adapted as Colbert, had been ordained in Paris in 1762 and became Gallican Bishop of Rodez in 1781.[41] The Highlands in the 1760s, in the aftermath of the Jacobite/ Hanoverian civil wars, was a place which knew the significance of difference in religion and the implications for questions of loyalty and sovereignty.

In Grenada, Macintosh also served as a justice of the peace for the parish of St Andrew and in 1771 encountered Olaudah Equiano, by then a free man. Equiano and others had sailed from London for the Caribbean as traders and in Grenada had sold goods to a white planter, who had failed to pay them. They applied to Macintosh for redress – 'but being negroes, although free, we could not get any remedy'.[42] This is a useful reminder of the limits to Macintosh's 'liberal' views.

Macintosh left Grenada and between 1777 and 1781 travelled to and from India, journeying through Europe and Africa. His access to senior levels of government in India had been facilitated by a letter of introduction from Sir Hector Munro of Novar, a soldier and politician – and an old neighbour of the Macintosh family in Ross-shire. Macintosh was 'scandalized by what he saw as the inefficient, corrupt, and cruel administration of British India' and argued that the East India Company must 'resolve to treat the Hindoos, not as slaves or inferior animals, but as fellow-men, entitled to protection, liberty, and justice'. It was ironic that Hector Munro had himself brought back

Figure 4.3 Olaudah Equiano. © National Portrait Gallery, London.

to Novar House an enslaved East Indian man named Caesar, who worked as a cook until he ran away in June 1771.[43] In 1782 John Murray published an anonymous work, *Travels in Europe, Asia, and Africa*, using Macintosh's writings but heavily edited and transformed by a William Thomson to take the form of a series of letters. It was a radical, highly critical and controversial book, which drew counter-attacks including a 'venom-filled tract' from Joseph Price, a captain in the East India Company. Price revealed Macintosh's identity and, in the course of his invective, described him as 'the son of a Scotch planter, by a French creole, on one of the West India Islands [and] as swarthy and ill-looking a man as is to be seen . . . on the Royal Exchange'. Elsewhere he described him as a 'half black fellow'.[44] This was incorrect but Macintosh, perhaps already a dark-skinned Highlander, was clearly weather-beaten by his years in the Caribbean.[45]

When Macintosh had returned to London from Grenada, and before his departure for India in 1777, he had estimated that his property was worth some £60,000. But on his return from India in 1781 he found that most of this was irrecoverable, allegedly because of 'the death of two of the purchasers of his estates, and the dishonesty of a partner, whom he had raised from being his clerk'.[46] He had earlier fallen out with his other partners, the Johnstone brothers, and in 1778 William Pulteney/Johnstone referred to Macintosh being in debt to him and as having 'run away to the island of Madeira, en route, apparently, to the French East Indies'.[47] As early as 1770 Alexander Johnstone had turned on Macintosh, despite them both being opponents of Governor Melvill.[48] It is further evidence of the fractiousness of the Scots in Grenada.

For much of the 1780s William Macintosh lived in Avignon with his wife and children, but moved to Germany after the French Revolution and was in Eisenach when he drew up his will in 1807. He appears to have lost all his remaining wealth in France and relied on the support of his brother George, the Glasgow merchant. Even in old age he remained 'a very intelligent, amusing man'.[49] Yet, despite his liberal views on the rights of French and Indian subjects of the Empire, Innes Keighren rightly draws attention to the 'ugly truth' of his slave-holding, embodied in the purchase of branding irons for the plantations jointly owned by Macintosh and Pulteney:

> Please to get made of silver set in a wooden handle, two such stamps as are underneath for marking our Tobago & Dominico [sic] Slaves.[50]

Although Macintosh branded at least some of his slaves, he held that some other forms of mistreatment could not be justified.

TORTURE

One of Governor Melvill's leading supporters, and an opponent of Johnstone and Macintosh, was Captain Peter Gordon, who took over command of the 70th Regiment on Johnstone's dismissal. The progression in plantation ownership of the Gordon family, from Knockespock (Clatt, Aberdeenshire), both captures the successive opportunities created for investors in the British colonies and also the brutality of which they were capable. The

Figure 4.4 Enslaved man branded with initials 'JGS'. Detail from 'Family of Negro Slaves from Loango', William Blake after drawing by John Gabriel Stedman. © Victoria and Albert Museum, London.

eldest son, James Gordon (1694–1768), was an associate of the Scottish merchant James Milliken and with him acquired land in St Kitts, which had been returned to Britain by France under the terms of the Treaty of Utrecht (1713). James inherited the family's Aberdeenshire lands in 1729, became Chief Justice of St Kitts in 1735, and acquired property in Antigua in 1741 and in Grenada in 1751. About 1749 he bought the estate of Moor Place in Hertfordshire, where a new mansion house was built (1775–9) for James' heir, his nephew James Brebner, Chief Justice of the Leeward Islands.

James Gordon's half-brother, Colonel Harry Gordon (1725–87), served in the army in North America and owned land in Philadelphia, which he lost as a loyalist during the American

Revolution. He was, however, on good enough terms with George Washington to write to him in 1783 in the following terms:

> Having been your Excellencys Fellow Soldier in some Campaignes of a difficult and dangerous operation, and as peace has Again Sanctified our Communication, and lessend your Cares; I presume to Ask your Interference and Friendship, on the Subject of my honestly earnd Small Property in America; which it Seems Was with others proscribed by Congress.

By this date Harry and his American-born wife had moved to Grenada, where he became Commander in Chief of Engineers. With two other half-brothers already in the Caribbean, the family's interests thus extended to at least five of the twenty-six colonies: St Kitts, Antigua, Grenada, Jamaica and Philadelphia.

In 1766 Captain Peter Gordon, by then a justice of the peace in Grenada, along with John Harvey (above) and a John Graham, responded to the murder of two white coopers by torturing five slaves belonging to a French planter, Monsieur La Chancellerie. The enslaved men had their hands tied behind their backs and were repeatedly hoisted up by their thumbs until they falsely confessed, first to witnessing the murders, then to having taken part, and finally to the involvement of La Chancellerie and his son, who were then imprisoned. Although charges were later dropped, and the killings blamed on Maroons, three of the slaves died of their injuries.[51] Gordon's fellow justice of the peace, John Harvey, was – as we have seen – also from Aberdeenshire and the third, John Graham, was another Scot. All three were soon appointed by Melvill to be members of his Council.

THE GRENADA MAROONS

Melvill was also accused by his opponents of having failed to suppress the Grenada Maroons who, under their leader Augustin, had been 'in open rebellion for the space of fourteen years'. It was alleged that Augustin had first run away after raping a white woman. But that charge would have been made in respect of any sexual relationship with an enslaved African. He was also accused of the murder of a French planter. In 1766/7 one of the Assembly members, Jersey-born John Dumaresq, who was both a plantation owner and a captain in the 70th Regiment, led a party of more than two hundred whites against Augustin and surrounded the Maroons at a French-owned plantation. At this point a French planter identified only as 'Mr P—y' arrived with instructions from Melvill that no attack was to be made. Other evidence indicates that he was Jean Baptiste Pichery.[52] It was alleged that the Maroons were then allowed to retreat and continue their raids on plantations, while Dumaresq's party was forced 'to remain inactive for seven weeks in the woods'. This only ended when Pichery agreed terms of surrender with Augustin, who was conducted 'as a valiant soldier' to the Governor's house. Melvill then had an Act passed in the island Council freeing Augustin, who remained in the Governor's house for a year until in the face of attempts to prosecute him he was spirited away to another island – some said to Melvill's plantation on Tobago, others to St Vincent to join the Black Caribs, to whom, according to Macintosh, Pichery had 'for many years past been a patron'. This was a reference to Pichery having bought a large tract of fertile land from the Caribs and of being on good terms with their chiefs.

Macintosh's explanation of all this was designed to shock. He claimed that Pichery was not only 'a near neighbour, intimate friend, and inseparable companion of Melvill' but that Pichery's hospitality to Melvill extended to 'his bed' and the company of his young mistress (an enslaved woman related to Augustin) whose 'personal qualifications [were] peculiarly suited to Mr Melvill's well known taste'. There was the added salacious detail that the girl was said to be both Pichery's daughter and granddaughter – that is, Pichery had had a daughter with an enslaved woman, followed by an incestuous relationship with the daughter, and a further incestuous relationship with her child, who was then offered to Melvill:

> Augustin thus stood in a very complicated degree of relationship to the whole of that worthy family into which His Excellency [the Governor] was said to have been, as it were, adopted.

This, according to Macintosh, was the reason why Melvill protected Augustin. It was an astonishing claim to have made, even under the cover of anonymity. It is not surprising that Macartney summed up the nature of the white population of the island in these terms:

[A] strange discordant mass of English, Scots, Irish, French, Creoles and Americans ... heated by various passions and prejudices far beyond any European idea.

Macartney added that there was among the white population:

[A] meaner sort composed of overseers, clerks, low planters and tradesmen [who] are mere banditti, averse to all order, discipline and obedience, turbulent, mutinous and impatient of any restraint whatsoever.[53]

This has more resonance with Cugoano's description of the white population than with Alexander Campbell's evidence to Parliament in 1790 and his description of the 'good conduct' of those 'men of some education and ability' – including the sons of Scottish gentlemen – who had become overseers and managers.

BEFORE THE FÉDON REVOLUTION

For the white planters, the Fédon Revolution was the culmination of a series of adversities. The island suffered an earthquake in 1766, in 1768 it was struck by the worst hurricane recorded in the Caribbean, a plague of 'sugar ants' destroyed crops in 1770, and there were two major fires in the capital Georgetown in 1771 and 1775. Then, in 1778, what had been thought of as a united British colonial presence in the Caribbean and North America was shattered by the Declaration of Independence by North American colonies. The French entered the subsequent War of Independence in support of the North Americans, took Grenada in July 1779, and held it until the peace treaty of 1783. The period of resumed French control had increased divisions in the island and, when British control was re-established, many British planters felt the French should now be dispossessed:

The Idea of converting a Frenchman into a good English Subject, however specious in Theory, is impracticable & absurd.[54]

The now marginalised white French planters were often as keen to sell their estates as British investors were to buy:

This departure of the white French planter class removed from Grenada's political stage the group that was of the same ideology as the white British planter class. Denied a place in the British colonial establishment by their religion and country of origin, they moved to Trinidad, where they formed part of the politically conservative, racially pure ruling elite.[55]

Yet Grenada's white British planters prospered. Sugar production had increased more than fourfold and Grenada had become, after Jamaica, the most valuable colony in the British Caribbean.[56] It was also boosted by a significant change in the supply of sugar from elsewhere in the Caribbean. Planters in the British West Indies sold their sugar in Britain, where they were protected from competition by the Government policy of placing high tariffs on cheaper sugar from other sources. Although this secured the British market – and average sugar consumption by each person in Britain increased by 50 per cent between 1750 and 1775 – British sugar planters and merchants remained very small players in the supply of sugar to the much larger market of continental Europe.[57] This changed in the early 1790s. The French island of St Dominique (renamed Haiti in 1804) was the richest colony in the Caribbean and produced about half of the world's sugar, at lower cost than in the British colonies. However, a revolt by the island's slaves in 1791 and a revolution in 1792 was followed by almost ten years of bitter warfare, with a dramatic decline in sugar production on the island. The result was a shortage in supply, consequently high sugar prices which continued until 1799, and a dramatic expansion of production in the Ceded Islands.[58] These investments were enabled by easy credit made available as the British financial system developed.

Grenada also became a centre for slave-trading, not only receiving enslaved Africans to work as labourers in Grenada but selling on slaves to other Caribbean colonies. This trade created as much wealth as all of its production of sugar, rum, cotton, coffee, indigo and cacao.[59] O'Malley's emphasis on the commodification of enslaved Africans, described in Chapter 2, helps us to appreciate the role of Caribbean islands such as Grenada as entrepôts in the international slave trade. During the eighteenth century Britain increasingly welcomed foreign traders to British territory to buy both enslaved people and British manufactured goods. As O'Malley points out, 'some of the first experiments with free trade were designed to facilitate intercolonial commerce in unfree people'. Re-export of slaves from Barbados was 'considerable' between the end of the Seven Years War and the American Revolutionary War – perhaps two thousand enslaved people each year. The Free Port Act of 1767 opened a number of other ports in British Caribbean colonies to foreign traders, allowing the onward shipment of slaves particularly to Spanish and French colonies. By 1787 St George, in Grenada, had been added to the list of designated free ports and the early 1790s saw the greatest number of slaves brought from Africa to Grenada – 25,000 in the three years from 1791 to 1793.[60] One Highland Scot to take advantage of this was George Robertson (1756–99), from Kiltearn in Ross-shire, who made use of Grenada's recently acquired free port status to trade with the Spanish colonies of Caracas and New Granada.[61] I will return to him and his partners in Chapter 10.

A final indication of the prominence of Scots in Grenada can be found in the militia lists. In plantation societies, being a senior officer in the local militia was a mark of social standing since these ranks were simply bestowed on individuals by their fellow planters. In Grenada in 1787, of the fourteen colonels, lieutenant colonels and majors commanding the five regiments of militia, and the troop of horse, half were Scots.[62] Among the most senior were four of the six colonels: Ninian Home, William Lucas, Alexander Campbell (of Islay) and his brother James Campbell. Lucas died in 1787 and had perhaps been ill, since under him was the only lieutenant colonel, James Baillie – probably the cousin of the Baillies of Dochfour described in Chapter 2. The cavalry troop was more prestigious than the militia's other regiments, and of the four officers and thirty-five troopers, twenty-six (66 per cent) appear to have been Scots. Their world was shattered by the Fédon Revolution.

THE FÉDON REVOLUTION AND AFTER

On 2 March 1795 an uprising began on the island involving both enslaved people and French-speaking free people of colour, led by the planter Julien Fédon and his brothers. It was to be a rebellion infused with the language and ideals of the French Revolution, holding out the prospect not only of liberty – including the abolition of slavery – but equality and fraternity between all citizens. Enslaved labourers from both British- and French-owned plantations were to the fore in the first attacks on the settlement at Grenville and on the colony's second town, Gouyave (originally Charlotte Town). In the first few days over forty prominent whites, including the Governor and many members of the Council, were captured. The capital St George held out against the attacks and when the deputy Governor, Kenneth Francis Mackenzie, refused to surrender Fédon ordered the execution of forty-eight prisoners. These included Governor Ninian Home, George Rose (son of the minister of Tain), James Farquhar (from Kintore, Aberdeenshire) and Cugoano's former master, Alexander Campbell. A bitter war followed, ended only by the action of British reinforcements brought from neighbouring colonies. Kit Candlin summarises its impact thus:

> [T]his rebellion against British rule all but destroyed the once-thriving colony. When the British finally, and at great expense, overcame the insurrection 16 months later, at least 7000 of the enslaved lay dead alongside over 1000 Europeans and free people of colour. Scores of plantations were ruined and over 40 'ringleaders' were rounded up and publicly executed along with many others killed out of hand. Over 400 rebels, mainly free people of colour, were sent to the penal colony of Honduras. It would take several years and a loan of over £100,000 from the Colonial Office for this colony to begin to recover from the damage wrought by the conflict.[63]

Those who continued to prosper after the Fédon Revolution were mainly those who had diversified into other colonies. Stephen Mullen has shown how the partners in the great Glasgow West India merchant house of John Campbell senior & Co. initially made their money in Grenada and the smaller island of Carriacou. The partners included John's younger brother Thomas Campbell. It was Thomas in particular who 'maintained a transient lifestyle' and was 'particularly adept at cultivating close relationships with Scots at home and abroad', for example travelling to north-east Scotland in 1786 to establish a long-term business relationship with the Urquharts of Meldrum and Craigston, who were leading plantation owners in Carriacou. Thomas became a full partner in John Campbell senior & Co. in 1791 and was planning diversification into Demerara from as early as 1792, when it was still a Dutch colony. When he too was caught up in the Fédon Revolution he fled there and, although he died of fever shortly afterwards, the partnership continued as a major player in Guyana.[64]

The rebuilding of Grenada as a profitable, slave-based plantation economy involved a generation of new Scottish merchants and adventurers, including many from the north of Scotland.

They are beyond the scope of this chapter but many played a prominent role in Highland life. In a former archive cupboard in Poyntzfield House on the Black Isle (Ross-shire) there is a docket hole marked 'Grenada', a reminder of the role of the Gun Munros on the island. In Dornoch Cathedral (Sutherland) is a large memorial window to the Hoyes family. Their wealth came from Lewis Hoyes (1786–1843), whose death was noted in the *Inverness Courier*:

> The death is announced of Mr Lewis Hoyes, merchant in the island of Grenada and Speaker of the House of Assembly, in his 58th year. Mr Hoyes was a native of Forres, but had been a resident of Grenada for about thirty-four years.

And writing in the 1880s Isabel Harriet Anderson wrote this of what is now Abertarff House in Inverness, then commonly called the Blue House because of its slate roof.

> An aged lady in Inverness has often narrated to the writer the delight with which, in her youth, she used to visit the Blue House, when it was the abode of a gentleman known as 'Mr Munro, Grenada' ... There were beautiful gardens and a delightful conservatory attached to the house, but the great delight of the young people, who sometimes went there on a Saturday ... was a room filled with foreign birds of brilliant plumage, having among them a parrot of such remarkable talking powers as had never been equalled by any parrot in Inverness.[65]

But behind these tranquil images of stained glass and the brilliant plumage of parrots there had been the reality of Grenada. It was a society which Lord Macartney had described as a 'strange discordant mass of English, Scots, Irish, French, Creoles and Americans ... heated by various passions and prejudices far beyond any European idea'.[66] Northern Scots had been among those who stoked the fires of cruelty and prejudice which fed that furnace.

5

A Family of Highland Carpenters
in the Ceded Islands

As early as 1752, Alexander Baillie (see Chapter 2) noted the 'great numbers' who flocked to the West Indies 'from a very mistaken Notion ... [that] Gold may be got for the gathering'. He was of the opinion that none were 'more deceived in this respect than the Scots'.[1] Baillie's plantation *Hermitage* in Grenada attracted its own share of hopeful young men from the Highlands and about 1770 Thomas Fraser, a carpenter from Inverness, arrived there to join his friend Hugh Fraser (who was probably also his brother-in-law). Hugh had left his wife and children behind in Inverness and had become a rum distiller in the island.[2] Over the next thirty years Thomas sent eight letters to his cousin Simon Fraser, a baker and merchant in Inverness, writing from Grenada, Tobago and St Vincent before his death in 1800. He died on board a ship from Virginia, where he had gone in a final, desperate attempt to recover his health. In 1774 another carpenter, a cousin also called Thomas Fraser, arrived and established himself in St Vincent. This second Thomas Fraser wrote thirty letters to Simon Fraser, the last arriving in late 1802 shortly after Simon's own death. There are a few more letters to Simon from other friends and relations, written from the Ceded Islands and from the Danish colony of St Croix, making a total of forty-four in all. This correspondence, held by the Highland Archive Centre in Inverness, is especially valuable because it preserves a view of life in the Ceded Islands from the perspective of men who were neither greatly successful nor well connected, but who embarked on an 'adventure abroad' and spent the greater part of their lives in the Caribbean.

The first Thomas Fraser – who I will call 'Thomas (elder)' –

had at least five 'mulatto' children there, one of whom was at school in Glasgow at the time of his death in 1800; the second Thomas – henceforth 'Thomas (younger)' – married a French-speaking woman in St Lucia in 1792 and had six children with her. At least another five family members were in the Ceded Islands and this extended family group were acquainted with many other Highlanders there, some of whom had made – or would make – their fortunes. But the Frasers' perspective, if not from the bottom of society, was generally from its middling reaches; and when it came to understanding the fickle lure of the West Indies, their experience of struggle and misfortune gave them deeper insight than many others who were better off, better educated or simply had better luck.

Both the Thomas Frasers were literate but Thomas (elder) struggled with spelling and with standard English. He was prob-ably a native Gaelic speaker. Thomas (younger) wrote more 'correctly' and elegantly – but surprisingly he was unsure how old he was. In 1791 he asked his cousin Simon to consult the local parish registers, explaining that 'I intend to go a Courting, and I look a little old so perhaps older than I am.' Both had learned a trade as house carpenters but this did not guarantee employment. From the time of his arrival in 1770, Thomas (elder) thought 'there is two [too] many here already which makes the wages very poor for all kinds of trades'; in 1778 he reported from Tobago that 'carpenter work is very slack since the beginning of the American war'; and in 1786 from St Vincent that 'carpenter work is very dull in this Island'.[3] His only advantage as he saw it was that he owned three 'negro carpenters' and five field slaves. Although they were reduced to three by 1784, this enabled him to rent an area of land on St Vincent and plant cotton when he could not find employment as a carpenter. After two years or so of profitable work from 1793, as a carpenter on government contracts in Martinique, he returned to St Vincent to join his cousin in more small-scale cotton- and coffee-planting. When it had been suggested that his younger brother might come out, he advised against it – indeed, 'he did not approve at all' unless the young man learned a trade more in demand, such as that of a blacksmith or better still a millwright. Even then it would be best to go to the 'south country' to learn about windmills. If he did come as a house car-penter, he should get a few years' experience in Inverness first.

Similar reservations were expressed by another of Simon Fraser's correspondents in the Caribbean, also called Simon Fraser, in the Danish colony of St Croix. In 1779 he was thinking of having his brother Hugh sent out from Inverness to join him but he too was cautious and thought it essential that Hugh could 'read, write, cypher, speak good English and [was] otherwise a smart, lively boy' – otherwise he should remain at school in Inverness. Twenty years later, Thomas (younger) thought the situation was no better:

> God help us have you no employment for your young men in Scotland, a Ship from Glasgow brought so many of them here the other day that it was said she was a Scotch Guinea man and that in spite of Mr Wilberforce and the Parliament we would get white negroes from Scotland enough to cultivate our plantations without buying them, the truth is we have too many here, lucky are those who get employment in any line.[4]

Thomas (elder) arrived in debt, probably because he had had to borrow money for his passage to the West Indies, and struggled to repay the loan. Like many other young Highland men who came to the Caribbean, he was struck on his arrival in Grenada by two things – the cost of basic provisions and the lack of respect for 'the Sabbath Day'. The first letter to Simon Fraser from Thomas (younger) in 1777 included an assurance that he was trying to recover both the balance due by his cousin, who was now in Tobago, and also money owed by 'friend Hugh', the distiller in Grenada. Even when they had money, repayment of debts was difficult both because there was no easy way of remitting small sums and because they all wished to retain and invest their small accumulated wealth. In the words of Thomas (elder), 'it is money that will make money'.

One option was credit. When William Fraser, the brother of Thomas (younger), arrived in St Vincent about 1775 he had credit of over £1,000 from John Fraser & Co., the London-based partnership of John Fraser of Achnagairn (see Chapter 2), who was himself in St Vincent. This enabled William to trade as a merchant in addition to working as the manager of an estate – but the risk taken by William did not pay off. Although he disposed of his first consignment of goods, he had another cargo sent out which was partly unsold at the time of his death the following year. The remainder was auctioned at less than cost and, since about one-third of the debts due to William could not be recovered, his own debt to John Fraser & Co. could not be paid. There were limits to what networks could deliver. Because the merchant house was known to the family – they were all from the parish of Kirkhill – Thomas's sisters had written to John Fraser 'to request him to see Justice done them in regard to their brothers effects'. But Thomas (younger), who was on friendly terms with John Fraser in St Vincent, gave this advice.

[They should not] deceive themselves, by thinking there is a substance when there is but a shadow. My Brother had no way of making money before he went home, more than I have at present. What small matter he could save of his salary as a Manager, he was robbed of by Doctors Charges ... he was cut off just as he was getting into a way of getting a Genteel living for himself ...[5]

Thomas (elder) had a nephew, Alexander (Sandy) Fraser – a sister's son – who was in St Kitts & Nevis from 1786 and died in Grenada in 1797. Thomas (younger) noted how Sandy had soon become 'discontented with his lot and thinks that some of his rich relations, by the father's side, have not done so much for him as they ought to have done'. Thomas's view was that it was a mistake to place too much reliance on family, for 'the moment a man begins to think that others are obliged to support him, I say that man is a fool and if he gives up his industry ... he is lost and undone'.[6] His cousin Thomas (elder), towards the end of his life, had a similar lack of confidence in their family connections: '... not one of you ever corresponds with me indeed it is not worth your while I am not Ritch of course a poor man is never linked on'.[7]

Nothing could be achieved without good – or at least tolerable – health. Of seven closely related Frasers mentioned in the letters – brothers, cousins, nephews and a brother-in-law – four died prematurely in the West Indies. Thomas (elder), although he lived for thirty years in the Ceded Islands, was beset by illness: on his arrival in Grenada around 1770 he 'suffered a great deal of sickness'; in Tobago in 1778 he spoke of 'four long years sickness which has taken away all the money I have turned before'; arriving in St Vincent in 1783 his cousin spoke of the loss of his health in 'that cursed country' such that 'it would be really a shock to you to see him the day he landed in [this] island'; and in 1785, about to leave the island to recuperate in North

America, he took the precaution of making his will. Although he lived for another fifteen years, he made little money, his affairs were in a 'deranged' state at the time of his death in 1800, and he had been in decline for some years. Only Thomas (younger) and his nephew Tom, a 'fine boy' who came to St Vincent in 1794, enjoyed long periods of good health – although Tom had been 'at the point of death' in late 1787. Escaping to the better climate of North America, although costly, was regarded at times as essential, both before and after the War of Independence, and five of the seven Fraser relations made at least one journey there. Thomas (elder) paid the substantial sum of £30 for his trip in 1786.

With a sound education at home and a trade which was in demand, with suitable contacts and credit when it was needed, with hard work and tolerable health – and with good luck – it was possible for men like the Frasers to achieve some success. In 1798 Thomas (younger), after a quarter of a century in the Caribbean, reckoned himself to be worth just over four thousand pounds. More than half of his capital was in the value of his slaves. This was a marked advance from his position in 1784 when he acknowledged that his financial state was a poor return on ten years in the Caribbean.

> If I was to pack up my all tomorrow I do not think that I could muster more than five hundred pounds currency after paying my debts in the Island, this you'll think is poor doings indeed for a man that has been ten years in the West Indies.[8]

Four thousand pounds was a sum similar to the capital accumulated in Jamaica by many of the men on the east coast of Sutherland mentioned by Donald Sage (see Chapter 2).

Hugh Fraser did not have the same success. He had left his wife and family in Inverness – and had also left behind him a bad reputation. According to Thomas (younger), he had become 'entirely altered from his old nature' and 'well beloved of his Masters'. Nevertheless, Hugh died in Grenada in 1777 still in debt to Thomas and to Simon Fraser in Inverness, who had advanced money to his wife.

THOMAS (ELDER) IN TOBAGO

Thomas (elder) had soon moved on from Grenada to Tobago. Although Tobago was regarded as strategically important – and Britain and France contested ownership for over a century – in the 1750s there were only a few dozen European settlers, living with a larger Amerindian population. This began to change after 1763 when the island became British, yet in 1765 the Commissioners responsible for the sale of lands in the Ceded Islands wrote to the Treasury explaining that 'such are the difficulties, dangers and expense which attend the clearing of land in this climate, that until persons of fortune and enterprise shall have made some progress in this colony, we are apprehensive the settlement thereof will go on but slowly'.[9] One individual, recently returned to St Vincent from the public sale of lots of land on Tobago in May 1766, believed that 'many people will raise very genteel fortunes in a very short time' but he was bemused that so few lots had been purchased by London merchants, 'which surprised me the greater, as upon my word, I do not know of any scheme where money could be laid out to so great advantage'.[10] Tobago instead came to be a 'Scots dominated island'. The Kennedy, Gordon and Forbes families described below are examples of the many northern Scots who seized the opportunity of investment and Thomas (elder), as a fellow Scot, may have expected this to be to his advantage.[11] Douglas Hamilton's analysis shows that Scots acquired over half of the land offered for sale and that by 1770 they owned thirty-three of the seventy-seven plantations, amounting to 15,517 of the 30,440 acres made available.[12] Only about one-fifth of this land was 'cleared' – that is, ready for cultivation – justifying the statement by the American historian Andrew Jackson O'Shaughnessy that 'Tobago was transformed from woods by the enterprise of "younger sons of Gentlemen of good families in Scotland" to become a producer of sugar, indigo, and cotton'.[13] That transformation was in reality based on the labour of more than ten thousand enslaved Africans who were brought to the island over the next decade.[14]

By the early 1770s 'Tobago was very much a frontier that promised opportunity and riches to ambitious investors ... mimicking the economic miracle that had already occurred in Grenada'.[15] Walter Kennedy (1732–75) was among the first purchasers and is an example of a Scot operating across the boundaries of national empires. Kennedy's father was Revd Hugh Kennedy, who served in the Scots Kirk, Rotterdam, from 1737 until his death in 1764. He both supported and wrote an account of the religious revival taking place in the Netherlands in the 1740s and saw this as part of a wider movement which included his native Scotland.[16] His children were brought up in Rotterdam and while the eldest son, William, became professor of Greek at Aberdeen University, three other sons – Walter, Charles and Robert – sought their fortunes on slave plantations in the Dutch colony of Suriname. Walter established himself in the capital Paramaribo and married a Dutch woman, with whom he returned to Holland. By the time of his death in 1775 he had also acquired lands in Tobago and left over £10,000.[17]

Hamilton shows that among the Scots planters there was a network with a specific connection to 'the area formed [by] a triangle between the towns of Elgin, Huntly and Banff'.[18] Among the most powerful men in this group was Alexander Gordon (d. 1801) of Cluny (Aberdeenshire), also known as 'Alexander Gordon of Belmont' after his Tobago estate. From unknown origins his father, John Gordon (1695–1769), had acquired a fortune through his roles as factor to the Duke of Gordon, as a merchant leasing the Spey salmon fishings, and as a landowner in his own right. He left a reputation that 'every shilling he got within his fingers stuck to them'.[19] Alexander Gordon, his third son, also became 'very rich' in Tobago before returning to London in the 1790s. I will return to Gordon of Cluny in Chapter 11.

A second Gordon family from Scotland's north-east were William, Alexander and James Gordon, the sons of Jane Findlater and John Gordon, a merchant in Portsoy. Through their mother they already had connections with the West Indies and when Alexander (1756–1824) was baptised it was recorded – an unusual addition to the parish records – that he was 'called Alexander after Alexander Findlater in Jamaica'. The three brothers all went to Tobago. William (1749–79) died there; Alexander amassed enough money to return to Scotland and buy the estate of Newton, near Insch, where he died in 1824; and James (1750–93) returned, married and became an improving farmer at Tillynaught near Portsoy. Four plantations in Tobago passed to Alexander's son, John Gordon (1802–40), who received £7,855 compensation for 392 slaves at emancipation in 1834.[20]

Other early investors in Tobago – from beyond the Elgin, Huntly and Banff triangle – were the family of William Forbes, gardener to the Earl of Sutherland at Dunrobin castle and subsequently the tenant of nearby Culmaillie farm. His sons William (d. 1789) and George (1740–86) bought three lots of land in 1763, one of which they named *Culloden*. Having become indebted to Miles Barber, a Liverpool slave trader, they mortgaged and subsequently sold one of the other lots, much of which remained uncleared woodland, in order to keep *Culloden*.[21] Both William and George, and a third brother Duncan, died in the West Indies and the estate having been 'at the mercy of managers' was of little value in 1806 when it was inherited by William Robertson, from Kiltearn.[22]

Another Forbes family – friends and probably relations – from Ribigill, near Tongue on the north coast of Sutherland, also invested in the island. Hugh and Duncan Forbes were the sons of Donald (also known as Daniel) Forbes, sheriff substitute for Sutherland. Duncan wrote his will in Grenada in 1789, referring to his eldest brother as 'Hugh Forbes of Tobago', with a codicil in November 1791 indicating that they had together bought a plantation in St Vincent. A third brother, Donald, succeeded their father in Ribigill.[23]

Tobago was recaptured by French forces in 1781, formally ceded to France in 1783 and remained under French control until 1793, but the culture of the British inhabitants, who had been allowed to retain their property and their Protestant religion, remained largely intact.[24] Yet Thomas Fraser (elder) did not succeed in the island which he called 'that cursed country'. He longed instead for the Highlands and wrote to his cousin Simon Fraser in Inverness:

> In case I could screap two or three hundred pounds together I would certainly go and see you once yet if God spars me and if not I must leve my bons in Tobago.[25]

And there had been a recurring theme in his letters of isolation and complaint at 'how carles [careless] my friends is of writing to me'.

THOMAS (YOUNGER) IN ST VINCENT AND ST LUCIA

From about 1774 Thomas Fraser (younger) lived in St Vincent and in the smaller island of St Lucia, fifty miles to the north. St Lucia had been returned to France at the end of the Seven Years War but had been reoccupied by British forces in 1778 after France joined with the North American colonies in the War of Independence. Thomas was caught up in the turbulence of the Caribbean in the 'Age of Revolutions' and lived through both the uprising known as the Brigands' War (1795–7) in St Lucia and, having fled the island, the Second Carib War (1795–7) in St Vincent.

Sales of land in the ceded island of St Vincent had begun in May 1764 but the commissioners appointed to oversee the process faced a particular challenge. The island had a substantial population of indigenous Caribs, who had absorbed into their number some escaped slaves, from Barbados and perhaps elsewhere in the Caribbean. They occupied the most fertile land on the windward (east) side of St Vincent and only on the leeward (west) side had they tolerated the settlement of a small number of French planters. Over the next thirty years British planters faced resistance from indigenous people which was more enduring than in any other British Caribbean colony. This resistance was both in the two Carib Wars – the first of 1769–73 ending in a stalemate and a peace treaty and the second of 1795–7 ending with the expulsion of the Caribs – and through the Caribs' cooperation with the French who recaptured the island in 1779 and held it until 1783.

The British authorities called the inhabitants in the east 'Black Caribs', portraying them as predominantly the descendants of Africans who had survived the wreck of a slaving ship, and distinguished them from the 'Yellow' or 'Red Caribs' in the west. This account is now challenged and seems to have been an attempt to deny the Black Caribs any rights as indigenous inhabitants by representing them as runaway slaves, who had themselves taken the land from its original owners.[26] A British expedition in 1769 to map the windward part of the island had been repelled by Black Carib warriors under their leader Joseph Chatoyer and a larger assault in 1772 was similarly resisted, leading to a peace treaty in 1773. The Governor, Sir William Young, had his artist Agostino Brunias (see Chapter 4) record

Figure 5.1 *Chatoyer the Chief of the Black Charaibes in St Vincent with his five Wives* by Agostino Brunias. © John Carter Brown Library, Providence, RI.

the surrender and signing of the treaty. Brunias also painted Chatoyer with his five wives.

As in Grenada, land grants had been made to British planters while the existing French planters were allowed to lease back their holdings. Initially over 15,000 acres were granted, of which just over 2,000 were for 'poor settlers'. There were only a few

Scots among the named holders of the larger lots on the island
– although these did include the MacDowalls and the Ingrams,
both Glasgow tobacco merchants, and the inter-related Gordon
and Brebner families (see Chapter 4) from Aberdeenshire[27] – but
there were opportunities both for poor settlers and for those
who took on lowlier roles as managers, overseers, bookkeepers
and tradesmen. As an example of such opportunities, an advertisement in the *Aberdeen Journal* of 30 October 1768 sought '4
masons, 4 house-carpenters and 2 mill-wrights to go at short
notice' to St Vincent. It is indicative of the role of Scots that
twenty years later a third of the officers in the island's militia
were Scottish.[28] Even more telling is the corps of white officers
who commanded a militia of five hundred armed slaves, embodied in 1795 during the Second Carib War. These were men one
would expect to be able to exercise control over the enslaved
men and to have an extensive knowledge of the black population. At least half of the twenty officers were Scots, including the major and three of the four captains.[29] Among them
were Captain William Fraser, possibly William Fraser (1763–
1843) of Culbokie who was said to have 'gained a great deal of
fame by his gallant behaviour during the present trouble', and
Captain William Alves (*c.* 1775–1835), whose father was from
Inverness.[30]

There were, as elsewhere, at least some cases of spectacular success for Scots from relatively modest backgrounds. The
Cruikshank family had farmed at Gorton in Strathspey for generations. Four or five brothers – James (1748–1830), Patrick
(1749–97), Alexander (1772–1846) and John (1766–1810)
and, probably, Donald (d. 1795) – went to St Vincent, arriving either as 'poor settlers' or as tradesmen. Patrick returned
to Edinburgh, where he married in 1776 and at the birth of
his daughter in 1779 was described as 'late of the island of
St Vincent, carpenter'. Yet, although he had begun as a trades-
man, by 1791 he was the owner of the estate of Stracathro,
north-east of Brechin; and the oldest brother, James, who had
also returned from St Vincent, bought land near Montrose
which had already been renamed Langley Park after a plantation in Jamaica.[31] The brothers married two of the daughters of
Gilbert Gerrard, professor of philosophy at Aberdeen, in 1791
and 1793. James and his wife Marjory had their portraits done
by Henry Raeburn and these now hang in the Frick Gallery in

New York. It was the two younger brothers, Alexander and John, who remained in St Vincent during the troubled 1790s, and possibly a fifth brother, Donald.

Thomas Fraser (younger) knew the Cruikshank brothers well. In 1777 Donald carried a letter home for him and he used James Cruikshank – then in Kingstown, St Vincent – as his return address. In 1782 he shared the cost of postage by enclosing his letter with one sent to the Cruikshanks' parents at Gorton and in 1790 he sat at the same desk as one of the Cruikshanks as they both wrote home. But although Patrick Cruikshank had been a carpenter like Thomas, by 1791 he had an income of £3,000 a year from a plantation, shared with his brother James. As Thomas saw it, the difference was that 'for some people their friends were here before them otherwise they might be toiling and working for other people to this good day as I am'.

But Thomas had moved on from work as a carpenter and had begun 'in the planting business' in 1776. The following year he was confident enough to write:

> I may safely say without vanity of affectation that there are several young fellows of much more experience and a more liberal education than I can boast of that have not met with such encouragement in the planting business as I have, tho I am only sixteen months in that way.[32]

ST LUCIA AND THE 'BRIGAND WAR'

In March 1792 Thomas Fraser (younger) was preparing to leave St Vincent for St Lucia, where he had been offered a position on a plantation partly owned by 'an old and intimate friend'. His salary was to be double what he had in St Vincent, he would have few expenses, and there would be 'no person to interfere' in his work. He had been lent £500 by his friend Thomas Scott, a captain in the West India trade, with which he planned to arrange his affairs in St Vincent so that they made a profit in his absence and, of great personal importance, he was about to make a proposal of marriage to the young French widow who he had known since she was a girl. He was confident she was his for the asking – and she had £3,000 to her name, shared with her young son.

He commented that, had he been better off, he could have married her ten years before. The wedding was celebrated on

14 July 1792, seven months before Britain and Revolutionary France went to war, and their first child, Katherine, was born in St Lucia eleven months later.[33] During that year there had been no communications between St Lucia and British colonies and no one had been allowed to leave the island.

On 4 February 1794 the French Constitutional Assembly passed a law abolishing slavery throughout its territories. To the north, a British fleet seized the French island of Guadeloupe, with the connivance of some French planters who opposed the emancipation of slaves. But in June a small French force commanded by the revolutionary Victor Hugues landed there, declared freedom for slaves and rallied an army of ex-slaves and 'free coloured' people. Within five days Hugues' enlarged army had taken the capital and by October he was in full control of Guadeloupe. From here he set about bringing the Revolution to other colonies.

On 18 April 1795 Hugues' force of 600 men landed in St Lucia, where they were joined by 250 local republicans and 500 enslaved, who then took the town of Soufrière on the west coast of the island. In 1791 this had been the scene of brutal executions of slaves who had protested against their enslavement. The heads of the leaders of the protest had then been displayed on spikes throughout the parish. Retribution came with the erection of a guillotine on the town square and the beheading of a number of Royalist French planters. Although a British force was sent from the island's capital, Castries, the 'brigands' – as they were dismissively called – defeated them. Both the British and the French Royalists fled the island on 19 June 1795 and Hugues' forces declared *l'Année de la Liberté* – the year of freedom – from slavery. Only a short time after this, British forces reinvaded but it was not until 26 May 1796 that the French garrison, consisting mainly of black soldiers, surrendered – on the condition that they would be treated as prisoners of war and not as slaves. Many others escaped to form *l'armée Française dans les bois* (the French army in the woods) and fought a guerrilla campaign over the next year, only surrendering at the end of 1797 on the condition, once more, that they were treated as prisoners of war.

Thomas (younger) had sent his family to St Vincent in December 1794 and had remained in St Lucia until early March 1795 when, feeling that things were more settled, he went to

St Vincent with the intention of bringing them home. He thus escaped Hugues' invasion of St Lucia on 18 April but in St Vincent 'the war or rather massacre began on the day of my arrival'.

ST VINCENT AND THE SECOND CARIB WAR

Victor Hugues' strategy was based on rallying marginal-ised groups and in St Vincent he looked to Chatoyer, leader of the Black Caribs, addressing him as a French general and sending him the corresponding uniform, sabre and hat. Hugues originally planned a coordinated attack on British forces in Grenada and St Vincent on 17 March, St Patrick's Day, but the Revolution in Grenada began on 5 March and by 9 March it was underway in St Vincent. At Chateaubelair, a settlement in the north-west of the island, on 'the twelfth day of March and the first of our freedom' Chatoyer drafted a proclamation addressed to the French inhabitants of the island, calling on them to join the Revolution. His army then marched to join with that of his brother at Dorsetshire Hill, twenty-five miles south, overlooking the capital Kingston. On the morning of 14 March Chatoyer had three British prisoners brought before him – Duncan Cruikshank, Peter Cruikshank and Alexander Grant – who had all been captured at Chateaubelair. Using the sabre which had been presented to him by Sir William Young to mark the peace treaty of 1773, Chatoyer hacked the three men to death. It is possible that these Cruikshanks were relations of the brothers from Strathspey. That night, in a surprise attack on Dorsetshire Hill by a small force of seamen, soldiers and armed slaves, Chatoyer himself was killed. The war continued with atrocities on both sides.

By October, Thomas Fraser (younger) was able to communicate again with his relations in Inverness and reported that:

> I lost part of my property both here [St Vincent] and there [St Lucia] to a very large amount and what I regret more than all my eldest child my poor tottie girle Kate, I have still thank God my boy Simon left and one coming so this is the sum total of my family.[34]

He praised the conduct of William Fraser of Culbockie, another Mr Fraser who was the partner of the Cruikshanks, and his own nephew Tom, who 'had a ball through his thigh but soon got well'. After the war, Thomas (younger) remained in St Vincent, rather than returning to St Lucia. He welcomed the defeat of the Black Caribs and their expulsion from the island:

> It is some consolation to us on this Island that the Government is determined to rid us at last of our ferocious Neighbours the Carraibs they are now actually embarked on board transports at Bequia a small island three leagues from hence and will proceed for the Island of Ratan under convoy of a frigate on the tenth of next month the very day two years that they began there bloody Tragedy. They are furnished with arms and ammunition tools and utensils of every kind and seeds and plants of every kind that will suit the country they are going to which is said to be fertile and to abound with game.[35]

In reality, when Thomas wrote this letter in February 1797, a total of 4,336 defeated Caribs – 1,002 men, 1,779 women and 1,555 children – had been disembarked and confined on the tiny island of Baliceaux, near Bequia, ten miles south of St Vincent. Exhausted, crowded together and exposed to a variety of infectious diseases, they began to die. When HMS *Experiment* arrived with other vessels in March to transport them to the Spanish island of Roatán in the Bay of Honduras, only half were still alive.[36] And so, in an act of ethnic cleansing carried out 'less than thirty-five years after formal [British] colonial rule was [imposed] ... the last people to assert that they were indigenous to the southern Caribbean were forcibly removed more than 1,800 miles beyond the region's borders'.[37] Only a small number of Black Caribs clung on in St Vincent and they were caught up in a natural disaster which also had an impact on Thomas and his family.

Of the French, free black and 'free coloured' soldiers who had surrendered to British forces in St Lucia and St Vincent on condition of being treated as prisoners of war, almost 2,800 were transported across the Atlantic in July 1796, arriving Portsmouth in October, where they were confined in Porchester prison. At least 218 died on board ship. The survivors were 313 white soldiers, 2,080 black and 'coloured' soldiers, and 99 women and children.[38]

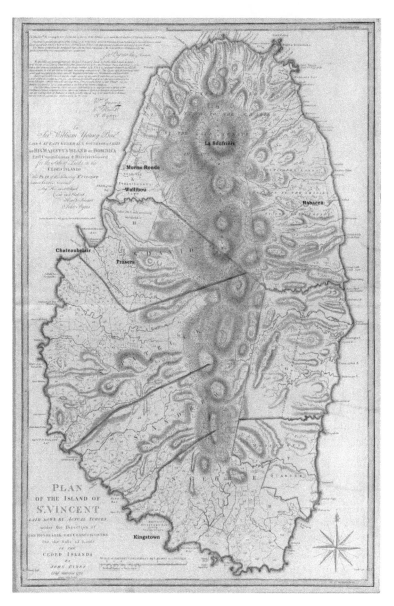

Map 3 'Plan of the Island of St Vincent' by John Byrne, 1776.
© John Carter Brown Library, Providence, RI. Annotated to show
Kingstown (where Chatoyer was killed), Chateaubelair, Frasers and
Wallibou estates, the Carib settlement at Morne Ronde, the volcano
La Soufrière and Robert Sutherland's Rabacca estate.

ST VINCENT: FRASER'S ESTATE

The property of Thomas Fraser (younger), which became known as *Fraser's Plantation*, was in the parish of St David, in the north-west of St Vincent. It was land which had been granted to 'poor settlers' in the 1760s and it later included at least part of a lot which had belonged to a French planter called Arseneau, who had been allowed to retain it under a lease after 1763. Arseneau's property then passed to a family called Fitzhugh, into which Thomas's wife had married. As a widow, with a son, she had retained rights to part of the estate.[39]

From early 1802, Thomas Fraser (younger) was also employed on the nearby plantation *Wallibou* (also spelled *Wallibo* and *Wallibu*):

> I have been living here these eight months where I have the conducting of a large estate a salary of £400 sterling a pipe of old wine a flock of sheep and two men to fish for me. I am near my own place that I can see it once in two days.[40]

The *Wallibou* plantation had been created in a controversial manner because it lay within the boundaries of the Carib lands, which under the peace treaty of 1773 had been reserved for the indigenous inhabitants, and the grant of *Wallibou* to Lieutenant Colonel George Etherington was a source of grievance. Etherington had gained the trust of the Black Caribs and claimed that he had been granted the land by Joseph Chatoyer himself – but this was disputed by Chatoyer, who said that he and his brothers had only intended to lease him a few acres. Etherington legalised his claim by a visit to London in 1777, after which he was described by the Secretary of State as 'Superintendent of the Charibbs in St Vincent'. This festering grievance was one reason why Chatoyer had made contact with French forces in August 1778 and supported the French invasion of the island the following year. By this time Etherington was commander of the island's garrison – 450 poorly trained men of the Royal American Regiment – many of whom, it was later alleged, he had diverted from their duties to clear his land at *Wallibou*. Etherington later faced a court martial, at which he was exonerated, on a charge of having too readily surrendered St Vincent to the French forces in 1779.

The subsequent ownership of his plantation is unclear.

Etherington retired from the army in 1788 but not before having his portrait painted, in uniform, seated looking over the coast of St Vincent, with bundles of what appear to be cut sugar cane at his feet.[41] When the insurrection of 1795 began, Chatoyer had led his force from the north through *Wallibou* to Chateaubelair and then south to Kingston, where he was killed on the night of 14 March. His force then retreated north to the Carib lands, destroying the canes and sugar mill at *Wallibou* – having, it was alleged, killed the overseer by feeding him alive into the sugar mill to be crushed by the rollers. His name was Grant. When the Carib and French force was resupplied from St Lucia in June, they reoccupied *Wallibou* plantation and skirmishing continued – one of the casualties being another Grant. When the Caribs surrendered in 1795 and were expelled from St Vincent, a few remained and continued to resist the British forces – indeed, the Second Carib War is sometimes considered as have only ended in 1805 with the surrender of those remaining fighters, the majority of whom were in the vicinity of Morne Ronde, just north of *Wallibou*. Against the wishes of the island's Council and Assembly, the few remaining Caribs – reported at the time as sixteen men, nine women and twenty children – were granted 230 acres at Morne Ronde.[42] Thomas Fraser (younger) was thus taking on the management of an estate with a violent past and, in 1802, a continuing threat from the remnant of the indigenous people – which may account for the generous salary of £400 and his various perquisites.

In June 1804 an Act was passed by which the Caribs formally lost their rights to land and which allowed the Governor to sell these to white planters. The largest tract was bought by John Cruikshank (600 acres) and other substantial purchases included those by his brother Alexander Cruikshank (300 acres); by Robert Sutherland (1776–1828) from Uppat in Sutherland (300 acres); and by his partner William Mackenzie (1773–1819) of Fairburn in Ross-shire (300 acres jointly with T. Patterson).

Both *Wallibou* and *Fraser's* were among the estates which sustained substantial damage through a violent eruption of the nearby La Soufrière volcano in April 1812, an event which was sketched by a local planter and became the subject of a powerful work by the artist J. M. W. Turner in 1815.[43] A well-planned and effective campaign on behalf of planters with estates on both the leeward (east) and windward (west) coasts in the north of St Vincent led to the setting up of a select committee of the House of Commons, a report to Parliament and the award of £25,000 in compensation.[44] Twenty planters claimed to have suffered losses which amounted to just over £79,000, although it is thought that these were exaggerations of their actual losses.[45] Of these, at least eight were northern Scots – the above-mentioned Robert Sutherland and William Mackenzie; Alexander Clunes, probably from east Sutherland; James, Alexander and John Cruikshank from Strathspey; Alexander Cuming, who was Cruikshanks' brother-in-law; and Thomas Fraser (younger). The *Wallibou* estate was now owned by John and Lewis Grant, who may also have been northern Scots. Together they received over 80 per cent of the compensation, largely because Sutherland received the largest payment of £5,300, against his reported losses of £19,378 for damage to *Rabacca* estate on the windward side, where the river which drove the sugar mill had dried up as a result of the eruption. Thomas Fraser received a modest £700.

A further casualty of the eruption was the Carib settlement at Morne Ronde. A description of the eruption submitted by the island's Chief Justice described how about sixty Black Caribs fled their houses.[46] Yet in the early 1830s Trelawny Wentworth travelled to Morne Ronde, met with Caribs and sketched a woman, Mary, with her child.[47] They were, however, a mere remnant of the indigenous population.

FRASER'S ESTATE AFTER THE ERUPTION

Thomas Fraser (younger) made the first return of slave numbers for his plantation on 27 March 1817, recording his ownership of seventy-seven enslaved people, including a five-year-old girl, Soufriere, named after the volcano and its eruption in the year she was born. By 1824 ownership had passed to Thomas' heirs and the return was made by a William Fraser, probably Thomas's second son, now twenty years old. The number of slaves had fallen to fifty-nine, in part because of the emancipation of five slaves on 1 February 1823. They were Amelia, a twenty-five- year-old 'mulatto' seamstress, and four children who were described as 'mestif(e)', a French form of the term 'mestee', used of a person born of a white father and a 'mulatto' mother. A possible explanation is that these slaves were freed

Figure 5.2 A Carib of Morne Ronde, 1833. © The Library Company of Philadelphia.

under the will of Thomas Fraser (younger) who must, if this is correct, have died about 1822 and, if so, it is probable that they were his children. By 1828 the plantation had an additional owner, Thomas Fraser, probably the third son of Thomas Fraser (younger), born in 1797, who would then have been twenty-one. In April of that year, almost all the plantation slaves were sold to another estate and the remainder were sold the next year.

Fraser's was unusual and this may account for the sale of the slaves in 1828. Of the island's plantations, only six had fewer slaves than *Fraser's* fifty-nine and it produced the smallest amount of sugar of any estate, a mere 6,974 lb from its 214 acres. Alexander Cruikshank's *Belmont* plantation in the same parish, with seventy-seven slaves, produced twenty times as much from a similar acreage, along with rum and molasses. Moreover, *Fraser's* was the only estate on the island noted as producing cocoa and coffee.[48] In 1791 Thomas had explained in detail to his cousin how, along with Thomas Fraser (elder), he had planted coffee bushes:

> He and I are in a kind of partnership about a spot of land that we rent on which we plant coffee with about twenty negroes, the coffee is a plant will not yield any crop before the fourth year after it is first planted, but after that if no hurricanes happen it will bear annually for 15 or 20 years and in good soil for 40 years, it is very expensive at first to find the negroes and Cloath them, and ones expences without making any crop, we have twenty thousand coffee plants some of which will begin to bear the crop and all of them after, it is allowed that on an average each tree will give a pound of coffee when they are in full bearing.[49]

It seems that Thomas had stuck with this commitment to coffee. To produce this there were in 1817, under a slave driver, thirty-seven fields slaves, twenty-six of them labourers aged from twelve to fifty-five, with a 'grass gang' of eleven youngsters aged seven to twelve who would have been used for lighter tasks. Two thirteen-year-old boys herded sheep and cattle; two men in their twenties were fishermen; and there was a carpenter and three coopers. Two old men were watchmen and four women were either too old or too ill to work. Fourteen slaves had domestic tasks – including a cook, a washer, seamstresses and a sick nurse – and, oddly, one African-born woman was described as 'working for her own family'. Eleven children under the age of seven brought the total to seventy-seven. Among them was the group – probably a family – who would be freed in 1823.

The plantation was also unusual in that eighteen slaves, almost a quarter of the enslaved people, had white ancestry, when the average for St Vincent as a whole was just under 5 per cent.[50] Eleven were 'mulattos'; three were described as 'mongrel' – that is, children of a 'mulatto' and a black slave; and four were 'mestif(e)'. It would appear to have been a plantation with a long history of sexual relations between masters and slaves, and with few, if any, manumissions of the children of these relationships.

WHAT MATTERED, WHAT DIDN'T MATTER AND WHAT THEY LEARNED

Like all letter writers, the Frasers selected what they revealed to their relation, Simon Fraser in Inverness. It was, for example, only after the death of Thomas (elder) that any references were made to his long-standing relationship with a 'free coloured' woman or to his five children. Yet despite long silences and failures to disclose, some things clearly were important.

Family at home mattered and, at least while he anticipated making money, Thomas (elder) expected to have influence in family affairs. In his first letter, after asking after his brothers and sisters, he made this request of Simon.

> Above all dont let them go on in aney Black Gard way or good for nothing marriages or otherways if they do so they will be sure thell never see aney of my favours.[51]

Two months later he made the same plea: 'I begg the favour of you to take care of my Sisters and not throw them to a careless marriage.'[52] By 1778 his brother Hugh had let him down: 'as fore Hugh I am told he is married so I am done with him especially on account of the Match he has got'; and he sent a warning message to his sister Mary, 'if shell [sic] take care of herself I am always ready to do all I can for her or otherwise she need not look me in the face'.[53] However, by 1786, his tone was less peremptory:

> I would wish much to know of . . . my own mother, brothers and sisters . . . please let us know something of our poor relations if we

cannot do them any great good will do them no harm especially as we are so far of.[54]

Thomas (younger), whose sisters were all married, offered more affectionate greetings and more practical assistance. When his brother-in-law Hugh Fraser died at Killachy, he was insistent on defending his sister Grizel's right to remain in the property against moves by others (the Frasers of Culbokie and Dunballoch) to acquire the tenancy.

> I would sell my coat of [sic] my back sooner than she would be turned out of possession . . . I would sooner sell everything I have in the world than see her fall a sacrifice to such hungry Tygers . . . I will send what money I can by the end of July. I beg you to write me fully about this matter.[55]

When his mother died in 1791 he renounced his small legacy in favour of another sister, Kate; in 1795 he gave up to her a further small legacy he had received on the death of his sister Grizel; and in 1801 he responded supportively to Kate's request that he find a position in St Vincent for her son, wanting first to ensure the boy had the capacity for this venture.

The cost and difficulty of communication, especially in war time, led to long uncertainties about close family members. 'Pray let me know if my Mother is alive,' wrote Thomas (elder) in 1778, and twenty years later there was a frustrated outburst, 'I heard that [my sister] was dead some years ago indeed you may all be dead unknowing to me for not one of you ever corresponds with me.'[56] Thomas (younger) recounted a dream of seeing himself with his mother and deceased father and brother – 'what the meaning is the Lord only knows'.[57] From the Inverness end, the family of Thomas (younger) had heard rumours of the birth of a child but, isolated in St Lucia by war, he later had to reassure them that 'the mother is not black but fair'.[58] Friends at home mattered too. But friendships were difficult to maintain and after only a short time in the Caribbean, Thomas (elder) complained, 'I am surprised how carles my friends is of writing to me others in this island get letters every week.'[59]

Property at home mattered. Two recent studies – Finlay McKichan's *Lord Seaforth* (2018) and Kathy Fraser's *For the Love of a Highland Home* (2016) – show how two families of landed gentry, Mackenzie of Seaforth and the Frasers of Reelig, turned to the West Indies in attempts to secure the income needed to maintain their Highland estates. Although on a much smaller scale, we see the same motivation in the Boblainy letters. When Thomas (elder) arrived in Grenada in 1771 he soon heard news of his father's poor health and his immediate concern was to secure the tack (lease) of Boblainy for the family. He offered to pay the annual rent and begged Simon Fraser to do all he could to ensure that it did not pass out of the family's hands. Simon had, as it turned out, already advanced money to Thomas's father and had secured Boblainy for the oldest brother Hugh – and on Hugh's death the lands of Boblainy came to Simon. Similarly, when his brother-in-law Hugh Fraser died in Inverness-shire in 1786, Thomas (younger) was willing to go to almost any length to ensure the lease of Killachy was retained. For more than ten years he encouraged Simon Fraser to do all he could, authorising him to take whatever action was necessary, sending him £30 in 1793 and promising a further £50 in 1796.

News from home was welcomed, not just news of their families but 'Country news' – meaning local affairs and the doings of the principal landowners. 'Country news will be a treat to me,' wrote Thomas (younger). And Thomas (elder) expressed the same thought:

> I would be glad to hear from you and a full letter. The postage is nothing at all to me in comparison to the pleasure I would feel in receiving your long letter full of country news . . .[60]

They were sometimes concerned by what they heard.

> We have dreadful accounts of your bad harvest and severe stormy winter that followed. Grain of course must be both dear and scarce consequently the poor must suffer.[61]

In return they attempted to convey information which would be of interest at home, mentioning men from the Highlands who they had met in the Caribbean or about whom they had news. More than twenty people, beyond the immediate family, are mentioned in the Boblainy letters, the longest reference being to the arrival of Lord Seaforth as Governor of Barbados in 1801.

> There are grand doings at Barbadoes the other day on the arrival of Lord Seaforth. After firing all the great guns of the fortifications they conveyed him to the church to hear the sermon, as if a deaf man could hear a parson preaching at the distance of several yards. They say his lordship is so deaf that he only talks by his fingers, if

so what use was the sermon to him, unless they had a copy of the discourse laid before him, then he might guess what the parson was about.[62]

For Thomas (younger), his marriage in 1792 to a young French widow, and the birth of children, was of immense significance and his ambition became focused on his children:

If it pleases the Almighty to spare me to see my three boys able to shift for themselves I shall think myself the happiest of mortals.[63]

An essential part of that ambition was to be able to send his four sons home for education in Inverness, something which he mentioned in five letters over as many years. This became more pressing than a visit home himself, although he still hoped that he would see his cousin Simon again: 'Who knows but you and I may sit by the fireside there yet before we die.'[64]

What did not matter to any of Simon Fraser's correspondents in the Caribbean was the condition of the enslaved people or of the indigenous Caribs of St Vincent. The first letter from Thomas (elder), written from Grenada, included a brief description of the island.

The island is a very mountainous place full of woods and two thirds of it uninhabited and great sight of runaway Negros how [who] destroy Plantations and wheat [white] people but the whole island rises against them once a year and destroys a great many.[65]

In his spelling of 'white' as 'wheat', we hear his native pronunciation of English.

Enslaved people were only referred to in relation to their work and their economic value. Thus in 1787, on his return from North America, Thomas Fraser (younger) lamented that while he was away 'a negro that cost me 100£ sterling absconded and it is fifty chances to one if ever I see him again as he has been absent now about six months'; and in 1796 he intended to return briefly to St Lucia because 'one of my negroes left there is still on the estate, a cooper by trade worth a hundred guineas'.[66] He attributed the loss of slaves by his cousin Thomas (elder) to bad luck: '. . . fortune seems determined to persecute him to the last . . . he loses negroes often, not through neglect or bad usage'.[67] There was no suggestion that being enslaved might itself be 'bad usage'.

We have already seen how in 1797 Thomas (younger) welcomed with relief the removal of the indigenous people – 'our ferocious Neighbours the Carraibs' – to the island of Becquia.[68] And when his cousin, Thomas Fraser (elder), died in 1800 there was little sympathy for his 'mulatto' children and certainly not for their 'free coloured' mother, who he described as 'an indolent worthless creature in no way capable of earning their bread'.[69]

INSIGHT

In the same letter, Thomas Fraser (younger) offered some of the most insightful comments on the lure of the West Indies. He had seen the Frasers of Belladrum invest in Demerara as early as 1790 and must have known from his cousin in Inverness that by 1801 word had spread around Inverness and the north that there was money to be made there. Thomas observed:

> Your Demerara planters have certainly made a large and rapid fortune but it is easily accounted for, those gentlemen went there as Guinea factors they were supported by money men their commission on sales and returns were enormous without the smallest risque and very little trouble they soon bought larger estates and became rich before they were aware of it.

It was similar to his own experience in St Vincent, where it was those with money who had made money. And he knew the reality for those – like himself and his relations – without these advantages, who had had to rely on their own 'industry':

> Now look at the poor adventurer who goes there to do his best by his industry only, he gets a grant of several hundred acres of Swampy boggs he commences draining with a few negroes he takes the spade often and works to forward the Settlement but alas all his endeavors to combat difficulties only serves to ruin his health and too often the poor man sinks under his distress before he gets a crop to compensate his labour.[70]

Thomas had the wit to understand why people were so misled. Conclusions are often reached on the basis of what we can easily call to mind, a systematic bias known in behavioural economics as the 'availability heuristic':[71]

> This has been the case with numbers. You have only seen the fortunate few and draw your conclusion accordingly.[72]

Among these 'fortunate few' was Alexander Cruikshank who, by the time of emancipation in 1834, had transferred his principal investments to Demerara, where he owned 620 enslaved people. In 1824, having acquired the Stracathro estate from the heirs of his brother Patrick, he commissioned the Aberdeen architect Archibald Simpson to build him a Palladian mansion house, surrounded by a deer park and gardens.

The recipient of all these letters from the Caribbean – Simon Fraser, the baker and merchant in Inverness – left no grand house or estate. He is commemorated on a simple carved stone plaque on the outer wall of the High Kirk of Inverness. But the forty-four surviving letters he received from relations in the Caribbean place him at the centre of a network of men and women of modest means who were, in one way and another, entangled with slavery and the slave-worked plantations of the Ceded Islands.

PART 2

Northern Scots in Guyana on the 'Last Frontier' of Empire

The next four chapters give an account of northern Scots in Demerara, Essequibo and Berbice – on the north coast of South America – former colonies which now form the Republic of Guyana. They were places where vast fortunes continued to be made up to and beyond the end of British colonial slavery and this distinguished them from the old English sugar islands and from the Ceded Islands, where soils had been depleted and returns reduced. They were also places where tropical fevers posed a greater threat to whites and where the drive for profit pushed slavery to – and beyond – previous limits. In proportion to their numbers, fewer whites exploited more enslaved Africans and their descendants than anywhere else in the Caribbean or North America – with a consequent reliance on systematic control through brutality and terror.

Chapter 6 describes the early involvement of northern Scots in Demerara, while it was still a Dutch colony, and the subsequent enthusiasm of Highland Scots to be part of the exploitation of land and people when Britain seized the three colonies in 1796. They subsequently became some of the most Scottish of the Caribbean colonies – and Berbice, on some measures, the most Highland.

Chapter 7 is an attempt to hear the voices of the enslaved, especially in Berbice – men, women and children, many held by Highland plantation owners and brutally controlled by Highland managers and overseers. A large part of this chapter is an account of a planned uprising of the enslaved in Berbice in 1814, its suppression and its aftermath.

In Chapter 8, I turn to the role of 'free coloured' women in these colonies, to their relationships with Highland Scots, and describe the powerful force they were within the colonies until emancipation.

Since it was in Guyana (and Trinidad) – less so than in the older colonies – that fortunes continued to be made, it was here that the most powerful West India merchant houses flourished. Chapter 9 explores the Scottish – and surprisingly Highland – origins of the two largest slave-holding partnerships at emancipation. This also carries the account forward to the end of British colonial slavery in 1838 and into the era of indentured Indian labour, pioneered in Guyana as a replacement for enslaved labour.

Map 4 Detail from 'Map of British Guiana' by John Arrowsmith (1844). © David Rumsey Map Collection.

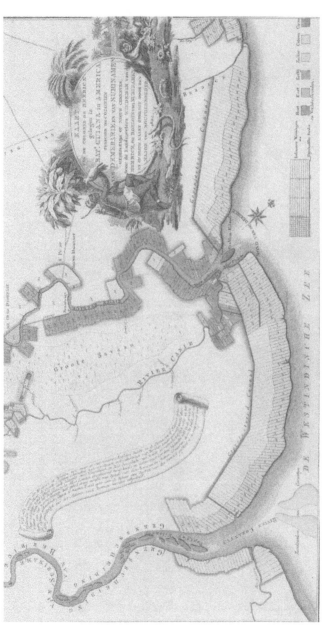

Map 5 Coastal plantations laid out on the coast of Berbice and Nickerie by 1802, detail from *Kart van de Colonie de Berbice* by Major von Bouchenroeder. National Archives of the Netherlands, Inventory number 1577A4. © National Archives of the Netherlands.

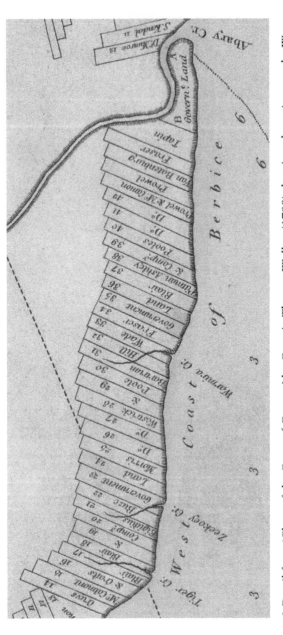

Map 6 Detail from 'Chart of the Coast of Guyana' by Captain Thomas Walker (1798) showing plantations on the West Coast of Berbice. © Nationaal Archief (Netherlands).

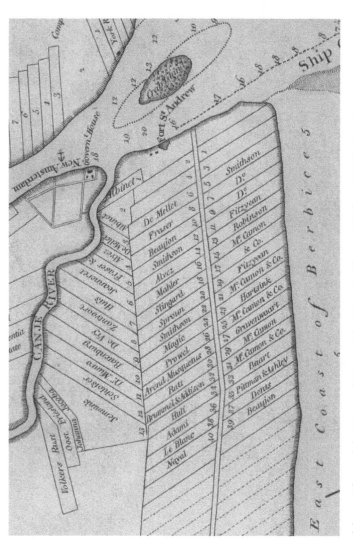

Map 7 Detail from 'Chart of the Coast of Guyana' by Captain Thomas Walker (1798) showing the entrance to the Berbice River. © Nationaal Archief (Netherlands).

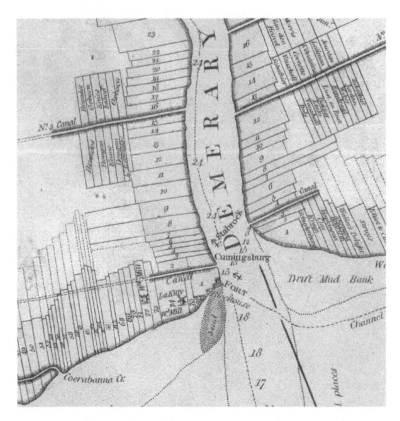

Map 8 Detail from 'Chart of the Coast of Guyana' by Captain Thomas Walker (1798) showing the entrance to the Demerara River, with Thomas Cuming's plantation *Kitty* and the new town of Cumingsburg.
© Nationaal Archief (Netherlands).

6

Guyana – A Last Frontier

On Sunday, 3 November 1799, in the parish of Urquhart near Elgin, the Cuming family gathered for the double christening of sixty-year old Thomas Cuming's daughter, Hannah, and his grandson Christopher, babies born within two weeks of each other. In 1798 Thomas had returned from Demerara, where he was the owner of two sugar plantations and six hundred enslaved Africans. He bought Innes House near Elgin, styled himself 'Thomas Cuming Esquire of Leuchars', had his portrait painted, and married for a second time. His young wife, Isabella Fraser, had been seriously ill since Hannah's birth and was confined to bed. Her three brothers – James, Simon and Evan Fraser of Belladrum – were all absent in South America as prominent plantation owners in Demerara and Berbice. But Isabella's sister Sarah had joined them with her husband William Fraser of Culbokie, recently returned from St Vincent.

Cuming's older daughter Catherine – baby Christopher's mother – had been born in Demerara in 1769 to his first wife, Catherina Gertrude Lossner, a Dutch widow. With Catherine was the baby's father, John Bagot, an Anglo-Irish officer in the British army, accompanied by his sister and brother. Then there were Thomas Cuming's five unmarried sisters from Dufftown, still supporters of the long-lost Jacobite cause – including the youngest, Eliza, dressed in her habitual black as a sign of mourning for the Stuarts' loss of the throne. It was not until twenty years later that she put on her brightest colours, on hearing news of the death of George III. They were joined by a nephew, the son of their older brother William Cuming – by now known as Guillaume. He had fled Scotland for France after the defeat of the Jacobite army at Culloden and had risen to become a chevalier of the Order of St Louis and aide-de-camp to Prince François Xavier of Saxony. Guillaume may have died by this time but his son – their French-speaking nephew – was there. He was Thomas de Cuming de Craigmillen and had been educated from 1786 at the Ecole Militaire in Brienne, where his older brother André had also been a pupil. Thomas de Cuming had recently arrived from Amsterdam and this was perhaps the first time they had all met. No doubt everyone was interested in his brother André's former classmate at the Ecole Militaire, a young Corsican – named Buonaparte.[1]

Collectively the extended family spoke English, French, Dutch and probably Gaelic; they mourned the defeat of the Stuarts and loyally served the Hanoverian state; and they were citizens of nations and empires who were at that moment at war with each other. Yet they were one family whose interests crossed all these boundaries. Demerara, which was above all a place to make money, engendered such entanglements.

But all was not well for Thomas. Concern about his financial situation was weighing heavily on him and in September he had written to his agent in Demerara:

> Since I had my property I never was in such difficulty for money as at this time . . . if I cannot get a purchaser for one of my Demerary properties I do not know how I am to be extricated from my present difficulties . . . I am so distressed in mind and cannot rest and [am] perfectly unhappy.[2]

Before the end of the year his young wife Isabella was dead and Thomas decided to return to Demerara, leaving his daughter Hannah to be brought up by the Frasers of Culbokie. His nephew Thomas de Cuming accompanied him.

In 1810, at the age of seventy, Thomas came back to Scotland for the last time and, when it was clear to his 'brother colonists' that he was not to return, 101 men in Demerara and fifty in Berbice subscribed to present him with a piece of silver plate costing 500 guineas (£525).[3] He died at Elgin in 1813, commemorated in the parish church of Dallas (Moray) as the 'principal promoter of [Demerara's] prosperity and wealth'.[4] Thomas Cuming is both an example of the involvement of northern Scots in the plantations of Guyana and one reason why so many others followed him there.

THE DUTCH GUIANAS

Between the rivers Amazon and Orinoco on the north coast of South America was an area known to Europeans as the Wild Coast – the Guianas. Nearest the Amazon, but still some distance from it, was the French colony of Cayenne and along the rest of the coast were four Dutch colonies – Suriname and then, from east to west, Berbice, Demerara and Essequibo. The last three were surrendered to British forces in 1796 and were formally ceded to Britain in 1814. They united to become British Guiana in 1831. Suriname was surrendered in 1799 but returned to Dutch rule in 1814. But there had been a significant British presence in Demerara and Essequibo from the 1740s, the result of the policies of Laurens Storm van 's Gravesande, who arrived in Essequibo in 1738, became Governor in 1742, and when Demerara was constituted as a colony in 1745 became the Director General of both colonies. Van 's Gravesande opened up Demerara and Essequibo to British planters, mainly from the British West Indies, who were desperate to develop new plantations as the fertility of the soils on the islands declined. Van 's Gravesande also enticed these British planters through low taxes and turned a blind eye to their illegal imports of enslaved Africans from British slave factors.

Demerara, which had been established from Essequibo, was particularly attractive and the number of plantations increased from thirty-eight in 1748 to ninety-three in 1762, thirty-four of which were owned by 'Englishmen' – the term being used to cover all English-speaking planters, including Scots and Irish. Essequibo had sixty-eight plantations, only eight of which were 'English'-owned. The Scottish presence in both colonies was initially small. Daniel Stewart owned plantations *Dundee* in Essequibo and *Dunoon* in Demerara; the Millikens of Kilbarchan (Renfrewshire) owned *Oranjesteyn* in Essequibo; and James Douglas of Springwood Park (Kelso) owned *Weilburg* in Demerara. On *Weilburg* the Scots employed on the plantation were as divided by personal and political fractiousness as in Grenada (see Chapter 4). The manager was Thomas Grant, with Lachlan Maclean as attorney, and Maclean headed one faction of the deeply divided white community. In 1765 the owner, James Douglas, sent his brother-in-law William Brisbane from Ayr to replace Maclean as attorney and the following year wrote to him, saying, 'for God's sake Willy don't run me into any more expenses than are absolutely necessary'. Brisbane failed to contain expenditure and a Robert Milne travelled out to replace him in 1767. While en route he heard rumours that Brisbane was a Jacobite and had held a 'celebration of the Pretender's birthday'. These rumours turned out to be false but they are further evidence of the factions among the colonists.[5]

The openness of Demerara to British planters is a particular example of the general nature of the Dutch Atlantic and of the response of Scots to the opportunities there. Esther Mijers describes Scots operating in both English and Dutch colonies as 'boundary crossers', people whose success arose from their tradition of emigration and because of the combination of their social status in the English empire and, in many cases, their shared religion with the Dutch. Alison Games uses the terms 'boundary crossers and middlemen' to describe the characteristic specialisation of the Dutch in the 'entangled Atlantics' where, with a willingness to assimilate others, they forged regional economic ties across boundaries of nation, language, religion and culture. Demerara is but one example of Scots adapting to and operating in that environment.[6]

Some Scots, and some parts of Scotland, had the additional advantage of a link with the Dutch Empire through traditions of enlistment in the Scots Brigade, a set of regiments in the service of the Dutch state. In the mid-1700s it consisted of four regiments and could muster around 7,000 officers and men, most of them Scots, who were considered to be 'the best in the Dutch army, the most courageous and trustworthy'. The Brigade had its origins in the 1580s and was not disbanded until 1782/3, although its right to recruit in Scotland came to an end in 1757. Many in the Brigade were from families who had served over a number of generations, often marrying Dutch or Flemish women.[7] So while James Douglas – a British naval officer and later Admiral – acquired plantation *Weilburg*, his brother, Lieutenant Colonel Robert Douglas, was second-in-command in the Dutch expedition which suppressed a slave rising in neighbouring Berbice in 1763. Colonel Douglas married into a prominent Dutch family, received promotions and honours in both Holland and Britain, and became involved in the trans-Atlantic slave trade.[8]

It would be a mistake to read back onto the early Dutch Guianas the notion of a well- ordered, nineteenth-century colony.

Essequibo (and its extension Demerara) was run by the Dutch West India Company (the WIC) and the colony had initially been established in the 1600s to trade with Amerindians. Indeed, a single part of the WIC – the Zealand Chamber – claimed exclusive trading rights. Bickering between factions continued until the mid-1760s, by which time this was no longer an economic backwater and investors in Amsterdam were funding a booming plantation economy. But rivalries continued despite attempts at reform and increased representation for planters – and the WIC did not succeed in its attempts to create an effective institutional structure. Nor was it able to meet the costs of protecting the colony, which was taken by British and then French forces during the Anglo-Dutch war of 1780–4. Both these occupations, although by opposing powers, gave planters a taste of access to the British slave trade, some limited economic reforms and the development of badly needed infrastructure, including the creation of a town on the Demerara River which would later be renamed Stabroek. When hostilities ended and the colonies were returned to Dutch rule, planters were united in their determination to resist restoration of WIC control and the imposition of taxes without representation of the planters' interests. During 1785 petitions were presented on behalf of planters in both colonies, showing that they were sufficiently united to challenge the WIC and its new director general, L'Espinasse. In Demerara, 109 signatories were listed – just under one-third were Dutch, just under one-third 'British' and the remainder a mixture of French, German and other groups. The 'British' included English, Scots, British Caribbean and British American planters. It was a mark of the diversity of the colony and of the considerable opposition to the director general, although in 1787 sixty planters presented a further petition expressing their loyalty to L'Espinasse. Behind these petitions lay the now vital importance of smuggling for the majority of planters – both the illegal import of enslaved Africans and the illegal export of produce beyond the control of the WIC monopoly. It was in this setting that Thomas Cuming rose from relatively humble origins to be a leading figure in the colony.

It had been a long journey from the north of Scotland, in every sense. Cuming's father had supported the Jacobite Rising of 1745 and, when Thomas was only six years old, he was taken prisoner. He died in prison in London in 1746, leaving their mother to bring up her family in difficult circumstances.[9] Thomas must have been in Demerara by about 1760 and he fits the description of British planters given by Dr Edward Bancroft, who was in the colony from 1763 to 1766.

> Many of these are unfortunate persons, whom the unavoidable accidents of life, or frowns of fortune, have induced to seek an asylum in distant countries where their industry is often so amply rewarded, that they are enabled to return with opulence and credit.[10]

From 1770 Cuming's name began to appear in Dutch legal documents, sixty-two in all before 1783. From these it can be seen that he acted as attorney for a number of planters and in 1774 for the heirs of a fellow Scot, Thomas Grand [Grant?] and his Dutch wife Jannetta van Baarle. He had also begun to acquire property, buying *Hof van Eden* (*Garden of Eden*) on the east bank of the Demerary, in partnership with Bernard Albinus. By 1786 it had been divided into a *steenbakkerei* (brickworks) and *De Wildernis* (250 acres), both owned by Thomas Cuming & Comp. (that is, Cuming and Albinus). The remaining 1,000 acres was in sugar. He had also acquired land near the capital Stabroek, on which he created the plantations *Kitty* and *Thomas*, and later he added *Cuming's Lodge*, on the east sea coast.[11]

By 1774 he had married a Dutch widow, six years his senior, Catharina Lossner, whose father had been Governor of Berbice and whose first husband, Johann Heyliger, had owned plantation *Ruymsicht* on the Demerary. It was a happy match and Thomas wrote to his first cousin William Rose in July of that year, saying, 'I have reason to be thankful for my choice of a wife with whom I enjoy a large share of conjugal Felicity.'[12] The couple had one child, the daughter Catharine (1769–1837) who was at Innes House with her baby in 1799. She was probably the 'Kitty' after whom he named one of the plantations.

By 1787 Cuming headed the British faction opposing the WIC, and his partner Bernard Albinus was one of the five leaders of the Dutch faction. He subsequently became a member of the Court of Policy, the governing body of the Dutch colony, and ironically he was therefore one of those who formally surrendered Demerara to British forces on 22 April 1796. Dr George Pinckard, who was in Demerara from then until May 1797, visited *Garden of Eden* and described Cuming as a 'very hospitable [man] . . . [whose] fortune was already amply made'.[13]

Although Cuming kept his plantation *Kitty* growing sugar, it was cotton which was becoming king in the explosion of interest in Demerara plantations in the 1790s. Lord Seaforth, who invested in Guyana in 1802, credited Thomas Porter as the driving force behind this development.

> In 1782 Mr Porter, a ruined man from Tobago owing £10,000 more than he was worth, left to recover a debt for 20 Negroes sold to Mr Elliott of Demerary. Having been accustomed to cotton planting, he acquired Lot 27 on the east side of the Demerary. His Dutch friends thought him mad but he succeeded in producing cotton, and that of better quality, and made an immense fortune. Over the next ten years this changed the face of the country.[14]

This crop was particularly suited to new plantations created on the coast by the Dutch technique of empoldering, and by 1798 lots for 126 plantations had been laid out on the east coast, almost all of them planted with cotton. Scots owned about one-sixth of these, sometimes in partnership with other British merchants.

By the early 1790s Thomas Cuming had been joined by his younger cousin Lachlan Cuming (*c.* 1756–1836) and by James Fraser (1766–1832), the first of the three Belladrum Fraser brothers to come to Guyana. It was their sister Isabella who married Thomas in 1798. James Fraser must have bought property in 1789 because by January 1790 he let it be known that he had purchased 'a good estate that is likely to turn out to great advantage'.[15] He was then in partnership with George Inglis (1764–1847), brother of the future provost of Inverness. Inglis was already in partnership in St Vincent with the slave trader George Baillie (see Chapter 2) and with William and Archibald Alves, from another Inverness family. When Inglis dissolved the St Vincent partnership in 1792, his brother Hugh (a shipmaster in the West India trade) wrote home to Inverness:

> George . . . reckons himself worth £6000. This is a handsome sum for a young man and acquired very speedily for George had not much to reckon on when he took it into his head to become a Demerary planter.[16]

This was an early expression of the prospects which Demerara was thought to offer, prospects which would become a lure for others in Inverness and the wider Highlands. Already the Baillies

of Dochfour, cousins of the Belladrum Frasers, had invested
and established a number of plantations and the slave-trading
Captain James Fraser (see Chapter 2), at his death in 1798/9, left
a share in a Demerara plantation to his cousin, Fraser of Reelig.
There was also the coffee planter Spencer Mackay (1764–1846),
London-born but from a family originating in Sutherland; Dr
William Munro (1752–1832) from Kiltearn (Ross-shire); and
the firm of Sutherland, McRae & Co., whose partners were
John Sutherland (of whom little more is known) and one of
the Macraes of Inverinate in Wester Ross, probably Alexander
(1756–1812), the oldest of three brothers and later four nephews
who went to Guyana.

There was also the Scottish lawyer, Kenneth Francis
Mackenzie, from a minor branch of the Mackenzies of Redcastle
(Ross-shire), who had purchased *Lusignan*, a 'very large' plan-
tation in Demerara which generally 'gave a very good income'
and supported the family for almost fifty years.[17] It also pro-
vided a refuge when Mackenzie, who had been appointed attor-
ney general of Grenada in 1793, was caught up in the Fédon
Revolution (see Chapter 4). He escaped with his life, having
served as President of the Council after the execution of Ninian
Home, and was living on his Demerara plantation in 1797.
His name, or at least his initials, live on in the KFM brand of
Demerara rum.

This involvement of Scots was summed up by Lord Seaforth
in a memorandum to the Duke of Portland written in early
1800:

> A considerable time before Britain acquired Dutch Guiana migra-
> tions of Britons to Surinam and Demerary had been frequent but
> at the period of us taking possession, the influx of English, and still
> more of Scots, adventurers was truly astonishing.[18]

Thomas Cuming's early success was based on his integration into the Dutch society of Demerara and on his ability to
operate across boundaries of nationality and religion. Although
he returned to Scotland twice, and died in Elgin, he was at home
in the colony. Similarly, both his cousin Lachlan Cuming and
his future brother-in law, Simon Fraser of Belladrum, married
Dutch women and established homes there, albeit Mr and Mrs
Fraser travelled to Scotland a number of times. Although he was
said to have hated the country, Simon Fraser spent £5,000 on

his Berbice house and more than £2,000 each year on running his household.[19] Neither of these marriages survived – Lachlan's wife lived separately, at least after Lachlan returned to Elgin in the early 1820s, and Simon Fraser's marriage ended in divorce after his wife, Suzanna van Batenburg, eloped with another Demerara planter. But they served the purpose of forming links with established Dutch planters in the colony. More commonly, British planters saw Demerara as a temporary residence, even if that might mean for twenty years or so.

BERBICE

All the Dutch colonies on the Wild Coast had been run by private companies operating under individual charters. In matters of trade and immigration, Suriname was the most liberal, followed by Demerara–Essequibo, with Berbice, under the control of the Berbice Association, the least so. There had, however, been a period of growth after Berbice received a new constitution in 1732 and by 1763 there were eighty-eight plantations on the Berbice River and twenty-seven on the Canje. In that year enslaved Africans rose up under their leader, Cuffy, in a well-organised revolt and held large parts of the colony until 1764. Although Dutch control was re-established, the colony's white population fell from 286 to 116 and the number of slaves from 4,251 to 2,464. A later map of 1771 shows 162 plantations on the Berbice and eighty-seven on the Canje, but many of these remained unoccupied.[20]

From 1791 new grants of land on the coast were made by the Governor, van Batenburg, but while this marked a revival of the colony's plantations, these were only available to Dutch buyers until the capitulation to British forces in 1796. There was the additional complication of a boundary dispute and it was Governor Frederici of Suriname who had made grants of land between the Corentyne River and Devil's Creek, an area which it was later determined was part of Berbice. Berbice had a number of disadvantages compared to Demerara. Hard sand bars made the Berbice River and the harbour at New Amsterdam more difficult to enter than at Stabroek, at the mouth of the Demerary. Fully laden ocean-going ships could only leave the river twice in every month and it was easier to use coastal schooners to move goods to Demerara. Moreover, after the capitulation in 1796,

Berbice retained its complex system of Dutch taxes on shipping, creating a further barrier to trade.[21] Yet, despite these disadvantages and despite the high death rate from fevers among newly arrived whites, Berbice would become – in terms of the proportion of its white populations – one of the most Scottish and most Highland of the Caribbean colonies.

As in Demerara, new plantations were being created on the coast by empoldering. On the west coast, from the Berbice River to the Abary, fifty-two lots were delineated and by 1802 twenty-three of these were in the hands of Highland Scots and their business partners. Of forty-five lots on the east coast, the same Highland Scots owned six plantations. The long-running dispute as to the boundary between Berbice and Suriname was resolved in 1799, while both colonies were under British control, with the boundary fixed at the Corentyne River. This allowed the delineation by the Berbice authorities of a further twenty lots on the Corentyne coast, eight of which were owned in 1802 by a group of Scots.[22] This meant that Scots, mostly with a Highland connection, were in possession of one-third of the new coastal cotton plantations and were directing vast engineering works to bring them into cultivation, work which required the labour of many hundreds of enslaved Africans. In the 1802 *Naamlyste* of plantation owners, twenty of the thirty-six Scottish-owned plantations belonged to 'James Frazer & Comp', that is, to James Fraser of Belladrum and a variety of partners.

As the colony opened up, money was to be made in land speculation as much as in growing cotton. This had already happened in the first wave of purchases in the 1790s, when Lambert Blair (*c.* 1767–1815), a presbyterian Irishman from Newry in Ulster, and his nephew John McCamon or McEamon (1769–1818), formed partnerships which bought plantations with money they had made in slave-trading. They sold some on and developed others. Blair was said to have sold an uncultivated lot on the Corentyne coast in 1801 for £7,000 – a lot which in 1800 had been valued at £5,000. Thus in a single year its value before cultivation had increased by 40 per cent.[23] The same land had been bought by Thomas Porter in 1782 for £500, when it was consider part of Suriname. In the words of one Highland investor, there were 'vast fortunes made by land jobbing'.[24]

Blair used the profits made from land speculation to meet

the costs of bringing his other plantations into cultivation. For example, he owned two lots on the east coast and hired a task gang of fifty enslaved Africans to empolder one of them, which involved digging a shallow canal two miles long and using the material dug out to create a coastal embankment or dam. This took fourteen months but the cost was met by an agreement to sell the second lot to the master of the gang at its original purchase price. The increase in value thus covered the cost of labour.[25]

BELLADRUM AND BERBICE

The allure of Berbice and the role of the Frasers of Belladrum can be seen in the affairs of a failed Highland entrepreneur, Donald Macintosh, who in 1787 had entered into an agreement with Colonel Baillie of Dunain to establish a bleach field on the banks of the Ness. Macintosh expected to spend about £200 but by 1790 the bleach field, still incomplete, had cost Baillie and Macintosh some £900 and to recoup this Macintosh was forced to pay a higher rent. He was soon bankrupt.[26] Macintosh went to London and then to Berbice, arriving in August or September 1795 with the expectation of being employed on one of the Belladrum properties. However, it was not until November that he found work – on another cotton plantation, at a low salary of £42. He remained there for four months until Fraser offered him the management of plantation *Golden Fleece*, at a salary of £100. In April 1796, when Berbice capitulated to British forces, Macintosh wrote to Colonel Baillie, reflecting on the opportunities in the colony:

> I see many young men here in a prosperous way who came but few years ago to the Country as bare as I did. It is true I came with greater embarrassments, but if so, I can easily avoid many extravagances which the generality of them enter into, consequently I look upon myself as on equal terms with them at least. I believe there is hardly any place where money may be made with more facility than here, the great difficulty is once to have a little; but when that little is in hand it can be increased by a rapid progression; and now that these colonies are under British Government, they will be more advantageous for Adventurers of all denominations than before.[27]

Macintosh also expressed his hope of returning 'to my native land with Fifteen Thousand Pounds, tho' more advanced in age by twenty years'.

In 1800 James Fraser of Belladrum entered into a new partnership with a group of Highland landowners and merchants
to buy the lands of the Society of Berbice, which had run the
colony from 1732 until the capitulation. They were Francis
Humberstone Mackenzie (now with the title Lord Seaforth),
who was chief of Clan Mackenzie, Edward Satchwell Fraser of
Reelig, Dr William Munro from Kiltearn (who already owned
plantation *Foulis* in Berbice) and Archibald Alves (a London
merchant and son of Dr Alves of Shipland, Inverness). Alves had
been in partnership as a slave trader in St Vincent with George
Inglis and George Baillie. It is the enthusiasm of Fraser of Reelig,
a struggling Highland landowner, which rings out from the surviving correspondence:

> What an asylum for those of broken fortunes from other colonies.
> What an opportunity to rival the French in Domingo.[28]

Reelig had also inherited a share in a plantation through his
relation, the slaver James Fraser, Master of the *Pilgrim*, and had
expressed his willingness to go to Guyana himself. This did not
happen but two of his sons were sent out.

The final partner was Anthony William Somersall, the son
of Anthony Somersall who from 1759 or earlier had owned a
2,000-acre sugar plantation, *Wismar*, sixty-five miles upriver
on the west bank of the Demerary. The father had come from
one of the Caribbean islands and like many others had been
engaged in smuggling – the illegal importing of slaves from
British merchants. But *Wismar* was now abandoned and his son
was seeking new opportunities.[29]

The partnership thus combined experience of slave-trading,
of plantation ownership and of plantation management, with
capital for investment – much of it based on credit. It was Reelig
and Seaforth who, lacking direct experience of the Caribbean,
were most concerned about what was 'honourable' but Reelig
believed that 'his friends Mr Cuthbert and Cllr Fraser can give
good advice on how an honourable man may acquire a fortune'.

There was a strong sense that the partnership had inside information and had stolen a march on other investors. In early 1801
Alves and Munro had rushed to Holland, despite Britain and
the Netherlands being at war, to complete the deal and Fraser
of Reelig observed with some satisfaction that Lambert Blair,
who had heard about this through 'blabbing', had expressed

his disappointment at having missed the speculation, declaring it worth £100,000. 'If so,' noted Fraser, 'it is tolerably cheap at £20,400.'[30] Their optimism had been fired by the 'chitchat' around Inverness that James Fraser of Belladrum had 'made £40,000 by his last trip [to Guyana]'.[31] Lord Seaforth laid out the reasons for his confidence in a Memorandum to the Duke of Portland:

> My attention was very early drawn towards this subject, from several Gentlemen in my neighbourhood being among the first speculators in Guiana. Of these, some never had any fortune, & others had exhausted what little fortune they were possessed of, yet, with very few exceptions . . . they all returned speedily with larger & some of them with immense fortunes.[32]

He went on to say that he had studied two or three of these men and so had an insight into the general conditions in Guiana. This may well be a reference to Thomas Cuming, James Fraser of Belladrum and George Inglis, all of whom had returned to the north before Seaforth made his investment.

Both the Belladrum Frasers and the Inglis family had already established trans-Atlantic trading and family networks. The father of the Belladrums, Colonel James Fraser (*c.* 1732–1808), served in Germany from 1759 to 1763 during the Seven Years War; in North America from 1777 to 1782 during the American War of Independence; and came out of retirement in 1794 to raise a Fencible Regiment, serving in Ireland until 1797. His brother Alexander (1738–84) was a merchant in Tobago and his wife was Hannah Baillie (1739–*c.* 1797), sister of the slave-trading Baillies of Dochfour.

In the case of the Inglis family, George's grandfather Alexander Inglis had two sons – Hugh (1711–82), an Inverness merchant, and George (1716–75), who emigrated to Charleston, Carolina. It was the next generation which created an international network of family and business interests. George established himself in Carolina as a leading merchant and one of his sons, Hugh Baillie Inglis (1770?–1830?), later managed his cousins' Demerara plantation, *Bellefield*, before moving on to Berbice. Hugh had five sons. Alexander (1743–91) and John (d. 1781) both emigrated to America, where Alexander died in a duel and John was murdered; William (1747–1801) became a leading merchant and provost of Inverness, before drowning himself by jumping from the town's bridge; Hugh (d. 1796) was a ship-master in the West India trade; and George (1764–1847) has already been described.

SURINAME: NICKERIE AND CORONIE

The boundary between Suriname and its neighbour to the west, Berbice, had been disputed but Britain had occupied both colonies by 1799 and an agreement between the governors, Frederici and van Batenburg, established the Corentyne River as the boundary. New plantations were laid out on both the Corentyne coast of Berbice and in Suriname.[33] Two years earlier, in 1797, Frederici had made grants of land on the Nickerie River, a tributary of the Corentyne on the Suriname side, and had himself established the first two plantations, *Paradise* and *Plaisance*, which he soon sold to John Stuart (1767–1808), an Aberdeenshire-born planter in Grenada. Frederici was said to have acquired enslaved people who had run away from Berbice and been recaptured by Amerindians, but Stuart brought his own slaves from Grenada. When the colony was returned to the Netherlands in 1816, the Nickerie River and the lower Nickerie coast had six coffee and fourteen cotton plantations that were worked by over 1,500 enslaved people. Plantations later included John Stuart's *Forgue*, named after his home village, and three others named after other places in Scotland's north-east – Lonmay (given as '*Longmay*'), *Rhynie* and Huntly (rendered as '*Huntley*'). These names probably reflect the involvement of a James Gordon from Huntly and a number of Cruickshanks from both Huntly and Forgue in Scotland, possibly all inter-related and some at least related to Stuart. There was also Glensanda (given as '*Glensander*'), probably connected to the presence of Camerons from Lochaber.

In 1801 an area of coastal land in Upper Nickerie, to the east of the River Corentyne, was laid out in lots. This became known by English speakers as the 'colony' and subsequently by Dutch speakers as 'Coronie', the name it bears today. In 1835 there were twenty-two working plantations, of which eight were, by 1850, named after locations in Scotland – *Clyde, Novar, Belladrum, Bantaskine, Cardross Park, Moy, Hamilton* and *Inverness*. Only three plantations had English place names – *Oxford, Leasowes* and *Totness* – indicating the preponderance of Scots involvement. The names *Belladrum, Moy* and *Inverness* are indicative of the Highland presence.

In addition, Adam Cameron (1772–1841), an illegitimate son of Colonel Sir Alan Cameron of Erracht (Lochaber), is credited with establishing *Burnside*, the first cotton plantation in Coronie, in 1808. And Alexander Cameron (before 1764–1821) younger of Invermallie, the son of a tacksman (principal tenant) on the estates of Cameron of Lochiel in Lochaber, went to the Virgin Islands before moving to Suriname, where in 1804 he described himself as operating 'on a pretty extensive scale and as far as I have gone my prospects are favourable'. Alexander was joined in Suriname by at least three of his brothers – Angus (1764–1854), Duncan (1788–1835) and Donald (1770–1837) – and by his sister Ann (1774–1854). Ann also brought to the colony William Mackintosh (1799–1848) and Alexander Mackintosh (1803–53), her sons by her first marriage in the Highlands, and she later remarried a James Munro 'of Surinam', whose surname suggests that he might too have had Highland origins. When Cameron died in Suriname in 1821, he left his four plantations – *Burnside, Clyde, Leasowes* and *Oxford* on the Coronie coast – together with 550 slaves to his brothers and nephews, his son Alexander having drowned at Nickerie in 1818.

When slaves were freed in the Dutch colonies in 1863, compensation was paid to slave holders by the Dutch Government. Nine per cent of this compensation was claimed by Scots and three per cent by English owners.

'BERBICE IS A POISON'

On 13 August 1814 an Anglo-Dutch treaty, known as the Convention of London, agreed the permanent ceding to Britain of Essequibo, Demerara and Berbice and the return to the United Netherlands of other former Dutch colonies in the Caribbean, including Suriname. But the stability brought by the treaty, and by the final defeat of Napoleon the following year, came too late for those who had speculated in cotton in Berbice. Exactly six months earlier, James Baillie Fraser had written to Lord Seaforth attributing the failure of their speculation to 'a ten years series of the most dreadful seasons ever known' and also to their overconfidence – the 'sanguine turn common to all Guiana adventurers at that period'. There had been the allure of good crops and high prices for cotton, but neither had been realised.[34]

James's father had reached the same conclusion in 1810. He wrote to Lord Seaforth, saying that he was 'determined to bring home my sons after 10 years unsuccessful trial' and he advised Seaforth against the idea that the two of them might go to the colony to investigate the state of their properties:

> At your age and mine what should we do ... we should have to compete with low cunning characters versed in every subterfuge and ravelling ... Berbice is a poison.[35]

He referred, of course, to the effects of Berbice on white planters like his sons. The cotton boom had failed and for those planters who remained, and the merchants who financed them, the future lay in sugar. But Berbice was a place much more toxic to the thousands of enslaved Africans who had been brought there. It was a place where the system of plantation slavery was being pushed to its extremes – yet where, as the next chapter will show, we can most clearly hear the voices of the enslaved.

7

Guyana – Voices of the Enslaved

Randy Browne of Xavier University, Cincinnati, introduces his *Surviving Slavery in the British Caribbean* with the claim that Berbice is perhaps 'the most well-documented slave society in the Americas ... [with] the single largest archive of first-person testimony from and about enslaved people'.[1] He is surely correct, at least for the period from 1819 until emancipation in 1834. This was the result of a coming together of two administrative systems. First, there was the Dutch legal system, continued under British rule, which provided enslaved people with a limited means of making complaints about their treatment to an official known as the fiscal. And, second, there were the attempts of the British governments, under pressure from abolitionists, to show that slavery could be reformed by 'amelioration' – using Berbice as a testing ground. This included the appointment of an official known as the 'protector of slaves', whose role was to enforce new regulations intended to improve conditions. The same individual acted as both fiscal and protector, and reported each year from 1819 to 1834. These reports, held at the UK National Archives at Kew, include 'near-verbatim testimony from thousands of individual slaves, free people of color, and European colonists':

> [These records] reveal, in astonishing and often painful detail, the world that enslaved Africans and their descendants confronted, their hopes and fears, and their efforts to survive horrific conditions ... This is the closest we are likely to come to the actual voices of enslaved people in the Atlantic world.

The archive, although rich and unparalleled, has of course its limitations. The voices are those of witnesses speaking in a formal setting and in relation only to very specific complaints. Yet, as Browne's study shows:

> [They] allow us to better consider enslaved people's ordeal and especially their struggles, successes, and failures in a world of violence, terror, and uncertainty. Their stories bear witness to remarkable courage, and human frailty. They are surprising, horrifying, and haunting. When we listen to them together, we are able to see Atlantic slavery at its core – a world where the central problem was one of survival.

We have too the Registers of Slaves which, from 1817, slave owners in all British colonies were obliged to keep. These also have their limitations but, used with care, they can shed further light on the lives of the enslaved. The complaint of Brutus is but one example among thousands of the ordeals of slavery and of the world into which young men from Europe entered when they became overseers, bookkeepers, managers and attorneys.

Brutus was an African-born slave employed as a watchman on the plantation walk of *Providence*, a sugar estate on the east bank of the Berbice River.[2] As watchman he would be expected to observe and control the movement of slaves on the plantation. In 1817 he was about thirty years old and his African-born wife Arabella, a field slave, was about the same age. They had a daughter Peggy (14), who the owner Matthias Rader (or von Raeder) employed as a maid in the plantation house, along with four other young female slaves – Rosalia (15), Frankje (14), Fanny (12) and Rosetta (9). Rader also had a personal slave, an African named Dick (30), and two house boys. He had already travelled – or at least planned a visit – to Scotland in 1816, including trips to Inverness and Cromarty. In preparation for this the manager of one of his other estates, John Gordon, had written to friends in Inverness asking them to take care of Rader as he would be 'a stranger' there.[3] In 1819 Rader sold his Berbice properties – *Providence* on the Berbice River and *Belair* on the west coast – and left for Europe, keeping only his slave Dick, who three years later was baptised in Lindau, Bavaria, taking the baptismal name Friedrich.[4] We will return to his master Matthias Rader later in this chapter.

Plantation *Providence* was bought by a William Henery, who appointed Hugh Bethune (1789–1821), from Alness in Ross-shire, as his attorney and a Robert McDermott as his manager.

By early 1819 McDermott had begun to exploit the female slaves on *Providence*. He 'kept the wife of Rule, and after having her a few nights, left her'. Rule was an African-born sugar boiler and field slave, aged about twenty-four. For women like 'the wife of Rule' there was, in addition to the abuse, the agonising calculation as to whether or not a sexual relationship with the estate manager might protect her and her family. But McDermott's attention soon turned to Brutus' daughter:

> The manager wants my daughter Peggy; I said no; he asked me three times, I said no ... Manager asked me Friday night; I refused, and on Saturday morning, he flogged me. It is not for my work. This thing hurt me, and I came to complain.

Brutus, according to the manager, had been punished for failing to flog a man and two boys who had all refused to work because they were debilitated by the disease known as yaws, a chronic bacterial infection of the skin, bone and cartilage. Brutus stated that he had been afraid of being infected himself if he whipped them.

When Brutus made his complaint to the fiscal, his daughter Peggy was sick and her sister Acquasiba gave evidence instead. There is no Acquasiba in the Register of Slaves for the plantation and so this might be her 'born day' name, given to a girl born on a Sunday, rather than her 'slave name'. She told how the manager had instructed the enslaved woman 'aunt Grace' to send Peggy to his bed and that, if she would not go, to send Acquasiba. Acquasiba reported, 'We said, daddy said we must not, I was too young.' After Grace tried to coax her, Acquasiba's response was the same: 'I would not, as my daddy had forbid it.' However, when Fanny was sent for – her age was given as twelve – she went to his room. Subsequently Peggy and 'all of us (the creoles) got orders to be watchmen at his door' – that is, to be available to him for sex. One of these girls was fourteen-year old Frankje, the daughter of aunt Grace.

Henery was in London at this time and the fiscal had a 'long conference' with the attorney, Hugh Bethune, who assured the fiscal that he had 'used every endeavour' to discover if Brutus had been punished for refusing his daughter to the manager, adding that had this been the case he would have dismissed McDermott. Bethune was the son of the parish minister of Alness (Ross-shire) and had been a fellow pupil of Donald Sage at Dornoch (see Chapter 3):

> Hugh's mental abilities were not of the highest order, but he had a good, working mind, suited not so much for the higher walks of literature, as for the business of the world.

Bethune, with his mind on the 'business of the world', had found no evidence – presumably the testimony of his own slaves was discounted – and the fiscal therefore 'forebore inquiry'. He did, however, admonish the manager whose conduct he clearly found distasteful but a complaint two months later by an enslaved man, Laurence, who alleged excessive punishment by McDermott, was also dismissed.[5] And by the end of the year, if not before, Peggy's father Brutus had lost the position of watchman and had been reduced to a field labourer.

Four years later, another complaint reveals that Peggy had become the housekeeper to the manager of *Providence*, although it is not clear if this was still McDermott. She was found wearing a coral necklace which had been stolen from an enslaved woman named Jenny. For this theft an enslaved carpenter, Michael, had already received a hundred lashes and been confined in the stocks. But because Peggy was the manager's housekeeper – and sexual partner – nothing was said to her.[6] The slave registers reveal that the other housemaids had been reduced to the status of field slaves, while Peggy had enhanced her position, at least for the time being. Meanwhile, her father and mother remained part of the sugar plantation, whose enslaved population had increased from 122 to 204 as its owner, William Henery, consolidated his workforce.

This is but one example of the painful detail of the lives of enslaved Africans and their children between 1819 and emancipation in 1834. In the rest of this chapter I turn to other sources through which we can understand how enslaved men, women and children struggled and survived – or died – earlier in the 1800s. It is also an account of how a remarkably small number of whites – in proportion smaller than in any other colony – exercised control over those who had been stolen from Africa in the final years of the trans-Atlantic trade.

CONTROL

Caitlin Rosenthal has recently used her background in management and accountancy to shed light on this 'most vexing historical question about the West Indian plantation complex ... how a small number of free whites maintained power over so many enslaved Africans?'.[7] It is an essential question in seeking to understand slavery in Berbice, where this challenge was greatest and an issue for the colony's Court of Policy, which expressed concern on a number of occasions about the need to augment the number of whites on the plantations. In 1808 they noted that on some estates only one white person was employed.[8]

Rosenthal, Browne and Trevor Burnard (see Chapter 2) are all unflinching in identifying the centrality of terror in the operation of large-scale plantation slavery – and the fiscals' and protectors' records are irrefutable evidence of this. Rosenthal shows how planters adopted multiple strategies all underwritten by that terror. Not simply fear of punishments – which included branding, nose slitting, gelding, whipping and pickling (rubbing salt into the wounds) – but spectacular displays of violence whose effects were believed to extend into the afterlife. Thus heads were severed from the bodies of those who had been hung and carcasses were left in chains to be devoured by vultures. But along with this were the systematic and daily methods of control – control of access to horses and to cutlasses, restrictions on travel, on social gatherings and on the spread of information, and crucially a system of management which extended into the enslaved population and offered rewards and incentives to head drivers, carpenters, distillers and so on. The Demerara planter Colin Macrae (1776–1854), from Inverinate in Wester Ross, later explained the importance of enslaved managers in his evidence to a Parliamentary Committee in 1827, stating that at one time he had 'as many as three thousand Negroes under my charge' and that the loss of 'an engineer, a head boiler, or a leading man' would have 'very injurious effects'and 'might cripple the whole concern'.[9] Later, Macrae's nephews Alexander Macrae (1787–1860) and Farquhar Macrae (1808–38) wrote manuals on plantation management which influenced practice in both the Caribbean and the United States.[10]

To exercise this control it was essential to know, through accurate and detailed record-keeping, who was on the plantation, what was happening, and where people were at any given time. Thus, 'accounting complimented violence and terror, binding multiple strategies into a rationalised web of control both on individual plantations and across the islands'. The plantations of both Berbice and Demerara with their tiny number of whites were, of necessity, at the forefront of the development of these systems. There is an extensive body of relevant material in archives in the United Kingdom and elsewhere, written from the perspective of slave holders, merchants, slave traders, plantation managers, overseers, bookkeepers and the many others who were active or complicit in the crimes of slavery. It is worth quoting Rosenthal again:

> Slaveholders (and those who bought their products) built an innovative, global, profit-hungry labor regime that contributed to the emergence of the modern economy ... [T]he fact that many slaveholders were accomplished managers should not be surprising. We know that large planters were among the wealthiest business people of the time. We know that slave-grown sugar was the most valuable commodity of the eighteenth-century Atlantic world ... We know that the textile industry – by most accounts the leading industry of the Industrial Revolution – wove cloth from [slave-grown] cotton. We know that the amount of capital invested in slaves was massive, by some measurements as large or larger than the amount of capital invested in factories ... Slave-holding business people – and those who bought their products – benefited from control over enslaved people. Control enabled them to manage with great precision ... [And] control has always been at the heart of modern accounting practice.

These developments in accounting practice included standardised, monthly reports which were designed to be scrutinised by absentee owners in Britain who had entrusted their plantations to attorneys and managers. Rosenthal sees this separation of ownership from management as proving a potential advantage, allowing owners to promote their interests in and around the UK Parliament, defend themselves against the movement for the abolition of slavery, and diversify their investments. A disproportionate number of these early standardised reports came from these colonies that would become British Guiana and among the earliest are reports from *Hope and Experiment*, a plantation on Berbice's west coast belonging to Hugh McCalmont (1765–1838) from Belfast. It was managed for him from the early 1810s by John McLennan (d. 1851) from Skye. These monthly reports continued, under successive managers, until emancipation in 1834. There is no doubt of McCalmont's success – his sons Robert and Hugh were among the richest men dying in Britain in the nineteenth century, leaving £1.4 million and £3.1 million respectively.

The operation of these systems required an increasingly skilled cohort of attorneys and managers. When a proposal was made in 1819 to settle a hundred displaced families from Sutherland in South Africa (see Chapter 3), a George Laing applied for the post of superintendent on the basis that he had 'been from 1797 to 1812 a Settler & Sugar & Cotton Planter in the Colonies of Demerara & Essequibo and during that period in the constant habit of following up and superintending the labour of Negroes in the cultivation and planting of new lands &c'. This was not, as might seem at first sight, a comparison of Highlanders with slaves but an expression of the complex management systems required on a large plantation.[11]

Confusingly, the meaning of the terms 'manager' and 'overseer' varied from colony to colony. In Berbice and Demerara, overseers were lowly figures but were expected to have some basic skills in literacy and numeracy. Both the Frasers of Reelig and Lord Seaforth sent out estate gardeners, or their own sons, as overseers – with the sons moving on to more senior roles. It was managers and attorneys who exercised greater control, the attorney being authorised to act on behalf of the owner to the extent laid down in the 'power of attorney', a registered legal document. Attorneys might act for a number of owners and on a number of estates. The most powerful attorneys on the west coast of Berbice included John Ross (from Golspie), John Cameron (from Lochaber) and Lewis Cameron (from Edinburgh). All three men figure in the following accounts of this area of Berbice and of the response of enslaved people to the conditions under which they suffered. So, too, do those owners who managed their plantations themselves or did so through their sons and other relations.

FRASERS OF REELIG (NO. 28) AND PETER FAIRBAIRN (KINTAIL, BRAHAN AND SEAWELL)

Plantation No. 28 on the west coast of Berbice was never given a name and, although it was managed for some years after its creation *c.* 1794 as a part of *De Unie* or *Union* (along with No. 29 and No. 30), it remained a number. Perhaps this was a daily reminder for the Reelig brothers, James and Edward, that this was a business venture, entered into with the purpose of sustaining their Highland home near Inverness.[12] The family's involvement with Berbice began when their father Edward Satchwell Fraser (1751–1835) of Reelig inherited a share in another plantation, *Dochfour*, from James Fraser, master of the slave ship *Pilgrim* (see Chapter 2). The other owner of *Dochfour* was James Fraser of Belladrum who, after some time and some acrimony, persuaded Reelig to give up his share in exchange for an interest in Belladrum's new venture – plantation *Union*, acquired in 1800. In this venture Belladrum was in a partnership with William Fraser (1763–1843) of Culbokie and Colin Mackenzie (*c.* 1767–1824) of Mountgerald (Ross-shire). For Culbokie this was both a reinvestment of the £10,000 or so he had made in St Vincent (see Chapter 5) and a further bond with the Belladrum brothers – in 1797 he had married their sister Sarah Fraser.

Two of Reelig's sons, James and Edward, shared the experience of life in Berbice, training as overseers and then running No. 28. They did so between 1801 when James arrived in Berbice at the age of eighteen and 1811 when he sailed for home. Edward arrived in October 1803, aged seventeen, and left in 1810. James had initially been apprenticed in St Vincent with the intention that he become a slave factor. Both learned to control enslaved Africans as overseers on *Novar*, owned by the man they called the 'growling doctor' – William Munro (1751/2–1832), a neighbour from the Highlands. Although they shared this experience, the brothers saw their interaction with their slaves in quite different ways.

When James finally left Berbice in 1811, he referred in his journal to the pain of leaving No. 28 and 'the negroes whom I love & consider as my children & friends . . . who all look up to me for redress or happiness'. Three years later he recalled that he had stolen away 'secretly through the plantation walk, that I might not have any more painful farewells for my unfortunate negroes and old servants'. When James had taken home leave in Scotland in 1809, Edward in a letter to their mother had praised James for his attention to their slaves, saying, 'It would do you good to see the care he takes of the sick and old people – and his tenderness even to the children.' Yet it was James who insisted on a level of discipline and was critical of

Edward's laxity during his absence. This was a long-standing complaint. In 1805 Edward told his mother that he was 'fond of the negroes' and that 'James charges me with being too familiar with them'. After Edward returned from his own period of leave in 1808, he admitted to his mother how difficult he found his role and insisted that she kept his letter from his father:

> I compare my self standing with the workmen up the burn [at Reelig] to standing over the Negroes of 28 obliged to keep on stern sour looks and scolding every moment.

Yet Edward has seen James lose his temper and strike a slave, which he thought was 'shocking and coward like' because a slave who retaliated 'must have his arm cut off if he attempts to return a white man's blows'. Both were also aware that their neighbour from home, Alexander Fraser of Clunes, had struck an enslaved man so hard that he died. And Thomas Staunton St Clair had, at about this time, witnessed such a punishment carried out behind Government House in New Amsterdam in front of a large crowd.[13]

Edward argued about slavery with both his brother and James Fraser of Belladrum – and about the relationship between slaves and slave owners. His brother had taken two of his personal slaves to the Highlands in 1809 and one of them, known as Black John, remained there until James returned in 1811. Similarly, James Fraser of Belladrum took his slave Archy to Britain – and probably to the Highlands – and returned with him to Berbice in 1812 or 1813. Black John was close to James and liked by the family at Reelig, yet Edward was clear in his opinion:

> If he [Black John] was to return to the country and there were an insurrection I am sure he would as soon see his master and me killed as not . . . People ought to feel no faith in their slaves for they all know they deserve nothing in return from them but such as is generally met with . . . James will give you other notions . . . but facts are facts.

After the brothers left Berbice, Lewis Cameron was appointed as Reelig's attorney and he in turn appointed a James McDougall as manager. Even if it is true that the Fraser brothers had managed No. 28 in a relatively benign manner – and there is no reason to doubt their sincerity – this gave their slaves no longer-term protection. In 1812 two sick slaves, Willitick and his wife

Dobie, were repeatedly and brutally flogged by the manager, as were the couple's young children when they intervened. Cameron declared that he would resign rather than connive at McDougall's behaviour. Cameron remained as attorney and McDougall was dismissed – and was in Cameron's view 'finished' in the colony since no other planter would give him a job.

This incident is illustrative of the fact that throughout the period of slavery there was a certain level of violence and sadism which disturbed at least some of the planters and which they attempted to suppress. For example, in 1812 the former manager of plantation *Welgelegen* accused the attorney John Broderick of 'murder and an unnatural crime' following the death of an enslaved woman, Sally.[14] And in 1810 Thomas Fryer Layfield appeared before the Court of Criminal Justice charged with the murder of a slave while acting in his role as a captain in the Burgher Militia. The sentence was merely a reprimand and Layfield was allowed to resign his commission. The court seems to have accepted that, while he had exceeded the intent of an earlier regulation aimed at curbing excessive punishment, Layfield was acting neither as the owner nor manager. Two other cases were dealt with in the same session. Richard Fowler, a manager and attorney, was fined 6,000 guilders for causing a slave named October or Quasi to be punished with 'extraordinary severity'. One member, Simon Fraser of Belladrum, voted that Fowler be subject to the greater punishment of whipping and banishment from the colony but he was overruled. In contrast, Caesar, an enslaved man on plantation *Hampshire*, was convicted of killing an enslaved woman – his wife Johanna, who had been 'given to another negro on the estate'. He was hung, beheaded, and his head stuck on a pole on the plantation.[15]

In addition to No. 28, Fraser of Reelig was, as we have seen, in partnership with Lord Seaforth, James Fraser of Belladrum, William Munro and others in the purchase of land on the east and west coasts belonging to the Dutch Society of Berbice. On the west coast, when these were divided among the partners, Reelig became the owner of No. 23 and Seaforth the owner of *Kintail* (No. 51 and No. 52) and *Brahan* (No. 34). Seaforth also acquired *Seawell* on the east coast and sent his secretary, Peter Fairbairn (1762–1822), to manage all three plantations. Fairbairn had worked for Lord Seaforth at Brahan Castle in Ross-shire from at least as early as 1794, an important position because Seaforth was both deaf and dumb, and so relied heavily on written communications.

Fairbairn arrived in Berbice in November 1801 and remained in Guyana until his death in 1822. He had never intended to stay. In 1808 he hoped 'to return next year after 8 years abroad' and felt, at this date, that he had stayed for the previous two years against his own interests and to the injury of his family and children, all 'to keep down the expenses of the concern and render it productive'. By July 1809, however, he was still unable to leave: 'In vain I attempted to close my arrangements to quit this country and find it impossible until I see results of the ensuing crop.' In 1810 he was still there and expressed his regret that he had not left in 1806. And so things continued, with perhaps some sense that he had become reconciled to life in the colony – by 1814 he was resident at *Kintail*, his 'favourite place', with both land and building neatly laid out 'like a European farm', where he had established a settled relationship with an enslaved African woman, Charmion, who between 1812 and 1821 bore him five children. Fairbairn made provision for their manumission in his will.

Finlay McKichan, in *Lord Seaforth: Highland Landowner, Caribbean Governor*, argues that Seaforth, acting through his manager Fairbairn, was a relatively benevolent slave owner, motivated by humanitarianism as well as commercial concerns. Seaforth served as Governor of Barbados from 1801 to 1806, but never visited his Berbice plantations, relying instead on frequent reports from Fairbairn. McKichan cites this extensive correspondence and argues that it demonstrates significant attention to the diet and health of slaves (including care of older non-productive slaves), an increase in the number of children, and a decrease in the number of slaves running away. McKichan accepts that slavery was inherently 'a brutal system' but holds that Seaforth was attempting to improve conditions for slaves within that system. The claim that Seaforth was a humanitarian is robustly and convincingly refuted by Stephen Mullen in his review of McKichan's book.[16] I will return to this in more detail in Chapter 11.

Fairbairn was not only a plantation manager but a member of the colony's Court of Policy and Criminal Justice from 1812, serving during some of the most troubled times for the white planters. This included their response to escapes and to threats of rebellion.

MAROONS AND THE BUSH EXPEDITIONS

Escape was the most common form of resisting slavery but the pattern of 'desertion' – as the planters called it – varied from colony to colony, depending on the geography, the extent of white settlement, and on borders beyond which there were different laws and practices. Bram Hoonhout's *Borderless Empire* shows how in the Guianas it also depended on relationships between the whites and indigenous Amerindians, whose knowledge of the forests and savannahs made them valuable allies in the recapture of runaways. In Suriname from the later 1600s, large Maroon communities were established in the interior, where the declining Amerindian population refused to assist the colonial authorities. They retained their freedom and members of the six Maroon nations of Suriname make up about 20 per cent of the country's current population, with about half of them still living in the forested interior. In the westernmost colony, Essequibo, escape across the River Orinoco into Spanish territory was an option. In Demerara and Berbice, however, alliances with Amerindians were vital to the white planters, especially because little military support had been given to the colonies under Dutch rule, and the bargaining power of the Amerindians increased considerably during the mid-1700s as Demerara's plantation economy grew. The same policy was continued by the British who maintained the Dutch system of post holders, strategically located up the main rivers, whose principal function was to maintain good relations with the Amerindians, providing them with guns and making formal, annual gifts of European goods.[17]

In these circumstances large settlements of Maroons in the forest were vulnerable and some of those who escaped instead established small camps surprisingly close to the plantations. This is sometimes referred to as borderland marronage to distinguish it from the *gran marronage* of the permanent settlements. In one striking example cited by Hoonhout, a community of about a dozen Maroons were discovered in 1789 living only 150 yards behind a plantation.[18] With borderland marronage escapees could maintain communication with those still enslaved in the plantations and this is a feature in the following account from the west coast of Berbice.

In January 1803 Fairbairn told Seaforth that two slaves had

run off but that he expected them back soon. However, the following January he had to report that 'desertion' had been 'furious during this quarter' and that an expedition had been mounted into the bush. This had encountered a camp of about fifty Maroons a day's journey away, on the Demerara side of Abary Creek, the boundary between the colonies. The camp was well provided with 'plantains, rice, tobacco, cassava etc in abundance'. Those in the camp included three of Seaforth's slaves – Peter, Dingwall and Inverness. Only Inverness was recaptured and Fairbairn reported that a 'military party' was being sought in order to pursue the others. By this time – January 1804 – the hundred slaves he had bought since 1801 for plantation *Brahan* had been reduced by five deaths and six runaways.

The dry winter season made easier escape across the savannah to the forest and in January 1808 Fairbairn reported that Quaco, who had been Seaforth's cook in Barbados, had absconded along with a boy, and had attempted to contact the 'maroons in the woods'. They were captured but Quaco escaped again in late 1809 along with another slave 'of much greater value than himself'. In an undated memorandum, from about the same time, Fairbairn gave a detailed account of the slave Favourite, who had been 'detected in the practice of Obie [Obeah]' and 'also in having communication with Runaways and having formed a plan to carry off a number of the women to the Woods'. Female Maroons were often described in this way – as if they lacked agency and were victims of kidnap.[19]

Favourite had been punished by 'confinement in barracks' and then returned to plantation *Seawell*. However, in November 1808 he had again been found practising obeah and had been 'delivered to the Governor to be put in irons and put to labour'. Although Fairbairn does not mention whipping, it was a standard punishment that runaways were 'condemned to be flogged and to work in chains' and those found guilty of practising obeah were also commonly flogged.[20]

Favourite escaped again and in May [1809?] he was caught at *Brahan* 'in the act of carrying off one of the negroes, assisted by a negro belonging to the estate and by one of the 'Brahan Runaways'. This was Inverness, who had been long absent but who according to Fairbairn 'knows the way back and holds correspondence with the coast'. Favourite was again 'confined

Figure 7.1 Charles Edmonstone's plantation on Mibiri Creek, Demerara, drawn by Thomas Staunton St Clair.

in barracks'. By this time Fairbairn reckoned that the Maroon camp had grown to number about a hundred and noted that 'if the Runaways . . . are not drove away I fear very serious consequences'. The Governor, van Batenburg, had promised to send an expedition the previous year, 'assisted by Indians', but had been prevented 'by the season'.

The promised expedition was mounted in January 1810, under Charles Edmonstone, and Fairbairn was able to assure Seaforth that the hundred runaways had been 'killed or taken' (see Chapter 2). The Demerara newspaper gave more detailed information:

> We now take leave to announce the return of the Party, with Seventy-six black prisoners, after having killed Twenty-six more in different skirmishes with the Banditti.[21]

Among those captured were Seaforth's old cook Quaco and his companion, who Fairbairn assured him would, like the other captives, be 'shipped to the islands' and the plantation would 'get the value'. Lewis Cameron also reported to Reelig the capture of a number of enslaved people, who had run away from both No. 28 and neighbouring *Union* (No. 29 and No. 30).

Fairbairn was appointed to the Court of Policy and Criminal

Table 7.1 *Berbice Gazette*, 20 February 1813 (Sale of Negroes captured in the Bush Expedition of 1809/10, sold in Demerary 9 June 1812)

Owner	No. of slaves	Adult male	Adult female	Child	Value at sale (guilders)
Morris, Alexander Bruce (heirs of)	13	7	4	2	14,470
Fairbairn, Peter	7	7			5,920
Fraser, Simon	6	1	3	2	5,730
van den Broek	6	1	3	2	5,400
Katz, Wolfert	6	2	2	2	4,650
Pln Hague	4	4			3,380
Pln Herstelling	4	4			2,620
Blair, Lambert	5	3	2		2,101
Others	19	15	4		12,545
Total	70	44	18	8	56,816

Justice shortly before it dealt with the outcome of this Bush expedition. It took more than two years to resolve disputes over the cost and how that was to be shared between the two colonies. Seventy enslaved men, women and children from plantations in Berbice had been taken and held in Pomeroon, in the west of Essequibo. They were eventually transferred to Fort Island, which had been the capital under the Dutch and where the Courts of Demerara–Essequibo still met. The sale of the Berbice slaves was one of the final acts of these courts before they moved to Stabroek (Georgetown).

I ended Chapter 2 with an account of the life and death of an African-born slave renamed Inverness, who first escaped from plantation *Brahan* in 1803. He was not among those captured in the Bush expedition. In addition to these slaves, at least a further ten had been caught and returned directly to Berbice, including two belonging to James Fraser of Belladrum. They were all condemned to be flogged and to work in chains.[22]

As these runaways were being handed over to the fiscal in Berbice, the Governor of Demerara (Bentinck) wrote to the Governor of Berbice (Gordon):

> I have ascertained from whence they are furnished with cutlasses, hatchets and every thing else they require which I rather not trust to paper but shall mention the whole to you the first time I have the pleasure of meeting you.[23]

This suggests another layer of suspicion within the colony about those who might have armed the slaves. The Court of Policy certainly felt that there was a continuing threat and agreed to 'guarantee to the postholder & Indians' – that is, Charles Edmonstone and the Arawaks – the 'usual barrack fees, the payment of the same reward as was stipulated on the outset of the Bush expedition for the taking of runaway negroes, namely one hundred guilders per head'. They remained 'convinced of the imperious necessity of routing out the settlement of any runaway negroes & particularly of the expediency of ridding the colonies of the head man of the runaways'. Payments were also being made to the postholder on the Corentyne and to the Amerindians there. In July 1811 Governor Gordon made one change by 'doing away with that barbarous custom of encouraging the Indians to bring in the hands of runaway negroes when with equal facility the negroes could be brought in alive . . . [it being] repugnant to the feelings of human nature'. In future, only half the reward was to be paid for a right hand.[24]

As this was happening, Edward Fraser, who had returned to Scotland in 1810, was approaching Portsmouth where, on 25 July 1811, he sailed for India. James was to leave Berbice a few weeks later and then follow him. During the five-month voyage Edward thought of their former slave, Black John at Reelig, and wrote urging James to bring him to India. He would be 'a treasure of no small value'. But this also made him think of the plight of the slaves on No. 28 under a new master: 'Indeed it is so painful a subject that when it comes across me I instantly go in search of someone to talk to and avert my attention other ways.'[25]

Black John and James were reunited in October 1811, and in the summer of 1812 they explored the West Highlands together, John mounted on their pony and James walking. In December John was baptised in the High Church in Inverness and in January 1813 they sailed together from Portsmouth for India. After ten years of loyal service – and friendship – in travels through India, Persia and Europe, John died in London in 1823, mourned by the Fraser family. In Black John's loyalty, James was proved correct. But Edward was closer to the truth in the case of another house slave, Archy, who had come to Britain with his master James Fraser of Belladrum and after his return to Berbice was implicated in an uprising of slaves in 1814.

RESISTANCE AND THE LOSS OF CONTROL

A further rich source in understanding slavery in Berbice is the outcome of cooperation between the National Archives of the Netherlands (Nederlands Nationaal Archief) and the National Archives of Guyana, under the former's Shared Cultural Heritage programme. This has led to the conservation and digitising of all documents in the 'Dutch Series' in the Guyana Archives – that is, all material dating before the formal ceding of Berbice and Demerara–Essequibo to Britain in 1814/15. This amounts to almost 100,000 scans, made freely available online, and includes significant material in English. Among these is a further body of testimony from enslaved people relating to an alleged plan for an uprising in 1814 on the colony's west coast – one of the most Scottish, and most Highland, parts of the Caribbean. This material provides a window into the lives of the enslaved in the period following the abolition of the African slave trade in 1807 and demonstrates how a fear of losing control affected the small white population.

CHRISTMAS 1813: 'THEY MUST TAKE CARE OF THEMSELVES AND DO THAT STORY'

James Fraser and Black John spent Christmas 1813 in Liverpool with the Gladstone family, on their way to London and then Portsmouth. That Christmas there were more than three hundred enslaved people on *Bath* and *Naarstigheid*, also known as No. 17 and No. 18, adjoining plantations on the west coast of Berbice. More than half were born in Africa, kidnapped and transported as children or adults – one eleven-year-old girl had been born on a slave ship. The rest had come into the world as slaves in Berbice, six of them – four boys and two girls – fathered by white men. Among the oldest of the African-born was a man of the Congo nation, also given the slave name John. Just before Christmas, John's child died and he sent word to other Congos, including those on nearby plantations, saying they should 'bring fowls or money or whatever they had to bury [the child] decently ... as he was an old man it was likely he should soon die & that when he did die they should bring fowls & money to his wife'.

John was concerned that their nation 'was not so good' – that

they were not doing enough to care for the sick and bury the
dead in a fitting manner, with a feast and dancing. And for the
past six years, since the abolition of the slave trade from Africa,
no more of their people had joined them. Ganges, a slave on
Hope, later said, 'no new negroes now come to the country
... [they were] obliged to work so much the more & ... they
must now begin to look about for themselves'. And Pompey on
plantation *Washington* was reported as saying, 'that as no new
negroes now came to the Country they must take care of themselves & do that Story.'

John, although enslaved, was a man with authority on plantation *Bath* – as a driver directing the work of other slaves and
more importantly as a leader among his own people. But also
because he practised what the whites feared – obeah. After Mr
McConchie, the manager of *Golden Grove* (No. 25), repeatedly meted out brutal punishments, their head driver George
(his 'day name' was Quasi) sent Queen, Barrington and Cudjo
to John with the message that 'the Buckra on we place punish
the negroe too much & beg Driver John to move him'. They
asked for 'something to kill the manager' and John gave them
'something which he was to put in a stick & put it on the dam
& that it would do the business'.

The manager may have been the William McConchie who
in 1821 was appointed to plantation *Berenstein* and who is
described by the Guyanese historian Alvin O. Thompson as both
'harsh' and 'morally reprobate'. McConchie used his power to
sexually abuse young enslaved women, punishing them if they
refused, sometimes whipping them when naked, and encouraged
others to abuse them by forcing them to bathe naked in the creek
in front of young white men from neighbouring plantations.[26]
Queen said they wanted to 'move' McConchie; Barrington that
the 'something' was to prevent him getting better if he fell ill;
and Cudjoe that it was poison, placed where he might stand on
the stick. But, despite this mundane explanation, Cudjoe was
certain that John practised obeah.

Christmas was a time when slaves were given extra provisions
and allowed time off work to hold their own celebrations. There
were gatherings all along the west coast to eat, to dance, to
drink illicit supplies of rum and to talk. From this emerged the
appointment of leaders for the African nations on at least some
of the plantations. With strange mimicry of the white authorities

in the colony, they were given the title of Governor and below them were fiscals, lawgivers and other officers, including a *schout* – an administrator in the Dutch courts.

Randy Browne shows how enslaved people, despite their enslavement, soon came to claim three customary economic rights: to be provided with sufficient food, clothing and other basic necessities; to have and enjoy their own private property, such as livestock, fowls and garden produce, with the necessary access to land; and to make and enforce bargains and to claim reparations for stolen or damaged goods.[27] These were rights which, as far as was practical, enslaved people attempted to regulate themselves and the appointment of 'officers' of the African nations on the plantations was in part for this purpose, as a Fulani slave on plantation *Washington* explained:

> Pompey told him he was the Fiscal that in the event of anything being stolen they should come to him and if the thief was found he was to make good the article stolen but if refused he the Fiscal was to take effects to make good what was stolen.

There is also evidence of attempts to regulate relations between enslaved people and punish unacceptable behaviour. Thomas of No. 28 said, 'they made a regulation in the event of their quarrelling that the common negroe should pay . . . for troubling each other'. Above all, these societies of the enslaved had the purposes of caring for the sick and burying the dead.

This Thomas, the head driver on Reelig's No. 28, was another man with moral authority who presided at funerals and festivals. He had made a musical instrument which he called a 'pump' and which he played for the first time at Christmas when Fanny, a twenty-six-year-old African-born woman, asked him to 'christen' the new house she had built. She paid him with two bottles of rum. Soon afterwards he was asked to play at No. 19, plantation *Catherinburg*.

> I came to 19, to the managers door & played Mr Ross door till 4 o'clock. Mr Ross approved of my play & gave me rum in a calabash. I went home, stayed home on Sunday till New Year.

At New Year he played and danced again at *Bath* (No. 19), *Belair* (No. 22) and *Golden Grove* (No. 25), and some time later at Seaforth's plantation *Brahan* (No. 34 or 35). According to Thomas, his people 'made him head man on account of his

being always ready to play'. Not all the plantation owners per-
mitted these celebrations. Sam, a Congo on *Washington*, said,
'Don't dance or sup at Washington, master won't let us dance.'
The master was Dr William Munro from Ross-shire.

At *Brahan*, managed by Peter Fairbairn, there had been gatherings of both Congo and Coromantee people. At a supper
held there, Thomas from No. 28 met Archy, a house slave on
Trafalgar and personal servant to James Fraser of Belladrum.
Archy had travelled with his master to Britain – and so probably to the Highlands – and on his return had begun to organise
among the Coromantees. He had a prized possession, a patch-
work quilt or counterpane, which he displayed at their gatherings. Archy sometimes made visits to George, the head driver
on *Golden Grove*, when they 'spoke together in their country
tongue'.

Among all this there were rumours of the appointment of
kings. Thomas, Archy, Pompey, Quamina on No. 17, and
Banaba, the head carpenter on No. 22, were all said to be
kings. More seriously, they were said to be plotting a revolt. It
was two other head drivers, Alexander on *Bath* and February on
No. 11, who reported this to the manager of *Bath*. He told John
McCamon, who acted for the owner, his uncle Lambert Blair,
now in England. And it was McCamon who spoke with the
Governor and requested an extraordinary meeting of the Court
of Policy to deal with the 'meditated rebellion of the negroes &
massacre of the whites'.

RESPONSE AND INVESTIGATION

The Court assembled on 14 February 1814 and the next morning
there was a dawn raid by a detachment of sixty men, with
officers, dispatched by Major Grant, the officer commanding
the garrison at Fort St Andrew, near New Amsterdam. They
seized the suspects and the Court later took evidence from over
seventy enslaved men and women. The evidence they gathered,
all given under duress, they took as confirmation of their suspi-
cions and as justification for their fears. Some slaves confirmed
the existence of a plot to seize control of the colony and kill all
the white population. But even if this had been little more than
talk, the planters and managers were deeply disturbed by the
extent of communication between slaves along the coast, by the

slaves' knowledge of earlier revolts, by the possibility they were in contact with Maroons in the bush, by their organisation in nations and by their use of military terms and military symbols.

It was John Ross – the manager in front of whose house Archy had played – who heard from his informers that there was regular communication between the slaves on the coast and the runaways 'settled aback'. None of the witnesses seem to have confirmed this – the records are damaged and incomplete – but a slave named John testified as follows:

> He had heard from an old man on 22 how the revolt was carried on here formerly, that the black got possession of the Country & that they kept it till they began to quarrel amongst themselves when the Whites took again possession; says the Congo's fought against the Coromanties the Mandingos against others & that then when the Whites came they caught them one by one & destroyed them.

This was a reference to the Berbice slave rising, referred to earlier in this chapter, which began in February 1763 at a plantation on the upper Canje River. Kofi (Cuffy), an enslaved man at *Lilienburg*, was soon accepted as leader and declared himself Governor of Berbice, with Accara as his military captain. He attempted to establish greater order among the rebels but there were disagreements between Kofi and Accara, with Kofi seeking to negotiate the establishment of a separate black state within the colony. An attack in May on Dutch planters failed because they had now been reinforced from Suriname, Barbados and St Eustatia, and divisions grew among the insurgents, who now numbered about three thousand, until this amounted to an internal war. Kofi committed suicide in October but the revolt continued under Accara, who was captured in April 1765. This was followed by the execution of 125 men and three women.[28]

Others talked of more recent events in Demerara, which they often referred to as the 'Demerary story'. According to one, 'White men oppress them, that the same fight they had with the white men in Demerary [and] they wished to renew now'; another that 'they would renew in Berbice a Story they had had in Demerara'. This earlier uprising – or at least a planned uprising – was later described by Thomas Staunton St Clair, at the time an ensign in the Royal Scots:

> On 23rd December, 1807 ... a young Scotchman, overseer of a plantation on the east coast ... requested to see the governor.

He reported ... there would be a rising among the Negroes on
Christmas-eve and that their intention was to march down to
Stabroek on Christmas-day, as they knew we Buckras made it a
day of rejoicing and dinner-parties, when it would be easy for them
to cut all our throats, and free themselves.[29]

The overseer had learned of this from 'a young Negress, my
friend ... who, for two days past, has been most anxious that I
should come down to Stabroek'. When threatened with pistols,
she confessed that it was her father who was planning the revolt.
Twenty slaves were arrested and her father and eight others
were executed. This was all the more disturbing to the plantation owners because the ringleaders consisted of 'the drivers,
tradesmen, and other most sensible slaves on the estates'.[30] This
was a threat to the core system of management which extended
into the enslaved population and on which the whole enterprise
of a large-scale plantation depended. The planters had also been
disturbed by the discovery of a document belonging to one of
the slaves, which appeared to be written in Arabic. It was a
reminder that some of the enslaved were literate and educated.

A key focus in taking evidence in 1814 was whether or not
the 'Governors' of the African nations had some role beyond
presiding at feasts and funerals. Congo, a driver on *Britannia*,
said that Archy, when he came to a supper at *Brahan*, wore
a sash and a cockade on his hat, and had a broad white flag.
Archy denied that he wore either and said that the flag was kept
by a herdboy on the estate. But all this suggested a military
bearing, and references to some individuals as 'King' or 'King
Father', with an implied authority in their nation beyond an
individual plantation, frightened the whites – as did the reported
use of terms including 'General' and 'Captain' and descriptions
of the slaves as 'soldiers'. The slaves who gave evidence could
only answer the leading questions put to them but some, who
later spoke with the missionary John Wray, explained that they
had organised themselves in 'imitation of the Freemasons'.[31]

The Court concluded that there had been a plan to rise up
and kill all the white population. On Tuesday, 19 April six men
– George of *Golden Grove*, John and Quamima of *Bath*, Banaba
of No. 22, Thomas of No. 28 and Pompey of *Washington* –
were taken from the prison in New Amsterdam and executed in
accordance with the sentence of the Court:

[To be] brought to the place where this criminal sentence shall be executed; there delivered into the hands of the public Executioner; by him to be hanged by the neck till death ensue; and after hanging for the space of one hour to be cut down and his head severed from his body; the body to be buried on Crab Island & his head conveyed to the Plantation to which he belonged; there to be stuck on a pole, as an awful example and to remain until destroyed by birds of prey.

The expenses associated with the execution included sixty guilders for porter supplied to the military in attendance.[32] Among those who witnessed the executions was Hugh Munro Robertson from Kiltearn in Ross-shire, who described it as 'an awful but necessary example of punishment in the execution of six Negro ringleaders'. He added the rumour that a document written in what was thought to be Arabic was found among the possessions of one of those executed, fuelling the speculation that 'their plot was laid with a degree of policy & subtlety'.[33]

The members of the Court of Policy and Criminal Justice who reached these verdicts were James Fraser (of Belladrum), George Munro (from Easter Ross), Peter Fairbairn (agent for Lord Seaforth), John McCamon (from Newry) and A. J. Glassius (a Dutch planter). Glassius, a Dutch speaker, found it difficult to follow all of the proceedings of the Court, which were in English. The owners of the slaves executed were the heirs of Alexander Bruce Morris (from Barbados), Lambert Blair (from Newry), Edward Satchwell Fraser (of Reelig), Dr William Munro (from Ross-shire) and Matthias Rader (from Bavaria). Two of the convictions – Thomas of No. 28 and Banaba of No. 22 – were majority verdicts. Shortly afterwards Rader described Banaba, the head carpenter on No. 22, who was 'white with age', as 'denying to the last that he had any bad intentions'.[34]

James Fraser's house servant Archy, who had travelled with his master to Britain, escaped death. He was convicted on a majority vote and, with eleven others, was sentenced to be flogged and sold to a plantation in the Caribbean Islands under a sentence of lifetime banishment from Berbice. Surprisingly, his master James Fraser of Belladrum proposed that he transport Archy to Scotland but, on being informed of this, the Governor intervened. After discussion by the Court of Policy, who concluded that Archy might indeed be sent anywhere in Europe, Fraser had him sent to Grenada.[35] This seems to suggest that some bond had been formed between Archy and Fraser, which survived Archy's role in the planned uprising.

Others slaves were whipped, sometimes branded, and returned to their plantations. Alexander and February, the drivers who had revealed the plot, were rewarded with pensions, medals and silver-topped canes – although they remained slaves and continued in their essential roles as trusted, enslaved managers.

REVERBERATIONS

Revd John Wray of the London Missionary Society returned to New Amsterdam from a brief visit to Demerara a few days before the executions. He had first arrived in Berbice, with his wife and children, in June 1813 after five years in Demerara. His appointment had been sought by the Crown Agent responsible for four Government-owned plantations now run by a Commission, which included prominent abolitionists including William Wilberforce and Zachariah Macaulay.[36] The commissioners' aim was to demonstrate the effectiveness of amelioration and Wray was to provide religious instruction and education. He initially concentrated his efforts on the town and on preaching to the 'Crown slaves' but he was planning for expansion to the west coast where there were '5000 slaves entirely without means of instruction'. He had also been encouraged to come to Berbice by James Fraser of Belladrum, who he had met in November 1812 at *Golden Fleece*, where they had 'much conversation on the instruction of the negroes'. Fraser, who Wray described as having five hundred slaves, wished 'to have a missionary establishment in the neighbourhood'. Fraser later introduced him to Matthias Rader and in May 1813 he 'had an opportunity of preaching . . . on the estates of Messrs Rader and Fraser, where the negroes were very attentive'.

Wray had spent Christmas 1813 in New Amsterdam anxious about the effect of 'dancing, drumming, rioting, and drunkenness' and preached eight times over the three-day holiday before falling ill with a fever. On 8 January 1814 he set off with his family to recuperate in the healthier climate of the Demerara coast where, other than a nine-day return to Berbice by Mr Wray, they remained until 1 April. It was while they were in Demerara that they were informed that a number of slaves on the Berbice coast had been seized in response to rumours of an insurrection and that 'private slander had been helping to do the rest ... regarding Mr Wray and his work causing the trouble'. It was alleged that the plot extended along eighty miles from the Corentyne to the east Demerara coast and that one slave named Philip, a member of Wray's former congregation in Demerara, was a conspirator. As well as rumour, the Crown Agent in Berbice had received a letter from a planter on the west coast, reportedly the owner of a thousand slaves, who fulminated against 'Wray and all Wilberforce's party' and asked the Agent to act in private to obstruct what Wray called 'their humane plans'.[37]

In July Wray travelled along the west coast, staying once more with Matthias Rader at No. 22, with James Fraser and his wife at *Trafalgar* (No. 29) and with the Frasers' manager at *Golden Fleece*. He had ample opportunity to hear about all that had happened and it seems, from the tone of his comments, that he remained sceptical about the alleged plot. Wray's perspective is a useful counterbalance to the partial evidence considered by the Court but it also shows how even those sympathetic to amelioration, like James Fraser and Rader, were incapable of standing against the tide of fear sweeping through the white community.

The convictions had strengthened the hand of those opposed to amelioration, and the London Missionary Society found another opponent in Lieutenant Governor Henry Bentinck, who had taken up his post on 4 January 1814 and who had presided over the trials. From the English branch of a Dutch family, Bentinck had already governed Demerara from 1809 to 1812 and was backed by planters who were later referred to as 'fellows of the old school'. Although Bentinck accepted the invitation to become patron of a bible society formed by Wray in November 1815, within a year they were in barely disguised conflict. Wray, his family and his black congregation in New Amsterdam were subject to repeated harassment. This included interruption of services by hitting sticks against the walls, breaking windows, and on one occasion disruption by a group of white doctors who threw a plank of wood down into the congregation from the gallery. Enslaved people trying to attend services were apprehended by the town guard, their passes were rejected as invalid and Wray's slave George was beaten. Mrs Wray was the subject of obscene verbal abuse and the town guard were instructed to beat drums and fire rifles near the house when she was heavily pregnant. Wray blamed Bentinck for lack of action on his complaints and it seems that the hand of the 'fellows of the old school' was strengthened.[38] The especially brutal punishment of an enslaved African woman named America in 1817, on one of the Crown estates which had now been returned to the Berbice Association, led Wray to travel to London to lay his complaints before the Colonial Secretary.

Meanwhile Bentinck, who was described by the historian Donald Wood as 'a touchy and difficult man', had fallen out with many of the leading planters. In his role as Lieutenant Governor he also presided over the colony's Court of Civil Justice, with whom he soon quarrelled and then dismissed all its members. In an attempt to resolve the problems, he persuaded the Colonial Secretary in London to separate the offices of Lieutenant Governor and President of the Court of Civil Justice. An English lawyer, Henry Beard, who had been lobbying for a West Indian appointment for two years, was appointed to the Civil Court in 1816.[39] Beard was the brother of Mrs Morris, the owner of *Golden Grove* whose slave George had been executed for using obeah or poison in an attempt to kill the manager. Beard, for quite different reasons, would have an important influence on slavery in Berbice. He became Lieutenant Governor in 1821 and, with the support of the British Government, pursued a policy of support for amelioration and reform – and personally supported Wray and the London Missionary Society. He was, however, now faced by a recalcitrant Council of Government – as the Court of Policy was now known – stubbornly opposed to amelioration and horrified by the notion of abolition. Their views were only strengthened by the Demerara slave rising of 1823.

This reactionary Council of Government continued until all members were removed from office in 1826. The sole Dutch member, with little influence, was Adrian Krieger and there was one Englishman, the former midshipman and colonial official John Downer. The other four were Scots. Two have already been mentioned: Dr William Munro and the attorney John Cameron, now acting for Davidsons & Barkly. The others were William Ross (1787–1840) of plantation *Skeldon*, the oldest son of Hugh Ross of Kerse and Skeldon in Ayrshire, a family from Ross-shire who had established themselves as lawyers in Edinburgh, merchants in Sweden and soldiers in India, and

Simon Fraser, the son of the minister of Kilmorack (Inverness-shire), who had given his Berbice estate the name of his Highland home. Fraser was described by Beard in a confidential memorandum as 'one of the most active opponents to every system of slave amelioration ... [and] notoriously insolvent'. Even a fellow planter, Wolfert Katz, had complained that 'his violence of temper was such as, or nearly, to approach insanity'. It was men like this who imposed the harsh discipline which was so characteristic of the Berbice plantations.

THE 'GROWLING DOCTOR' AND THE MOVE FROM COTTON TO SUGAR

One of the members of the Council, the 'growling doctor' William Munro from Ross-shire, has appeared a number of times in this chapter. On the evening of 14 January 1804 young Edward Fraser, newly arrived in Berbice, had sat on Munro's plantation *Novar* with an enslaved African woman as her four-day-old child died of tetanus. There is no indication from Edward that the baby received any attention from Dr Munro, who had graduated from Edinburgh University in 1783 with his thesis *De Tetano* (On Tetanus). Edward had remained 'melancholy' and had predicted, correctly, that he would be laughed at by Mr Arthur, the overseer under whom he was training – 'a capricious conceited little body'. This was nineteen-year-old Innes Arthur (1785–1816), son of the minister of Resolis in Ross-shire, who later pushed his own slaves so hard that one of them died of exhaustion in the Bush expedition of 1810.[40] If Munro sensed any of Edward's unhappiness or his concerns about slavery he did not reveal it when he wrote to Edward's father saying he had every reason to be satisfied with him: 'I know not a better or more promising young man. He is stout & hearty, grown taller & now quite seasoned.'[41]

Munro was an early Scottish settler in Guyana. By late 1783 he had arrived in Grenada, where he became a corresponding member of the Society of the Antiquaries of Scotland, and for some time he worked on the island in a partnership with Dr Colin Chisholm, from Inverness. In that year Chisholm contracted yellow fever and was successfully treated by Munro.[42] Munro left for Demerara in 1793, so avoiding the Fédon Rebellion, and his only child, a daughter Eliza, was born there *c.* 1796. Nothing is know of Eliza's mother.[43] About this time he acquired plantation *Novar* in Demerara, so close to Berbice that it was sometimes described as being in that colony.

Munro was in Britain from about 1800 and he took time in late 1801 to travel to his home in Easter Ross, visiting Revd Harry and Mrs Robertson at the manse of Kiltearn, along with the Demerara planter Mr Labalmondiere. He was already known to the Robertsons and Mrs Robertson remarked, 'He is a sensible agreeable man much improved in his appearance since he was formerly in this Country.'[44] Munro returned to Guyana, arriving in December 1803 after a frantic year or more negotiating for himself and his partners the purchase of the uncultivated lands of the Berbice Association on the east and west coasts. When these were divided, he acquired what would become plantation *Foulis*, close to *Novar* but on the Berbice side of the Abary Creek. Munro had also acted quickly in 1802 to buy, with his cousin and fellow planter George Munro of Alness (Rossshire), an area of land beyond Devil's Creek on the Corentyne coast. He had almost immediately sold a lot and a half lot for three times the purchase price but the deal fell through when a discrepancy was revealed between the area of land sold and the colony chart. George Munro and the surveyors had failed to check the measurements and William Munro was forced to return almost £4,000 to the purchaser. In the meantime, and no doubt to Munro's frustration, Simon Fraser of Belladrum had sold a single lot for £5,000. The market for land had then collapsed and this also affected the partners' plans for their lots on the west coast – plans which had always included an element of 'land jobbing' to finance the cost of bringing the rest into cultivation. Munro confessed:

> I now clearly perceive the folly of entering into so many speculations. For a man so moderate in his wants & desires as I am it is folly in the extreme. I shall now however profit by my experience & shall remain here (much as I wish to be with my friends on your side the water) till I again get into my depth.

A few years later, Munro probably bought plantation *Washington*, which was later managed as a single plantation with *Foulis*. After the alleged conspiracy of 1814, more slaves from *Washington* were indicted and convicted than from any other plantation on the west coast. It was also the one plantation where the slaves were not permitted to dance at Christmas, an indication of Munro's harsh regime.

When it became clear that cotton would not return the vast profits predicted in the early 1800s, Munro turned to sugar. In 1817 he moved a hundred enslaved people from *Novar* in Demerara to Berbice and by the following year he had converted *Foulis* and *Washington* to sugar, creating one of the brutal 'plantation machines' described by Burnard and others. At the end of that year there were over three hundred slaves, and this had increased to 320 by 1822. It was on 30 May 1822 that a group of men from *Foulis* came to complain to the fiscal about their treatment by Dr Munro.[45]

There were five of them, all field slaves. Sharp (43), a 'stout' Mocco, had a Papa wife Hagar (40) and a Berbice-born son Frank (13). Spencer (38), a Coromantee, had a daughter Dorinda (6) and a young wife Thisbe (19), both born in Demerara. Her parents Caesar, a Mandingo, and Sappho, a Congo, were also on the plantation. Thomas (29) and his wife Laura (37) were both Congos, with a daughter Kate (10) born in Demerara. Dick (44), a Papa, and his Demerara-born wife Onetta (21) had a son named Hislop (3). And there was their spokesman Quasi Reynolds (34), a Papa, 'well made, clean limbed' and 'handsome'. Standing 5 ft 11 in tall, he was the tallest slave on the plantation. He told the fiscal how they were poorly fed, with just a small bunch of plantains each week and no salt fish and so little or no protein. They had had no new clothing for four years and that had only been a jacket, and they worked long hours, sometimes a shift of up to twenty hours in the boiling house. They had 'suffered this for many years, but at present . . . cannot suffer it any longer'. This was not a complaint of especially brutal punishment but of the dull and persistent pains of hunger and fatigue.

The fiscal travelled the twenty-five miles to *Foulis* from New Amsterdam, accompanied by a burgher officer. They found 'some irregularities' which they attributed to the overseers, who were duly admonished. They gave Dr Munro a copy of the colony's 'ordinances respecting the feeding and clothing of negroes', with the warning that there would be penalties if these were not complied with. And then they had two of the complainants whipped in front of the other enslaved people – for insolence and disobedience.

DEMERARA RISINGS

Revolts continued. In May 1818 letters arrived in London with accounts of an uprising among the enslaved people on plantation *Beehive* on the Mahaica Creek in Demerara, which resulted in the killing of two white overseers, one of them the brother-in-law of the owner, Charles van Baerle.[46] Between fifty and one hundred people from *Beehive* and *Greenfield* had established a camp in the forest. Those from *Greenfield* agreed to return on condition that a new manager was appointed but the *Beehive* slaves continued their resistance and, with the assistance of some men who had remained on the plantation, lured the two overseers into their camp, where they were killed and their bodies mutilated. The heads of the dead men were severed and placed on poles on the back dam of the estate 'as a defiance'. Shortly afterwards, two more whites were killed by the enslaved sailors on a plantation boat. One correspondent gave the assurance that every effort was being made 'to send a formidable party of whites and Indians to endeavour to destroy them' – but the outcome is not clear. The events yet again exposed the fragility of white control, leading another correspondent to express the fear that 'the charm which held the negroes in subjection is completely broken asunder'.

The uprisings of 1807 in Demerara, of 1814 in Berbice and of 1818 in Demerara are largely hidden from history but reveal a continuous pattern of resistance and revolt, which can be linked back to earlier risings. These include the Berbice Rising of 1763 and a conflict with Demerara Maroons in 1795, in which seven encampments were destroyed and from which the raiding party returned with '70 black arms on points of bayonets'. The encampments – villages might be a better term – were well provisioned and defended, and some has been established for fifteen years. Brutal torture and executions followed, including that of one leader named Amsterdam, who refused to betray his people despite having his flesh torn with red hot pincers and being burned alive.[47]

It was, however, events in 1823 in Demerara which, for the public in Britain, decisively broke the silence. On 18 August

1823 an uprising of slaves began on the sugar plantation *Success* on the east coast of Demerara, led by an enslaved cooper named Jack Gladstone (*c.* 1795) and his father Quamina. Jack was named after the owner of the plantation, the Scottish-born Liverpool merchant John Gladstone. The rebellion has passed into history – including popular history in Guyana – as a revolt of more than 10,000 enslaved people. The rebellion was well documented and publicised at the time, in part because the planters falsely accused the missionary John Smith of encouraging the revolt, as they had earlier accused John Wray in Berbice. Smith was tried, condemned and died in prison before his execution. The most thorough study to date is still Emilia Viotti da Costa's *Crowns of Glory, Tears of Blood*. But more recent investigations suggest that the numbers were exaggerated, the product of white paranoia at the time and of the planters' justifications, after the event, of the brutal acts of suppression and revenge which followed. Almost all the violence was from the white authorities. In that respect it was similar to the Berbice rising of ten years earlier. And as in Berbice, what is easily missed – and in many ways lost – are 'the nuanced and sophisticated ways in which slaves considered the options available to them to better their lives'. It served the narrative of the planters and of their white chroniclers to ignore this and to articulate instead 'their greatest fear [that] slaves would take white men's place along with all rights [and] privileges'.[48]

Jack Gladstone gave evidence for the authorities and was exiled from Demerara to Bermuda, where he was condemned to labour as a convict. His father, Quamina, was shot by one of the 'hunting party' who had tracked him down, either an Amerindian or an enslaved man.

> He apparently would not surrender, never pausing in his stride as the man hunting him took aim ... It seems entirely possible that Quamina ... realizing that to the authorities his role was a foregone conclusion, he refused to be captured, tortured, and humiliated, instead dying with his self-respect intact.[49]

Quamina and Kofi, the leader of the 1763/4 revolt, are now national heroes of Guyana.

8

Guyana – The 'Free Coloured' Moment

Under British control the enslaved population of the colonies of Demerara and Berbice grew rapidly – to over 100,000 by the end of the African slave trade in 1807. Indeed, in the last years of the trade most newly captured Africans transported to the Caribbean were bound for Guyana. Meanwhile, the white populations of these colonies remained small. Berbice never had more than six hundred white inhabitants in the era of slavery and it had the highest ratio of slaves to whites of any British colony. Even in Demerara, where the white population increased in the 1820s as sugar fortunes continued to be made, there were only three thousand white inhabitants in 1827. And in both colonies there were relatively few white women. In 1827 only one in five of the white population in Berbice was female, and in Demerara about one in three.

Across the southern Caribbean the populations of free people of colour had increased to dwarf the white populations. In Trinidad by 1829 there were around four thousand whites and almost sixteen thousand free people of colour – a ratio of one to four. In Dominica the ratio was one to five. And while there were relatively more whites in Demerara and Berbice, with a ratio of one to two, this was against the background of the smallest number of whites relative to the enslaved black population of anywhere in the Caribbean. This was at its most extreme in Berbice, where there was one white to every forty enslaved people – and many of these whites were in the town of New Amsterdam, not on the plantations. The hard fact for the planters was that Berbice and Demerara could only function with the involvement of their 'free coloured' populations. This was part

Table 8.1 Guyana Population, 1827 (Robert Montgomery Martin, *History of the British Colonies*, 5 vols (London, 1834), ii, 32)

	White			Free coloured and free black			Enslaved (1829)		
	Male	Female	Total	Male	Female	Total	Male	Female	Total
Demerara and Essequibo	2,100	906	3,006	2,530	3,830	6,360	37,092	32,276	69,368
Berbice	419	104	523	454	707	1,161	10,998	9,420	20,418
Total	2,519	1,010	3,529	2,984	4,527	7,521	48,090	41,696	89,786

of what Kit Candlin and Cassandra Pybus have called 'the free coloured moment'.[1]

Since the early 1790s, free people of colour had been especially visible and active in communities across the southern Caribbean. They identified themselves as 'free coloured', so distinguishing themselves (and being distinguished by others) from enslaved people, from the tiny number of free black people and from whites. But they aspired to come as close as was possible to the social and economic status of whites. Many, especially 'free coloured' women, were mobile and responded to the emerging opportunities in the Guianas, relocating from older colonies such as Barbados, Grenada and Martinique. This in itself aroused suspicion. In a petition presented in 1822 by white planters and merchants in Berbice, it was asserted that the majority of the free coloured population were foreigners 'if not by birth, at least by education' and that some had even served in the French imperial armies.[2] Since free coloured people had been to the fore in the revolution in Haiti in 1791 and in the Fédon Revolution in Grenada in 1795, reliance on the free coloured population could make whites feel that not only their own status but also their safety was under threat.

More female than male slaves were manumitted in the era of colonial slavery – because they had become the sexual partners of white men and the mothers of their children. A number of these freed women – and their female children once they became adults – entered into relationships with other white men. Free coloured women were notably mobile in their pursuit of these opportunities, both in making relationships and in developing the businesses open to them. In their aptly titled *Enterprising Women* (2015), Cassandra Pybus and Kit Candlin have rescued a number of these women from the oblivion and prejudice of history – women including Elizabeth Sampson in Paramaribo (Suriname), Rachel Pringle Polgreen and Rosetta Smith in Bridgetown (Barbados), Judith Philip in Carriacou (the Grenadines), Susan Ostrehan in Grenada and Dorothy Thomas in Demerara.

The pre-eminence of women over men in the socially distinct population of free coloured people made these colonies unusual places when compared to any society in Europe. The fluid relationships of race, gender and class could confuse and bewilder. When Governor Beard of Berbice issued a proclamation in

1822 removing the prohibition on free coloured men holding the position of plantation manager, he was thereby allowing plantations to categorise these men as white and so comply with the otherwise impossible requirements as to the number of whites required to be resident on an estate. Yet he was shocked at the opposition from the leading planters, expressed through the colony's Council, and he was bewildered that they should react in this way:

> I could never have anticipated a future objection on their part, more particularly so when I consider (as the fact is) that every member of the Council has a large family of coloured children himself . . . I really thought they would feel these appointments a compliment to themselves and their connections.[3]

In the previous year a new arrival, John Castlefranc Cheveley, had also been bewildered by attitudes, behaviours and distinctions. He sailed from Britain on the *Sir John Cameron* along with a small number of passengers that included Benjamin James Hopkinson (b. 1785). Cheveley, who was to take up a position as a clerk in Georgetown, had noticed during the voyage that when Hopkinson removed his wig his hair 'had all at once become black and frizzled' but it was not until he disembarked at Georgetown that he discovered Hopkinson's background:

> Hopkinson was a 'man of colour', which although he was somewhat dark I had not suspected supposing him of French extraction . . . [And] with all his accomplishments [he] could not be admitted into the society of white people! He had gone to live with 'Miss Johanna', his mother, a mulatto woman.[4]

Yet Hopkinson had attended both Oriel College (Oxford) and Trinity College (Cambridge). His mother thought that this had been a mistake:

> Ben shame' of his mother, better he been bring up a carpenter as I tell he father, but Missa Hopkinson say no, Ben must be gentleman, so he 'spise he poor ole mother, but Ben be good son for all that.[5]

Men like Hopkinson were isolated. Not only was he excluded from white society but had he appeared at one of the balls, where young white men and 'coloured ladies' mixed freely, Cheveley believed 'he would have been told that there was no place for *him*'.[6] The position of the leading free coloured women was different. The most prosperous of them were not only independent and enterprising but they also controlled key aspects of economic and social life in the colony.

Cheveley took up his position as a clerk with John & William Pattinson, merchants in Georgetown, who imported European goods and sold much of their stock through the 'black and coloured ladies who kept huckster's stores ... all over town'.[7] Another clerk, Henry Bolinbroke, had earlier described these women as he saw them in 1807:

> Hucksters are free women of color, who purchase their commodities at two or three months credit from merchants and retail them ... Many of them are, indeed, wealthy, and possess ten, fifteen, and twenty negroes, all of whom they employ in this traffic.[8]

Nora Leeds was one of these hucksters. She owned twenty-four enslaved people and when they were freed in 1834 she received compensation of £1,148 – about £100,000 in today's purchasing power. Twelve years earlier Nora was already renowned in the colony for the forceful way in which she ran the team who sold her goods around the town. In 1822 Cheveley often saw her on Sunday mornings 'seated in her shop in great state' holding her slaves to account, praising those who sold well, warning those who did not, and ordering those who had lost goods to be flogged. Then she got ready to attend St George's Church, with the other 'gaily attired coloured ladies':

> [Each] with two or three Negro girls walking behind carrying their prayer-book, umbrella or reticule in great state, [they] clattered

Table 8.2 Free coloured women in Demerara owning 20+ slaves (1817)

Owner	Slaves: male	Slaves: female	Total
Thomas, Dorothy	34	36	70
Rogers, Rebecca (estate of)	28	25	53
Ritchie, Rebecca	15	22	37
Langevin, Jean	24	12	36
Robertson, Jean	10	20	30
Bourdeau, Queen	14	16	30
Blair, Eleanor	10	20	30
Ruysch, Magdalane	16	12	28
Telfer, Martha Ann	15	13	28
Martin, Magdalena	15	8	23
Colongue, Maria Magdaline	13	7	20
Ostrehan, Mary	6	14	20

upstairs into the gallery, the place for all coloured people . . . It was curious to watch the formality of these old ladies, black or mulatto: a large prayer book, finely bound with gilt edges, was indispensable, although they could not read a word.[9]

This common inability to read or write allows us to identify the many women like Nora Leeds who were free women of colour – either 'free black' or 'free coloured' – and who owned slaves. Although there were some white women slave holders, it is inconceivable that these white women would be illiterate.

'FREE COLOURED' WOMEN AS SLAVE HOLDERS IN DEMERARA

In 1810 the *Essequebo and Demerary Royal Gazette* listed 275 'free-coloured persons' who had paid the colonial tax levied on slave holders from 1808. Of these, 195 were women. Nine years later, in 1817, slave owners throughout the British West Indian colonies were required to make a return detailing the enslaved people in their possession. In Demerara 2,376 returns were made by the deadline set in the legislation.[10] Of these, 404 were made by women who could not write and so, like Nora Leeds, they made their mark – usually a simple '+' on the form. Thirty-five men also made their mark, three of them on behalf of female relatives, bringing the number of women to 407. It is almost certain that all these non-literate women were 'free coloured' or 'free black', and sixty-five can be matched with names in the list of free coloured slave holders in 1808.[11] From other sources a further forty or so free coloured women slave holders can be identified – women who signed their names or who were represented by someone who could – bringing the total in 1817 to around 450 women.

Acquiring literacy had become important for the new generation of free women, many of whom had been born free. In 1815 Sarah Waterton and Louisa Chapman, both young free coloured women in Georgetown, announced their intention to open 'a Seminary for Young Ladies . . . wherein will be taught English, French, Writing, Arithmetic, and Fancy Work'. They added the assurance to 'those who may entrust their children to their care' that 'every attention will be paid to their morals, and that they will ever keep in view their improvement'.[12]

The total number of free coloured men who were slave owners was little more than seventy. These included the descendants of two brothers from Halifax (England), Benjamin Hopkinson (1758–1801) and John Hopkinson (1761–1821). Benjamin had two children with the 'mulatto' woman Johanna (quoted above), while John had three children with the free coloured woman Rebecca Rogers (d. 1809), who was a significant slave holder in her own right, and a further seven children with Elizabeth Rogers (1789–1850), possibly a sister of Rebecca. These inter-related families were represented by the survivor of the two brothers, John Hopkinson, who had by the late 1810s established himself at Aigburth Hall in Liverpool, but all the heirs were free coloured men and women. Yet the men, although wealthy and well educated, found no future for themselves in Demerara. Fifteen years later, in 1837, the abolitionist William Lloyd visited Demerara and Berbice and reported that:

> From society, balls, and parties, the coloured people [i.e. men] are excluded, though many of them are fairer than Europeans, and as well educated. A very respectable creole coloured neighbour of ours . . . told us she had lost her eldest son; for after he was expensively educated in England, where he was treated as a gentleman, he would not return to Demerara to be despised, and therefore went to the East Indies.[13]

This might be another reference to Benjamin James Hopkinson, Cheveley's fellow passenger.

Leaving out of the equation for the moment these few very wealthy individuals, other free people of colour owned 3,850 slaves, almost 5 per cent of the slaves in the colony, and most of these were in the hands of women. Among them were an elite of successful and powerful women who owned twenty or more slaves. These included the redoubtable Dorothy 'Doll' Thomas, who in 1817 registered her ownership of seventy slaves. When Cheveley 'called on Miss Doll' he noted that she received him 'with the air of a superior' and it was her imperious manner which stuck in the minds of many who met her.[14] The sailor, writer and journalist Matthew Henry Barker encountered her in Georgetown about 1827, describing her as 'the richest person in the colony'. Barker recounted how Doll had gone to London with a memorial from the free coloured women of Demerara addressed to the king and parliament, where she claimed to have had an audience with the king. When any one offended her she would exclaim:

> Ky, who are you, for peak of me, eh? You low fellow – you hangman. I hab *sit down* wib King George.[15]

As Barker pointed out, her insistence that she had sat down with the king was astonishing in a colonial society in which 'no one with a drop of negro blood in their veins . . . was allowed . . . to be seated in the presence of a white man or woman'. There are two other accounts of Doll's supposed encounter with royalty – from Captain Samuel J. Masters, the American consul to Demerara from about 1846 to 1849, who met Doll Thomas soon after his arrival, and from Marianne Holmes, the wife of Joseph Henry Hendon Holmes, an English lawyer in Demerara, who had been in the colony from the time of their marriage in 1817. In Holmes' version, Doll Thomas met William IV in London in 1827 – presumably Holmes meant the future monarch, who was still Duke of Clarence in 1827. Holmes added that this was a renewal of their acquaintance, for Doll Thomas, it was said, had danced with him when he had served in the West Indies as a young midshipman in the Royal Navy. Holmes' version chimed with popular ideas of the 'sailor king' William IV. The satirist James Gilray had produced a cartoon in 1788 showing the young Duke of Clarence sharing a hammock with a young black woman. Whatever the truth, Doll Thomas clearly let it be known in Demerara that she had made her presence felt in London.

Doll Thomas was notably mobile during her life of more than ninety years. Born in Montserrat, she lived in Dominica, Grenada and then Demerara. She appeared in Glasgow in 1810 to place her grandchildren in schools. And from London in January 1824 her son-in-law, Gilbert Robertson, wrote to relations in Liverpool, saying:

> Mrs Thomas is here well & hearty & sends her best respects. She makes herself quite at home among a numerous circle of acquaintances.[16]

On her return to Demerara later in 1824 she was presented with a silver cup and plate by 'a few Coloured Ladies of Georgetown' as a token of their thanks for her successful efforts to have the 'oppressive tax' removed.[17] The tax had

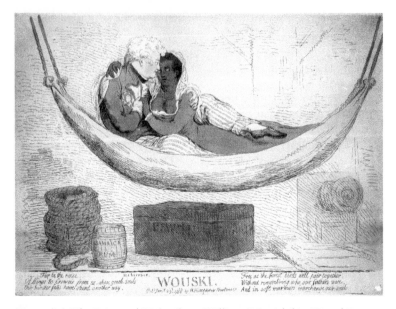

Figure 8.1 The Prince of Wales (later William IV) with his 'Wouski', James Gilray, 1788 [Wouski was a character in the popular opera *Inkle and Yarico*]. © British Library.

been levied on free coloured women only, free coloured men being exempted on the grounds that they were required to serve in the colony militia. Doll lived in London again in the early 1830s, renting a house in Kensington with another free coloured woman from Georgetown, Lucy Vanden Velden. And then she returned to Demerara, where she lived for another ten years or more. She died in Demerara in early 1848.

'FREE COLOURED' WOMEN AND SCOTTISH MEN IN DEMERARA

Table 8.2 lists twelve free coloured women who, like Doll Thomas, owned twenty or more slaves in Demerara in 1817. John Cheveley's neighbour Nora Leeds as yet owned only nine slaves but she was on her way to greater success. She had a son, William, who may have been the son of Amos Leeds, a cooper who ran a store in Georgetown. After Amos died or left the colony, his partner Robert Arnot – a 'douce canny' Scot – took over the premises and, in Cheveley's words, 'cast his lot in' with Nora.[18] The nature of their relationship is not specified but Cheveley remarked scathingly that Doll Thomas, 'like most of her contemporaries . . . had in her establishment a white gentleman who was not rich but submitted to the degradation of being domineered by this imperious old Dame'.[19] Nora, too, was imperious.

Of the others, Jean Robertson has the most obvious Scottish name. I can find nothing more of her but three of the Robertsons of Kiltearn (Ross-shire) were in Demerara from the early 1790s, where at least two had children who would have been adults by this time. Four others in this elite group of free coloured women were entangled with Scottish families, including Doll Thomas who had six daughters, three in relationships with Scotsmen. Doll's daughter Eliza was the partner of Gilbert Robertson (son of the minister of Kiltearn), Charlotte of John Fullarton (son of the minister of Dalry, Ayrshire) and Dorothea Christina of Major John Gordon (of Kildonan, Sutherland). The third of these relationships is yet another example of how the West Indian colonies had an impact on society in the north of Scotland, as described in Chapter 3. Donald Sage, whose father had been parish minister of Kildonan, remembered Major Gordon's father, Adam Gordon, the tacksman of Griamachary, describing him as 'a shrewd, worldly-wise man'. Perhaps his shrewdness helped to ensure that the Gordons were one of the families who were not cleared from Kildonan. Instead Adam and his wife 'lived in the exercise of the most unbounded hospitality, and at the same time economised so as to realise a good deal of money'. Adam's eldest son, John Gordon (1782–1850), joined the army in 1804 and was promoted to the staff of the Duke of Kent, through whose influence he obtained commissions for his three younger brothers. By 1817 John, now a lieutenant colonel, was in Demerara. His second wife had recently died in Trinidad and John was soon smitten by Doll Thomas' daughter Dorothea Christina. In 1819 he persuaded her to leave her mother and live with him, on the strength of a promise of a church wedding when he left his regiment. In the meantime the couple had a private ceremony in which they exchanged vows and John put a ring on Dorothea's finger:

> She took the name Mrs Gordon and was seen on his arm on social occasions, while he openly wore the gold watch and chain she had

given him. Of an evening he 'rode out with her' . . . she managed his household, stocking it with fine pieces of furniture and silver that belonged to her, as well as supplementing his meagre salary with an allowance from her mother.[20]

The history of the relationship between Colonel Gordon and Dorothea Christina illustrates the contrast between her status as a free coloured woman in Demerara and the growing prejudice of British society. From Demerara, where Gordon relied on the wealth of Doll Thomas, the couple came to Britain in 1821 and their son Huntly George Gordon was born in Glasgow in August. When John, now a major, finally resigned his commission in 1823 he sought what he considered a suitable dowry from Doll Thomas before entering into a formal marriage with Dorothea – and when Doll refused to offer more than £5,000, set against Dorothea's future inheritance, Gordon prevaricated. The couple continued to live together in Edinburgh and entertained friends at home, including Major Gordon's three brothers who treated her as a near relation.[21] However, they were not seen together at public events as they had been in Demerara – a decisive factor in what followed – and by 1826 Gordon had met another woman, a widow with an annual income of £300. He proposed marriage.

Dorothea believed she was already married to Major Gordon under Dutch law which pertained in Demerara and she went to court to seek a 'declarator of marriage' under Scots law, which allowed for marriage by 'cohabitation with habit and repute'. It was an action which Dorothea lost, largely because those who gave evidence on her behalf – as to the couple being commonly known as man and wife – were servants, shopkeepers and landladies rather than those who moved in John Gordon's social circle, who regarded him as a single man. In that higher society Dorothea had not been publicly seen, accepted and acknowledged. The case helped to define the requirements for establishing marriage by cohabitation by habit and repute, which remained a form of marriage under Scots law until 2006.[22]

But even more revealing was Doll Thomas' attitude during this dispute. According to Gordon, she simply did not want her daughter in this kind of formal marriage – in which she would lose all rights to her own property. In his evidence Gordon stated, 'She did not care for your getting married and that you were not better than your other sisters who are living in a different way.' Dorothea, against her mother's wishes, had sought respectability rather than that independence, but it was denied her by the Scottish court. Instead Dorothea received a financial settlement from John Gordon and gave up her child, Huntly, to be brought up in Britain. She returned to Demerara. When John Malcolm Bulloch, the author of many works on the Gordons, published *The Family of Gordon in Griamachary* in 1907 he began with this observation:

> Adam Gordon, tacksman, Griamachary, Kildonan, who died in 1831, gave thirteen Soldiers – all commissioned officers, and two of them honoured Generals – to his Country. That is a remarkable record even for the Gordons, whose ruling passion has always been Soldiering . . .

These included Dorothea's son who became Surgeon Major Huntly George Gordon – but the book was silent on Dorothea, whose existence was not acknowledged.[23]

Fifty years later, a Scottish court had again to deal with what was to them the surprising financial independence of a free coloured woman – once again to her disadvantage. Frances MacLeod (1823–1908) was the daughter of Hugh MacLeod, a Demerara planter, and an unidentified mother, who inherited £3,000 from her father at his death in 1843. MacLeod continued as a slave owner in neighbouring Dutch Suriname. In Edinburgh in 1847, Frances married her cousin, Hugh Wright, who was also a Suriname slave owner. Wright visited her in Edinburgh from time to time, and they had three children, but he also maintained a Suriname family with an enslaved domestic servant, who he finally freed in 1856. The issue which came to court was the failure of the City of Glasgow Bank in 1878 and responsibility for its debts. Frances had invested in the bank. In Scotland at that time a married woman would normally have had only the legal capacity to act as agent for her husband, who would have acquired her capital on their marriage. However, such was the degree of financial independence displayed by Frances that the court held that her husband must, after their marriage, have re-gifted to her the money left by her father. While this might seem a welcome recognition of her financial independence, the outcome was that her investment of a few hundred pounds left

her with a liability through the Bank's failure amounting to
£4,000 and she was ruined.

Another two of these elite free coloured women in Demerara,
Rebecca Ritchie and her daughter Martha Ann Telfer, had an
involvement with a much wealthier Scot – John Douglas (1768–
1840), a partner in the Glasgow-based merchant house of J. T.
and A. Douglas & Co. At emancipation the firm ranked twelfth
among the mercantile beneficiaries of compensation, receiving
£57,862.[24] Rebecca and Martha Ann had moved from Barbados
to the town of New Amsterdam in Berbice probably in the late
1790s. Here John Douglas and Martha Ann had two children
– Alexander (c. 1801) and James (1803–77). John Douglas
returned to Scotland, where in 1809 he married the daughter
of a Greenock merchant, but when he returned to Guyana he
resumed his relationship with Martha Ann, and their third child
Cecilia was born in Demerara in 1813. The boys were educated
in Scotland, at Lanark Grammar School, from where James
went to work at the age of sixteen for the North West Company
and then the Hudson's Bay Company. He rose to become the
first Governor of British Columbia and on his retirement in
1864 he was knighted by Queen Victoria.[25] It was a remarkable achievement for a man of colour but, although he visited
relatives in Scotland towards the end of his life, he remained
in Canada. His wife's ancestry was part Irish and part Cree
and their daughter Martha, while at school in Berkshire, was
instructed by Sir James not to draw attention to her mother's
heritage.[26]

The fourth of these wealthy free coloured women to be linked
with a Scottish man was Maria Magdaline Colongue. She was
born a slave and when she registered her own slaves in 1817 –
thirteen male and five female – she unusually named the nations
to which the African-born belonged: 'Congah, Cramanti,
Longanba, Popah, Mandingo, Eabo and Watime'.[27] Perhaps
her own African nation remained important to her. Maria had
seven children with at least two white men. These children
included John and Hugh, whose father was Hugh Fraser (d.
1812), the joint owner of a plantation on Wakenaam Island in
the Essequibo River. We can tentatively identify him through
the will of a John Fraser who in 1818 died at Findhorn (Moray),
where he had been cared for by a 'free mulatto woman' named
Henrietta Fraser, who had left Demerara with him the previous

Table 8.3 Free coloured women in Berbice owning 10+ slaves (1817)

Owner	Notes		Slaves
Bannister, Elizabeth Swain		Signed 'E. S. Bannister'	30
Katz, Miss Sally		Her mark	18
Harris, Phoebe	New Amsterdam	Her mark	15
Ostrehan, Susannah		Her mark	14
Burgers, Maria		Her mark	11
George, Susan		Her mark	11
Chalmers, Eliza & children	free coloured woman	Her mark	10
Fransientie	free negro	Her mark	10
Meed, Sabina	free black woman	Her mark	10
Stoel, Eva		Her mark	10

year. In his will John Fraser left 2,000 guilders to these two children of Maria Magdaline Colongue. John Fraser was from the parish of Kiltarlity (Inverness-shire) and with his brother Alexander had gone as a clerk to St Kitts in the 1760s. They bought plantation *Good Intent* in Demerara shortly after 1804. The legacy in John's will makes it likely that Hugh Fraser – Maria's partner – was a relation, probably also from Kiltarlity.[28]

THE OSTREHANS

Using the same methods for neighbouring Berbice in 1817 – including signing by mark – I can identify one free coloured man and ninety-three 'free coloured' and 'free black' women who owned 395 slaves – 1.6 per cent of the 24,570 slaves in the colony. The most prosperous of the free coloured women in Berbice, listed in Table 8.3, owned fewer slaves than their peers in Demerara. Members of the extended Ostrehan family were active across both colonies and the family is illustrative of the mobility and enterprise of such women and of the importance of their family networks. The Ostrehan women were the descendants of enslaved people in the oldest of the English sugar islands, Barbados. A woman called Susannah Ostrehan (d. 1809) was born a slave there, gained her freedom, and began to acquire property in the colony from the late 1770s. As her wealth increased she bought the freedom of her own mother and of other members of her family. By 1793 her sister

Mary Ostrehan (d. 1829) was described as a 'free mulatto' and by 1806 Mary's children – Henry Magee and Mary Ostrehan Brett (*c.* 1793–1846) – were also manumitted. Two cousins were also freed – Elizabeth Swain Bannister (d. 1829) and a younger Susannah Ostrehan. Responding to the opportunities in Demerara and Berbice, the younger women moved on from Barbados to Guyana.

It was not only the free coloured women who were mobile. Tables 8.3 to 8.9 show the origins of the slaves held by the five leading free coloured women in Guyana. Together they owned 187 enslaved people and of these, thirty-seven – one in every five – had been born in Barbados. A further seven had been born in Grenada and there were seven more individuals from seven different Caribbean colonies.

In *Enterprising Women*, Candlin and Pybus stress the importance of looking beyond the stereotypes, common at the time, of prosperous 'free coloured' women as either wily concubines exploiting a white male elite deprived of white female companions or as madams running brothels under the guise of hotels and boarding houses. The relationships described above – using those with Scottish men as examples – were more than short-term liaisons for profit and, while not formal European marriages, they were varied and complex relationships. They show women exercising power and control but also as vulnerable once they moved beyond the colonies in which they flourished. Their power and control was, of course, exercised in part through the exploitation of others in their role as slave owners.

While there were brothels, especially in port cities such as Bridgetown (Barbados), the 'hotel trade' extended well beyond this. In 1821 John Cheveley had attended Doll Thomas's 'balls and entertainments', over which she presided 'with the deportment of an empress'. This was no brothel but a sophisticated meeting place for young white men and free coloured women. It cannot be forgotten that enslaved females were, as a matter of course, the targets of entirely legal sexual abuse. The 'sexual leverage' of free coloured women was used by them to greater advantage, as was the case with Mary Ostrehan:

> If these women were happy, or at least willing, to provide intimate companionship [for white men] . . . that was well, but it was not their sole or even primary aim. Mary Ostrehan was such a woman

– and what better place to build an hotel than in a place without one?[29]

Mary Ostrehan's path to wealth was much longer than Candlin and Pybus suggest and it was probably huckstering and related businesses – together with relationships with prominent white men – which gave her, and other free coloured women from Barbados, a foothold in their new home in Guyana. In 1817 Mary Ostrehan's adult slaves were two male labourers and eight women – four hucksters, a seamstress, a washer, a domestic and one invalid. This was similar to Nora Leeds' team of hucksters. And this was not, at the time, a place without an hotel. There was already at least one thriving establishment in Stabroek (later named Georgetown), the Union Coffee House run from 1802 by a Scot, Malcolm Campbell. In 1806 the Coffee House moved to new premises in front of plantation *Vlissengen*, on a corner site which allowed a substantial building to be erected on three floors. The brick-built ground floor was a storage area; above that were a billiard room, coffee room and bar; the next floor had two halls, each over fifty feet long, with a pantry where they joined; and above that were six attic bedrooms. Other buildings contained the kitchens, stables and more bedrooms. After Campbell died in 1808, the lease was taken on by Thomas Marsh who again enlarged the buildings, with more bedrooms and stables for fourteen horses, and from then it was also known as Marsh's Hotel and Marsh's Assembly Rooms. Nearby from 1811 was the Columbian Hotel, run by Frederick Kent.[30] In 1819 Marsh's Hotel became known as the Demerary Exchange, whose crowning glory 'both in expensive decoration and superiority of size [was] the Ball or Assembly Room; with a gallery convertible to an Orchestra.'[31] It was perhaps Marsh's Assembly Rooms which Mary Ostrehan took over sometime after 1819, more than ten years after she had arrived in the colony. The scale of the building is a mark of the wealth she had accumulated. It is referred to in a description of celebrations on St George's Day (23 April) 1823:

There was a dinner by the governor at Camp House, a subscription ball at Mrs Dolly Thomas's in Cumingsburg, a dinner at Miss Rebecca Ritchie's, a subscription ball at the Royal Hotel Vlissengen and several other parties . . . But the event of the day was the Ball and supper at Miss Ostrehan's Assembly Rooms given by the Sons of St George.[32]

There are some unexplained oddities in the households of these women. Rebecca Richie's daughter Martha Ann Telfer owned twelve women – four field slaves, three domestics, three washers, a huckster and a nurse – and this might have allowed her to run an hotel or similar establishment. But the nurse was significant. Telfer's remaining slaves included twelve children and all but one were boys, including two 'mulattos'. Another woman, called Queen Breda by Cheveley, was described by him as a woman 'of darker hue and unmitigated ugliness ... who had a fine house and retail store in Robb Street'. She also appears as Queen Bourda in 1810 and as Queen Bourdeau in 1817, when she registered nineteen adult slaves. There were three tailors, a carpenter, six hucksters, four seamstresses, three washers, a sick nurse and one blind African woman. There was one girl, an eleven-year old who worked as a seamstress – and then, like Mary Ann Telfer's household, there were ten boys. The youngest was a nine-month-old 'mulatto' called Prince William. We simply know too little about these women and their households to understand the possible influence on them of the African heritage shared by their grandmothers, a heritage which might include both traditions of female leadership and of family structure.[33]

Most surprising in all these households are the slaves owned by Dorothy Thomas. Of her twenty-five adult female slaves, twelve were described as sickly or invalid. Three of these were reported as being in their late nineties – Betty (97) and Diana (98), both born in Africa, and the mulatto Madlain (98) born in St Kitts. There was also Bridget (87) born in Africa. Most of the twenty-five other adults were of working age and thirteen of them were porters. And so it seems that in 1817 Dorothy Thomas was making money from her male slaves who worked as porters, perhaps around Georgetown's busy docks, while creating a safe environment for a number of old female slaves. The cost of manumission was prohibitive and these older women would have little to gain, so late in life, from the formal grant of their freedom. Strangely, one of her male slaves – a twenty-year-old, Demerara-born porter named Jim – was categorised as 'white'. Was he perhaps albino and also vulnerable?

This is an aspect of Doll's character that does not emerge in other accounts, in which she appears as a harsh mistress. Her young grandson George Augustus Sala could just remember her in London in the early 1830s bellowing and swearing at her many 'sable handmaidens':

> These damsels, with coloured pocket-handkerchiefs tied round their black heads, used to sit shivering on the stairs of the red brick house, and cry to be sent back to their own country.[34]

OSTREHANS IN SURINAME AND BERBICE

Mary Ostrehan's cousins – Elizabeth Swain Bannister and the younger Susannah Ostrehan – also left Barbados. It is difficult to distinguish the various women named Susan or Susannah Ostrehan and while Candlin and Pybus believe that there was one woman of that name, who was a hotelier in Suriname, Berbice and Barbados, I believe that there were two different women. One woman named Susannah Ostrehan had two 'natural' children in Suriname – John Henry Wilson in 1804 and Edward Francis Wilson in 1808 – and was listed in Paramaribo in the census of 1811, described as both an hotel owner and as a 'foreigner' in Suriname.[35] A Susannah Ostrehan was later the owner of fourteen slaves in Berbice in 1817; these were African-born adults whose enslaved children were born in Barbados in 1805, Demerara from 1812 and Berbice from 1815. There is also a reference in 1814 to 'Susanna Ostrehan's hotel' in Bridgetown, Barbados – five years after the death of the older woman of that name. Given that there was a popular story in Barbados that a Susanna Ostrehan had come there from Suriname, the most likely explanation is that one woman of this name went to Suriname, where she had at least two children, that she remained there until at least 1811 and then returned to Bridgetown. And that a second woman left Barbados sometime after 1805, was in Demerara with her enslaved household by 1812 and had established her own business in Berbice by 1815. The nature of the Berbice household is consistent with a small hotel or boarding house, with a number of domestic or house servants.

Although she had a different surname, Elizabeth Swain (or Swayne) Bannister was an Ostrehan whose manumission was secured in 1806 by her cousin, the older Susannah. The method of achieving this was for Susannah to sell Elizabeth to a trusted sea captain, in this case a James White, who would then complete the process in Britain, thus avoiding the prohibitive costs of manumission imposed by the colonial authorities in Barbados. In Berbice, Elizabeth formed a relationship with William Fraser (1787–1830), the son of a house carpenter in Cromarty (Scotland), who had arrived in the colony in 1803, aged sixteen.[36] This relationship probably began about 1809 and they had four children: John (1810), George (1815), Elizabeth (d. before 1822) and Jane (*c.* 1821).[37] Fraser also had a daughter, Anna Maria (*c.* 1810–93), born to another 'free coloured' woman, Mary Stuart in Barbados. This allows for the possibility that Elizabeth had come to Berbice with William, who had set out to find a suitable companion in Barbados, to live with him in the new colony.

Fraser had arrived in Berbice before the abolition of the African slave trade and this would have made it easier for him to begin to purchase his own slaves, which would have been essential if he worked as a carpenter in the colony. With a 'task gang' working for him while the coastal plantations expanded in the early 1800s, he was well placed to make money and perhaps this made possible his trip or trips to Barbados and his liaisons with both Mary Stuart and Elizabeth Bannister. A parallel example of success is another young man from the north, Donald Grant (1776–1851) of Inverness (see Chapter 2), who arrived in neighbouring Demerara in 1801 with little more than a sound education and a letter of recommendation. Having built up his own slave-holding, with credit allowed him by his employer, he was able to enter into a partnership in 1811 to buy a sugar estate in Essequibo and subsequently retire to England. In 1815 William Fraser entered into an even more ambitious partnership with Richard Clarke Downer (1780–1828), secretary to the Court of Policy in Berbice, in which they purchased seven plantations and by 1817 registered ownership of 684 slaves. By 1821 Downer had left the colony and the business was focused on sugar production at *Goldstone Hall*, with 330 slaves and a modern steam-powered sugar mill. These assets were valued at almost 2.2 million florins (about £183,000).[38]

Elizabeth Bannister meanwhile advanced her own position. In 1817 she owned thirty slaves, while Fraser had made returns for twenty-six slaves that he held in his own name, rather than in the name of the partnership, and for sixteen slaves belonging to his children by Elizabeth.[39] But by 1822 Fraser had only fourteen slaves of his own, while Bannister's slave-holding had increased.

By 1819 the enslaved people who had been held by her jointly with her children were transferred into her sole ownership. And in 1820 there were further transfers by purchase from the part-nership of Fraser and Downer. With three births and two other purchases, Elizabeth owned sixty-six slaves by the end of April 1822. Like Doll Thomas and Mary Ostrehan, Elizabeth's slaves were a mixture of those kidnapped from Africa and creoles from a variety of colonies – from Barbados, Antigua and Suriname, as well as those born in Demerara and Berbice. Her oldest slave, a domestic named Quashi, was from Suriname.

She was also ensuring a good education for her children. John and George were attending Paisley Grammar School, where John was among the prize-winners in 1827, and Jane was at school in Liverpool. She had visited 'England' about 1825, a trip which probably included Scotland and which was likely to have been made in connection with the education of her children. We only know about this visit because she had taken with her an enslaved woman, Betsey Ann (*c.* 1786–?), who in 1827 brought a complaint about her mistress to the Protector of Slaves.[40] Betsey Ann, who had worked as a huckster for Bannister for twenty years, had a son John, a cooper born in Barbados about 1806, and a second son Archibald, a 'mulatto' born in Berbice in 1821. Her dispute with Bannister was about whether or not Bannister would sell Betsey Ann and her chil-dren to Betsey Ann's sister, a free woman in Demerara, and, if so, on what conditions. It is from the details that we learn that Betsey Ann had accompanied her mistress to Britain, where Bannister had found Betsey Ann's conduct 'so bad that I twice threatened to turn her out of the house'. The complaint also reveals that Bannister had given Betsey Ann's older son John to her 'young master' – presumably to John or George Fraser, both still in Scotland. The Protector found in favour of Bannister and 'impressed upon the complainant the injustice of her accusation against so kind a mistress, and a woman much respected in the Colony'. Bannister it appeared had never had a slave flogged and had subsequently sent Betsey Ann to Barbados 'at very great expense . . . for the recovery of her health'.

Elizabeth Bannister died in Berbice in late March or early April 1829, leaving property to 'her reputed children, John Frazer, George Frazer, and Jane Frazer', including £3,000 'to be applied to the maintenance, education and support of my daughter Jane Frazer who is at present at school in Glasgow'.[41] These were impressive legacies and a further £2,400 was left to other relatives. In the words of the Barbadian historian Pedro Welch:

> Such growth clearly sent a message. If some free colored women could, within a few years of manumission, accumulate enough economic resources to rival those of wealthier whites then, others could achieve similar success.[42]

The children's father William Fraser had taken the unusual step, while resident in London in 1823, of seeking a grant of 'letters of legitimation' from the Privy Council through the Colonial Secretary so that his free coloured children could inherit. Marriage to Elizabeth would have achieved the same outcome but William described himself in his petition as unable to 'marry satisfactorily'. It would seem that Fraser intended to repatriate his wealth and establish himself as a gentleman in Scotland, while at the same time providing for Elizabeth, whose slave-holding in Berbice was now on the same scale as that of Doll Thomas in Demerara. The house carpenter's son from Cromarty was on his way to becoming a landed gentleman, and the enslaved woman born in Barbados had risen to be perhaps the most prosperous free coloured woman in Berbice. There are no accounts of her appearance and personality and nothing to suggest the flamboyance of Doll Thomas, but she was an effective business woman, selling cotton in her own name and regarded as the owner of plantation *Lewis Manor*, even if this was never formally transferred into her ownership. And despite being born a slave, she was able to sign her own name on the Slave Register in 1817.

When Elizabeth died in early April 1829, William may have been with her. He was certainly at plantation *Voorburg* on the east bank of Canje Creek in January 1830 when he drew up his own will dividing his estate between his sister Elizabeth Bain in Cromarty, his wife-to-be in Scotland and his four surviving free coloured children – all still minors under the age of twenty-one. The oldest, Anna Maria, the daughter of Maria Stuart, was in Berbice and had been treated by Elizabeth's doctor during two bouts of fever, but all three of Elizabeth's own children were in Scotland. She may have continued the family tradition of securing the emancipation of relatives because there was also a Jane

Bannister at *Voorburg*, who was provided with a plot of land and who lived on until 1848. And there were certainly people to grieve for Elizabeth. The estate accounts detail the purchase of seven pairs of ladies' shoes, along with crepe and ribbons, as mourning dress.[43]

Elizabeth's ambitions for her children were only partially realised. William Fraser returned to Scotland, where he married forty-three-year-old Elizabeth Munro (1787–1859) of Munlochy (Ross-shire) and sold his Berbice estates to Eric Mackay, by that date Lord Reay. In a codicil to his will added in June 1830, only a few weeks before his death, he wrote that he had made an offer to purchase the mansion house and estate of Braelangwell on the Black Isle, five miles from his native Cromarty. Knowing that his end was near, he expressed the wish that his new wife should live there along with his two daughters, Anna Maria and Jane. Anna Maria was now twenty and had probably travelled back with William from Berbice, having survived the bouts of fever, and Elizabeth's daughter Jane, who was ten, was probably still at school in Glasgow. The offer of £10,000 for Braelangwell was not successful and Fraser's financial affairs turned out to be much less sound than he had hoped. It was not until 1846, sixteen years after his death, that a compromise settlement was reached with his creditors. There were insufficient funds to pay all the legacies, and the ante-nuptial agreement he had made with Elizabeth Munro brought her into conflict with Fraser's children. His fond hope that she and his girls might live together as a family was not realised – and might always have been unrealistic. His daughter Jane married a 'merchant and manufacturer' at the age of seventeen and lived in Rothesay and Devon, along with her half-sister Anna Maria, until Jane's death in the 1850s, after which her widowed husband left for Chicago with their children.

Elizabeth's elder son John was apprenticed in 1832, at the age of twenty-one, to the surgeon in Cromarty under an indenture registered with the Royal College of Surgeons in Edinburgh. But he became mentally incapacitated and died unmarried sometime before 1845. Only her younger son George prospered – but in South America, not Scotland. Before he left Berbice, William Fraser had bought plantation *L'Esperance* in Suriname, 'a fairly large sugar plantation with a slave force of 157 people, and a steam-driven sugar pressing plant'.[44] George managed and owned this plantation until at least 1859 and was thus, since slavery was not abolished in Suriname until 1863, one of the last Scots to be a slave owner.[45] Only Anna Maria, Mary Stuart's daughter, returned to the Highlands to live in Inverness, where she died in 1893.[46] In 1834 she had claimed compensation for her ownership of one slave.

A FREE COLOURED MOMENT?

In 1955 Rawle Farley argued that, as a result of the particular population structure in Guyana in the early nineteenth century and the economic necessity of running the plantations, free coloured people in Berbice came to 'enjoy rights far greater than the coloured free in the rest of the British Caribbean'.[47] He referred to the role of free coloured men. More recently, Candlin and Pybus have widened these horizons to an understanding of the place of free coloured women on this new frontier of the southern Caribbean in the late 1700s and early 1800s. But this 'free coloured moment' did not last long beyond the era of slavery.

When Dr Henry Dalton (1818–74) published his *History of British Guiana* in 1855 he was clear about the changes which had taken place as a result of the 'arrival of European females'. Their 'moral influence was obvious and considerable' and although change was slow it brought to an end the cohabitation of white men and free coloured women. These free coloured women now aspired to acceptance in white society but did not achieve this status. Dalton blamed this on the otherwise 'gentle and virtuous ... European female' who would not accept 'mixing with a colour and class to which she considered herself superior'.[48]

But there also appears to have been wider opposition to the continued use of these categories. In 1838, as the era of slavery in British colonies drew to a close with the end of forced labour under 'the apprenticeship', the now united colony of British Guiana conducted a census. This sought to identify all inhabitants by 'complexion', that is, as either white, brown or black. According to evidence given to a Select Committee of the House of Commons in 1842:

> A census was proposed to be taken at the time of emancipation but it was disallowed by the Home Government, because they thought it would perpetuate recollections of the conditions of the people at that time, which had better be buried in oblivion.[49]

But surviving census returns in the National Archives of Guyana show that it was complete – except for that categorising by 'complexion'. Analysis of one ward of Georgetown with a population of 1,991 reveals that a quarter of households had not been willing or able to comprehensively identify their members as white, brown or black.[50] It was a minor but telling act of resistance which seems to have forced a U-turn by the 'Home Government'. But it also marked an end to the role in the colony of women such as the remarkable Dorothy Thomas.

FREE COLOURED WOMEN IN GUYANA AND THE ORIGINS OF THEIR SLAVES

Table 8.4 Origin of Elizabeth Swain Bannister's slaves (1817)

	Age over 9	9 and under	Total
Africa	10		10
Demerary	2		2
Antigua	1		1
Barbados	6		6
Berbice	4	6	10
Suriname	1		1
Total	24	6	30

Table 8.5 Origin of Mary Ostrehan's slaves (1817)

	Age over 12	12 and under	Total
Africa	3		3
Barbados	6	6	12
Martinique	1		1
St Lucia	1		1
Demerary		2	2
At sea on schooner		1	1
Total	11	9	20

Table 8.6 Origin of Dorothy Thomas's slaves (1817)

	Age over 12	12 and under	Total
Africa	36		36
Demerary	4	17	21
Grenada	6	1	7
Barbados	1	2	3
St Martins	1		1
Montserrat	1		1
St Kitts	1		1
Total	50	20	70

Table 8.7 Origin of Rebecca Ritchie's slaves (1817)

	Age over 12	12 and under	Total
Africa	19		19
Demerary	2	12	14
Barbados	1	3	4
Total	22	15	37

Table 8.8 Origin of Queen Bourdeau's slaves (1817)

	Age over 12	12 and under	Total
Africa	9		9
Demerary		9	9
Barbados	10	2	12
Total	19	11	30

Table 8.9 Summary of above

	ESB	MO	DT	RR	QB	Total
Africa	10	3	36	19	9	77
Demerary	2	2	21	14	9	48
Antigua	1					1
Barbados	6	12	3	4	12	37
Berbice	10					10
Grenada			7			7
Martinique		1				1
Montserrat			1			1
St Kitts			1			1
St Lucia		1				1
St Martins			1			1
Suriname	1					1
At sea		1				1
Total	30	20	70	37	30	187

9

Guyana – The Merchant Houses

At the time of emancipation, British West Indian estates were as a whole heavily indebted, to the extent that this sector of the economy was effectively bankrupt. This led Eric Williams in his still influential *Capitalism and Slavery* (1944) to the conclusion that the fundamental drivers behind the emancipation of the enslaved in 1834 were economic rather than humanitarian. Slavery, he argued, ended because it was increasingly inefficient. Slave holders sought to extract their wealth from the slave plantations and invest in more productive enterprises and they therefore embraced the process of emancipation with compensation which liquidated their assets in the Caribbean and allowed them to reinvest where returns were higher. Williams' 'decline thesis' is still debated. It is now clear, however, that the overall indebtedness of the plantation economies was not the result of operating losses but because value was being extracted to fund investment and consumption in Britain. Money was being borrowed against projected future returns on what were still, in general, profitable enterprises. These enterprises were, however, particularly vulnerable to fluctuations in the price of the products of the plantations – costs were largely fixed – and were at risk whenever income fell below what had been projected.[1]

The vote in Parliament in 1833 for the Abolition Bill was brought about in part by the foreseen consequences of the Reform Act of 1832, which by widening the franchise for elections in Britain allowed more abolitionists to be elected as Members of Parliament. But there was also the fear among slave holders that the uprising of enslaved people in Jamaica in the winter of 1831/2 might lead to the loss of the colony altogether. Emancipation with compensation suddenly seemed an attractive option.[2] What is also clear is that returns were quite different across the colonies of the British Caribbean and South America, and a key conclusion of Nick Draper's study of the compensation records is that by 1834 there was a pattern and variety in the system of slave ownership in Britain.

> The slave-system was not homogenous. Both in economic terms and in the structure of metropolitan slave-ownership, there was little in common between the old and new colonies. British Guiana and Trinidad attracted modern capitalists; the old territories remained the domain of long-standing owners and merchant dynasties.[3]

The 'modern capitalists' referred to by Draper made their fortunes in Guyana and Trinidad during the 1820s and to the end of slavery. The economic importance of Guyana – and often its very existence – faded long ago from memory in Scotland. There were few reminders, as there were in streets and squares named after Jamaica or St Vincent. Yet at emancipation Glasgow's merchants held more wealth in Guyana than in any other Caribbean colony and, for the UK as a whole, Guyana ranked only second to the much larger colony of Jamaica. Compensation paid to owners of slaves in Jamaica amounted to £6.12 million and in Guyana to £4.28 million, although there were almost four times as many enslaved people in Jamaica as in Guyana – 311,455 as compared to 84,075. This was because compensation was calculated as a proportion of the average value of a slave in each colony, amounting to just under £20 in Jamaica but almost £51 in Guyana. This was a reflection of the fact that it was in Guyana and Trinidad (where owners were also compensated at an average of just over £50) that fortunes continued to be made after the abolition of the slave trade in 1807. Slaves were valuable because of the money they made for their owners. And these fortunes were made in sugar, not in the cotton which had led Scots to flock to Demerara and Berbice in the late 1790s and early 1800s.

Sugar can be made from both sugar cane and sugar beet. Sugar cane dominated world sugar production until about 1850 but was being successfully challenged by the development of beet sugar production, which then dominated until the early

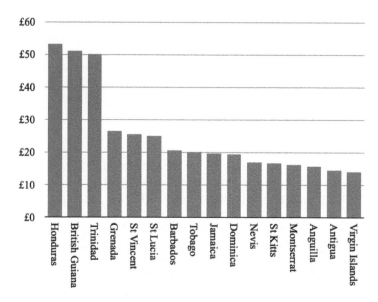

Figure 9.1 Compensation value of slaves (1834) in different colonies.

twentieth century. However, the possibility of making sugar from the sugar beet plant had been discovered much earlier, in Berlin in the 1740s by the German chemist Margraaf, but this was of little practical interest until the French and Napoleonic wars reduced or cut off supplies of cane sugar to continental Europe. By 1812/13, as a result of government support, there were 334 factories producing sugar from beet, 309 of them in France. However, the peace of 1815 and the consequent avail-ability of cheaper 'slave-grown' sugar, brought their operations to an end.[4] Meanwhile, British sugar consumption per head was slowly increasing, by about 50 per cent between 1800 and 1840. It was this renewed market for their product which particularly benefited the plantation owners of Berbice and Demerara after 1815 and especially in the 1820s.

Two merchant houses with Scottish origins – indeed, with largely Highland origins – embraced these opportunities to the extent that when slavery ended they were the two largest mercan-tile recipients of compensation in Britain. They were Davidsons & Barkly and Sandbach Tinné. All of Sandbach Tinné's slaves were held in what was by then the united colony of British

Guiana. Other firms with Scottish connections were also heavily involved and the principal investments of Glasgow-based John Campbell senior & Co., of Bogles and of J. T. & A. Douglas were now in Guyana – as were the assets of the Liverpool-based houses of John Gladstone and C. W. & F. Shand, and of the Baillies in Bristol, all with Scots among their founders.[5]

DAVIDSONS & BARKLY

In later life Henry Barkly (1815–98) reflected on the year of emancipation and compensation payments. At four o'clock in the afternoon on most Saturdays in 1834, then a young man, he set off from London's Lime Street Square mounted on a chestnut mare, Meg Merrilies. His groom, who rode behind, had brought the horse from Highbury Grove, the family house set in twenty-five acres of garden and parkland to the north of the city. Riding through London's streets, he was 'enjoying the reputation of the only son of a rich man . . . puffed up by conceit and vanity'.[6] There was much to be done preparing and making claims in the counting houses of London businesses with interests in the Caribbean and he was a partner in the firm which would receive the largest payment – the West India house of Davidsons & Barkly, whose compensation would amount to £164,875 (equivalent purchasing power today of £14.25 million).[7] This sum was shared among the four partners: thirty-two-year-old Henry Davidson and his younger brother William, sixty-six-year-old Aeneas Barkly and his nineteen-year-old son Henry.

And the Davidsons? Writing in this same year, Hugh Miller described the old parish school of Cromarty, a predecessor of the school I referred to in Chapter 1:

> I am not making too much of my subject when I affirm, that the little thatched hovel . . . gave merchants to the Exchange, ministers to the Church, physicians to the Faculty, professors to Colleges, and members to Parliament. One of the pupils reared within its walls – the son of old Clerk Davidson, a humble subordinate of the hereditary sheriff – became a wealthy London merchant, and, after establishing in the city a respectable firm, which still exists, represented his native county in Parliament.[8]

Miller was referring to Duncan Davidson (1733–99), the second son of the sheriff clerk to the small hereditary jurisdiction of Cromarty. It was Clerk Davidson's oldest son, Henry Davidson

(1726–81), who first made the move to London, where he became an apprentice to the Scottish lawyer George Ross. Duncan was to follow him. By the early 1760s Henry was a partner in Ross's business as an army agent, acting as middlemen between regimental colonels and the contractors who supplied clothing and camp necessities, and rivals viewed with envy the firm's access to government ministers.[9] From his relatively modest beginnings, Henry acquired the estate of Tulloch in Dingwall, and when he died without children in 1781 this passed to Duncan.

Duncan, meanwhile, had become the junior partner in the London merchant house of George Chandler (1721–79), whose father Captain Sabine Chandler (d. 1750) had spent much of his life at sea, trading sugar between Jamaica and London. By the time of his death in 1750, Captain Chandler was regarded as 'an eminent West-India merchant' and the business grew until George Chandler's death in 1779.[10] Davidson then formed a new partnership with Charles Graham (before 1757–1806) of Drynie on the Black Isle (Ross-shire). The extent of Charles Graham's family network can be seen by considering his siblings and first cousins. His older brother Colin (d. 1799) was a professional soldier whose career took him to North America and the Caribbean; and his younger brother Alexander was a merchant and British consul in the Azores, a group of Portuguese islands strategically situated in the Atlantic. His first cousins included Charles Graham, another soldier who rose to the rank of major general and died in the West Indies; Colin Dundas Graham (1751–1828), who served in the Scots Brigade of the Dutch army and, through his marriage to a Dutch woman, acquired a plantation in Dutch Suriname; Colin Munro (1756–1825), a successful merchant and slave owner in Grenada who returned to Inverness; and John Munro (1762–1831), a merchant in Trinidad and Grenada who returned to live in Edinburgh.

This well-connected partnership of Davidson & Graham, operating from Fenchurch Buildings in the City of London, prospered in the sugar trade for over a quarter of a century and Duncan Davidson, the product of the Cromarty school who had inherited the Tulloch estate in 1781, extended his influence in 1790 when he was elected to Parliament for Cromartyshire. After his death in 1799 the business continued, with his son Henry Davidson (1771–1827) as a partner. Just as George Ross had brought the Davidsons to London from Cromarty, the Davidsons were the patrons of Aeneas Barkly, born in 1768 on the farm of Kirkton, six miles west of Cromarty. Indeed, Barkly may have been another pupil at the Cromarty school, since his father owned a substantial house in the town. Aeneas prospered in London, rising to be a partner in the merchant house. He was said to be a cool and reserved man and seldom mixed with his London neighbours. His preference was always 'to have a few old friends – chiefly Scotchmen – to dine and sleep' at Highbury Grove or to enjoy long visits from 'Country Cousins'. It was, after all, to such a network that he owed his success. Later Duncan Davidson's grandsons, Henry (1802–86) and William (1808–93), became his partners in Davidsons & Barkly, owning slaves and plantations in Antigua, Grenada, St Vincent, Trinidad and British Guiana.

The fortunes of this firm, which benefited beyond all others from the whole bloody business of slavery, was thus in 1834 in the hands of two families originating in one small community in the north of Scotland. It was a place to which Aeneas still felt attached, for when he died two years later he recommended in his will that the Cromarty property 'should on no account be sold or alienated the same having remained in the family for a long series of years'.[11] Yet neither Aeneas nor Henry Barkly, nor the Davidson brothers, ever set foot on a plantation during the time of slavery. However, the partners in the next firm in the league table of mercantile compensation were unlike the Barklys and the Davidsons – their founders had got their hands very dirty indeed.

SANDBACH TINNÉ

Ranking second in compensation were the members of the Sandbach Tinné partnership – Philip Frederick Tinné (1774–1844), George Rainy (1790–1863), James Patrick McInroy (1799–1878), Charles Stewart Parker (1800–68), George Parker (1806–60), Henry Robertson Sandbach (1807–95) and John Abraham Tinné (1807–84). Like Davidsons & Barkly, the details of compensation required attention and in November 1835 Charles Stewart Parker's younger brother Patrick wrote:

> All the partners in the house will be kept very busy . . . in order to
> see that everything goes on right about the Compensation. Henry

Sandbach goes to London next Monday in order to be on the spot when the awards are made.[12]

Other than Philip Frederick Tinné and George Rainy, these men were second-generation members of the business founded in the late 1700s by four men. Two had been Highland Scots – George Robertson and James McInroy – while Charles Parker was a Lowland Scot whose father had prospered in Virginia until the War of Independence. Only the fourth founder, Samuel Sandbach from Cheshire, was still living in 1834. These men, and the rise of the partnerships they founded, are described below.

James McInroy (1759–1825) was from a modestly wealthy farming family in Highland Perthshire. His father had made a loan to the laird of Edradour in 1756 and in return became the *wadsetter* of the farm of Balnabruich, where James was born.[13] By 1782 he had established some form of trading concern in the Dutch colonies of Essequibo and Demerara, taking advantage of the opening up of trade which was a result of occupation by the British (February 1781–February 1782) and then by the French (February 1782–March 1784). Although Essequibo and Demerara had welcomed non-Dutch settlers from the 1750s, legal trade had still been restricted by the Dutch West India Company (WIC). The British occupation, which did not disturb property rights, allowed the planters access to British trade networks, including the African slave trade, and this allowed an increase in the number of enslaved Africans brought to the colonies. The French occupation again left property, and prosperity, intact. At the end of the Anglo–Dutch War in 1784, the colonies were returned to the control of the WIC at a time when the Dutch slave trade was at a standstill. Continued prosperity and growth relied on the now illegal import of slaves and on the export of produce of the slave-worked plantations to the most profitable markets – and not necessarily to the Netherlands. When the WIC attempted to impose greater control through a new governing Council, the planters resisted and rejected the Council as unconstitutional. This was, in their words, a state of *regeringloosheid* (anarchy) but it was an anarchy they welcomed – as long as anarchy meant the freedom to smuggle. Bram Hoonhout sums up their position in the most recent study of the colonies:

> The colonists ... were so dependent on illegal trade that they strongly resisted anyone who tried to put an end to it ... The situation reflected the three Orwellian characteristics that capture Essequibo and Demerara's development: (institutional) weakness as strength, anarchy as stability, and smuggling as a right.[14]

In this contest James McInroy proved to be an effective smuggler. His essential link was to Grenada, which would soon be making as much from the re-export of slaves as from all its crops. In 1787 Britain recognised the commercial importance of inter-colonial trade – particularly this inter-colonial slave trade – and partially legitimised it by the establishment of free ports like St George (see Chapter 4). From the perspective of the WIC and the Dutch Government, it was still smuggling.

One merchant to take advantage of the emerging opportunities in Grenada was George Robertson (1756–99), the youngest son of the minister of Kincardine (Ross-shire), a family which was developing links across the Americas. While the oldest son Harry became a Church of Scotland minister like his father, the second son John Robertson (1751–98) became a lawyer in Tobago and their cousin Gilbert Robertson (1759–1836) worked in Trinidad before moving to Philadelphia, where he served as British consul from 1817 until his death.[15] George was established in Grenada when St George became a free port in 1787, and in 1789 he engaged young Charles Stewart Parker as a clerk. Parker had worked in the Port Glasgow Customs House before being sent to Cadiz to learn Spanish, which allowed him to assist Robertson in developing trade with the Spanish colonies of Trinidad, Caracas and New Grenada.[16]

Parker's father then provided him with £1,000, which was enough for him to become Robertson's partner, along with a Daniel Gordon. They were joined by James McInroy, whose foothold in Demerara allowed them to illicitly import slaves and to illicitly export cotton from the Dutch colony to both Glasgow and Liverpool. Their cotton business was to prove immensely profitable and although fully aware that it relied on smuggling this at no point seems to have been a problem for them. They were, however, certain that one partner must always be resident in Demerara. McInroy moved between Demerara and Grenada but Gordon was unwilling to settle there semi-permanently, and so the proposal was made to take in a new partner. This was one cause of a bitter dispute with Gordon, who declared that he would never 'turn Dutchman for such a small object as my share in the profits in our Demerara concern'. There were other disagreements, Gordon was accused of 'underhand plots' and the partnership was dissolved in 1792.[17] It was reformed with a new partner, Samuel Sandbach (1769–1851), who had worked as their clerk from late 1790.

Sandbach came to Grenada with an existing family network. His uncle, also Samuel Sandbach (1730–1800), was a planter in Grenada, and a nephew, William Sandbach (1762–1829), joined him to manage the plantation. Both were senior officers in the island's militia in 1787. His mother-in-law later said of Sandbach that a legacy from an uncle had been 'the foundation of his being arrived so early in life at independence' but it seems more likely that this was an advance from his uncle William, who was in London in 1792 and was 'desirous to forward him'.[18] Whatever the source, Sandbach was able to come up with £2,000 and became a junior partner with McInroy, Parker and Robertson, who each invested £4,000.

Parker described them in 1792 as having 'a very respectable footing in Demerara' and things only got better. In 1795 they made a profit of £14,512 on their total invested capital of £36,514 – a remarkable annual return of 40 per cent. Parker's personal aim had been to be worth £3,000 in 1796 at the agreed end of their partnership but in that year, with British occupation, their trade became legal, their exports (mainly now to Liverpool) grew and the partnership continued. Although they had had problems maintaining their lines of credit from financiers in Britain, these had been resolved by a visit by Parker and Robertson to Scotland in 1794.

They had also had remarkable luck at the outbreak of the Fédon Rebellion in Grenada in 1795. McInroy had not only avoided capture but had been able to load about £9,000 of goods onto their sloop *Rambler*, which had been anchored in the harbour, and had then reached Tobago after surviving three attacks by a French privateer. Parker and Robertson were already in Tobago, or quickly went there, where they oversaw the sale of the cargo, while McInroy returned to Demerara. He had been wounded in the skirmishes with the French privateer but only slightly.

The partners were also investing in ownership of plantations and slaves. McInroy had acquired a cotton plantation on Leguan

Island in the River Essequibo in 1792; by 1795 they owned
Woodlands on the Mahaica Creek, on Demerara's east sea
coast; in 1800 they bought *L'Amitie*, a 500-acre cotton estate on
the west sea coast; and by 1803 they also had plantation *Coffee
Grove*. By the early 1800s they had created an extensive and
integrated business. They not only grew and exported cotton
but imported both provisions, mainly from North America, and
manufactured goods from Britain. And once Britain had re-
established control in Grenada, they once more became slave
factors. An essential part of their success was their ownership
of ships. The *Rambler* was probably their first vessel but it was
soon replaced by larger ships, like the 265-ton *Elbe* built in
Hamburg, the 409-ton *Demerary* built in Lancaster for McInroy
and launched in 1801, and the *Duke of Kent*. These three ships
were captained by Scots – Charles Downie, from Urray (Ross-
shire), who died on board in 1805; Peter Inglis, who settled in
Liverpool but was born in Scotland; and James Dougall.[19]

George Robertson brought two nephews from the Highlands
to help manage the growing business – Gilbert Robertson (1774–
1839) and Harry Robertson (1776–95), sons of his brother
Harry, the minister of Kiltearn. Harry drowned in the Demerara
River not long after his arrival, having survived two bouts of
fever, and in March 1799 George Robertson himself contracted
a fever and died a week later. It was twenty-five-year-old Gilbert
Robertson, the older of the two surviving nephews, who wrote
to Charles Parker, then in London, breaking the news. Parker
now had a more personal connection to the Robertson family,
since in 1797 he had returned to Scotland and married Gilbert's
cousin Margaret Rainy (1774–1844). She was the daughter
of his aunt Anne Forbes and Revd George Rainy of Creich
(Sutherland). George Robertson, Parker and McInroy all had
other family who were less openly acknowledged. Robertson
had a son known as 'Black George', who was being educated in
London; Parker had fathered two 'mulatto' boys, Charles and
James, who were sent to Scotland for education in 1791; and in
1810 there was a Catherine McInroy, a 'free coloured' woman,
in Demerara.

There was another significant strengthening of the network
in December 1802 when Samuel Sandbach married Elizabeth
(Eliza) Robertson (1782–1859), daughter of Revd Harry
Robertson and sister of Gilbert. Sandbach had returned to

Britain in 1801 and had already made a trip to Holland in September 1802, during the fourteen-month Peace of Amiens. In 1803, after his marriage, the couple went there together and, among other visits, dined with a Mr and Mrs Tinné – Tinné's son was in Demerara and later became a partner in the business. They were back in the family home by late May, leaving Holland as the Peace ended, and thereafter Sandbach was based in Liverpool, where a branch of the partnership was established in 1804. This later became its head office.

Despite his marriage, Parker was remarkably mobile over these years. He may have been in Demerara in the winter of 1799/1800. He certainly made trips in the winters of 1801/2 and 1803/4, leaving in November and returning about April, and he sailed again in late 1804, returning sometime in 1805.[20] Since McInroy was also in Glasgow in December 1804, and possibly before that, the partnership increasingly relied on a new generation of men on the ground in Demerara. Parker's brother-in-law Gilbert Rainy (1782–1808), the oldest son of Revd George Rainy and Ann Robertson, was there by 1799; McInroy's nephew Peter McLagan (1774–1860) was recruited and was there from at least 1806; and two more of George Robertson's nephews, Hugh Munro Robertson (1787–1819) and George Rainy (1790–1863), arrived in 1806 and 1807. McInroy and Sandbach had also formed a partnership in Demerara with William McBean (1776–1822) from Tomatin (Inverness-shire), who had been in the colony with his brother Lachlan from before 1799. This continued until 1808.

When Gilbert Robertson wrote to Parker in 1799 to inform him of George Robertson's death, he also assured Parker that the business was in good hands, since he [Gilbert] had now 'been long enough in the country to acquire a thorough knowledge of all the affairs of the concern'.[21] With Parker, McInroy and Sandbach back in Britain, Gilbert Robertson had the opportunity to take the lead in the business in Demerara. But over the course of the next ten years Parker lost confidence in him and in 1810 he wrote to his wife, saying:

> I am sorry to say that accounts of Gilbert Robertson (from him we have heard nothing) are far from flattering, he is over his head in debt, I see nothing for it but compulsive measures to get what can be got out of his hands.[22]

It was instead George Rainy, Parker's brother-in-law, who rose to become the acting partner for the firm in Demerara, until he left the colony in 1837. He left a vivid impression on a clerk in another business who in 1821 paid a visit to 'the tall gaunt-looking store of Messrs McInroy Sandbach & Co., looked up to as the Rothschilds of Demerara, rich and influential':

> Many estates were heavily mortgaged to them, their whole business connected to the arrangements to which the mortgagers were strictly tied down. All the sugar must be shipped home in THEIR ships, under THEIR agency both here and at home, and so much every year; all plantation stores to be bought of THEM; and other pickings, highly profitable to the mortgagee, who got full rates and commissions: considerably more so than planting was to unfortunate mortgagers, who got about as much as would just keep them on their legs. Other produce such as coffee and cotton was subject to like conditions. Here I found the Executive of this formidable establishment, Mr George Rainey, whom Mr Pattinson had told me I would find 'very keen': slow-spoken, he had a sharp visage, high thin nose, and a cold quiet calculating grey eye. He and his coadjutor Mr George Buchanan brought enormous gains to the Liverpool House and to McInroy Parker & Co. in Glasgow, though they dealt fairly: their business was money-lending.[23]

Robertson, Parker, McInroy, Sandbach, McBean and Rainy had all worked on plantations. They had all, almost certainly, ordered punishments of slaves. This was in marked contrast with the desk-based Davidsons and Barklys, who were London merchants and financiers who looked to Guyana after the end of the Napoleonic wars as it became a place to make money. It was not until 1839 that young Henry Barkly visited British Guiana.[24]

THE DAVIDSONS & BARKLY PLANTATIONS

In 1817 the partnership of Davidson & Graham (the predecessor of Davidsons & Barkly) owned no land in Berbice and only one plantation in Demerara, with just eleven slaves. The following year, along with John Cameron and Donald Charles Cameron, they acquired the estates of the Dutch-owned Berbice Association (which had been returned to them when war ended in 1815) along with 682 slaves, for a purchase price of £66,000.[25] These estates were then divided and, in part, renamed. Against the background of a burgeoning demand for sugar, there was something triumphal in the replacement of the old Dutch plantation names – *Dankbarheid, Dageraad, Sandvoort* and *St Jan* – with *Lochaber* after the Camerons' homelands in Scotland and *Highbury* after the Barklys' London estate. *Highbury* had 450 slaves and at emancipation was the largest West Indian plantation owned by Davidsons & Barkly.

Just as Sandbach Tinné increasingly relied on the relations of their co-founder George Robertson to be on the ground managing the business in Demerara, Davidsons & Barkly relied on these two men from the West Highlands – Donald Charles Cameron, later of Barcaldine (Argyll), and John Cameron (1782–1862) of Glen Nevis. Stephen Mullen's study of the Glasgow merchant house John Campbell senior & Co. shows how, in much the same way, that firm relied on another West Highland network, the Macraes of Inverinate.[26] Both the Camerons and the Macraes were from the class of tacksmen, men like those in Sutherland described in Chapter 2, all seeking ways to maintain their income and status.

In Guyana they were, first and foremost, professional attorneys and managers. I referred in Chapter 7 to two of the Macraes who became leading exponents of systematic plantation management, influencing practice in both the Caribbean and the southern states of the USA. D. C. Cameron & Company of Berbice were similarly methodical. A series of their account books, running to thirteen journals and ledgers, is held by the National Records of Scotland and cover the years 1816 to 1840, giving detailed accounts of the mercantile life of Berbice, including shipments to Europe of coffee, cotton, rum and sugar. They also detail the costs of plantation management, the sale and hire of named negro slaves, and dealings in general merchandise, including cattle.[27] The company owned some plantations in their own name, some in partnerships, and managed others for absentee owners. They also had their own network of contacts and in 1817 Donald Charles Cameron returned to Scotland and married Elizabeth Matheson of Bennetsfield (Ross-shire). Two of her older brothers were already in Berbice and, a month before, her older sister Martha had married a Demerara planter.

Donald Charles Cameron returned to Berbice the following year and when the second slave returns were made in early 1819 the two Camerons were responsible for almost 1,300 enslaved people.

Table 9.1 Plantations managed by John Cameron and Donald Charles Cameron (January/February 1819)

Owner(s)	Return made by	Plantation	Slaves
Alves, William & Cameron, John	Cameron, John	*Rosehall* and *Inverness*	204
Cameron, John & D. C.	Cameron, John	*Rosehall*	87
Cameron, John & D. C.	Cameron, John	No. 1, Corentyne Coast	45
Cameron, D. C.	Cameron, D. C.		14
Cameron, John	Cameron, John	*Heversham* and *Epsom*	8
Cameron, John	Cameron, John		13
Davidson, Henry; Barkly, Aeneas; Cameron, John; Cameron, D. C.	Cameron, D. C.	*Sandvoort*	230
Davidson, Henry; Barkly, Aeneas; Cameron, John; Cameron, D. C.	Cameron, D. C.	*Dageraad*	141
Davidson, Henry; Barkly, Aeneas; Cameron, John; Cameron, D. C.	Cameron, D. C.	*Dankbarheid* and *St Jan* (later renamed *Highbury*)	309
Smithson, Henry	Cameron, John	*New Forest*	75
Smithson, Henry	Cameron, John	*Smithson's Place*	160
			1,286

Donald Charles Cameron's wife remained in London, where his first two children were born, but by the mid-1820s the family were back in Scotland, where Cameron had bought a small estate near Linlithgow. Thereafter it was John Cameron who remained in Berbice until he was joined by no fewer than six nephews of his partner, Donald Charles Cameron. In the 1820s John Cameron became a member of the Berbice Council of Government, which, as described in Chapter 7, was intransigent in its opposition to any amelioration of the conditions under which slaves worked until all were removed from office by the Governor in 1826.

HIGHBURY

John Cameron was the attorney for *Highbury*, a large and innovative sugar estate, its cane mill driven by water power using a sluice from the river.[28] Aeneas Barkly and Henry Davidson became the sole owners in 1822, retaining Cameron & Co. as attorneys, but it was not until November 1838, at the age of twenty-three, that Henry Barkly first visited his Berbice properties. When he did so he was able to draw on almost two decades of reports on their management. These included monthly reports which he said 'were sent home to every merchant'. They appear to be of the kind, described by Caitlin Rosenthal in *Accounting for Slavery*, prepared for 'analysis from afar' and synthesising 'the content of larger journals ... in a simple format which facilitated review and accountability'.[29] Barkly knew how to make use of this material and of the more detailed Day Ledgers held on the estates because he had left school at seventeen and started work with the junior clerks in the London counting house, learning every detail of the business. And unusually, his education, at Bruce Castle school, near Tottenham, had emphasised science and mathematics rather than the classics, leaving him with a 'lifelong interest in statistics'.[30] This grasp of detail was on display when he confidently gave evidence in May 1842 to a Select Committee of the House of Commons, established to consider the supply of labour in the West Indian colonies.[31]

His particular qualification was his knowledge of a later innovation on the *Highbury* estate – the use of indentured labourers brought from India. The scheme had been promoted in Demerara by John Gladstone & Co. and Andrew Colville, by John & Henry Moss in Essequibo and by Davidsons & Barkly in Berbice. Two British ships embarked 414 men, women and children (but mostly men) at Calcutta and disembarked 396 in Guyana in May 1838 – eighteen had died during the four-month voyage. From the *Whitby* 176 people were allocated to *Highbury* and *Waterloo*, both plantations belonging to Davidsons & Barkly. Henry Barkly met these workers during his six-month residence in the colony from November 1838 to April 1839. There were six women, five girls and four boys; the rest were men. The experiment was deemed a failure after credible reports of ill treatment, mainly in Demerara, led the Anti-Slavery Society to campaign successfully for an embargo. But in 1842 Barkly was arguing before the Select Committee for a resumption of this migration to provide what he regarded as essential labour.

It was central to his argument that *Highbury* was a profitable plantation which had brought an average profit of more than £5,000 a year since its purchase and had continued to do so during the period of 'apprenticeship'. It had been bought outright in 1822 for £54,000, and a further £10,000 had been spent purchasing more slaves. In 1834 the capital value of the plantation and its slaves was assessed at £60,000, most of that (£48,500) 'invested' in the ownership of the slaves. The annual profits at over £5,000 thus represented a healthy and reliable 8½ per cent return on capital, significantly more than the standard 6 per cent interest on loans to the colonies.

With regard to the enslaved population of *Highbury*, Barkly did not provide evidence of numbers before the time of emancipation, but these are available from other sources. In 1819 there had been 450 slaves on the three plantations which were to be renamed *Highbury*. By 1822 there were 386, a consequence of 81 deaths and of only 17 children being born and surviving. By 1825 there had been a further 73 deaths and 22 births, leaving only 335 enslaved people. A quarter of the enslaved population had died in a six-year period. From the perspective of Davidsons & Barkly this was a serious depletion of their capital, to which they responded by an injection of funds. In September 1827 their attorney, John Cameron, bought eighty-five slaves, described in the notice of sale as 'very fine people', from the estate of Donald Ross (d. *c.* 1824). The purchase of these slaves brought the numbers up to 390 in 1828. Numbers

Table 9.2 Workforce on *Highbury* (Berbice), 1 August 1834

	Male	Female	Total
Headmen and tradesmen	43	0	43
First-class field labourers	71	111	182
Second-class field labourers	24	39	63
Aged, diseased and non-effective	Not specified	Not specified	60
Children under six	Not specified	Not specified	38
'Inferior' domestic	0	1	1
Total formerly enslaved			387
'Effective' labourers			288

rose to 439 in 1831 – probably the result of a further purchase – but this had fallen to 387 at the time of emancipation in August 1834. This was almost exactly the number on the plantation in 1822 when Aeneas Barkly and Henry Davidson had bought it outright. But behind this was an appalling death rate – and in the earlier period between 1819 and 1822 it had included three suicides.

Until emancipation all slaves on *Highbury* over the age of six were regarded as part of the 'effective' labour force. Barkly's annual profit was also augmented by a regime under which, unlike most colonies immediately before emancipation, slaves still worked on Saturdays – providing a fifth more labour than if they had been free, as on Sundays, to cultivate their own plots. It was only questioning by the committee which drew out this fact. Barkly also omitted any mention of discipline. On *Highbury* in the course of the year 1832 about eighty-eight punishments were meted out for every hundred slaves and in 1830 there had been about ninety-two punishments. About a quarter of these probably involved whipping, the rest confinement in the stocks.[32] This was more than twice the average in the colony. While it is difficult to know how accurate these records of punishments were across the colony, they will not have been overstated. The manager at this time was John Ross, perhaps the 'John Ross of Berbice' from Golspie (Sutherland) who later returned to Inverness. If so, there is other evidence that Ross favoured what he would have regarded as a strict approach. In preparation for the regime of unpaid labour for forty hours a week under 'apprenticeship', he stipulated to his own slaves 'that every day lost by skulking in the hospital must be made good by the party out of his own spare time'.[33] And in 1837 he wrote from Inverness recommending the appointment of a manager for another plantation, commenting that the manager 'being a little bit of a disciplinarian is no favorite with Blackie'.[34] There is, however, no evidence that he strayed beyond the limits of what was regarded in the colony as acceptable punishment.

John Cameron remained as attorney until the end of apprenticeship, and the large plantation was run by a small white staff consisting of a manager, three overseers/bookkeepers and, at least from the 1830s, an engineer. Production consisted of sugar, rum and molasses – and during the apprenticeship Barkly invested £3,000 of his £18,555 compensation in additional machinery. This included a steam engine (powered by coal imported from Britain from 1836), a still and two elevators for cane and megass (waste used mainly as fuel), in order to reduce labour costs at the sugar mill. But Barkly was clearly frustrated, even distressed, by the reaction of his former slaves to the freedom which they enjoyed from September 1838.

A group of sixty former slaves immediately left for the now abandoned coffee plantation from which they had been taken ten years before. They were probably the survivors of the eighty-five slaves sold in September 1827 from *Spring Garden*.[35] They had belonged to the estate of the deceased Donald Ross, one of three brothers from Boath (parish of Alness, Ross-shire) who had originally run it as a cotton plantation on the west bank of the vast Corentyne River. Fifty years later, in the 1880s, *Spring Garden* had become part of a larger area of 'homesteads' inhabited by an ethnically mixed population of Chinese, Portuguese from the Cape Verde Islands and the descendants of enslaved Africans. It was the opportunity for such independence and self-sufficiency that was sought by most former slaves. Those who remained on *Highbury* generally chose to work on the plantation for only two or three days a week, devoting the rest to their own plots of land. This was common across the colony and, although Barkly himself refused to sell ground, many former slaves purchased plots, either individually or in groups.

The *Highbury* people included ninety or so who did no work on the plantation and resisted attempts to charge them rent for their houses and plots, which they held to be theirs. It was, they said, 'All nonsense that the Queen had made them free, without giving them free houses and free land.'[36] But it was their 'independent footing with regard to [their] employer' which Barkly found most difficult, the consequence of the unmet demand for labour and the unwillingness of the former slaves to work as full-time labourers. Since the very existence of a sugar plantation, with its dams and canals and the need to process cane immediately, depended on control of a labour force, he was led to the conclusion that a proprietor 'cannot be master of his own property as long as he is dependent for its very existence upon the supply of labour that the labourer may choose to afford him'. Yet, while others wanted to drive down the cost of labour by coordinated action, Barkly argued for large-scale Indian immigration.

He painted a favourable picture of the conditions of the indentured Indian labourers allocated to *Highbury* but this was contradicted by the abolitionist John Scoble, who had visited the colony in 1839. While the most serious abuses were in Demerara, and there were favourable reports of their treatment on *Highbury* by the stipendiary magistrate, Scoble disputed these claims:

> When in the presence of them they know to be their friends, and really interested in their welfare, they give full vent to their feelings, and exhibit their real sentiments, and with tears and clasped hands, and in broken English entreat to be sent back to their native country and to their kindred from whom they have been wantonly separated.[37]

He added that in April or May 1839 'upwards of twenty of them' had left the estate and had travelled east, through the bush, in the hope of 'reaching Bengal'. This was condescending to the intelligence of the Indian labourers. They were, however, following in the footsteps of the sixty former slaves who had left for *Spring Garden*.

Barkly's analysis of the accounts of *Highbury*, and the evidence he presented to the Select Committee, show him convinced that the sugar plantations of Berbice could remain profitable with indentured labour. He had an interest – as owner, merchant or mortgagee – in six of them, which amounted to a fifth of the thirty or so sugar estates in the colony. To source that supply of labour he argued for the resumption of migration of indentured Indians, which would not, as it turned out, be resumed until 1845/6. He was also exploring other options. In Grenada in 1839 he was involved in a scheme which brought 165 labourers and their families from Malta and in 1840 his agents, D. C. Cameron & Co., welcomed two black Americans to New Amsterdam, Nathaniel Peck and Thomas S. Peck. They had been elected at a meeting of free coloured people in Baltimore as delegates to visit British Guiana and Trinidad in order to assess the possibility of coloured people migrating there. They were 'proffered [Cameron's] house as a home, as long as [they] might choose to remain in the colony', and visited several plantations but nothing appears to have come of the proposal.[38]

In Berbice in 1841 Barkly's attorney also willingly accepted an allocation of 'captured Africans'. These were people who had been 'liberated' from foreign slaving ships, which had been intercepted by the Royal Navy and taken to Rio de Janeiro, where an international British–Brazilian judicial commission allocated them to British Guiana. Although saved from slavery, they were unwilling migrants with no practical option but plantation labour. Twenty 'captured Africans' came to *Highbury* – eight men, three women and nine children – and there were almost five hundred across the colony, including 224 children.

Despite these efforts, in 1841 Barkly's accounts showed a loss of £3,500 for the plantation and Barkly suggested to the Select Committee that if this continued he would feel inclined to 'abandon production . . . and transfer machinery, stock, and whatever else could be removed to the neighbouring slave colonies, Surinam or Cayenne'. This was a bold statement, given that it was illegal for British citizens to engage in the slave trade in any part of the world. In fact, his response was to cease further investment and lease his two plantations, *Highbury* and *Waterloo*, to local planters.

Barkly's partnership with the Davidsons was dissolved and when he returned to Guyana it was as its Colonial Governor (1849–53), the beginning of a long career which took him to Jamaica, Australia, Mauritius and South Africa. Indian immigration had resumed in 1845 and in the next three seasons 11,841 migrants arrived in British Guiana. The 'supply' then dried up for two years and the 1851 British Guiana census revealed an Indian population of only 7,682. There were 2,218 recorded as having died on estates, in jail or in hospitals – but the rest must be presumed dead. That is, more than four thousand had died.[39] Yet Barkly, as Governor, promoted the expansion of Indian migration, in the face of opposition at home from the Anti-Slavery Society. And it was this which gave Sandbach Tinné a further opportunity for diversification.

SANDBACH TINNÉ AFTER EMANCIPATION

At emancipation Sandbach Tinné & Co. in Liverpool and its related partnerships in Glasgow and Demerara were by far the largest slave holders in British Guiana, submitting thirty claims for 3,324 slaves. After emancipation they faced the same challenges as Davidsons & Barkly. Yet their partner George Rainy, who remained in the colony until June 1837, expressed the same belief that 'there is nothing in the inherent constitution of the new system incompatible with the continued prosperity of this valuable colony'. He felt, however, that the crop of 1834 had suffered because of the attitude of the former slaves, who were still obliged to work unpaid for forty hours a week:

> A good deal of sugar would have been made on some estates but for the turbulent . . . state of the Negroes, in regard to which things are still very far from being in a satisfactory state.

He laid the blame at the door of the colony's Governor, James Carmichael, who was seen as sympathetic to the former slaves.[40]

Rainy's principal clerk, Peter Miller Watson – who would head the business in Demerara after Rainy's departure – expressed the same view, which was passed on by his mother in Scotland to friends in Orkney:

> The poor deluded blacks have got idle and independence & freedom has not as yet had a good effect upon them.[41]

In 1836 Watson was sent, with a chartered vessel, to recruit labour from other West Indian colonies but the venture was 'nearly an utter failure'. Watson brought back only about sixty people, several of whom were children, and most had only engaged themselves for two years at 'a pretty high wage'.[42] It was to be the migration of impoverished peasants from the Portuguese islands of Madeira which provided the first, large influx of new plantation workers.

One effect of compensation was, however, to allow Sandbach Tinné to expand their trans-Atlantic trading fleet and, when the migration of indentured Indian labourers expanded in the 1850s, they also specialised in Indian Ocean trades with the

Atlantic, principally the transportation of labour.[43] Among
their first purpose-built vessels were the *Fairlie* (named after the
Ayrshire village which had become a retreat for the inter-related
Parker, Rainy, Sandbach and Robertson families) and her sister
ship *Kiltearn* (named after the Robertsons' home parish in Ross-
shire). Later there were the *Sandbach* and *George Rainy*, and
perhaps reflecting their ownership of Clyde yachts which sailed
around the Scottish islands, the *St Kilda*, *Rona*, *Jura* and *Ailsa*.

Peter Miller Watson (1805–69) remained principal clerk
in Demerara until the late 1850s. He was the great-nephew
of George Robertson and a nephew by marriage of Samuel
Sandbach, two of the company's founders, and the last family
member to remain on the ground in the colony. Other children
and grandchildren of the founders had become part of the elite
of British Victorian society – businessmen, scientists, natural-
ists, supporters of various churches, and patrons and collectors
of the arts.

Perhaps despite himself, Henry Barkly relayed to the Select
Committee of the House of Commons the attitude of the former
slaves on *Highbury* to their own children. In slavery all children
from the age of six had been required to perform 'light field
work' and Barkly, faced with a labour shortage, was frustrated
that after 1838 none of them were sent to work:

> I have been repeatedly told by negroes, when I have asked them why
> they did not make their idle children work, who were running about
> doing nothing; I have been repeatedly told that they were born free;
> and I think they would ... have worked their own fingers to the
> bone before they would have made their children do the slightest
> work.

PART 3

Entangled Histories – Legacies of Slavery in the North of Scotland

The previous nine chapters have shown something of the extent and the nature of Highland Scots' involvement in the African slave trade and in the plantation economies of the Caribbean. In panoramic view it was an involvement which began in earnest in the English 'sugar island' of Jamaica after 1707, then grew through the new opportunities presented by Britain's acquisition of the ceded islands of Grenada, Tobago, Dominica and St Vincent in 1763, and continued from the mid-1790s on the 'last frontier' of empire in Trinidad and in the Dutch colonies of Demerara, Essequibo and Berbice, which were to become British Guiana. It was on this frontier that fortunes continued to be made up to and after the end of British colonial slavery, and in British Guiana that the largest of the West India merchants built their commercial empires.

But seen in closer view, there was Scottish and Highland involvement from an earlier date in English Barbados, where Irish and Scots indentured servants were transported in the mid-1600s, and an early Highland presence from the same time in Suriname on the north coast of South America. Scots were also involved in Suriname after the end of British colonial slavery and when the Netherlands finally freed slaves in 1863, more than 9 per cent of the compensation paid to slave holders went to Scots.[1] Other Scottish and Highland entanglements are to be found beyond the bounds of British empire, including for example in French St Lucia, Danish St Croix and in trade to Spanish colonies. And the extensive Northern Scottish presence in British-controlled Guyana after 1815 grew from the Scottish presence there while its constituent colonies were part of the Dutch Atlantic.

The next four chapters will consider the impact and some of the legacies of this involvement and complicity in the crimes of slavery. Chapter 10 describes how wealth from the Caribbean was used in attempts to transform the Highlands and how the economy of the Highlands was intertwined both with trade to and from the British colonies and with the financial systems on which the slave plantations depended. In earlier chapters I have shown the extent of Highland involvement with slavery and here I argue that it is important to reject the claim that the Highlands in the era of British colonial slavery can be thought to be a colony of, or an 'internal colony' within, the British Empire.

In Chapter 11, I use five case studies of Highland landowners to capture the variety of ways in which they used wealth from the slave plantations not only to transform, for good and ill, the economy of the Highlands but to sustain, develop, adopt, invent or abandon, as an elite, their Highland identity. This does not address the question – which is beyond the scope of this book – of how more ordinary Highlanders thought of themselves in the Caribbean and whether or not Highland identity was as important to them as it was to many later migrants to Canada, the United States, Australia and New Zealand.

In Chapters 12 and 13, I turn to the human legacies of Scotland's involvement with slavery and, in particular, to Highland 'Black History' – the presence in the Highlands of enslaved black people, of free black servants and of the children of Scots and both enslaved and 'free coloured' women.

10

Northern Scotland – Investments

The culture, society and economy of the north of Scotland were transformed in the hundred years or so between the Jacobite Rising of 1745 and the Highland famine, which began with the failure of the potato crop in 1846. It was a century in which traditional clan-based social structures, already in decline, gave way to a culture of commerce in which land became regarded as a resource and its inhabitants as a source of labour. Wealth, often gained from Britain's growing empire, provided the capital with which to invest in new ways of doing things – in new ploughs, dykes, farm buildings and machinery, fishing boats, spinning wheels and looms – and in entirely new industries which would create further wealth. And all that was needed, it was believed, was the transforming power of 'enterprise' – the understanding, drive and willingness to choose well and venture what one had for future gain. This commercial land-lordism enabled the convulsive changes in rural society known as the 'Highland Clearances'. The period ended in the 1850s with the beginnings of a mass emigration of Highlanders in the wake of the famine and this in turn brought further changes to the Highlands and to the British colonies of Canada, Australia and New Zealand.

This was also a period of a hundred years or so which had begun with the appearance of Highland Scots in prominent roles in what had been the 'English sugar islands', especially Jamaica, and had ended with both the final freedom of enslaved labourers in 1838 and the arrival in the Caribbean of the first indentured labourers from the Indian sub-continent. In Chapter 2, I quoted the bard Robb Donn Mackay, who described the dream of returning to the Highlands from the West Indies with 'as much gold as will fill a flagon'. Some adventurers to the Caribbean and South America made that dream a reality and this chapter considers both the impact of these fortunes on the Highlands and the variety of ways in which Scotland – and the Highlands in particular – profited from and were transformed by slavery.

THE TRANSFORMATION OF SCOTLAND

In the 1750s, in the wake of the civil war between Hanoverians and Jacobites which had ended in 1746 at Culloden Moor, Scotland as a whole was a relatively poor country. Its transformation in the three decades from *c.* 1760 was the more startling. In central Scotland, especially in the Lothians, farming became a model for agricultural improvement, admired abroad; textile manufacturing flourished with the development of mechanised cotton-spinning, concentrated in the Clyde valley; and the country began to become a nation of town and city dwellers rather than of country folk, urbanising at a pace unprecedented in Europe. These were also times of radical social upheaval, with winners and losers across the country. There is a clear connection between these agricultural, industrial and social revolutions in Scotland and the slave plantations of the Caribbean. This lay most obviously in the importance of cotton as a raw material, the West Indian colonies being the principal suppliers after the American War of Independence (1775–83) and until the early 1800s. But the Caribbean was also an increasingly important and dominant market for Scottish exports, including 'slave cloth' (rough linen fabric used for clothing) and salt herring (used as a cheap source of protein on the plantations). By 1813, 65 per cent of Scottish exports were to the West Indian colonies.

In 2011 Thomas Devine posed the question 'Did slavery make Scotia great?' and revisited the question in his contribution to *Recovering Scotland's Slavery Past* in 2015.[1] In both he suggests that, since Scotland's economy was much less developed in the 1750s, it was more in need of external economic stimulus than was England, with its more developed home markets. Trade in tobacco and sugar had created a 'deep association with the two slave-based economic systems in the eighteenth-century Atlantic empire: Virginia, Maryland and North Carolina on the American mainland, and the sugar islands of the Caribbean'.

From the profits of these enterprises came the necessary economic stimulus for Scotland's 'clear and decisive break with the past' which can legitimately be described as an 'Industrial Revolution'.

But slavery and the slave plantations provided more than an economic stimulus and to understand this we should consider the work of Eric Williams, both an insightful historian and the prime minister of Trinidad and Tobago from independence in 1962 until his death in 1981. Williams' *Capitalism and Slavery*, published in 1944, argued against the idea that the abolition of slavery in the British Empire was mainly motivated by moral and humanitarian concerns. He proposed that the abolition of slavery was, by that date, in the economic interest of British capitalists because the continuation of slavery would have been of greater benefit to their competitors. He was especially scathing of those who presented the British Empire, and even slavery itself, as fundamentally benevolent. He had, for example, a particular dislike for the influential nineteenth-century Scottish writer Thomas Carlyle, whose *Occasional Discourse on the Negro Question*, published in 1849, claimed that the abolition of slavery had been a mistake. Williams described the book as 'the most offensive document in the entire world literature on slavery and the West Indies'.[2] Carlyle, who peppered this claim with many insults about the appearance and intelligence of black Africans, is but one example of the emergence of the pseudo-scientific racism which had become established by the middle of the nineteenth century.

Capitalism and Slavery, based on Williams' doctoral thesis at Oxford, was intended to be challenging and politically influential. It was about much more than the reasons for the abolition of slavery but, as a result of the controversies which followed, his view – known as the 'Williams thesis' – was at times reduced to a caricature: slavery had become unprofitable and so it was abolished. Williams' argument was much more subtle and his research was much less concerned with theory – in his case, Marxist theory – than with understanding the full impact of slavery on the growth of British industry, commerce, shipping and financial institutions. His insights have been developed, notably by Joseph Inikori, in *Africans and the Industrial Revolution in England* (2002), and by others since then.

Slavery both provided a workforce for the British colonies

in the Caribbean and made profits for British slave traders, increasingly by selling on slaves to non-British colonies. The slave-worked plantations, both before and after the abolition of the British trans-Atlantic slave trade in 1807, provided the raw materials for consumer goods in Britain; they generated profits not only for plantation owners but for those who had invested in plantations or who held mortgages on the plantations; they provided a market for the food and clothing needed by slaves and for the manufactured goods and luxuries required by the planters and their employees; and the profits from all this were in turn a source of investment in industrial development in Britain and an opportunity for the display of wealth in grand houses, public institutions and patronage of the arts. But more than this, slavery was the foundation for a whole system of trade across the Atlantic, which grew under the protection of British naval power, and which, as British manufacturing became more innovative, included the re-export of manufactured goods to consumer markets in the colonies. And this required not only a growing fleet of merchant ships, with all the associated trades in British ports, but also increasingly sophisticated systems of marine insurance and extended credit provided by financial institutions. It was the whole of this system, unique to Britain because of the protection provided by its naval power, which meant that British manufacturing, commercial and financial institutions were able to take abolition in their stride, bolstered by the astonishing £20 million paid out in compensation for emancipation. In this context Pat Hudson, a leading historian of the industrial revolution, has recently summarised the importance of Inikori's work:

> Before Inikori's contribution the marine insurance sector, along with other linkages between the slave trade and the financial sector, had escaped serious estimation regarding its importance to the British economy of the eighteenth century ... [as had] the unique importance of the slave trade and associated bills of exchange in bringing about the integration of London and provincial money markets, without which the major manufacturing regions of the industrial revolution might well have floundered.[3]

Thus Britain reaped 'greater rewards from slavery in the home economy, in the development of its broader financial institutions and payments systems'.

Even although England as a whole had a more developed domestic market and the transformation of Scotland's economy was more dependent on external stimulus, the success of the 'industrial revolution' in both countries was the result of their integration into British financial and trading systems. These systems did not guarantee success and 'the growth of the British economy in the eighteenth and nineteenth centuries is a story of distinctive regional "take-offs" alongside stasis or industrial decline in other parts of the country'.[4] It is therefore less helpful to compare or contrast Scotland and England as a whole than it is to consider how regional economies responded to the opportunities. How then did the north of Scotland fare after 1760 as these profound changes took place?

THE TRANSFORMATION OF LOWLAND AGRICULTURE IN THE NORTH

Earlier chapters have shown how real or imagined prospects in the Caribbean shone bright in Highland imaginations from the mid-1700s and how these opportunities were seized by many enterprising individuals seeking 'adventures abroad'. There are a few examples of early profits from these adventures being invested in agricultural improvements on the model of the Lothians. From the 1760s to the 1790s this was money from Jamaica, the other English 'sugar islands' and the Ceded Islands. Thus, as described in Chapter 2, when the agriculturalist Andrew Wight visited Sutherland in 1781 he saw how Joseph Gordon had used wealth gained in Jamaica to improve the farm of Navidale in Sutherland. But this was a small and isolated instance and in the Highlands large-scale agricultural change did not come until after the 1790s, a generation later than in the Central Lowlands, even on the fertile east coast of the northern Highlands. By the mid-1790s there was a marked contrast between Moray, where agriculture has been 'infinitely improved', and the rest of the fertile coastal fringe in the counties of Nairn, Inverness, Ross, Cromarty and Sutherland, where there were only a few examples of improved farms.

Improvement in Moray began in 1768 when the largest landowner, James Duff (1729–1809), 2nd Earl of Fife, began to grant long leases of land, formerly occupied under joint tenancies, to 'particular substantial and intelligent farmers'. This was a key step in encouraging enterprising individuals to invest in change, since long leases allowed them to reap the benefits of their efforts and single, rather than joint, tenancies gave them greater control over what was done. Wight visited one such farm at Sheriffstown in Moray:

> The Earl was very lucky in getting James Duncan as a tenant. He had made his fortune in the island of Tobago as a planter. It required money to subdue his obdurate farm, and he bestowed plenty of money upon it.[5]

Duncan took a nineteen-year lease but had to return to the West Indies after eleven years. His improvements had, however, substantially increased the value of the property. Since Wight visited in 1780, Duncan must have been in Moray from about 1768 to 1779.

Other proprietors followed his example and by the early 1800s single-tenant improved farms were the norm on Duff's estates.[6] He was heavily committed in London through his involvement in politics and so his extensive landholdings in Aberdeenshire, Banff and Moray were managed by his factor, William Rose (1740–1807) of Montcoffer and Ballivat. While it seems that improvement was largely funded by Duff's inherited wealth, both the Duff and Rose families soon became involved in the West Indies. Duff's oldest illegitimate son, James Duff (1752–1839), became a general in the British army and married in Jamaica. In the words of one commentator, 'marriage brought him financial independence and a sugar plantation'.[7] As for Rose, he was a cousin of Thomas Cuming, who was active in Demerara from the 1760s (see Chapter 6); Rose's son Andrew (1783–1832) became a land surveyor in the colony; and his daughter Anne (1778–1827) married there. Anne's husband was Philip Frederick Tinné (1772–1844), later to be a partner in the highly successful West India house of Sandbach, Tinné & Co. (see Chapter 9).

While attempts at improvement further north did not immediately lead to the revolution in agriculture which was seen in the Central Lowlands or even to the more modest transformation which had occurred in Moray – mainly because of the lack of a local market for grain – there were nevertheless significant attempts at improvement.[8] When Sir John Sinclair produced his *General View of the Agriculture of the Northern Counties and*

Islands of Scotland in 1795, his principal source of information was George Gun Munro (d. 1806) of Poyntzfield on the Black Isle. Munro had inherited the estate from his uncle George Gun Munro (d. 1785), the prosperous son of a Caithness minister. The details of Munro's early career are obscure but he became involved in military procurement and by 1761 he was Commissary of Stores for North Britain, receiving a knighthood in 1779. He had earlier married a wealthy widow, Mary Poyntz of London, whose fortune was at least in part based on slave plantations in Jamaica. In her honour he renamed his Scottish estate Poyntzfield and, according to the parish minister, was 'the first in this part of the country who began improvements in agriculture on a large scale'. Meanwhile, his own illegitimate son, also George Gun Munro (1779–1829), became a plantation owner in Grenada.

In Inverness-shire there was a similar link between Caribbean wealth and attempts at improvement. James Robertson, in his *General View of the Agriculture of the County of Inverness* published by the Board of Agriculture in 1808, included a letter from 'an unnamed gentleman . . . who, perhaps of all others, is best acquainted with the former and present state of the county'. This letter traced the 'course of improvement' in Inverness-shire and identified the seven leading exponents:

Col. James Fraser (1732–1808) of Belladrum
George Ross (1708/9–86) at Kinmylies, but later of Cromarty
John Fraser (1712–95) and his brother Simon Fraser (1727–
  1810) of Ness Castle
Alexander Baillie (1733–99) of Dochfour
Col. John Baillie (d. 1797) of Dunain
David Davidson (1720/1–1804) of Cantray

A further twenty were praised for their extensive planting of woods.[9]

The seven named leading improvers were all local men who had made money outside Scotland. The interests of the Frasers of Belladrum and the Baillies of Dochfour, whose wealth was from slave-trading and plantations, has already been described – although Robertson at no point mentioned the source of their wealth. Of the others, Colonel John Baillie of Dunain and his older brother William served in the army in India in order to restore their family's fortunes; David Davidson of Cantray had prospered in London as a merchant and broker; and the three other improvers, George Ross and the Fraser brothers of Ness Castle, had – like Munro of Poyntzfield – made their money in military contracting as commissaries or army agents and had subsequently extended their investments to the West Indies.

Some further detail on the Frasers of Ness Castle and on George Ross will help explain the extent of their influence and the significance of their roles as army agents. John and Simon Fraser were two of the children of an Inverness merchant, and while John practised as a lawyer in Edinburgh, Simon became a merchant in Gibraltar. Some later sources describe him as the commissary there and certainly government contracting in Gibraltar was considered particularly lucrative.[10] He returned to London and rose to be the senior partner in the West India merchant house Fraser, Alexander, Neilson & Co. of Coleman Street, which had interests in Dominica. Fraser seems to have been among the second wave of purchasers of estates in Tobago in the early 1770s and then became owner of plantation *Good Hope* in Guyana in 1795. He was also, from 1791, a director of the East India Company and a founder subscriber of Lloyd's of London. It was in the 1770s that he had purchased the estates of Borlum and Kinchyle near Inverness, which were renamed Ness Castle.[11] George Ross, from Pitkerrie in Easter Ross, established himself in Edinburgh and then London, where he flourished under the patronage of influential Scottish politicians, particularly the Duke of Argyll. He was renowned for his effectiveness in deals made behind the scenes – 'by the candle' in the slang of the day – and at the time of his death in 1786 he too owned West Indian property, possibly in St Vincent. What Fraser and Ross had in common was the experience of operating as army contractors in a time of international conflicts and in a system of supply 'whose most remarkable feature . . . was its efficiency'.[12]

The interplay between army agents, making money abroad and improved farming is well captured in a letter from Donald Calder in London to his cousin Simon Fraser, the merchant and baker in Inverness described in Chapter 5. Calder, as confidential clerk to George Ross, was well informed about prospects in the army. In 1771 Simon Fraser was hoping to secure a commission as an officer, which Calder referred to as his 'project of getting into the army to assist your Rural Scheme'. Calder warned his cousin that things had 'a very pacifick appearance' and that the East India Recruitment Bill before Parliament would, in order to contain public expenditure, require that officers on half pay were brought out of retirement before new officers were commissioned. His advice was frank:

> In the meantime the ploughshare is a very good instrument to exercise your ingenuity, and the wished for event of a war having once taken place, I hope you will have no difficulty of converting your ploughshare into a truncheon.

A 'truncheon' was an officer's baton carried as a symbol of his authority.

Peace did not last. It was high grain prices during the French and Napoleonic wars, increasingly commercial approaches by landowners and the arrival of a second generation of skilled farmers, often the sons of the first wave of farm managers in the Scottish Lowlands, which from the 1790s created the conditions for a revolution in farming in the north of Scotland. However, in the previous thirty years, for want of opportunities at home, the region had already lost through emigration many of its own 'middling sort'.

MANUFACTURES – SLAVE CLOTH AND INVERNESS BAGGING

There had, nevertheless, been sustained attempts to introduce manufacturing to the Highlands. During the 1700s flax-spinning and linen-weaving became Scotland's staple industry and, after agriculture, the largest employer of labour. During the course of the century the west of Scotland, especially around Glasgow and Paisley, specialised in finer, high-quality linens; while in the east, in the counties of Angus, Perth and Fife, there was specialisation in cheaper, coarser linen. A type of loosely woven, unbleached linen cloth – known as osnaburgs because it had originally been made in Osnabrück in Germany – was first produced in Forfar in the late 1730s and came to dominate coarse linen production. It had another name – 'slave cloth' – and was exported in increasing quantities to provide the cheapest of clothing for enslaved labourers on plantations in North America and the Caribbean. Exports were encouraged under the Bounty Act of 1742 by payment of a government grant for each yard of linen exported, a subsidy which was increased after 1745 and continued until 1832. By the 1790s about nine-tenths of linen exported from Scotland was for the plantations.

The demand for coarse linen was such that it was difficult to recruit enough labour in and around the east coast centres of production and from the 1740s female hand-spinners were being recruited beyond the traditional textile-working areas. The principal developments in the north came after 1747 when the British Linen Company (BLC), in response to a buoyant market and rising labour costs, turned to the Highlands to satisfy their requirement for a cheap and dependable supply of yarn. The Company judged that they could tap a pool of female labour in the Highlands and that the area's remoteness and absence of alternative employment would meet both their requirements of cheapness and dependability. The Company also wanted relatively unskilled spinners to satisfy the demand for coarse linen. The BLC believed that the benefits of employing spinners in peripheral areas would outweigh the additional costs of transport – both of unprocessed flax to the north and of spun yarn to the weavers of Fife and elsewhere – and this was borne out by 1749 when the cost to the BLC of yarn spun at Cromarty was 8d a spindle, while in Dundee the cost was 14d. There was a further motivation in promoting the spinning of linen yarn – the vision that the introduction of manufactures would be a means of integrating the Highlands into the economic, political and social systems of the rest of Britain. The BLC was supported in its pursuit of this objective by both the Board of Trustees (established in 1727) and by the commissioners administering the annexed estates of the principal Jacobite families who had supported the 1745 rising.

When it became clear after only a few years that Scotland could not grow enough flax, it was determined that the raw materials for spinning in the north would be imported to Cromarty, mostly from Riga and St Petersburg, and distributed to a number of spinning-masters who would recruit and train local spinners. By 1752 William Forsyth, a Cromarty merchant, emerged as the chief agent for the BLC in the north, distributing imported flax to a number of sub-agents. Crucially, Forsyth was more successful than others in recruiting female spinners, mainly because of his local standing in the community and his staunch support of the local church against what was perceived as interference by their Roman Catholic laird.

An image of a labour 'pool' which could simply be tapped would, however, be misleading. Flax-spinning was monotonous and the BLC quickly became aware that in years of good harvest and low grain prices production fell because the spinners were under less economic compulsion to submit to the drudgery of spinning. Moreover, production on the scale required by the BLC required the use of spinning wheels rather than the distaff and this marked a break with a traditional way of life. The distaff was used while going about other tasks, whereas the spinning wheel tied women to the house and made them unavailable for farm work. It was by no means clear to those faced with the 'opportunity' that the change would be economically justified, especially given the low rates of pay – and even if justified, it was a sacrifice of a more social lifestyle for one bound to the house. Indeed, the BLC's only similar scheme in the south of Scotland, at Leadhills, foundered because spinners were not willing to work at the rates offered. Yet home-based employment for women, using a spinning wheel, was an enduring and significant social change in the Highlands. And it was a change driven by the use of enslaved labour in North America and the Caribbean.

The demand for cheap clothing for slaves drove a similar development in rural Wales, where impoverished rural households in Montgomeryshire and Merionethshire produced a woollen fabric also used as 'slave cloth'. In the Caribbean and the Southern States of the USA it was called 'Welsh Plains'. Its production was described by Thomas Pennant in 1778:

> The abundance of sheep, which enliven these hills, brought, at the time I visited the country, great wealth into it. The flannel manufacture, and that of a coarse cloth for the army, and for the covering the poor negroes in the West Indies, is manufactured in most parts of the county. It is sent and sold in the rough to Shrewsbury.[13]

A similar durable woollen fabric was woven in the Yorkshire and Lancashire Pennines ('Penistones') and, to a lesser extent, in the Kendal area of the Lake District.

Producers of Scottish woollen cloth had also found expanding markets in the Caribbean and North America after 1707. The requirement was for a relatively light but durable cloth and, since it was price that mattered, lower labour costs meant that Scotland possessed an advantage over English producers.[14] In 1766 James Stirling of Keir (Stirling), then in Jamaica, wrote to his brother in Scotland:

> If the tartan comes out cheap I will have all my Negroes decked with it as it will help to encourage our own Woollen manufactory. Instead of jackets make a sort of short coats which I don't imagine will stand with the Philabeg above [8d?]. The tartan must be strong and the cloaths well shewed [sewed?] that they may last two years. The Kendall Cottons which came out last dont keep the couller they turn purple then white in a few days wearing.[15]

There was a similar purchase of Scottish woollen products in 1767 by the *Montrose* estate in Grenada, with an order for twenty dozen 'Kilmarnock caps', the heavy wool bonnet now known as a Balmoral.[16] But despite James Stirling's enthusiasm, the later account books record only the purchase of osnaburgs and 'Welch plains'.

Until the early 1800s undyed and durable woollens such as Welsh plains vied with coarse linens as the favoured fabric for slaves' working wear in both North America and the Caribbean, but from the 1820s linens and cottons or mixed cottons/linens were the preferred material. Although slaves generally wore cottons and linens for working, they were supplied with woollen blankets, mostly from Yorkshire, for sleeping, with large quantities exported from the 1760s.[17] This was more of a necessity further north in the southern American states, where slavery continued until the 1860s, and we have already seen in Chapter 2 how Henry Laurens in South Carolina complained about the condition of enslaved Africans sent by Smith and Baillies of St Vincent, stating that he expected 'healthy new Negroes to be pretty well clothed and have a blanket each'.

A key driver in the transformation of the Highlands was the creation of large sheep farms, a process which accelerated in 1792 – *Bliadhna nan Caorach* (the Year of the Sheep) – in response to higher wool prices, resulting from the loss of supplies from Spain and Portugal during the Napoleonic wars. The new breeds of sheep which were introduced, especially the Cheviot, had a much higher wool-bearing capacity than indigenous breeds. It is not clear what proportion of British wool manufacture was for the plantations but it was possibly one of the economic drivers for the introduction of the Cheviot to the Highlands.

In Cromarty, William Forsyth had ambitions to weave linen cloth as well as spin yarn, despite a lack of enthusiasm from the BLC. His attempts to produce higher-quality yarn and weave fine linens were not encouraged but he was able to promote his schemes by joining with others to meet another need of the plantations – for the bagging in which cotton was transported. The idea of a 'factory' (originally a shortened form of the word 'manufactory') suggests two things – the bringing together of a large number of workers in a single place and the use of machinery, increasing both the output and efficiency of a manufacturing process – and once the industrial revolution was in full swing these two aspects of a factory were inseparable. But it was not always so. The first manufactories simply brought workers together in one place, without water- or steam- powered machinery, so that their labour could be more controlled, their efforts integrated and the flow of production increased. The modern jargon for such a place is a 'proto-factory' and I will use the term because it helps to identify this important early stage in the industrial revolution. This could, of course, also be a description of a sugar plantation which was, in its own brutal way, a proto-factory.

No successful, large, mechanised factory was established in the Highlands in the late eighteenth or early nineteenth centuries. However, two large proto-factories were set up in Inverness *c.* 1765 and in Cromarty in the early 1770s, providing employment to about a thousand and 850 people respectively, and a branch in Invergordon followed in the early 1800s. They were as near as the Highlands came to joining the industrial revolution of the late 1700s, at least in terms of the numbers employed. The market for their principal product depended on the labour of enslaved Africans in the Caribbean. They made hemp cloth for the bags in which cotton was packed for shipping. This was known in the West Indies as 'Inverness bagging', a brand that was still recognised sixty years later in the southern states of the USA.[18]

These 'manufactories of hempen cloth' emerged out of the Government-backed promotion of linen-spinning in the Highlands in the 1750s, which had created a workforce of female spinners. A few entrepreneurs like Forsyth, with the right connections, saw the opportunity to use the labour of both these spinners and the increasing number of poor, displaced Highlanders who were drifting into the region's towns. Hemp could be imported from the Baltic ports of St Petersburg and Riga, the same source as for the flax used in linen production, and the promoters had connections, through London, to the markets in the Caribbean.[19] The proto-factories were praised by leading proponents of improvement. In 1777 David Loch noted the 'number of young people employed in spinning and otherways much to the good of the country, which prevents idleness and beggary', and in 1781 Andrew Wight found that a great part of those employed were children or young persons under the age of fifteen. Wight considered the employment of young people 'most advantageous . . . because there is no other method so certain of spreading industry among a people'. The employment of the destitute, especially the young, was not only economically advantageous but also socially desirable and Lord Kames commended the Inverness manufactory in 1765 as having in this respect 'more utility than any other branch of manufacture in Scotland'.[20] A substantial number of those employed in the Cromarty manufactory were not residents of the town but Gaelic-speaking Highlanders, who 'on the breaking up of the feudal system . . . began to drop into the place in search of employment'.[21] The influx of Gaelic speakers was sufficiently large to warrant the erection of a church for services in Gaelic.

The Inverness and Cromarty manufactories continued for more than half a century, adapting to rope-making as the demand for ships' rigging for the Royal Navy grew in the early 1800s. The Cromarty establishment struggled on into the 1850s but then declined and and failed because jute replaced hemp as a cheap source of sacking. Most of the Cromarty factory survives and is, today, the most significant remnant of a proto-factory in Britain. Only one part of the Inverness manufactory remains – its clock and stone-built clock tower, misleadingly called Cromwell's tower. It is a powerful symbol. It houses one of the earliest public clocks in the Highlands, marking the moment in 1765 when a large labour force began to work to the tick-tock rhythm of a clock and the sound of a bell – a faint echo of the sound of the conch shell which called enslaved labourers to the cane fields.

Because there was water power in the Highlands there were

some attempts to mechanise production of cloth, just as was happening in the north of England and Central Lowlands of Scotland. The most ambitious of these was 'a little beginning ... towards converting Sutherland into a Lancashire' with the erection in the early 1790s of a cotton mill at Spinningdale, on the shores of the Dornoch Firth. This was the most northerly of the large number of cotton mills being constructed in Scotland from the mid-1780s. The development was backed by George Dempster, an innovative landowner who bought the Skibo estate in 1786, and implemented by a partnership that included David Dale (1739–1806), who had founded New Lanark, and George Macintosh (1739–1807). Macintosh was a Glasgow dyer who was the brother of William Macintosh, then in Avignon but formerly of Grenada (see Chapter 4). It was said that the managers of the cotton mill found it difficult to impose work discipline on their local labour force, a further reminder of the impact of these changes on traditional ways of life. In any event, the building was sold and subsequently destroyed by fire in 1806.

FISHERIES

From the mid-1700s there was another growing source of employment in Scotland's fisheries. Keeping slaves alive and working required a supply of at least a bare minimum of protein. This was most commonly Newfoundland salt cod and by the 1820s adult slaves in Berbice, for example, were usually supplied with two pounds of salt fish each week. However, there was also a significant market for salt herring from Britain. When a Parliamentary Committee took evidence on the state of British herring fisheries in 1798, exports to the West Indies had increased to 84,782 barrels, of which 51,892 barrels (61 per cent) were from Scotland, almost all shipped from Greenock. Exports to Ireland – almost entirely from Greenock – were similar and there were no other significant overseas markets. This gave Scotland 79 per cent of British exports of salt herring. Merchants on the Clyde reported that they had difficulty in meeting demand and that the West India fleet was sometimes delayed by a month or six weeks waiting for supplies of herring. These were fish taken as far north as Lewis and Lochbroom but, since most was caught and processed by large fishing 'busses' and not by a local 'boat fishery', the benefits accrued to Rothesay,

Campbeltown and Greenock. This also created openings for local seamen. One of the Greenock merchants, Hugh Crawford, said that he had to replace his crews every three years because those who had served as fishers and coopers on the busses were sought after by the masters of West India ships, often becoming second or even first mates.

Demand for salt herring continued after the end of the African slave trade in 1807 because there was then a greater economic imperative to keep slaves alive and 'breeding'. In 1816 Samuel Laing (1780–1868) of Papdale in Orkney, by then established as a merchant in Leith, travelled to London to meet his brother James (1766–1827), who had gone to Jamaica at an early age. James suggested that a herring fishery in Orkney might supply Jamaican estates. An agreement was entered into with Thomas Spenser & Company and a curing station was established at Papay Sound on Stronsay. The following year, four hundred boats were fitted out and for a number of years the salt herring were exported directly to the Caribbean.[22] This is a particularly clear example of the impact of the West India market on Scottish fisheries, and Stronsay later became the main base of the Orkney herring fishery.

Exports to the West Indies from Scotland were reported to have been between 50,000 and 80,000 barrels for a number of years before emancipation.[23] But freedom for slaves brought a collapse of the market and in June 1836 James Loch MP presented two petitions to Parliament:

> One was from the merchants and fish-curers of Wick, in the county of Caithness, and the other from similar parties in the town of Cromarty. The petitioners complained of the loss of the market which they formerly had for their fish in the West-India Islands, and of the impossibility which they found of opening new markets on the Continent.[24]

For the same reasons there had been earlier petitions in 1824 from both Tain and Cromarty opposing the immediate abolition of slavery.

THE FINANCIAL SECTOR AND BANKING

The work of Inikori and, more recently, of scholars such as Nick Draper has revealed the extent to which slavery drove the development of financial institutions in Britain. This was also true of regional banking, as is illustrated by the career of John Ross, the carpenter's son from Golspie in Sutherland who later became known as John Ross of Berbice (see Chapter 7). On his return to the Highlands, he built a small but elegant house in Inverness on Godsman's Walk, looking out over the River Ness to the mountains of the north and west, which he named Berbice Cottage. Ross was a key figure in the establishment of the Caledonian Bank in Inverness, which had twenty branches in the Highlands by 1845. On 12 November 1840 the directors and shareholders held a dinner at the Caledonian Hotel at which they presented Ross with a piece of silver plate in the form of a Scottish thistle, inscribed with their thanks to him for his services 'as Manager of the Bank at the period of its commencement, and subsequently as Chairman of the Board of Directors'. The new chairman proposed a toast, beginning with the following words:

> I happened to hear, this very day, of his honourable conduct abroad, and of his patriotic behaviour in the colony of Berbice, in a case which involved a concerted plan for the massacre of all the whites of that colony. Indeed, I have heard of several instances of his spirited conduct, and I am sure the gentlemen present will agree with me in thinking that such men are best fitted for promoting our home improvements.

He was referring to the slave rising of 1814 described in Chapter 7. In his reply, Ross expressed his particular appreciation that their gift was 'emblematical of *tir nam beann, nan gleann, nan gaisgeach*'.[25] This was the Gaelic motto, usually translated as 'land of mountains, of glens, and of heroes', which appeared on the bank's notes from its foundation in 1838. With the exception of a single note issued by the Leith Bank, its use of Gaelic was unique. The motto surrounded a panorama of Inverness and figures of a kilted man hunting deer and a young woman holding a sheaf of corn and tending sheep, all intended to inspire customer loyalty from the bank's clientele who were 'farmers, Highland gentry, fishermen, whisky distillers and grain factors'. The panorama changed over the years as new buildings appeared in the town but until the bank's demise in 1907 images 'of misty mountains, waterfalls and lochs, bountiful harvests and successful hunts coexist[ed] with castles and tartan-clad figures as well as prosperous cityscapes'. It embodied and promoted a sense of tradition, reliability and solidity combined with modernity. The Caledonian, in part established on the profits of slavery, thus asserted ownership of 'the picturesque national identity that had been popularised by Sir Walter Scott (and others) and appropriated to represent the country as a whole'. This was a period in which banknote symbolism was being widely deployed across Scotland to articulate loyalty to the Union while representing a distinctive Scottish identity. The Caledonian added to this iconography a further layer of a corporate Highland identity adapted to the changing and increasingly commercial world of the mid-1800s.[26]

IMPROVEMENT, CONTROL AND DISPOSSESSION

Common to both the exploitation of enslaved labour in the Caribbean and to developments in Scotland – to plantation, farm, factory and fishing boat – were the concepts and importance of 'control' and 'accountability'. 'Control' itself was originally a term from accounting – the *contreroulle* or counter-roll, a duplicate document which allowed cross-checking and verification. Its meaning expanded to encompass the supervision and management that was required for such verification. In Chapter 6, I used the work of Caitlin Rosenthal to examine the importance of management systems in Berbice in the early 1800s, in a colony where the challenge of control by a tiny white population was greater than anywhere else in the Caribbean. This was made possible in part by what has been called 'an accounting revolution with its locus in Scotland' which began with John Mair's *Book-keeping Methodiz'd* first published in 1736. New material specific to tobacco plantations was added in its 1741 edition and it did the same for sugar in 1757. The book, popular on both sides of the Atlantic, went through twenty-nine printings and eighteen numbered editions between 1736 and 1807. It was an approach rooted in the rationalism of the Scottish Enlightenment – and indeed in Scottish Presbyterianism's emphasis on moral and social accountability.[27]

There is a parallel with the systems of control which landowners began to seek through their rent rolls, through single tenancies and through long 'improving' leases. Prior to improvement, a typical rent roll for a lowland estate in the north would list the constituent *davochs* (a *davoch*, pronounced 'doch' – rhyming with the Scots word *loch* – was a unit of land relating to its productivity) and the principal tenant or tenants of each davoch. There would be a number of sub-tenants and others with minimal or no land (known variously as cottars, cottagers, mailers or scallags). The latter were, in an important sense, of no interest to the laird. His (occasionally her) relationship was with the small number of principal tenants, who paid rent and, in a traditional clan-based society, had also provided hospitality and men for military service in support of the chief. A commercial approach, however, meant both surveying the land (in order to have accurate data on its nature, extent and 'improvability') and recording who was on the land. This became the responsibility of the estate factor (land manager), holding delegated responsibility from and reporting to the landowner. The notion that the laird would want to have access to the detail of who was in which house and what rent, if any, they paid was novel. Once landowners had this baseline, they could consider who should be granted leases, on what terms and for how long – and the standard became a nineteen- or twenty-one-year lease, with detailed terms controlling the improvement and management of the land, granted to a single, enterprising tenant who was willing to invest in the land and benefit from the improvements. The mentality of control also made it seem more appropriate for landowners to move the population within their estate, mainly from inland areas, which could be converted to large 'sheep walks', to small holdings on the coast, where fishing and manufactures could be established. Finally, the simple 'clearance' of tenants was an option.[28] There was a common mentality of control linking estate management in Scotland and plantation management in the Caribbean. There was, however, no similarity between the treatment of Highland tenants and the brutality of slavery.

In his most recent work, *The Scottish Clearances* (2018), Thomas Devine presents an account of the changes across all parts of rural Scotland through which so many people lost their place on the land and became labourers on larger farms, workers in rural and urban industries or sought a new future through emigration.[29] Devine uses the terms 'dispossession' and 'the dispossessed' to capture the experience common to the Scottish Lowlands and Highlands and to identify the people who thus lost their traditional places and their sense of belonging on and to the land. He also articulates the distinctiveness of that experience in different locations and within the different cultures of Scotland.

This transformation of Scotland through changes in agriculture, the development of manufactures and other industries, and the growth of small and large urban centres all led to dispossession in the southern and central Scottish Lowlands and in the Border hills. But this was what Devine calls a 'dispossession by stealth' and very much a silent revolution, which neither provoked radicalism such as Thomas Spence's call in England for the common ownership of land nor passed into folk memory in song, verse or story. In contrast, the clearances of rural populations in the Highlands were traumatic and the memory of them became central to a sense of Highland history and of Highland identity. On a personal note, I can remember in Sutherland in the 1960s one man, who worked on the Countess of Sutherland's estate, whose relations would not speak to him because of the Sutherland family's role in the clearances; and another, a shepherd, whose family had come from the Borders generations before, but who still felt unwelcome in the parish church.

One reason for that difference between Lowland and Highland clearances was the thirty-year delay between the beginning of the Scottish agricultural revolution in the 1760s and the beginning of sustained agricultural change (including the introduction of sheep-farming) in the northern counties in the 1790s. It was a period during which the Highlands lost a significant number of its 'middling sort' – including many of the indigenous class of tacksmen and minor gentry – who might otherwise have become the entrepreneurs and administrators of the new order. It was men such as these who led early migrations of whole communities from the Highlands to what would become Upper Canada, after its acquisition from France in 1763. But many others, as individual adventurers, sought their fortunes in the East India Company, in British and Dutch military service, and above all in the colonies of the Caribbean.

The gap they left was recognised in 1808 by the Revd James Robertson in *A General View of the Agriculture in the County of Inverness*. He acknowledged a lack of initiative among Highland tenants but rejected the notion that this was the result of 'constitutional indolence'. He attributed it to the decay of traditional Highland society and a resulting social structure in which there were few 'in the middle ranks of life'. As a result, examples of good farming practice were not disseminated. Small tenants could not identify with the few rich farmers who were engaged in improvement and could not emulate them on a smaller scale because of the absence of examples from people 'of their own rank'. In Robertson's view, such was the resulting torpor among the tenantry that 'rather than relinquish their slovenly habits ... they adopt the desperate resolution of removing to America'.[30] Subsequent changes were consequently the more traumatic because they were imposed by an ever more distant elite and were often implemented by 'strangers' from the south. There were also fewer alternative sources of employment in the north. Ventures such as extracting soda and potash from kelp for use in soap-making and glass manufacture were short-lived and, despite slave cloth and Inverness bagging, no Highland industrial revolution took place.[31]

In both Highlands and Lowlands it was the same educated and increasingly professional class of estate factors and surveyors who carried out the practical business of agrarian reform, inspired by the spirit of the Scottish Enlightenment in general, the ideas of Adam Smith in particular, and the methodology of accounting. They worked to the principles summarised by Devine:

> Virtually all aspects of the traditional rural social and economic structure were vigorously condemned for irrationality and inefficiency. Uncritical intellectual legitimacy and credibility were afforded instead to virtually everything that was novel and innovative.
>
> ... the enthusiasts for improvement sometimes seem like religious zealots determined not only to take more profit from the land but to do so as an essential part of an ideological mission to modernize Scottish society.[32]

They sought the control and accountability which was simultaneously being pursued, of necessity, on the plantations. And the factor of a Highland estate reporting to an absentee landowner, whose social circle and business interests were in Edinburgh or London, was in some ways similar to a plantation attorney sending monthly reports across the Atlantic. These parallels and the language and attitudes of some estate factors have made it tempting to portray the transformation of the Highlands – or at least of the *Gàidhealtachd* (the Gaelic-speaking Highlands) – as a case of 'internal colonialism' within the British state. In the words of Devine, 'the Highland experience seems more akin to one of colonial dominion imposed on the region by outside influences' than it is to 'the pattern in Lowland rural society, where rulers and ruled shared broadly similar sets of social and cultural expectations'.[33]

COLONIAL OR COLONISED?

To the professional estate factors and managers who, as described above, were engaged in an ideological mission to transform the Highlands, the attitudes of the indigenous people appeared 'not only archaic but wholly irrational'. This was also true in the rural Lowlands where, although there were arguably more shared expectations between 'rulers and ruled', there was little sympathy from landowners' agents for 'traditional rural and economic structures'. The difference in the Highlands, Devine suggests, lay in the improvers' sense of inherent superiority. He describes Patrick Sellar, for example, who engineered the clearances on the estates of the Duchess Countess of Sutherland, as having 'nothing but racialized contempt for the people, dismissing them scathingly on more than one occasion as primitives or aborigines'.[34]

The language, actions and attitudes of men such as Sellar have led some to wonder if the *Gàidhealtachd* (the traditional Gaelic-speaking part of the Highlands and Islands) was itself an 'internal colony' of the British Empire. This is an important question. Does the application of a set of concepts developed in the study of colonialism enable a better understanding of Highland history, in particular a better understanding of 'clearance' and 'improvement'? The idea has acquired a following, I suspect in part because it places Highlanders on the right side of history as the victims of colonialism and as fellow actors in the process of de-colonialisation.[35] The most recent and nuanced argument for the use of the concept of internal colonialism is that of Iain MacKinnon, who is cited by Devine as the principal source in his discussion.[36] But I believe that for the era of British colonial slavery it is an unhelpful analogy.

We can certainly find some comparisons and connections

with colonialism in what was happening in the Highlands. Eric Richards has said of the Sutherland estate factor James Loch, who described his own role in terms of 'the governance of a small kingdom', that he was engaged in what was to him 'evidently a kind of colonization of the Highlands'. Elsewhere Richards noted that Loch's predecessor, William Young, more than once referred to the Sutherland estate as 'the new colony'. It was, Richards observed, an 'interesting reflection on his general attitude'.[37] And Allan Macinnes described the Malcolms of Poltalloch, who ordered evictions at Arichonan in Argyll, in similar terms:

> [They were] . . . attempting to impose a system of estate manage-ment in the Scottish Highlands that he and his family had already carried out successfully in Jamaica and in southern Australia . . . Mid-Argyll was being turned into the Argyll Colony of Jamaica.[38]

But Macinnes is clear that although there was an influence from practices in the Caribbean, the case for 'internal colonialism' in the Highlands is merely superficial.[39]

A key writer here is the German historian Jürgen Osterhammel, whose definition of colonialism is worth reproducing in full:

> Colonialism is a relationship of domination between an indigenous (or forcibly imported) majority and a minority of foreign invad-ers. The fundamental decisions affecting the lives of the colonised people are made and implemented by the colonial rulers in pursuit of interests that are defined in a distant metropolis. Rejecting cul-tural compromises with the colonised population, the colonisers are convinced of their own superiority and their ordained mandate to rule.[40]

Defined in this way, Devine comments that 'the Highland experience seems *more akin* [emphasis added] to one of colo-nial dominion' while acknowledging that 'there is no exact fit between this definition and the course of nineteenth-century Highland history'. Most obviously, 'the Gaels were not being dominated by a foreign power'.[41] In expanding the comparison, he identifies 'several aspects of their experience which suggest the impact of internal colonialism on Gaeldom'. These are the acquisition of most estates by 'affluent southerners', the man-agement of the larger farms by men recruited from outside the Highlands, and the ideology of improvers which was 'shaped by an ethos of market capitalism ultimately derived from the

Lowland and wider British experience'. That ethos which developed in the 'Lowland citadels of learning during the Scottish Enlightenment' included a theory of human development which, although it 'did not automatically lead to the racialized differentiation of Celts and Anglo-Saxons . . . did provide a foundation for Victorian intellectuals to do so in later years'.

Earlier in this chapter, I described how the loss of the tacksman class led to the improvement of agriculture from the 1790s being implemented by improvers who came from outside the traditional structures of rural society in the Highlands – something recognised at the time by the Revd James Robertson. It is the language and attitudes of some of these men which can make them seem like colonisers. But both the racial theories, which had their impact on perceptions of and attitudes towards Gaels, and the widespread acquisition of Highland estates, often bought with compensation money, were features of the Victorian period, not of the era of British colonial slavery. The timescales are important. The most intensive period of clearance in the Highlands was between 1790 and 1850, but it was only in the latter part of this period that such racialised views of Gaels became widespread, influential and intellectually respectable.

In the course of the nineteenth century, differences between 'races of men' were increasingly presented as determined by biology and on this basis it was asserted that there was a hierarchy which justified the domination of the lower races by the superior. This not only justified the existing subjugation of blacks by whites but encouraged a similar domination of 'Celtic' peoples by the higher 'Saxon or Teutonic' race and consequently of Gaels by Lowlanders (whether Scots or English). From the 1820s this pseudo-science of fixed racial types gained traction and, in reaction to the campaign for the abolition of slavery, these views were embraced by the pro-slavery lobby – and indeed by some abolitionists. But, in the words of Catherine Hall, it was not slavery but the prospect of emancipation 'which provoked new ways of categorising racial difference, for it raised the spectre of black peoples as free and equal'.[42] This can seem counterintuitive. We imagine that emancipation was a move away from racism and we struggle with the idea that there were racist abolitionists.

Intellectual debate in Scotland about race can indeed be traced back further, to Henry Hope (Lord Kames), who in 1774 floated the idea that the differences between races were so great that they could not have a common origin in a single act of creation. This generated much controversy, with most supporting a single origin in line with biblical accounts of the creation of Adam (and then Eve) as the 'first parents' of humankind. Race became an acceptable subject for medical papers and theses by the early 1800s and there was also an emerging cultural agenda of racialism at home, promoted first by John Pinkerton, who claimed that differences had long existed in Scotland between a 'Teutonic super-race and an inferior Celtic people'.[43] For some, including the Scottish doctor Robert Knox – who published his most influential work in 1850 and has been described, with some justification, as 'the real founder of British racism' – this led to an anti-colonial stance since in his view the races could not and should not mix and war was the natural relationship between them.[44] But more commonly it came to provide an intellectual justification for the colonisation of large parts of the world, including the 'scramble for Africa'. Thus both racism and colonialism – in its fullest sense as defined by Osterhammel – flourished by the mid-1800s after the end of British colonial slavery.

But in the late 1700s there were strong voices raised against the assertion of 'Saxon' or 'Teutonic' superiority. James Robertson (1739–1812), quoted earlier, was a commentator and not a professional factor or surveyor, but he was an enthusiast for improvement and produced three of the *General Views* commissioned by the Board of Agriculture in the early 1800s, for the counties of Inverness, Perth and Kincardine. He concluded *A General View of the Agriculture in the County of Inverness* (1808) with a spirited attack on the Earl of Selkirk's promotion of emigration to Canada, in Selkirk's recently published *Observations on the present state of the Highlands of Scotland*.[45] Robertson believed that Selkirk with his 'flowing prose' and 'rounded periods' was seducing the public into believing that 'the improvement of Highlanders required their expulsion' through emigration. Selkirk's assumption and his prejudices against Highlanders were, he argued, ill founded. Robertson can hardly be accused of 'racialized contempt' towards Gaels. He believed that their virtues were the product of a traditional 'tribal' and martial society – they were '*true men*; of strong passions, firm to the purpose they had in view, steady in their

resolution, unshaken in the cause they had adopted, and reso-
lute to accomplish their object'. Moreover, they were adaptable
and the opinion of those who knew Highlanders and spoke their
language was, 'Give an object to a Highlander, and let him be
ensured in the fruit of his labour; and no man in Britain will
exert more ardor and perseverance.'

Robertson reminded his readers that he had spent more than
fifty years in the Highlands as a parish minister, unlike the
'Noble Earl, who took a ride through the Highlands in 1792,
during the course of his academical studies'.[46] Robertson had a
significant impact on the portrayal of Highlanders in another
sphere. As the parish minister of Callander he was among the
first to promote the beauties of the Trossachs with the claim
that they 'beggar all description'. He was followed, and quoted,
by Dorothy Wordsworth and Lady Sarah Maitland – and by
Walter Scott, who Maitland believed should have dedicated *The
Lady of the Lake* to her as the person who 'discovered' the
area.[47] While the long-term impact of such romanticising of
the Highlands and of Highlanders had its negative aspects, it
would be perverse to class these views of the late 1790s and
early decades of the 1800s as part of a project to colonise the
Highlands.

Nor was Robertson a lone voice. In her study of the Highland
Society of London founded in 1778, Kate Louise McCullough
concludes that it built on its members' social and political connections in order to preserve Highland culture, provide charity
for poor Highlanders in London, and develop industries and
employment in the Highlands and Islands. This was not simply a
'top down' charitable venture. The network they created sought
views of 'common Highlanders', supported discussion of economic and social improvement, and brought ideas formed by
Highlanders and other intellectuals into the 'institutional fold'.
All this was with the aim of enabling 'common Highlanders [to]
pull themselves out of poverty and into the modern era, develop
markets for Highland goods, and preserve Highland culture'.[48]

The institutional framework and networks developed by the
Society allowed them to influence groups of Highland Scots
located in Great Britain, India and British North America:

> They succeeded in elevating the status of Highlanders in the public
> sphere not only as heroes of British conflicts abroad but also

as inheritors of an ancient race with a sophisticated culture . . . [P]airing this ancient sophisticated culture with modern economic and social development facilitated much of the HSL's support by the British government and the British public for their improvement projects.

McCullough argues that an overview of the activities of the members of the HSL, who sought development of the Highlands from within, provides a balance to the view that Highland landowners sought to integrate into Edinburgh and London-based elite society and apply economic ideas, formed in these circles, which were unsuited to the Highlands and Islands. Rather, an 'improvement plan' was conceived of at various HSL meetings in the late eighteenth century and implemented by colleagues in Edinburgh. It was a programme which sought alternatives to emigration. It did indeed include both the creation of new settlements in which industry would develop and the 'clearance' of land to increase grazing. But McCullough argues that 'improvement . . . was the method used by members of the HSL and their colleagues to preserve a culture perceived to be rapidly disappearing'.[49] While we can certainly find examples of individuals such as Sellar, Loch and Young who displayed an objectionable sense of cultural superiority, the prominence of opposing views among other 'improvers' is strong evidence against the conclusion that a form of colonialism was integral to these plans.

We should be particularly wary of drawing conclusions simply from the language used at the time. The wealth which might be generated in the colonies was enticing and it captured imaginations throughout Britain. A new field brought into cultivation might be thought of as a conquest – 'my America! my new-found-land'. For example, above the village of Porth in the Rhondda were *America Fawr* and *America Fach* (big and little America), fields created in the late 1700s, and above my own home in Cromarty is the American Road, which I suspect may have run past similar fields which were once someone's 'America'. In the same vein, a colony might be any settlement which would generate wealth on what was perceived to be uninhabited, unused or underused land. Or it might be the bringing together of people into larger settlements on such land. George Gun Munro of Poyntzfield, who provided much of the information for Sir John Sinclair's *Report on the state of agriculture in the northern counties of Scotland* in 1795, favoured the settling

of mailers (smallholders) on moor ground and advocated settling them in such 'colonies'. Sinclair described the mailers as
'the aborigines of improvement' but this was because they were
to be the first settlers, to be followed by 'the common farmer,
the farmer of the higher or last polish, and the land-owner'.
The inequity was one of class – not of 'race' – since these first
settlers would then be moved on to do the same on yet more
new-found-land. The Colony, above Munro's Poyntzfield estate,
five miles from my home, is still there, although its houses are
now in ruins. Further afield, in the later 1800s, the founder
of the Salvation Army, William Booth, created what he called
'labour colonies' in rural locations in the south of England for
destitute men from the cities. It was a model derived from an initiative of penal reformers in France who in 1839 established the
progressive Mettray Agricultural Colony to rehabilitate young
offenders. While Booth's scheme had a colonial link in that he
encouraged emigration, it would be superficial and misleading
to regard this use of language as in itself indicating an internal
colonisation of the Scottish, English or French countryside.

One of the most helpful analyses of the distinct nature of
the Highland economy in the era of slavery is that of Andrew
Mackillop, who proposes that military recruitment be considered as a 'regional response' to the 'market niche' opened for the
Gàidhealtachd in the expanding empire. The process of internal
colonisation, in which (if it were applicable to the Highlands)
value would be extracted from the 'colony' for the benefit of the
colonisers and the 'mother country', was thus inverted:

> State revenue in the form of army commissions for the Highland
> elite, Chelsea pensions and volunteer companies for the tenantry was
> redirected for use on the periphery. In this way military employment
> can be envisaged as simply one of the specialised economies that
> emerged from the region's inclusion within the empire – Gaeldom's
> equivalent of Glasgow's tobacco trade.

There was a degree of contempt for Highland soldiers, notoriously summed up in the comment of General Wolfe in 1751
that they would make excellent irregulars to combat Native
Americans and that it was 'no great mischief if they fall'. But
any such contempt did not prevent them being used, in a vivid
and suggestive phrase quoted by Eric Richards, as 'the shock
troops' thrown at the frontier – 'one of the population reserves

upon which colonial legislators and land speculators drew to subdue the wilderness and civilise the continent'.[50] While Richards described this attitude towards them as 'semi-colonial', it is important to remember the disproportionate presence of Highland Scots in the running of slave plantations – where, 'to terrify slaves, they needed people willing to inflict terror'. The plantation system – and this was where money was being made – relied on systematic barbarity in the treatment of blacks and a degree of solidarity among whites. This extended to those whites towards whom there might be such a degree of contempt:

> Ordinary whites did not have to be inveigled into white supremacy. They supported great planters because the economic system great planters established gave ordinary white men economic benefits, access to consumer goods, and the possibility of acting as domestic patriarchs.[51]

The last thing planters could afford to establish or encourage was the presence of a class of disaffected and poor whites who worked alongside enslaved Africans and felt themselves to be similarly victims of a colonial power.

In the era of British colonial slavery, the 'colonies' were principally the twenty-six colonies of North America and the Caribbean, reduced to thirteen by the American Revolution and added to by further acquisitions in 1815 following the French and Napoleonic wars. Their subject populations were their indigenous peoples, who died in large numbers from violence and from introduced diseases to which they had little resistance, and a 'forcibly imported' majority made up of enslaved Africans and their descendants. There is no parallel in the population of the Highlands. And crucially, as we have seen in earlier chapters, many of the people of the north of Scotland, including the people of the *Gàidhealtachd*, were active and often enthusiastic participants in the exploitation of enslaved Africans.

11

Landowners, Caribbean Wealth and Highland Identities

Wealth derived from slavery led to what has been called a 'revolution in landownership' in the Highlands and Islands of Scotland. The most recent study by Iain MacKinnon and Andrew Mackillop demonstrates that between 1726 and 1929 at least a third – and almost certainly much more than a third – of the land in the western Highlands and the islands passed through the hands of those enriched by slavery. In addition, wealth derived from slavery enabled a number of traditional land-owning families to maintain their ownership. In the combination of these traditional families and what has been called the 'new elite', more than half of the area was in the hands of families who had benefited significantly from slavery. The number of estate sales doubled in the 1830s, with a particularly high number in the years after 1834 when compensation was paid to slave holders, thus allowing them to reinvest the capital they had accumulated in the Caribbean.[1]

Although Devine had claimed in an earlier analysis that the 'new elite' came from 'outside the region', MacKinnon and Mackillop's research suggests that a substantial minority of slavery-related estate buyers after 1829 had strong pre-existing connections with the region. The landowners who had benefited from slavery thus included traditional owners, members of the new elite originating from within the region and members of the new elite from beyond the region. There were also those who had come from traditional land-owning families and who used wealth derived from slavery to lead lives elsewhere but in a style which made use of their Highland origins. In different ways these families used the proceeds of slavery to sustain, develop, adopt, invent or abandon a Highland identity.

The case studies which follow are examples of a variety of such responses. For the first four families their Highland identity, albeit in different guises, remained important. Lord Seaforth sought Caribbean wealth in order to sustain the traditional role, at least as he saw it, of a clan chief, benevolent to his tenants but giving up none of the luxury to which he felt himself entitled. The Malcolms of Poltalloch over four generations transformed themselves from a client family of the Dukes of Argyll to become powerful landowners in their own right, successful in business and creators of their own sense of identity in the fashion of the Victorian Highlands. The MacLeods of Colbeck, having failed to rise into the elite of Jamaican society, used continued profits from slavery to lead a fashionable life in Cheltenham, where they promoted what they saw as the Highland values of loyalty and service to the monarch. And the MacKinnons in Antigua maintained a sense of the importance of their Highland origins for over a century and a half – but it was an identity which adapted itself to embrace first loyalty to the Hanoverian state and later the romanticism of Walter Scott and what was to become the Victorian love affair with the Highlands. None of this addresses the sense of identity – or identities – of ordinary Gaels and other Highlanders. But it is important to explore how wealth from the plantations allowed some of the elite – both new and traditional – to sustain or invent a relationship with the Highlands. Finally, both Gordon of Cluny in South Uist and Benbecula and George Rainy in Raasay brought cold calculation and apparently unfeeling hearts to the management of their estates – Cluny with a contempt for Gaels which he did not have for his Aberdeenshire tenants and Rainy with an approach which seems to draw on his own experience in Demerara.

LORD SEAFORTH

Francis Humberstone Mackenzie (1754–1815) was the second son of the fourth son of Kenneth Mackenzie, 1st Earl of Seaforth and chief of Clan Mackenzie. As a young boy Seaforth caught scarlet fever, was left profoundly deaf and had some form of speech defect. Yet he overcame these disabilities and became proficient in signing, which he learned from Thomas Braidwood who laid the foundations for British Sign Language. Despite his distant relationship to the 1st Earl – and contrary to his expectations – he succeeded to the chiefship and lands in Ross-shire in 1783 and was raised to the peerage in 1797 with the title Lord Seaforth. His life and his roles as a Highland landowner, Governor of Barbados, and slave holder and plantation owner in Berbice are the subject of Finlay McKichan's *Lord Seaforth* (2018).[2] Seaforth was born and educated in England and served as a midshipman in the Royal Navy. McKichan argues that, since Seaforth's knowledge of the Highlands came largely from his father who died when Seaforth was seventeen, he grew up with 'what was becoming an old-fashioned view of the nature of a clan and the powers of its chief'. McKichan shows how Seaforth managed his Highland estates with a benevolent pater-nalism, resisting the clearance of tenants, turning down offers of higher rents from sheep farmers who would have removed them, and in general 'accepting a lower level of income . . . than many of his fellow Highland proprietors'. This did not cause him to lower his expectations of living in a style which was beyond these means and which included being elected twice as an MP, raising a regiment, and moving in a social circle in London which included the Prince of Wales. To balance his lower income with his lavish expenditure, he turned first to developing the kelp industry in Lewis, in which he 'showed least concern for the welfare of his small tenants . . . [who] were obliged to participate in a trade they heartily disliked . . . and creamed off for himself the vast bulk of the revenues'. He then used his political influence to secure an appointment as Governor of Barbados (1801–6) and, as described in Chapter 6, became part of a consortium which invested in Berbice. The equation was financially straightforward and morally reprehen-sible: if he could make enough money from the exploitation of enslaved Africans in Berbice, he could save his Highland estates, keep his tenants and maintain his personal lifestyle.

   McKichan is too sympathetic to Seaforth in attributing to him humanitarian motives in his role as Governor of Barbados, where he was, in reality, simply doing his job in implement-ing government policies. Moreover, as Stephen Mullen shows, he was closely associated with those in government who were opposed to abolition and who were working to undermine or delay moves to end the slave trade and chattel slavery. There is also no evidence that Seaforth's Berbice plantations were any different from others in their run-of-the-mill brutality.[3] But McKichan's research on the management of the Highland estates is illuminating and is an example of how Caribbean wealth might be used to stave off growing commercialism in the Highlands.

Three paintings commissioned by Seaforth illustrate key aspects of his life and character. In the mid-1790s Thomas Lawrence portrayed him resplendent – if rather formal and awkward – in full Highland military dress as colonel of the 78th Regiment, raised by him in 1793 for service in the French and Napoleonic wars. This was, McKichan suggests, Seaforth as he aspired to be: a soldier-chief leading his loyal Highland men into battle. A second portrait from about 1806, also by Lawrence, shows him seated and dressed as a modern gentle-man. This might be the Seaforth described by Walter Scott as a 'nobleman of extraordinary talents' who was a man of science, a fellow of the Royal Society, the Royal Society of Edinburgh and the Linnean Society, and after whom a genus of palm tree was named *Seaforthia*. And, third, is the monumental 'Alexander III of Scotland Rescued from the Fury of a Stag by the Intrepidity of Colin Fitzgerald', which he commissioned from Benjamin West in 1783 and which was completed the following year.[4] This displays the foundation myth of the Clan Mackenzie, in which their ancestor saves the King from being gored by a stag, giving the clan their motto and battle cry *Cuidich'n Righ* (Help for the King) and their emblem *Cabar Feidh* (The Stag's Head). It celebrated heroism and loyalty, and was painted by George III's own favourite artist. This is Seaforth at the centre of royal and political power. What is missing is any portrayal of Seaforth as slave holder. But, ironically, the work has left us one of the few portraits of a Scot in Berbice in the early 1800s. The model used by West for Seaforth's heroic ancestor Colin was said to have been Farquhar Macrae (1764–1806) of Inverinate, a doctor who, after a short time in China, joined his older brother in Demerara. He died in 1806 of wounds received in a duel occasioned by a petty, drunken quarrel over precedence between officers of the colony militia.[5]

In the end, Seaforth's speculation in Berbice, from which he hoped to reap one of the 'rapid and splendid fortunes' which he saw being made in the colony, was a failure and the Mackenzie lands in Kintail – the homeland of the Macraes – were sold.

Farquhar's older brother, Alexander Macrae (1756–1812), the last chief of Macrae, died far from his Highland home in the heat of a sugar plantation on the Demerara River and the Macrae family's legacy, through his brother and nephew, were the manuals of plantership described in Chapter 6, which enabled the more effective and efficient exploitation of enslaved labour.

MALCOLMS OF POLTALLOCH

Allan Macinnes' study of the Malcolms of Poltalloch (Argyll) shows how they transformed themselves by wealth made in Jamaica from the MacCallums, a satellite family of Clan Campbell in the earlier 1700s, to the Malcolms, independent landowners who had been able to 'break free from reliance on the patronage of Campbell Dukes of Argyll'.[6] They were among those, described in Chapter 3, who seized the opportunities created by the Union of 1707 and became a part of the 'Argyll colony' in Jamaica. As merchants they adopted the 'store system' which had been developed by Glasgow merchants in the tobacco trade in the Chesapeake (Virginia). That is, rather than simply shipping and selling produce on behalf of planters in return for a fee, they acted through local factors to buy the product (in this case, tobacco) and shipped and sold on their own behalf. This transferred risk from the planters to the merchants, but enabled the merchants, if successful, to make higher profits.[7] The Malcolms used the store system in Jamaica, Tobago, Antigua and Honduras, managing the higher levels of risk by spreading it between these operations and consistently repatriated wealth in order to build up and reinvest capital. By 1786 their business was based in London and they had become major, rather than minor, landowners in Argyll.

After John MacCallum (d. 1773), the first family member in Jamaica, their expanding business empire and their Argyllshire lands were owned over three generations by heads of the family named Neil Malcolm – Neil I (1732–1802), Neil II (1769–37) and Neil III (1795–1857). In 1848 the last of these lairds cleared the traditional township of Arichonan, a survivor of earlier changes in which between the 1730s and 1820s townships were broken up to 'make way for sheep-walks, cattle-ranches, and crofting communities in the first phase of Clearance'. Like Seaforth, the Malcolms had also used the opportunities during the Napoleonic wars to expand their interests in cattle, timber, lime and kelp while access to foreign markets was restricted. But with the Malcolms there was no counterbalance in a desire to maintain traditional ways of life. In the words of Allan Macinnes:

> Highland landowners were not only aspiring members of the Anglo-Scottish ruling elite. They were members of the imperial exploiting classes as planters, slave traders, colonial officials, military commanders and merchant adventurers. Ultimately, as demonstrated by the Malcolms of Poltalloch at Arichonan, the issue linking land ownership, land use and enterprise was that of mentality . . . Under Neill III, Mid-Argyll was being turned into the Argyll Colony of Jamaica.

The same view of Neil III is echoed in his entry in the ODNB.

> He represented the archetypal West Indian slave owner, the reactionary opponent of change embedded in the ancien régime: other such slave owners were more inclined to adapt to a changing world in Britain. When emancipation became imminent, he was among the slave owners who insisted on measures to ensure that the colonial plantations continued to be cultivated and on 'adequate compensation to the West Indian proprietors' (*Royal Cornwall Gazette*, 1 June 1833).[8]

By Neil III's death in 1857 the Malcolms had 'amassed so much land in Scotland and England on account of their investment diversification and West Indian credit lending that its total value stood at approximately £400,000'.[9] Macinnes' study is pioneering in tracing the Malcolms' success in repatriating capital from the colonies, enabling them to diversify into enterprises which included Australian sheep farms. This is in contrast to Lord Seaforth, and while Seaforth had unsuccessfully attempted to preserve an old-fashioned and increasingly anachronistic notion of the role of a Highland landowner and clan chief, the Malcolms could now create a new way of being Highland, under the influence of the romanticism of Walter Scott, the craze for tartan boosted by George IV, and later Queen Victoria's 'Balmoralism'. In the late 1840s, as Arichonan was being cleared, Neil III commissioned the architect William Burn to design the extravagant and now ruinous Calton Mor, later known as Poltalloch House, built in Jacobean style, with an orangerie lit by large panes of plate glass. There had been an earlier Poltalloch, later known as Old Poltalloch, which had been 'designed along colonial lines'.[10]

Either Neill III or the next head of the family, John Malcolm (1805–93), indulged in the re-creation of their family history by bringing together 'a series of sculptured gravestones of Gaelic chiefs and warriors from the later Middle Ages which he lodged in Kilmartin churchyard'. They were defaced by engraving on them the word 'POLTALLOCH', an act of historic vandalism which goes unremarked by Historic Environment Scotland which now cares for them. In death John Malcolm also reclaimed his Gaelic name and ancestry, being described as 'one of the most respected landlords in the West Highlands . . . chief of the Argyllshire sept, the Clan Challum or the M'Callums'.[11]

MACLEODS OF COLBECKS

In Chapter 3, I described how the MacLeods of Colbecks failed to rise into the elite of Jamaican society, but then in the person of John McLeod (1758–1822) combined Jamaican wealth, a military career and pride in Highland ancestry with life in fashionable society in Cheltenham. Indeed, Mrs MacLeod (of the Raasay family) was credited as a woman 'to whose fascinating manners, and elegant hospitalities, may in a very great degree be attributed that social intercourse, almost characteristical of Cheltenham, and which has had no small influence in inducing strangers to settle here'.[12] Both husband and wife brought a Highland element to this: he by raising the Princess Charlotte of Wales or MacLeod's Loyal Fencible Highlanders, of which he was colonel, and she as the hostess of the annual suppers and balls, with Highland dancing, which they held to celebrate the birthday of young Princess Charlotte. The family were presented to her in 1802, with the six-year-old princess dressed in MacLeod tartan. And in 1809, aged thirteen, on behalf of her father she presented MacLeod with an inscribed Highland broadsword. MacLeod described this as expressing the 'future king's . . . strongest favour for the clans, the representatives of those ancient "heroes of the mountains" . . . [and] his desire of instilling the same sentiments in the growing mind of his illustrious daughter'. A strathspey, 'Miss MacLeod of Colbecks', was composed about this time for one of their five daughters and on the Colonel's death in 1822, Raasay's piper John MacKay composed the piobaireachd 'Lament for MacLeod of Colbecks'. John MacLeod's death came shortly after George IV's visit to Edinburgh, with its celebration of rediscovered and invented Scottishness choreographed by Walter Scott. Colbecks, still funded in part by the Jamaican plantation, had been an active and enthusiastic participant in that creation.[13]

Meanwhile in Jamaica, *Colbeck* plantation was managed by relations – by a Raasay cousin, Malcolm McLeod (1765–1842), and by Alexander McLeod (1753–1839), a brother or half-brother of Colbeck senior's wife. There is a salutary reminder of the source of the McLeods' wealth in the diary of Alexander Innes (1792–1875) from Banff, who spent six weeks on the *Colbeck* plantation in 1824.[14] There were three hundred enslaved people and three white men, including the overseer, Mr Spenser. Almost immediately Innes had been 'shocked ... beyond measure at the inhuman, cruel manner Mr Spenser directed a poor old Female Slave to be punished who is large in the Family way ... Such conduct ... is enough to rouse the spirit of revenge in any people.'

Spenser was dismissed a few days later and replaced by an Orkney man named Simpson, a 'vulgar looking fellow' who 'commenced his career by flogging six old Slaves'. Innes also described the ferocious Porto Rico bloodhounds used to hunt down runaway slaves.

THE MACKINNONS IN ANTIGUA

As with the Malcolms of Poltalloch, the maintenance, redis-covery and reinvention of Highland identity can be see in the Mackinnon family in Antigua. In his study of Antigua between 1730 and 1775, Richard Sheridan showed that thirteen of the sixty-five families on the island who could be characterised as 'colonial gentry' originated in Scotland. It is, once more, a strik-ingly high figure in what had been until 1707 an English 'sugar island'. By 'colonial gentry' he meant those who, in the words of a contemporary writer, were 'able to return to *Europe* and to live there in affluence and Splendour' on the profits of their plantations, as distinct from '*mere* Planters', many of whom owed 'more than their estates were worth'. Almost all of these thirteen Scottish 'dynasties' were of Lowland origin.[15] However, one of the earliest of the Scots families to become established in the island was from the Highlands – that of Donald or Daniel MacKinnon (1653–1720) from Skye.[16]

MacKinnon was the second son of Lachlan Mor MacKinnon, the clan chief who had fought for Charles II at the battle of Worcester in 1651. Attachment to the cause of the house of Stuart would remain important to the senior line of the family. At some point, according to tradition as a result of a quarrel with his father but perhaps simply to seek his fortune, Donald went to Antigua, where he first acquired land in 1693. Shortly afterwards he married Elizabeth Thomas, the daughter of an English plantation owner and widow of the colony's Governor. Through this, and other advantageous marriages, the Mackinnons came to own over 1,200 acres of land and over two hundred enslaved people.[17]

Two portraits from the Mackinnon family give us some insight into British, Scottish and Highland identities in the island during the long eighteenth century. William Mackinnon, the son of the original Mackinnon settler, married in Antigua and had four children, two of whom – Elizabeth (1729–80) and William (1732–1809) – were the joint subject of a portrait by William Hogarth known as 'The Mackinen Children', painted about 1747. This is now held by the National Gallery of Ireland. While it is possible that the portrait was painted from miniatures of the children, it is more likely that they had come to London from Antigua with their parents. If so, then the family may have been survivors of the fleet of 120 ships which sailed from the Leeward Islands in August 1747, of which only thirty-five vessels reached England. In a detailed analysis of 'The Mackinen Children', the art critic Arthur Marks teases out the messages embedded in the painting. The children, aged eighteen and fifteen if the date is correct, stand on a terrace by a two-headed sunflower, while a small dog looks on. Marks argues that one function of these objects, for a contemporary audience, was to symbolise loyalty – in this case to the monarch, as the faithful dog gazes at the sunflower. In 1747 this had a particular significance as the chief of the clan, the children's great-uncle John 'Ian Dubh' Mackinnon, stood accused of treason as an active supporter of the Jacobite Rising of 1745. Perhaps, Marks suggests, the children had come to London with their parents who were there to press the claim of the junior line as loyal Hanoverians? It is a coincidence which Marks describes as 'striking' but which, he admits, relies on much surmise. Other items in the picture, particularly the shells which Elizabeth holds in her lap, indicate the children's exotic background in the Caribbean.

The older of the two Mackinnon children in Hogarth's portrait of 1747 was Elizabeth Mackinnon. In 1752 she married Dr Thomas Fraser (1726–60) of Balnain (Inverness-shire), who had graduated from Glasgow University in 1749 and established a medical practice in the island. Douglas Hamilton points out that by 1750 nineteen of the thirty-two doctors in Antigua were Scots.[18] Half a century later, in 1808, the fifteen-year-old William of the portrait became, at the age of seventy-six, the 31st chief of the clan, following the death without a direct heir of John Mackinnon, the grandson of the Jacobite, Ian Dubh. Although William died the next year, and despite the fact that all the Mackinnon lands in Skye had been sold off by 1791, the chiefship was immensely important to William's heir, his grandson William Alexander Mackinnon (1784–1870), who became the 32nd chief in 1809. In 1810, when he joined Walter Scott on a visit to Staffa and Ulva, Scott noted that:

> Mackinnon of Mackinnon, a young gentleman born and bred in England but nevertheless a Highland chief ... now visits the Highlands for the first time [and] is anxious to buy back some of the family property which was sold long since.[19]

Scott believed that it was Mackinnon's father who had 'acquired wealth' but it is more likely that it was his grandfather, the William Mackinnon of Hogarth's portrait, who had successfully begun to repatriate funds from Antigua. The family continued to own the plantation *Mackinnon's Estate* and in 1834 William Alexander Mackinnon, the 'Highland chief' who had accompanied Scott on his tour, received a third of the £3,942 compensation payment for 276 enslaved people.[20] He became a long-serving Member of Parliament and an early supporter of the RSPCA. At the annual meeting of the Society in 1836, two years after receiving compensation, Mackinnon without irony expressed his pride in the fact that 'to Englishmen alone is the credit due, of having been the first to take up the cause of the suffering dumb creation'.[21]

Mackinnon's enthusiasm for his Highland heritage led him to have his portrait painted in Highland dress, possibly by the artist Sir George Hayter, the portrait and history painter to

Queen Victoria. Hayter produced works which were 'unexciting in their handling but composed with dexterity and accomplished grandiloquence'.[22] There is certainly such grandiloquence in the portrait of Mackinnon, who no doubt read and appreciated lines by Walter Scott in *The Lady of the Lake*, published in 1810, the year of their tour together:

> Hail to the chief, who in triumph advances,
> Honour'd and blest be the evergreen pine!
> Long may the tree in his banner that glances,
> Flourish the shelter and grace of our line.

As enthusiasm for all things Highland developed in the Victorian era and weighty matters, such as clan tartans and badges, were codified, Clan Mackinnon declared its traditional emblem to be the evergreen Scots pine.

The two portraits are widely different in style and message, moving from a presentation of exoticism combined with British loyalty to a reassertion of a largely imagined ancient identity, now safe and acceptable in the culture of nineteenth-century Britain. But that in itself reflects the fluidity of British, Scottish and Highland identities in the period and we should recognise that negotiating these identities was as much a part of life in the Caribbean as 'at home'. However, as these identities developed, the link to the wealth generated in the Caribbean was conveniently forgotten. Information on today's Clan Mackinnon website includes the following:

> The brutal but well-known clearing of the Highlands to make room for the more profitable sheep saw the MacKinnons, after more than 1000 years in the Hebrides, scattered around the globe.[23]

There is no mention of the Mackinnons' involvement in the Caribbean slave plantations.

Two further case studies show how wealth from the plantations was applied to the transformation of the Highlands in ways which were brutal, uncaring and displayed contempt for or indifference to the Gaels who were cleared from the land. The clearances in Uist and Barra by John Gordon of Cluny in the late 1840s were among the most callous. Finally there is George Rainy and his clearance of Raasay. This is of particular significance because it is one of the few examples – perhaps the only one – of clearance carried out by an individual who had himself managed a plantation where, if he did not hold the whip, he certainly instructed the slave driver.

GORDON OF CLUNY

In Chapter 5, I described how Alexander Gordon of Cluny (Aberdeenshire) became 'very rich' in Tobago before returning to London in the 1790s. At his death in 1801 he left his estates to his nephews John Gordon (1776–1858) and Alexander Gordon (1779–1839). This John Gordon (who became IV of Cluny) received £12,483 compensation in 1834, and in 1838 bought Benbecula and South Uist from Reginald George Macdonald, last Captain (chief) of Clanranald, and Barra from the bankrupt Macneills. Eric Richards has written scathingly about him:

> In the demonology of the Highland clearances [John] Gordon of Cluny ranks high ... [His] Barra evictions in the late 1840s were the most sensational model of a Highland clearance. They combined violence, forced emigration, landlord trickery, starving peasants, conniving factors, premature deaths and the fawning collusion of the minister of the established church.[24]

Cluny was also responsible for the extraordinary rebuilding of Cluny Castle (Aberdeenshire) between 1836 and 1840, to a design by John Smith which has been described as having 'something possessed' about it.[25]

Over three generations the family had a reputation for a miserliness which amounts to a caricature of the mean Scotsman. Towards the end of his life John would drive miles out of his way in order to avoid toll bars on the roads, and similar tales were told about his father.

> As he advanced in years his passion for saving became a perfect disease. He declined to move about for fear of incurring expense, and latterly he refused to get up out of bed on the ground that he could not afford it.

His grandfather had founded the family fortunes by ensuring that 'every shilling he got within his fingers stuck to them'. By the time of his death in 1858, John Gordon was reputed to be 'the richest commoner in the kingdom' of Scotland and left an estate valued at £2 million.[26]

Other than a military tour through Egypt in 1804/5 – where he carved his name on over a dozen monuments – and four years as a Member of Parliament (1826–32), Gordon mainly concerned himself with expanding and managing his estates. Thomas Devine describes Gordon as the 'classic case' of an adventurer who purchased lands in the Western Isles 'partly *because* rentals were low and the land was poor in the hope of transforming its prospects and so making huge gains in the long term'.[27] It is perhaps no coincidence that his rival bidder for the Clanranald lands was the notorious Patrick Sellar, responsible for implementing the earlier Sutherland Clearances.[28] Devine describes Gordon as 'an extremely hard-headed businessman who undertook very careful supervision of his properties; it was said that nearly every receipt of rent was signed by his own hand.' Yet the speculation produced minimal returns on his investment and by 1848 the rental value of his estates had been halved and he had been obliged to pay out nearly £8,000 in famine relief. Gordon turned to clearance, evicting around three thousand people and forcing or cajoling them into emigration to Canada. Immediately before this, the Revd Norman MacLeod (1783–1862), an influential parish minister, Gaelic scholar and educationalist, known as *Caraid nan Gaidheal* (Friend of the Gaels), described his visit to Gordon's estates:

> On the beach the whole population of the country seemed to be met, gathering the precious cockles ... I never witnessed such countenances, – starvation on many faces – the children with their melancholy looks, big looking knees, shriveled legs, hollow eyes, swollen-like bellies, – God help them, never did I witness such wretchedness.[29]

The evictions and migration involved handcuffing some individuals and hunting down 'runaways' with dogs. The contemporary historian of the Highland clearances Alexander Mackenzie (1838–98) remarked: 'For cruelty less savage, the slave-dealers of the South have been held up to the execration of the world.'[30] As so often, this comment is at best 'tone deaf' to the sufferings and status of the enslaved people of the USA. Yet it reveals the moral effects of geographical distance. Mackenzie knew, and empathised, with the people of Uist and Barra; he did not know the enslaved of the American South. And, in the same way, Gordon of Cluny enacted these barbarisms on the people of Uist and Barra, but was regarded in his native Aberdeenshire, among his own people, as 'an assiduous, innovative and generous landlord'.[31] It was said that, 'He liked to have about him the old tenantry, seldom parting with any who had occupied his land for any considerable time and were willing to remain on it.'[32]

GEORGE RAINY OF RAASAY

George Rainy's role as a partner in 'McInroy Sandbach & Co., looked up to as the Rothschilds of Demerara', has been described in Chapter 10. At emancipation he was the primary claimant for over £50,000 compensation for almost a thousand slaves and a secondary claimant for a number of other plantations. After having spent more than thirty years in the colony, he returned to Britain in the autumn of 1837, dining with John Gladstone on his arrival. He was now usually described as 'George Rainy Esq of Liverpool'. He probably brought with him (if they had not been sent ahead) his two 'coloured' daughters, Mary Augusta (1828–54) and Elizabeth Jemima (1830–99), who in 1841 were attending a boarding school for girls in Minchinhampton (Gloucestershire). Both girls later emigrated to Australia.

Rainy then married three times. His first wife, who he married in 1839 when he was forty-eight, was Margaret Janetta Louisa Darroch, the daughter of General Duncan Darroch of Gourock – almost certainly a man of colour since he was an illegitimate child born in Jamaica. Rainy's niece, Susan Parker, was already married to Margaret's brother. Margaret died only twenty months later and in 1844 Rainy, now fifty-three, married twenty-four-year-old Margaret Elizabeth Haygarth, with whom he had his only surviving legitimate child, George Haygarth Rainy. In late 1844, or in 1845, Rainy had left Margaret – who was either pregnant or a new mother – for an extended tour of the continent with his nephews Robert Rainy and James Brown. His last marriage, in 1860 at the age of sixty-nine, was to the former infant prodigy, the harpist Isabella Rudkin, now a widow of forty-one.

It was in 1845 that he became a landed Highland gentleman, buying the island of Raasay from the struggling MacLeods (see Chapter 3). All the evidence suggests that he was a ruthless landlord, clearing the island of many of its people and before that exercising a level of control over their lives which was reminiscent of the owner of a plantation. When evidence was taken from crofters in 1883 by the the Government-appointed

Napier Commission, seventy-eight-year-old Donald McLeod recalled this:

> Mr Rainy enacted a rule that no-one should marry on the island. There was one man there who married in spite of him, and because he did so, he put him out of his father's house, and that man went to a bothy – to a sheep cot. Mr Rainy then came and demolished the sheep cot upon him, and extinguished his fire, and neither friend nor anyone else dared give him a night's shelter. He was not allowed entrance into any house.[33]

Rainy subsequently cleared his estate of many of its people. In the words of Donald McLeod:

> I don't remember the first removing, but I remember Mr Rainy about thirty years ago clearing fourteen townships, and he made them into a sheep farm which he had in his own hands ... [He cleared] Castle, Screpidale, two Hallaigs, Ceancnock, Leachd, two Fearns, Eyre, Suisinish, Doirredomhain, Mainish ... The only occupants of that land to-day are rabbits and deer and sheep.

Rainy's clearance of Hallaig has become an icon of the wider Highland Clearances through the poem of that name by Sorley Maclean – an 'icon' in the true sense of an image through which a greater reality can be glimpsed. The poem was described by Seamus Heaney as 'haunted by the great absence that the Highland clearances represent in Scots Gaelic consciousness':

> 'Hallaig' is at once historical and hallucinatory, a poem in which the deserted homesteads of a little settlement on the Island of Raasay are repopulated by a vision of 'a fair field full of folk'. It arises out of MacLean's sense of belonging to a culture that is doomed but that he will never deny.

Yet Rainy is often misleadingly described as, for example, a 'pious gentleman from Edinburgh' or 'a Lowland business man who had made a fortune from the West Indies sugar trade' or 'a wealthy merchant trader'. All of which omit the two salient facts that he was a slave holder directly involved in the slave plantations of Demerara and that he was born and raised in the Highlands, a son of the manse in the parish of Criech.[34] He was a highly intelligent man, educated at Marischal College (Aberdeen), where he was awarded the 'silver pen' as top student in Greek in his year, and at the University of Glasgow. And he must surely have been aware of the idealistic 'Constitution of

Creich', a charter of tenants' rights proposed in the 1790s for his native parish by the philanthropic landowner George Dempster of Skibo and Dunnichen. We know nothing of Rainy's inner life, his portrait is lost, and we are left only with the chilling description of him as 'slow-spoken . . [with] a sharp visage, high thin nose, and a cold quiet calculating grey eye'.[35]

A DANCE ON THE BACK OF BEHEMOTH

In Cheltenham on 7 January 1809, the MacLeods' celebrations for the thirteenth birthday of Princess Charlotte continued into the evening. The dancing began with a reel which the newspapers reported as '*Bannah Vochrierchattah*' – a rendition of *Ban Mhorair Chataibh*, the Great Lady of Sutherland. A footnote explained that she was 'The Chieftain Countess of Sutherland, now Marchioness of Stafford'.[36] Her English husband later became the first Duke of Sutherland and at his death in 1833 he was described by the diarist Charles Greville as 'a leviathan of wealth; I believe the richest individual who ever died'. That wealth was the return of about £200,000 a year from the Duke's portfolio of English and Scottish estates, investments in railways and canals, and the interest on government and private stockholdings. The phrase was used as the title for Eric Richards' account of the family and of the clearances in Sutherland for which they were responsible: *The Leviathan of Wealth: The Sutherland Fortune in the Industrial Revolution*.[37] It was in 1809, the year that the MacLeods danced in Cheltenham, that William Young and Patrick Sellar, the architects of the Sutherland clearances, arrived in the county.

The Sutherlands were so rich that they appeared to sit above the scramble for profits in the slave trade and the slave-worked plantations. Certainly there is no record of compensation payments but the Countess' mother, Mary Maxwell, had inherited £5,000 in 1741 from her father who was 'mostly in trade and plantations in Jamaica'.[38] It no doubt aided her progress to marriage with the Earl of Sutherland. The diarist Greville meant no disrespect to the Duke, or his wife, in his use of the phrase 'leviathan of wealth'. A 'leviathan' had come to mean a great whale and by extension a hugely powerful person or institution.

But the Leviathan in many early traditions was primordial – a monster of the deep along with its fellow creature of chaos, the land monster Behemoth. Both were vast, overwhelming, and – without divine aid – beyond human control. Much attention has rightly been focused on the Highland clearances and on this Leviathan of Wealth straddling Sutherland and Staffordshire. But we lack a term for the great crime and the monstrosity of all that was chattel slavery. The refinements and niceties of polite society – the world of the Duke of Sutherland and the Duchess Countess Elizabeth, with its growing romanticism of the Highlands – were but a dance on the back of this Behemoth.

12

Enslaved Blacks and Black Servants

In July 1750 a party of the 6th Regiment of Foot, stationed on Loch Leven in Lochaber, arrested a man they described as 'a Black belonging to Mr Stewart of Appin, dressed in tartan Livery, turned up in yellow'.[1] The description suggests that this was a coat in Lowland style, lined in yellow, but the use of tartan nevertheless contravened that section of the Act of 1746 for the *Abolition and Proscription of the Highland Dress*, which stated that 'no tartan or party-coloured plaid of stuff shall be used for Great Coats or upper coats'. And so he was sent on to the nearest Justice of the Peace. His master was Dougal Stewart, the last chief of the Appin Stewarts, who although from a Jacobite family did not take part in the Rising of 1745. He has been described as 'existing between two worlds':

> In the Highlands, amid scenery (soon to captivate all Europe) of Ossianic romance, he dwelt in a classical mansion. In his Edinburgh tenement flat, he hung a portrait 'in Highland garb' alongside Piranesi etchings. He spoke Gaelic; he read the *Spectator*; he kept a broadsword in the attic; he bred canaries; he dabbled in Freemasonry; and he dressed his black servant, Orinoce, in tartan livery.[2]

Even his servant's slave name – Orinoce – had connotations in the culture of the genteel Edinburgh society in which Stewart moved. *Oroonoko: or, the Royal Slave* was a work of prose fiction by the pioneering female author Aphra Behn (1640–89), portraying a noble African prince enslaved in Suriname. It was adapted for the stage in 1695 and was frequently revived during the first half of the 1700s. Thus Stewart's Orinoce was not only a servant but a curiosity, a fashionable accessory and a conversation piece.

A domestic slave was a symbol of status and, until the early 1700s, had been mainly associated with the aristocracy and the royal court. The Restoration of Charles II as monarch of Scotland and England in 1660 increased contacts between the English court and courts abroad, and as a result black grooms and pageboys became both more fashionable and, it can be said – since they were regarded as chattels – more 'readily available'. In 1662, for example, Samuel Pepys noted in his diary that the Earl of Sandwich had brought back for his daughters 'a little Turk and a negro' along with 'many birds and other pretty noveltys'. Three years later, Pepys was entertained by Sir Robert Vyner, a rich banker and goldsmith who was then Lord Mayor of London. He was shown 'a black boy that he had that died of a consumption; and being dead, [Vyner] caused him to be dried in a Oven, and lies there, entire in a box'. The Lord Mayor might have lost a servant, but he had kept an exotic curiosity.[3]

BLACK SLAVES AND SERVANTS IN SCOTTISH PORTRAITS

Across both kingdoms the figures of black servants began to appear in portraits, often wearing a locked, silver neck-collar – a symbol of both wealth and control.[4] The fashion spread to the Scottish aristocracy and when the Flemish artist John Baptiste de Medina (1621–1710) settled in Edinburgh about 1690, with a virtual monopoly on portrait-painting for the upper classes, he included a young black boy in his portrait of James Drummond (1673–1720), the son of the fourth Earl of Perth.[5] It was probably painted about 1700 after James had returned from his studies in Paris, and the enslaved boy may have been 'acquired' there. The unnamed and unknown boy is the only black figure in Medina's many Scottish portraits and to date we know of only one other enslaved pageboy in Scotland in the early 1700s, a six-year-old kidnapped from the Guinea Coast of Africa and given the Latin name Scipio. He was brought from Jamaica to Scotland in 1702 by a naval officer, Captain Andrew Douglas. Scipio, aged eight, became a servant to Douglas's daughter Jean and her husband Sir John Kennedy of Culzean, who she married in 1705. He was their servant at Culzean Castle (Ayrshire) until 1725, when he was baptised and then manumitted at the age of twenty-eight. He took the surname Kennedy, remained as a servant to the family, married (after being rebuked before the Kirk Session for fornication) and had eight children.[6]

In 1733 another prominent Scottish nobleman had his portrait painted with a black servant, a young groom holding the bridle of his horse. George Keith (1692/3?–1778) was the tenth and last of the Earls Marischal of Scotland. He forfeited the title – and his estates – for taking part in the Jacobite Rising of 1715, in which he fought alongside James Drummond at the battle of Sheriffmuir. In 1719 he commanded the 300-strong Spanish force which landed on the island of Lewis in support of a further attempt to place James VII (the 'Old Pretender') on the throne. Keith was seriously wounded at the battle of Glenshiel in Wester Ross and fled to Valencia in Spain. He remained a Jacobite but came to detest James's heir, Charles Edward Stuart ('Bonnie Prince Charlie'), and took no part in the Jacobite Rising of 1745. It was *c.* 1733 that he had this portrait – an oil on copper – painted by the Italian artist Placido Costanzi.[7] Although it shows his family seat of Dunnottar Castle (Stonehaven) in the background, the portrait was made on the continent and the Earl did not return to Scotland until the 1760s, and then only briefly. The enslaved boy in the portrait was Mocho (also given as Motcho and Motchô).

Mocho was given to the Earl Marischal by a fellow officer in Spanish military service, the Chevalier Blaise-Marie d'Aydie (1692–1761). In the portrait he wears silver earrings, a silver collar on his neck and fine clothes, and his gaze is fixed on his master. If he was, say, ten or eleven years old, he would have been born *c.* 1722. George Keith also had a Turkish slave called Ibrahim and they were soon joined in the household by a young prisoner of war – Stepan, a Kalmyk from the north Caucasus. Kalmyks were the only Buddhists in Europe and Stepan was said, by some, to be related to the Dalai Lama. Keith, nominally a Scottish Episcopalian but in fact a sceptic, made no attempt to convert any of his servants to Christianity and referred to the Buddhist Stepan as his 'chief chaplain'. Later a Turkish girl, Emet Ullah, joined them. It was a remarkable and unusual household. The Earl would later describe Emet Ullah as his daughter, Ibrahim as his illegitimate son, and Stepan and Mocho as his bastards – but none of these were literally true. He also called the philosopher Jean-Jacques Rousseau his son and Rousseau addressed Emet Ullah as 'my sister'.

Figure 12.1 Motchô, an enslaved boy in the household of George Keith, 10th Earl Marischal. Detail from portrait attributed to Placido Costanzi, oil on copper, *c.* 1733. © National Portrait Gallery, London.

By 1736 Mocho had become the valet to the Earl's younger brother, James Francis Edward Keith (1696–1758), who had also fought in the '15 and the '19 Jacobite risings and gone into exile. James Keith went on to a distinguished career as a soldier in Spanish, Russian and Prussian service. As a postscript to a letter written in June 1736 by George (in Avignon) to his brother James (now in the Russian army), there is a playful note to Mocha, written in Spanish:

> Mr Mocho, You are a very big scamp, not to send me or Stepan a word. Try to take a Tartar man for me, and a Tartar lady for Stepan, and every time my brother writes to me, you must write to me too; if not I will go and pull your ears. Stepan shaves me like the best of barbers; you know how to shave, to eat, to drink. Good bye.

Stepan, the Kalmyk, added his own note: 'Friend Mocho,— place me at the feet of your master. Try to treat him well, for he deserves it, and send me your news.'

Mocho served James 'faithfully through all his campaigns'. This included James's participation in the coup d'état of 1741 which brought the Empress Elizabeth to power in Russia, a short time as *de facto* viceroy of Finland, and then in Prussian service under Frederic the Great as a Field Marshal commanding the siege of Prague and the defence of Leipzig in the Seven Years War. After James Keith's death in battle at Hochkirk in 1758, Mocho rejoined the household of the Earl Marischal, then serving as Prussian ambassador in Neuchâtel, an independent canton now part of Switzerland. He continued to live there, provided with a pension, after the Earl's death in 1778. Although Mocho never set foot in Scotland and never saw Dunnottar Castle – unless he accompanied the Earl Marischal to Edinburgh and the north-east in 1763/4 – he lived his life in two important Scottish households in Europe, part of what another Jacobite lord called the Earl Marischal's 'ménagerie of young heathen' which was known not only to Rousseau but to Voltaire and David Hume.

With the growth of English and Scottish involvement in the slave trade – from Africa and within the Caribbean and North America – and with the increase in slave-holding, the possession of a black enslaved domestic servant in Britain became a more common and more affordable luxury, no longer the sole preserve of the old aristocracy around the royal courts.[8] In 1765, for example, a young black slave/servant – possibly named Jolly – was painted along with his master, Sir William Maxwell of Monreith (Galloway).[9]

ENSLAVED SERVANTS AND RUNAWAY SLAVES

In 1771 Dougal Stewart would probably have considered himself to be the owner, rather than the master, of Orinoce and there were certainly other black slave-servants in the north of Scotland. In the same year the slave trader James Baillie, the middle of the three Dochfour brothers (see Chapter 2), returned from St Kitts and travelled north with his cousin Edward Fraser of Reelig, from whom he had agreed to rent the small estate of Moniack (Inverness-shire). With them was James's nineteen-year-old personal servant, 'a Negro young man born on the Coast of Guinea'. He had been given his master's name – James Baillie – and was baptised at Balchraggan, above Loch Ness, in the presence of two other servants and the local schoolmaster.[10]

In the same year an enslaved black East Indian man, Caesar, ran away from Novar (Ross-shire), where he was a cook for Colonel Hector Munro (1726–1805). Munro was not an aristocrat but a soldier from a minor family in Ross-shire who used the fortune he made in India to expand his landowner-ship and improve his estates. About 1785, after his final return to Scotland, Munro had his portrait painted with his Indian career indicated by a battle scene in the background and, in the foreground, a palm tree and a cannon, inscribed 'Buxar' and 'Ponticherry' – two of his victories. A black servant holds the bridle of his horse, but by this date servants were dressed in livery not in silver slave-collars.[11]

Also in 1771, an enslaved East Indian, a woman from Bengal named Bell or Bellinda, was convicted of killing her newborn child and disposing of the body in the River Leven. She was the 'slave or servant' of John Johnstone and his wife, and had been with them in London for four years before they moved to Balgonie Castle (Fife). The involvement of the extended Johnstone family in Grenada has been described in Chapter 4, and John Johnstone's household included another black 'slave or servant' named Molly. Bell claimed that her son had been stillborn but under Scots law the death of a child when the pregnancy had been 'concealed' and no medical attention had been sought was itself a crime equivalent to murder. Bell took the only course open to her by petitioning to be banished to the colonies for life, an established practical means under Scots law of securing a reprieve from capital punishment and not therefore, in any meaningful sense, freely entered into. This was normally accompanied by a contract of indenture as a servant in the colony for a specified number of years – but because Bell was a slave in Scotland she was to be sold in America as 'a slave for life'. This was the last occasion on which a British court would try someone as a slave and sentence them into slavery.[12]

Scots law was, however, grappling with at least some aspects of slave-holding in Scotland. In that same year, 1771, in an appeal to the House of Lords in a divorce case, the issue was whether or not an unbaptised enslaved servant could be called as a witness. The witness in question was Latchemo – who was a 'pagan' rather than a Muslim or a Jew – a servant in the household of Sir William and Lady Maxwell at Springkell House (Eaglesfield, Dumfries-shire). Latchemo was a witness to a liaison between Margaret Porterfield, the wife of Lady Maxwell's brother Stewart Nicolson, and a young estate overseer. She had been left at Springkell in the autumn of 1768 without her husband and had been discovered in the attic bedroom of the overseer. The courts avoided a decision on the admissibility of Latchemo's testimony and the divorce was granted on other evidence, but the case is a reminder of the proximity of black servants to the most intimate details of the lives of their masters and mistresses. What was more significant in legal terms were the arguments brought forward about the status of people such as Latchemo – were they possessions or persons?[13]

The legal status of these servants in Scotland was to change – or be clarified – in January 1778 when the full Court of Session found in favour of Joseph Knight (*c.* 1750?–?) in his action against his master, the merchant John Wedderburn (1729–1803). 'Joseph Knight' was a slave name given to him after he was kidnapped from Africa and transported to Jamaica in the *Phoenix* of Bristol, captained by a John Knight. Joseph came to Scotland as a personal servant to Wedderburn, who had bought the Ballindean estate on the north shore of the Firth of Tay. Wedderburn's wife was Margaret Ogilvy, a niece of John Johnstone (above), and these were circles in which the possession of black domestics had its own prestige. In 1772, aware of the judgement in the Somerset case in England (see p. 56), Joseph Knight demanded his freedom – and back wages – and when Wedderburn refused, Joseph took action through the Justices of Peace, the Sheriff Court and finally the Court of Session. The final outcome in 1778 was unequivocal and widely reported: 'The freedom of negroes has received it first *general determination* in the Supreme Civil Court of Scotland.'[14]

Until this judgement, advertisements had appeared regularly in newspapers throughout Britain seeking the return of runaway slaves and warning the captains of ships not to take them on board. A database compiled by the University of Glasgow contains sixty-seven such advertisements from Glasgow and Edinburgh newspapers, placed between 1719 and 1779, with details of forty-nine runaway slaves (all but one were men), of which forty-six absconded in Scotland or from ships calling at Scottish ports. Of these, thirty-five were of African descent, ten were Indian or 'Asiatic' and one was a native North American. At least five jumped ship, including two men who escaped in a ship's longboat in Stromness (Orkney).[15] Most of the runaways in Britain were male domestic and personal servants, and were aged under thirty. This was because when wealthy, white slave holders returned from the colonies with servants, they chose trusted domestic slaves. As with the earlier slaves of aristocrats, the preference was for young boys (and occasionally girls), who had become favourites. Ninian Home (see Chapter 4), for example, sent a young 'mulatto' girl back to Scotland from Grenada, perhaps to work as a domestic servant at Paxton House. He planned for her return to Grenada in 1782 but this did not happen and her detention in Scotland may corroborate the oral tradition in Grenada that Home had taken away the wife of an enslaved man named Orinooko – who in revenge betrayed Home's whereabouts to Fédon's supporters.[16]

The extension of slave-holding into the households of the 'middling sort' and tradesmen in Scotland is well illustrated by the example of William Colhoun, a ship's mate based in Sierra Leone, who bought a ten-year-old girl in 1773. Two years later he planned to send her home to Scotland and was determined not to sell her because 'she serves me more than any white woman that ever I know'd except Mother ... [When] I come home, she will be more careful over me in my old age than any white I can get.'[17] Similarly, many young white men on

Caribbean plantations had become used to the personal attention of domestic servants. In the words of Edward Fraser in
Berbice, 'servants at home are not accustomed to serve in the
way the blacks do'.

Life as an enslaved domestic servant was easier than back-
breaking labour in the field but, both in Scotland and on the
plantations, employment as a domestic servant might not continue into adulthood. The enslaved man Quamina (*c.* 1771–
1823) – who was later shot and his body gibbeted in front of
John Gladstone's plantation *Success* for his suspected role in
the Demerara slave rising – had been a houseboy from the age
of nine to eighteen. His duties included waiting on table, but in
addition 'Overseers, Managers, etc used to send him to fetch
young negroes, (good looking girls) to fornicate with'.[18] But
after that, he was trained as a carpenter and subject to the harsh
discipline applied to the other enslaved people on the plantation. About 1811, for example, he received a hundred lashes for
failing to complete the day's work. Similarly, in Barbados, Lord
Seaforth's cook Quaco was reduced to the level of a field slave
and sent to Berbice, where he escaped more than once and was
finally captured and sold at public auction. In Britain the threat
of a return to field labour in the plantations was a powerful tool
in the control of enslaved domestic servants. In 1753 one man
in Derby who was threatened in this way hung himself in his
master's coal cellar.[19] Simply being turned out of the house in
Britain was likely to mean a life in poverty. The enslaved African
Ottobah Cugoano (see Chapter 4) gave a first-hand account of
the events which took him from Africa to Grenada and then, as
a fifteen-year-old personal servant, to England in 1772. After he
was baptised the following year, a number of fellow black servants who had helped him were dismissed, some probably joining
the growing numbers of 'black poor' in London.

We do not know the number of black servants in Scotland
and Iain Whyte is ambiguous in his conclusion that 'all the
indications point to the presence at this time of about seventy
black slaves in Scotland' – a figure which he contrasts with a
black population in England of about 15,000 by 1800.[20] Rather
the evidence provides details of a number of enslaved people in
Scotland – now, with additional research, more than seventy –
whom we have every reason to believe are part of a much larger
number of unknown and unrecorded enslaved servants. The

database of runaways does suggest that there may have been proportionately fewer domestic slaves in Scotland. It details 622 individuals, of whom forty-six absconded in Scotland. That is 7.4 per cent of the total at a time twenty years before the first national census in 1801, when Scotland's population was about 15 per cent of the British population. By this date the great difference in the black population between Scotland and England lay in the growth of the number of 'black poor' in London, as described by Gretchen Gerzina:

> Up until 1783 Britain's black population consisted mainly of servants and former servants, musicians and seamen. Suddenly, with the end of the war with America, England felt itself 'over-whelmed' by an influx of black soldiers who had served the loyalist cause and who crossed the Atlantic for their promised freedom and compensation.
>
> At the end of the war 14,000 blacks ... left with the British from Charlestown, Savannah and New York, and went to Halifax, Jamaica, St Lucia, Nassau and England. Hundreds more were sent to Nova Scotia, expecting to receive allotments of land and funds from the British government, but found themselves continually put off and their claims denied.[21]

As a comparison, between 1750 and 1800 something in the region of 17,000 Scots left Scotland for the West Indies. This black migration, over a much shorter period, had a significant impact in London but bypassed Scotland, which was nevertheless benefiting disproportionately from the plantations of the Caribbean and North America.

Five of the runaways in Scotland were servants in houses in or bordering the Highlands. In 1758 a fourteen-year-old boy ran away from Mrs Campbell of Askomill, in Kintyre; in 1765 a 'mulatto boy', Sam, who also called himself Donald, absconded from Charles Robertson of Balnaguard in Atholl; in 1768 a slave called London left Kinloch House near Blairgowrie, the property of Captain George Oliphant Kinloch; in 1771 an East Indian slave, Caesar, ran away from Novar in Ross-shire; and in 1773 John London (or Quashy) ran away from Pitleavlis castle, just outside Perth.

Runaway personal servants were usually well dressed. One named Cesar, who ran away in 1740 from Leven in Fife, was dressed, like Orinoce, in tartan – a tartan vest and coat in one advertisement, tartan trews in another. Yet he belonged to

Captain William Jones, from Middlesex, master of the ship *St David* of London and Dysart. Why did an English sea captain dress his African slave in tartan? Cesar was an imposing six feet tall, spoke little English and his head was marked with ceremonial cuts. Had checked cloth already become associated with slave clothing? Or did it make Cesar appear even more exotic? Only a few years later, William Hogarth painted a much grander Scottish captain, Lord Sir James Graham (1715–47), son of the 1st Duke of Montrose, at ease in the cabin of HMS *Lark*. Behind him a well-dressed black servant plays on a drum and whistle.[22]

Further evidence that black enslaved servants were not altogether uncommon in the Highlands can be found in the case of the American-born man James, who absconded in 1769 from the house of David Finlay, a hairdresser in Edinburgh's Lawnmarket. At least that was where anyone who found him could claim the reward. Advertisements were placed in both Edinburgh and Glasgow newspapers. The second, in the *Glasgow Journal*, stated: 'He has been seen at this place [Glasgow] and may, if he cannot get service here, make off for the Highlands.' James, aged about sixteen, was described as speaking 'remarkable good English' and as being 'very artful'. It seems that it was not beyond the bounds of possibility for a well-dressed black person, fluent in English (or in the case of another runaway, 'broad Scots') to travel in Scotland, including in the Highlands, perhaps claiming to be on an errand or carrying a message for their master. After all, had it not been for his tartan coat, Orinoce might have been allowed to go on his way along Loch Leven in 1750.

Other than the portrait of Sir William Maxwell and his servant, the only other known Scottish painting to include a black house servant from this period – before the Joseph Knight judgement – is the portrait of John Glassford's family, painted between 1764 and 1766. A black servant stands at the side, long obscured by centuries of dirt until revealed by cleaning and conservation in 2007.[23] It is an apt metaphor for much of Scotland's relationship with its 'slavery past'.

After the Somerset case in England in 1772 and the Knight case in Scotland in 1778, it was clear that enslaved people brought to Britain could not, under the law, be forcibly returned to a state of slavery in the colonies. Yet some did return. In

Chapter 7, I described how Archy, an enslaved Coromantee and personal servant to James Fraser of Belladrum, was taken to Britain – and so probably to the Highlands – but went back to Berbice, where he was later convicted of taking part in a plot to seize control of the colony and kill all the white population. And yet he was still protected by Fraser, who at one point proposed sending him back to Scotland.

One indication of the number of enslaved servants in the colonies comes from Demerara, where those intending to leave the colony were obliged to notify the Secretary to the colony, who published their names in the local newspaper, thus giving notice to creditors who might otherwise be left with unrecoverable debts. By 1813 these notifications included details of both servants and other enslaved people – and almost all servants would have been enslaved. In 1815 there were 296 notifications, covering about 440 people who intended to leave the colony.[24] Of these, eighty were servants – that is, 18 per cent of the passengers. Six of them were in the service of free people of colour. If children and other enslaved adults are removed from the equation, then there were eighty servants to approximately 304 free adults: a ratio of just less than 1 to 4. An analysis of those leaving in 1813, when numbers were lower with fifty-four servants and 205 free adults, gives almost exactly the same ratio. Some of the servants would have been travelling within the Caribbean, with only a proportion continuing their journey to Britain or North America, but at least within the Caribbean they were up to a fifth of the adult passengers – enslaved labourers were considered as 'cargo'. Some families had up to four servants. In 1813 there were fifty-four servants accompanying 191 individuals/families and in 1815 there were eighty servants accompanying 276 individuals/families.

The relationship which might emerge between a slave holder and a personal servant often began in the childhood of the enslaved boy or girl. It could be lifelong or they might be cast off and replaced. The unconscious and disturbing naïveté betrayed in the letters of Hugh Munro Robertson, written after his arrival in Demerara in 1806, brings home the extent to which such children were on a par with pets:[25]

> Gilbert [his older brother] has presented me with a little boy newly imported from the Gold Coast, he is of the Madingo Country. He

is about 11 years old, a very good natured smart little fellow. I am training him as a servant for myself.

And three weeks later:

> I believe I mentioned to you before that Gilbert presented me with a boy – he was just bought when I arrived here – so that I will have the complete training of him myself, I can make him do anything I please, he is really a fine creature – he has always a complacent smile on his countenance & seems (& I think really is) quite happy. I have got him smartly rigged out – he is very desirous to please & I really think the poor little [creature?] has conceived an attachment to me already.

When Robertson temporarily left the colony in 1813 he was accompanied by a servant and in 1817 he had a new servant, eleven-year-old Henry, born in Demerara.

At the same time in neighbouring Berbice, the Reelig brothers James and Edward Fraser both had their own boys and favourite slaves. In 1809, when James was preparing for a period of leave in Scotland, Edward wrote to his twelve-year-old sister Jane Anne telling her about the black children on the plantation who were 'just like little monkeys' and would amuse her. These included three-year-old Cuffy:

> [He] comes every day to breakfast to beg for a bone or a crust of bread ... indeed he is hardly ever out of the house at meals when he fights with the dogs (of whom we have a plentiful stock).

James was to take with him Black John and Toby. On their arrival at Port Glasgow, 'Toby Fraser a negro late of Berbice', probably the older of the two, was indentured to James as a footman. This regularised Toby's status, binding him to James' service while in Britain. Edward had already described him to Jane Anne:

> James is going to take a black boy called Toby with him who will amuse you I think – he cannot speak intelligible English – and he has his face all cut and marked after the fashion of his country in Africa. You must be good to him for he is a very good boy in his way – and sat up many a night by me when I have been ill, and the same with James in many illnesses.

From the family's perspective, Toby was a great success in Scotland, serving them well and amusing Jane Anne with his dancing and singing during their musical evenings. Although under the law he could have refused to step on board the ship which took James back to Berbice – and took Toby back to slavery – he returned with his master.

In the same way, the enslaved man Cesar (*c*. 1803–?) went to England from Demerara with his master Thomas Hopkinson (1800–37), a younger cousin of Benjamin James Hopkinson (see Chapter 8). Cesar was a servant to Thomas while he attended Trinity College (Cambridge) from 1819 and probably when he trained as a barrister at the Inner Temple before returning to Demerara in 1828. Back in Demerara, although a slave, 'Mister Caesar' was a man of some status described by the journalist Henry Barker who met him *c*. 1828:

> [He was] a good-looking young man, about three-and-twenty . . . He had been allowed to ride one of his master's horses . . . [and] was arrayed in buck-skin breeches of bright yellow, handsome top-boots and spurs, a fine frilled shirt, with an immensity of cambric round the neck, and a large bow in front – a scarlet waistcoat, trimmed with sable fur, and a blue surtout be-frogged and be-furred, with braiding enough in every part to have satisfied a French field-marshal. A natty little hat upon the half-cock, a gold chain and quizzing-glass, a milk-white cambric handkerchief just thrust within the breast of his coat, and a silver-mounted riding-whip, completed his visible costume.[26]

While we do not know what became of Toby, the other Reelig servant, Black John, formed an enduring personal bond with James Fraser, who he accompanied to India (see Chapter 7). He also went with James to Tehran in 1821 and continued with him to the remote province of Khorasan in 1822. When the party were detained at Resht, James plotted an escape, sharing the details only with Black John, in whom he could 'implicitly confide'. Ten years later, on a journey to Constantinople, James regretted Black John's absence:

> It is now that I miss my faithful John, who was so capital a hand on a march, and who used to look after so much which I now must see to myself, whether weary or not.

James was at John's bedside in St George's Hospital, London, when he died there in 1823. His mother described the scene in her diary:

The Surgeon told him there was not a hope of his recovery and accordingly it appears he expired about 3 hours afterwards – he knew his Master however but could say little and was not quite Collected in what he attempted to say – poor John – never will he be remembered without a sigh of regret – or a pitying tear – after being associated with James in many afflicting and interesting scenes and having proved himself the attached faithful friend as well as the devoted Servant – and when James looked to making him as comfortable as possible for the remainder of his life – the regret at his unexpected loss is sincerely felt – and his attached service will be cherished in the memory of us all with affectionate regard.

It is inevitable that we know more of such 'devoted servants' than of others.

SCOTLAND'S LAST SLAVE-BORN SERVANT

In the previous chapter I described how Scots continued to be slave holders in the Dutch colony of Suriname until emancipation in 1863, even though it was illegal for British citizens to own slaves in a foreign country. Among these was James Balfour (1777–1841) from Dalgety in Fife who owned plantations on the Nickerie River in Suriname. A Dutch soldier described him as 'a strange man who had boundless wealth and always wanted more' but who, despite his success, lived 'alone, without wife or children, except for a mulatto, who he fathered with one of his slaves'.[27] This 'mulatto' was Harriet (or Herriet) Balfour (1818–58), who was born a slave and only freed at Balfour's death, when she was given the surname Schoonebeek. She later changed her name to Balfour.[28] Two of James Balfour's Scottish nephews, Robert and David Kirke, came to Suriname, where David married Harriet, his first cousin. They moved to Scotland, where two children were born, Helen (1842–5) and Harriet (1844–5). Harriet and David returned to Nickerie, where she had a son James (1847–52). David died there in 1850 and Harriet probably remained in Nickerie, where she died on 3 December 1858. She was commemorated, along with her husband and children, on a Kirke family memorial at Cairneyhill, Fife.

David's brother Robert Kirke married in Dunfermline in 1850 and brought his wife to Nickerie, where a daughter was born in 1851. In 1852 Kirke manumitted a slave named Petronella, who was given permission to travel to Europe with Kirke's wife and infant daughter. Petronella remained as a servant with the family until she died in 1917, commemorated by a gravestone in Burntisland:

> In loving remembrance of PETE (Petronella Hendrick),
> born at Providence, Surinam, 20th August 1829
> died at Hilton, Burntisland, 28th November 1917.
> For over 60 years the faithful and devoted nurse and friend of the
>   family of
> Robert Kirke, of Greenmount, and Nickerie, Surinam.[29]

WELCOME

Not all master and servant relationships were happy ones. The African who was given the name Welcome was born *c.* 1792 and by 1817 was an enslaved domestic servant to Lachlan Cuming (*c.* 1756–1836) on the sugar plantation *Chateau Margo* in Demerara. We glimpse a little of his personal life because he was known to the missionary John Smith, later unjustly convicted of fomenting the 1823 Slave Rising. In May 1817 Smith wrote this in his diary:

> Welcome, Mr Cumming's [sic] servant came to complain of Caliwander our servant. Welcome said he had caught him 3 times with his wife, Minkie, Mr Van Cooten's servt. Caliwander is a bad boy: he goes out at night (after we are in bed) & gets with other's wives. He has now 3 wives; yet must commit adultery with Minkie, tho' her husband Welcome was his most intimate friend.

From the slave registers we know that Welcome was about twenty-five at this time, as was his wife. John Smith and Lachlan Cuming had a poor relationship, mainly because Smith was willing to conduct marriage ceremonies for slaves and so, in Cuming's view, 'teach them the pernicious principle, that their owners have no right to separate them'. Cuming was a prominent and influential planter, and was chairman of both the Demerara Agricultural Society founded in 1815 and of the committee which established the first Scots Kirk in the colony in the same year. In 1798 he bought the estate of Blackhills near Elgin, part of the larger Innes estate, which was acquired at the same time by his cousin Thomas Cuming (see Chapter 6).[30]

Lachlan Cuming was appointed a Justice of the Peace for

the county of Elgin in 1821 but did not settle permanently at Blackhills until the mid-1820s, taking Welcome there with him. Their relationship had deteriorated by 1830, when Cuming first drafted his will. He included a bequest to Welcome, who 'was my slave but is now free', but the legacy was double-edged:

> To my Negro servant, Welcome, £50, and also to pay his passage money from the county to Demerara by way of Greenock provided that he agrees to proceed thither immediately after my decease; and if he shall refuse to do so I forbid my said trustees to pay such passage money for him thereafter; and I particularly direct that he shall not be permitted to remain one day on the Estate of Blackhills after my funeral, seeing that although he was once faithful and attached he is now no longer entitled to that character and has entracted evil habits.

From 1835 Cuming adjusted his will, which runs to over a hundred pages, rescinding his bequest to Welcome, now described as his 'late servant', and forbidding his trustees 'from affording him the least portion of my means'. Welcome had walked away from Lachlan Cuming and from Blackhills, a free man with 'a wife and large family in Demerara'. He walked out into a society increasingly hostile to people like him – and out of any history accessible to us.

13

Children of Colour

In April 1804 Anne Robertson, wife of the parish minister of Kiltearn (Ross-shire), wrote one of her many letters, rich in gossip, to her daughter Christy, then married and living in Orkney. On this occasion she recounted the visit she and her husband had made to friends in Dingwall:

> On Monday we called at Millbank. They are all well there. They had just got home two little Foreigner's children of their Brother the late Doctor George Bethune. Their mother was a Brigand. They are yellow, ugly things. I think it would be best to leave them in their own country but their aunt seems very tender of them and much interested. Miss Jenny goes to live with them to her own house at Dingwall at the term.[1]

Three things are worth noting. First, there is the casual racism which came so easily to Mrs Robertson, despite this being a family which was otherwise kindly, broad-minded and remarkably free from prejudice, certainly in matters of religion. When the Revd Harry Robertson had been awarded a Doctorate of Divinity by the University of Aberdeen in 1800, the Robertsons with their daughter Annie and two younger sons had travelled there. Mrs Robertson had told Christy that on their first Sunday, while 'your Father and the boys went to our own church', Annie went 'with the Miss Boyles to the English [Episcopalian] Chapel [and] in the evening to the Roman Catholic and Methodist Chapel which shows she wants to see everything she can'. And the following day, when they dined with a Professor Stewart, Mrs Robertson and Annie 'slipt away' to the theatre to see Sheridan's latest play *Pizarro*.[2] This is markedly different to the strictness of much Scottish Presbyterianism. Yet her reaction to Dr Bethune's children showed no comparable tolerance or breadth of outlook.

Second, Mrs Robertson's reaction suggests that she was unaware of – or chose to forget – the existence of her own black relations. Her husband's two brothers, George and John, had already died in the Caribbean. George had a son known as 'Black George' who was educated in London, and John had two 'mulatto boys', Charles and Daniel, who had been sent to school in Glasgow. And by 1804 the Robertsons' own son Gilbert was in a relationship in Guyana with Doll Thomas's daughter Eliza (see Chapter 8). Ironically, their first child would be named Ann, after Mrs Robertson.

And, finally, kindness and kinship did to an extent prevail. The children were cared for by their aunt and one of them, Agnes Bethune (1803–after 1851), lived in Dingwall with 'Miss Jenny' (Janet Bethune) until the aunt's death in 1849. But after Miss Jenny's death there was no network of support for Agnes, despite her family's connections. Her father's cousin, Elizabeth Robertson, was the mother of the future prime minister, William Ewart Gladstone. But in 1851, still in Dingwall, Agnes was described in the census as a pauper and she then disappears from the record. In other circumstances she might have had better prospects.

Agnes Bethune had other relations. Her grandfather had been a surgeon in Dingwall and his sons Dr George Bethune (1760–1803) and his brother Divie (1771–1824) had gone together to the Caribbean about 1790, first to Tobago and then to Demerara. Divie found 'the pestilential moral atmosphere was so thoroughly distasteful . . . that at the risk of forfeiting his brother's affection he left him, and in 1791 came to New York City, at the age of nineteen'. He founded the New York merchant house Bethune & Smith in 1798; his wife, Joanna Graham, was a noted philanthropist and leader of the Sunday school movement in New York; and their son, the Revd George Bethune, Agnes' first cousin, was a noted preacher in the Dutch Reformed Church and writer of the once popular 'O sing to me the Auld Scotch Sangs'.[3] The birth of these 'two little Foreigner's children' fathered by Dr George Bethune would perhaps have been regarded as an outcome of the 'pestilential moral atmosphere' which had driven Divie from Demerara.

Agnes Bethune is as clear an example as any of the difficulties faced in Britain by children of white fathers and enslaved or 'free coloured' women in the Caribbean, especially from the early 1800s. The most extensive study to date has been Daniel Livesay's *Children of Uncertain Fortune: Mixed-race Jamaicans in Britain and the Atlantic Family, 1733–1833* (2019), which tracks 360 children who were sent to Britain, either for education or to join white families. Livesay uses these case studies to map changing attitudes to family and race in Britain and Jamaica over the period.[4] In the 1730s, when Scots were becoming well established in the 'English sugar islands', those children who were sent to Britain were from the richest among the white planter class and it was intended that they become part of the elite white families whose interests spanned the Atlantic. Both British identity and the notion of the family were more 'porous' at this point and these children were accepted into society because, when it came to identity, class trumped race. At the same time, the future of colonies like Jamaica was seen as depending on such family units, which brought together both European and, to a carefully limited extent, African heritages. Indeed, in Jamaica from 1733 anyone with less than an eighth African ancestry could become white in the eyes of the law. This vision of colonies run by a carefully enlarged white plantocracy, resident in the West Indies but fully British, was shattered by a series of slave revolts, especially Tacky's Rebellion in Jamaica in the 1760s. This, as described in Chapter 3, led to an increased defensiveness among white planters on the island and the elite increasingly became absentee owners. Twenty years later, prejudices in Britain were fed by the influx of thousands of poor blacks, in the wake of the American War of Independence, and 'Britishness' increasingly came to be seen as an identity for whites only. Popular newspapers and pamphlets routinely ridiculed and vilified 'mixed race' migrants. But, at the same time, the growing 'free coloured' population in the Caribbean colonies was becoming even more important in managing the brutal regimes on slave plantations, the white population being simply too small – the more so in the new colonies of the Ceded Islands and, from the 1790s, in Trinidad and Guyana. Even if 'free coloured' children were increasingly unwelcome in Britain, being educated in Britain and returning to the West Indies with enhanced skills could help to bolster the security of British investments there. There were public debates about slavery, abolition, identity and race. But it was within families that the questions of family membership, of belonging and excluding, were negotiated – and thus even a relatively small number of 'mixed race' children in British families of wealth and status engendered much angst. Through their presence these children had an influence beyond their numbers.

Livesay concludes that 'by 1820 Britons were less tolerant of those with African blood'. The success and acceptance which might have been possible in the past had become much more difficult:

> These were children of an uncertain fortune. Their lives balanced between colonial repression and metropolitan acceptance, Caribbean riches and British poverty. They descended from an enslaved class brutally suppressed by white colonists, yet they held a place within their fathers' Atlantic networks. Indeed, they embodied the complex realities of race and status in the West Indies.

Some of Livesay's case studies come from colonies other than Jamaica, and of particular importance are the children of an enslaved woman in Berbice, given the name Countess in slavery and renamed Harriot when freed. Their father was William Macpherson from Blairgowrie and their lives have been explored by Steven Foster in *A Private Empire* (2010). The children – Eliza, Matilda and Allan – were brought to Scotland, to the great distress of William's mother, who refused to call them by their names and referred to them as the 'little moonlight shades'. They were children from the shadows of family life and, while she gradually became reconciled to their presence and did her duty in ensuring them a decent education, she was insistent that they could not be known as Macphersons. Instead they were given the surname Williams. Nor could they expect good marriages or genteel occupations. Allan Williams eventually emigrated to Australia and there is no record of Matilda beyond the early 1820s. But Eliza, who died single at the age of thirty, remained in the household and cared for her grandmother in her old age.

What is unusual – and perhaps unique – in the Macpherson archive is the extent to which discussions of these issues of race and belonging are reflected in the family correspondence. This is also true of William Macpherson's relationship with Countess.

Both William and his younger brother Allan, who arrived in Berbice in 1802 and 1805 respectively, came with letters of advice from their father, Colonel Allan Macpherson, based on his own experience in India. This advice ranged from their duties to their employers, through how often to change their clothes, to the importance of avoiding the company of 'loose women . . . [a] certain destruction to your health, character, money & happiness in this world & ruin to your Soul in the world to come'. But in his letter to Allan he was particularly frank:

> I by all means recommend to you to keep a decent Native woman of the Country where you may be as your constant concubine in preference to running after the loose & debauched Females.

The births of the 'little moonlight shades' were a consequence. William's mother had been shocked to hear of these illegitimate children and it seems that Colonel Macpherson had hoped to keep her in ignorance, since he wrote to William advising him to leave the girls in Glasgow rather than bring them to the parental home. But William did not receive this letter.

The men in the Fraser family of Reelig took the same approach, sharing information among themselves while partially shielding the women from such knowledge. By the mid-1820s James Baillie Fraser (see Chapter 6), who had known the Macpherson brothers in Berbice, had returned to Scotland and married, after spending some years in India. His younger brother William, who had established himself in Delhi, had a close friend, James Skinner (himself the son of a Scot and an Indian woman). Skinner sent his two illegitimate sons to be educated near Edinburgh and asked that James and his new wife look out for 'his poor Black Boys'. When James declined, William was furious and this led James to persuade his wife Jeannie to have the boys at their home in Inverness-shire. After their visit she conceded that they were 'fine boys' but added 'I only wish for our credit in the country they were white bairns.'[5]

James had also been keeping an eye on his brother William's own 'olive skinned' Indian daughter, Amy, who was at first passed off to their mother (and perhaps to James's wife) as the daughter of a Major Young. Amy was being boarded and educated in Nairn, along with a daughter of James Skinner, at a small school run by a Mrs Grant. Mrs Grant's initial reaction had not been encouraging:

[She was] a little confused and hardly pleased when she received the little half caste [Amy] who is much darker than Maria Skinner; but she could not throw her off, and the child has turned out so amiable & docile that the family are quite delighted with her.[6]

Amy was later invited to the Frasers' home at Moniack, where she got on well with James's niece Jane and the other children. James described to William how 'it was strange to see [Jane] wreathing her little white arm about Amy's olive coloured neck on the green before the house and all playing uproariously together'. Throughout her life Amy remembered the happiness of these days which she described, in a telling phrase, as 'a joyous liberty after the streets of Nairn'.

Livesay notes that such 'children of uncertain fortune' were to be found from one end of Britain to the other, citing in the north the Hay brothers who were at school in 'the small seaside town of Dornoch, nestled in the Scottish Highlands'. Here, in 1801, Donald Sage (see Chapter 3) and his brother Aeneas made friends with Fergus, John and Sandy Hay – 'the offspring of a negro woman, as their hair, and the tawny colour of their skin, very plainly intimated'. Fergus, who had 'the manners of a gentleman', was about twenty years old and the schoolmaster sometimes left him in charge of the other pupils. On one such occasion early in their acquaintance he unjustly administered 'thirty lashes' to Donald but later acted with kindness towards him. Fergus was only at the school for one year but after he left the other four remained close friends. Donald and Aeneas went home each 'harvest vacation' and one year John and Sandy came with them and spent the week at Kildonan. Sage tells us that Fergus was there to learn mathematics in order to 'fit him for commercial duties', perhaps in the complex business of managing a plantation (as described in Chapter 7), and a similar return to the West Indies was probably planned for his brothers.[7]

SCHOOLS

Black pupils were to be found in schools throughout Scotland. I began this book by describing Hugh Miller and the 'mulatto' boy who sat with him at school in Cromarty in 1818. At the same time, and only two houses away from Miller's home, Miss Elizabeth Bond ran a 'dame school' whose pupils included Jacobina Maria Nicholson (*c.* 1810–26), an illegitimate child born in Goa in the East Indies. Such schools, like the one in Nairn run by Mrs Grant, at their best could provide a homely setting otherwise denied to these children.

The best documented school in the north of Scotland is Inverness Royal Academy, whose admissions registers survive from 1803 to 1810. In the calendar year 1804 about 280 students attended classes at the academy, of whom either twenty-four or twenty-five were from the Caribbean – sixteen or seventeen from Jamaica, six from Demerara, two from Grenada and one from St Croix. That was almost a tenth of the school roll. There were also five students from Canada and one from Calcutta. Men from the north with white children in the West Indies certainly aspired to send them to the Academy. In 1798 Thomas Fraser in St Vincent (see Chapter 5), whose wife was French, wrote to his relation in Inverness:

> I understand you have a very good Academy in your town furnished with good teachers in several branches of education, if it pleases the Almighty to spare me to see my three boys able to shift for Themselves I shall think myself the happiest of mortals. If not, his will be done, poor things they must then look up to you as a father.[8]

Those with 'coloured' children had the same ambitions. John Noble from Inverness had a son John and a daughter Mary Ann with Susan Ross, a free coloured woman in Demerara. In 1811 his son left Demerara with a friend of Noble's on the ship *Sisters* of Glasgow. Noble later wrote to James Grant, provost of Inverness, saying: 'I hope in God they are both safe at Inverness long ere this.' He also sent bills of credit and asked that his son John 'be placed at the Inverness Academy as a boarder with one of the Masters or at any other Genteel Boarding House'. John was awarded a prize for handwriting in 1818.[9] Four children of the 'free coloured' woman Susannah Kerr in Demerara and George Inglis (a younger brother of Provost Inglis of Inverness) attended the school from 1804; and three brothers named Macrae, described as 'coloured' in later school rolls, were there from Jamaica.

At Fortrose Academy in 1818 the prize for handwriting – penmanship – was won by another girl from Guyana, Eliza Junor (1804–61). She and her brother William (1809–73) had arrived in Rosemarkie in 1816 with their father, Hugh Junor (d. 1823), who owned a share in a timber plantation in Essequibo.

William won the prize for French in 1822. At Elgin Academy in 1817 the prize for the 'best writer' went to James Botar, from Demerara, and he also came first the following year – but having already won the prize it was awarded to another pupil.[10]

At Tain, on the south shore of the Dornoch Firth, a new Academy was founded by Royal Charter in 1810 with funds raised between 1800 and 1809. The subscriptions amounted to just over £4,500 and of this £1,616 came from the Caribbean and South America – and a number of pupils were sent to the school from these colonies. From Demerara there was Marion (Minny) Iver (*c.* 1809–80) and the 'mulattos' Eve Oudkerk (b. 1807/8) and George Oudkerk (1806/7). They were in Tain from 1822 but in 1817 their names were still entered in the plantation slave register because they were 'free but not yet manumitted'. The Oudkerks' father was in a partnership in Demerara with George Rainy from nearby Criech (see Chapter 10) and this may have been why they attended a school in the north of Scotland. As Livesay points out, a father might want his 'coloured' children to be educated at a distance from his own home, perhaps more so as prejudices hardened. The Tain pupil Minny Iver was the illegitimate daughter of Archibald Iver (d. 1845), a merchant in Georgetown (Demerara). He had returned with her to his home town of Edinburgh, where he married Mitchell Shaw, the daughter of an Inverness merchant. It may have been his wife's origins which led to the choice of a school in the north. And after he returned to Scotland in 1837, George Rainy's two daughters were educated in Minchinhampton, near Stroud.

Some regarded education of this kind as a mistake. After the death of a cousin in St Vincent, the same Thomas Fraser who had wanted to have his white children educated in Inverness wrote from the colony to relations:

> There is a Mulatto boy [the son of a cousin, Thomas Fraser] in Glasgow on whose account there is now due to the woman at whose house he boards at least one hundred pounds sterling, it was a piece of foolish extravagance to have him sent home for I never saw one of the colour sent home that came to any good.[11]

But it was not always or only fathers who paid for this schooling. In Chapter 8, I noted that the free coloured woman Elizabeth Swain Bannister in Berbice, when she died in 1828, left £3,000 for 'the maintenance education and support of my daughter

... Jane Frazer who is at present at school in Glasgow'. Many others paid the emotional price of never again seeing their children and yet they encouraged their move to Britain, as was the case with Peter Grant (to whom I will turn later in this chapter). His 'free coloured' mother, who would never see him again, wrote from Jamaica to his father in 1796 making this plea:

> I was happy to hear of the safe arrival of ... little Peter; and ... I earnestly entreat you will make no delay in placing him to a good school ... and tell Peter all here joins me in kind love to him, & we hopes to hear he is a good boy.

THE UNIVERSITIES

Ambitious parents of 'coloured' children, both white fathers and 'free coloured' mothers, not only paid for schooling in Britain but sometimes funded university or professional education. Thomas Cuming (c. 1800–30), the illegitimate son of Lachlan Cuming (see Chapter 6), although baptised in Scotland in 1801, was described as 'of Demerara' when he graduated as a doctor from Edinburgh University in 1824. The 'free coloured' woman Dorothy Thomas (see Chapter 8) funded the studies of her grandson Henry Robertson (1807–81), which enabled him to pass the examinations set by the Society of Apothecaries in London in 1828. And William Davidson from Jamaica, who will be considered below, attended school in Edinburgh, studied in Aberdeen and was articled to a lawyer in Liverpool.

Before 1834 Marischal College in Aberdeen educated at least eighty-three students identified as being from the Caribbean: fifty from Jamaica, eleven from Barbados, seven from Grenada, four each from Guyana and Tobago, three from Dominica, two from St Vincent and one each from St Kitts and St Croix.[12] Other than exploring their individual histories, there is no way of knowing whether or not they were the children of women of colour. But some were, including, unusually, the three sons of an enslaved woman in Berbice, Susannah Munro (c. 1799–c. 1853). Their father was George Munro (1766–1824), owner of plantation *Alness* on the Corentyne coast, and if the records kept by the plantation were accurate, then Susannah was no more than twelve years old when, on 30 October 1808, she gave birth to her first child, named George after his father. Two more children were to follow, John born in July 1810 and William in

May 1812. Susannah and her sisters Charlotte and Diana were 'mestees', that is, the children of an unknown white father and a 'mulatto' woman, Amelia, an enslaved domestic servant on *Alness*. Susannah, who grew to be 'slender and a good make', was born when Amelia was about eighteen or nineteen.

This George Munro, from Easter Ross, was a prominent inhabitant of Berbice and a member of the colony's governing body, the Court of Policy – the Governor described him as 'the richest and the most impertinent' member of the Court. His cousin was Dr William Munro (see Chapter 7). Under the laws of the colony, these boys George, John and William, as the children of an enslaved woman, were born into a state of slavery. Yet their names, unlike those of their grandmother, mother and aunts, were not entered in the Register of Slaves which the plantation was obliged to keep after 1817. George Munro died at Falmouth in August 1824, returning from Berbice. His mixed-race son George had already begun his studies at Marischal College in 1822, attending the third-year lectures but for only one year; John matriculated in 1825 and graduated four years later; and William studied for three years from 1826 without graduating.

In his will, George Munro had provided rather meanly for Amelia and her three daughters, including Susannah, allowing them to reside on the plantation with a small allowance which he thought 'with the fruit of their own labour may be sufficient'. He divided his estate between his three Berbice-born sons and three nephews in Scotland, with legacies to the poor of the parishes of Alness and Kiltearn in Easter Ross. When Susannah made her own will in 1850 – making her mark because she was not literate – she instructed her executors to recover the inheritance which should have been paid to her sons George and John, now deceased. It was a spirited move by someone born into slavery, only possible because she could rely on her literate nephew John Millar, the 'free coloured' son of her formerly enslaved sister Charlotte, who was now the manager of plantation *Alness*.

AFTER SCHOOL

To get some handle on the numbers of children sent to Britain, Livesay examined 2,245 wills executed in the late 1700s and early 1800s. These wills reflect the attitudes of wealthier and more successful whites in Jamaica, who had the means to provide for their 'coloured' offspring and in some cases have them educated in Britain. Their actions must be seen in the wider context that the great majority of the children of white fathers were born and remained slaves. In the 1790s, when the proportions were highest, for every hundred white men who wrote wills, about thirty-four made provision for children of colour and of these, seven or so made provision for children presently resident in Britain or soon to be sent there.[13] But we do not know how many fathers of 'free coloured' children died without making a will. If one in every four made a will, then perhaps for every hundred children of colour, roughly eighty remained as slaves, while five were provided for under their father's will, and of these, one was sent to Britain for education. Livesay's study shows how these children could flourish if they had financial resources, were unchallenged by white relatives and were eager to succeed – but it is also clear that colour, and shades of darkness, mattered.

There were, however, some children who simply did not wish to stay in Britain. Livesay describes Robert and John McGregor, two of the four 'natural' sons of Patrick McGregor in Jamaica, who were sent to be educated and apprenticed in Edinburgh in the 1820s. Both in effect 'sabotaged' their prospects by a series of petty thefts from their employers and demanded to be returned to their home. After turning down the offer of living in the country rather than the town, they were put on board a ship for Jamaica. Perhaps, as Livesay suggests, '. . . it was owing to regular taunts along the Scottish streets, bad treatment by guardians, or simple disaffection with their new location'.[14] Their experience may have been little different from Amy Young's on the streets of Nairn. Yet there were some clear examples of success in adult life.

SUCCESSES: PETER GRANT

Success and integration were possible for some. Peter Grant (1787–1878), who later added the surname Peterkin, navigated a course to social acceptance in the north of Scotland despite what was regarded as the disadvantage of his birth as the son of a 'free coloured woman' in Jamaica. His father was George

Grant (1739–1819), a son of Patrick Grant of Glenmore (said to have sheltered 'Bonnie Prince Charlie' after Culloden and received the gift of a fishing rod from the Prince). While George's younger brother Patrick Grant (*c.* 1746–1809) became a Church of Scotland minister, George made money as a slave holder in Jamaica and at his death in 1819 owned 119 enslaved people, valued at £10,305, on his sugar plantation *Airy Castle*.[15]

Peter's mother was Elizabeth (Betty) McDermot (or McDermit), who also owned both slaves and a plantation, *Richmond Hill*. She was from an elite among the 'free coloured' population of the island – those who had not only been manumitted but who were the subject of private Acts of Parliament granting them further, but almost always limited, civil rights. These additional rights were given very sparingly to 'inheritors of large estates in the island' and in this case the private Act of 1781 was for the benefit of 'Johanna Gaul, of the parish of St Thomas in the East ... a free mulatto woman, and several children and grand-children', including 'Elizabeth McDermit'.[16] Elizabeth, as the child or grandchild of the 'mulatto' Johanna, was either (in the language of the time) a 'quadroon' or 'octoroon' – and her children, Peter and his three sisters, were one shade further removed from their African ancestry. This would turn out to be important to Peter, whose father had returned to Scotland where he had purchased the estate of Burdyards, near Forres. In 1795 Peter was sent 'home' to Scotland and was soon followed by his three sisters. Elizabeth McDermot would never see her children – or their father George Grant – again.

Peter's education in or near Aberdeen was overseen by Roderick MacLeod (1727–1815), professor of philosophy at King's College and from 1800 principal of the University. MacLeod also had responsibility for some other children from the Caribbean, who were named MacLeod but were apparently no relation. In August 1800 he wrote to Peter's father:

> I was out a few days ago to see Peter & I am happy to inform you that he was in good health & doing well he seems to be a fine boy & has a much better complexion than my young namesakes though they are not very black but rather swarthy & have a little of the woolly hair. I should suppose that Peter's mother had no African blood.

He was assuring George Grant that others might think Peter was white. A miniature of Peter shows that he had red hair. Perhaps that helped. At any rate, he had an advantage over the 'swarthy' – and therefore less fortunate – MacLeod boys.

Peter went on to a cadetship in the East India Company and a military career in India, rising to be appointed in 1823 to the command of the Guard at Delhi Palace, the ancestral seat of the Moghul Emperors. Until the early 1830s he had charge of the Imperial family, keeping a watchful eye on them on behalf of his British masters. He received honours from Muhammad Akbar Shah II, titular King of Delhi and last but one of the Moghul Emperors, and appears in a painting of a Royal Mughal procession – sitting atop an elephant, dressed in a black coat and wearing a top hat. Among the exotic surroundings of the Delhi court, he remained carefully poised as a white, British soldier and official. It is something of an irony that at the same court his younger contemporary William Fraser of Reelig, an entirely white Highlander, was 'going native'.

Grant returned to Scotland where, in 1836, he married Mary Ann Peterkin, the second daughter of a Jamaican planter, James Peterkin. Peterkin was born in Forres, the son of a merchant of the same name, and made his money in the Caribbean. This allowed him to buy the estate of Grange, outside the town, and other properties around Forres. He built the elegant mansion house of Grange Hall *c.* 1805 and improved the farmland around it, to the extent that it was described in 1811 as 'the first house in the district next to Darnaway Castle' and of such style that it bespoke 'the residence of opulence conjoined with the most accurate taste'.[17] When Peter Grant married Mary Ann in 1836 he added her family name to his to become Peter Grant Peterkin and acquired Grange Hall and its estate. This suggests that, despite the improvement of the estate, it was Peter's fortune from his career in India which was required to keep and develop it. The Grant Peterkin archive from Grange Hall has recently been deposited with the Highland Archive Centre and further study of these papers will provide an important example of how both West Indian and East Indian fortunes were directed to the improvement of estates in the north of Scotland. Peter Grant Peterkin himself made the transition from soldier in India to a fully accepted and integrated member of the land-owning class, combining through his marriage the fortunes of two Jamaican planter families.

Figure 13.1 Portrait of Nancy Graham by Henry Raeburn, photographed by John Bain *c*. 1900.

SUCCESSES: NANCY GRAHAM

Nancy Graham (1804/5–83), referred to briefly in Chapter 1, is an example of a girl of colour from Jamaica who also grew up to pass as white. Or at least that is how she was presented in her portrait by Henry Raeburn, painted *c*. 1812 when she was a young girl. It is now held by the Louvre.[18]

Nancy's father, the Jamaican attorney Francis Graham, married in Scotland the following year but died on his estate in Jamaica in 1820, leaving Nancy, his only surviving child, a legacy of £4,000. Nancy's mother, the 'free coloured' woman Eliza Jackson, remained in Kingston, where she died in 1827, leaving to her 'beloved daughter Nancy Graham at present in Scotland' money from the sale of six slaves. The legacy from her mother proved difficult to recover but Nancy, now aged twenty-one, still had a substantial inheritance.[19] In 1833 her guardian, Sir Michael Benignus Clare (the former physician general of Jamaica), died in Cromarty and Nancy married Alexander Gordon Graham (1803–78). Her new husband was a brother of Nancy's stepmother, the wife of her guardian, Sir Michael.

Whatever Nancy's feelings in the matter – and we do not know – the match kept her fortune in the family. And it was a family which, having inherited a plantation in Suriname thorough Alexander's mother, would continue to be slave holders beyond emancipation in the British colonies.[20]

VULNERABILITIES

Both Peter Grant and Nancy Graham may have passed as white but as prejudices against visibly 'coloured' children in Britain increased, boys who had been sent 'home' for schooling, and were now educated young men, were more likely to pursue careers in the colonies where they became part of a growing class of professional, free people of colour. But girls who had been sent 'home' were often in a more vulnerable position, especially after the death of their white fathers. When Peg (Margaret) Williamson (1779–1863) died in Highland Banffshire, she had served as midwife to the parish of Mortlach for more than half a century. But were it not for a local story recorded in 1899 and a brief obituary in the *Huntly Express*, which described her as 'a Mulatto born in Jamaica', we would not know that she was black – nor that she had been the victim of envy, deceit and prejudice. The story was of John Duguid, the parish schoolmaster, who liked to have a friend join him in the evenings for discussions on Scottish literature. Because of the distance between their houses, the evening would end with a bowl of *sowens* (fermented oats) before one of them walked home. On one occasion, while they were reading Walter Scott's *Waverley* novels, they were interrupted by the schoolmaster's housekeeper, who wanted to know how much treacle she should put in the sowens:

> 'Hoot, woman,' said young Duguid, loth to be disturbed in his reading aloud, 'gang awa' an' mak' them the verra colour o' Peg Williamson's face.'[21]

A footnote records that Peg, as well as being the midwife, had married the local blacksmith and kept a small shop. While this could be read as a tale of acceptance in the local community – and that may be true – Peg had earlier been deprived of a valuable inheritance. When her father Alexander Williamson died in Scotland in 1791 he left his estate, valued at about £3,000, to be divided between his sister and his twelve-year-old daughter Peg, who had come back with him from Jamaica. However, the will was stolen and a forged substitute was produced by the estate factor, apparently signed by Williamson on his deathbed and witnessed by other beneficiaries of the forged document. One macabre detail was that it was alleged that the dead man's hand had been used to sign the will and a bee had been caught and put alive into his mouth – allowing the witnesses to swear on oath that 'there had been life in him'. The sister appealed the case as far as the House of Lords and won – but the lawyers' fees had consumed all the inheritance and Peg was left with nothing of her father's Jamaican wealth.[22]

Some like Eliza Junor, who excelled in penmanship at Fortrose Academy, were taken advantage of by more powerful men. We catch only glimpses of her life. At the age of twenty-one she had become the owner of two slaves in Demerara but we do not know if she had returned to the colony with her father. We know she was in Edinburgh in 1828, aged twenty-three, and on New Year's Day called on an old friend from Fortrose.[23] But ten years later she was in Wapping (London), the unmarried mother of a daughter named Emma, fathered by a Scottish 'gentleman', Thomas McGregor. By 1851 Eliza had returned to live near Fortrose, working as a seamstress, while Emma had probably been sent to a small boarding school in Somerset. Just before Eliza died in 1861, Emma visited her – but was recorded in the census return as a visitor, a governess. Only on the registration of her mother's death did she reveal that Eliza was her mother.

Helen Inglis was sent with her three brothers to be educated in the Highlands, in her case at Inverness Academy, where she attended the English classes in 1803 and 1804. Her mother was Susanne Kerr (d. 1814), a 'free mulatto woman' from St Vincent, and her father was George Inglis (1764–1847), part of an international family and business network originating in Inverness, which by the 1790s included the burgh's provost, a captain in the West India trade and merchants in Carolina and the Caribbean. George had been part of a highly profitable partnership in St Vincent and subsequently acquired property in Demerara. He returned to Scotland, where in 1798 he married Helen Alves, the sister of his former partners in St Vincent. But he brought with him his four 'coloured' children, leaving Susanne in Demerara. Both George's expanding Scottish family – he had nine children before 1810 – and his 'coloured' children lived in Inverness, at least for part of these years. While there were openings for her three brothers – the eldest, William, joined the East India Company army – Helen eloped to marry a Royal Navy captain, William Hepburn, in Edinburgh in 1813. The following year her father concluded a marriage settlement with Hepburn, who left the Navy to become a captain in the Demerara trade, based in Port Glasgow and Greenock. Helen died sometime between 1824 and 1828. Her children were now three generations distant from their African great-grandmother. Their eldest son, George Hepburn, moved to Demerara and their three daughters married in Scotland – but something pulled or drove them away and all three, with their families, sailed for Otago (New Zealand) in 1848.

Some other 'coloured' women who married in Scotland are known to have had difficult relationships. Amy Fraser (c. 1818–1901), the daughter of William Fraser of Reelig, was also known as Young (an assumed name) and Surawen (her mother's name). I have described her above at school in Nairn. She later moved to Keith, where her exotic looks – and perhaps an expected inheritance – attracted admirers. In 1835 she married a John Forsyth, but only after Peter Grant, as a friend of William, had met with and approved the young man. It was not a happy marriage. Although they had twelve children, Forsyth formally separated from Amy in 1862 and in 1865 he divorced her for adultery with a John Fraser, who lived in Rothes and was by then a bankrupt wood merchant.

REJECTIONS: ROBERT WEDDERBURN AND WILLIAM DAVIDSON

We know of two Afro-Scots children from Jamaica who lived in Britain, in the environment increasingly hostile to those of visible African ancestry, and who turned to radical politics in response to their experiences. The better documented is Robert Wedderburn (1762–1835/6?), born in Kingston, the son of an enslaved African woman and James Wedderburn of Inveresk, near Edinburgh. The other, whose Scottish roots were near Aberdeen, was William Davidson (1786–1820). He became part of a revolutionary group in London who plotted to kill the ministers of the British Government and who, with four other conspirators, was hung and beheaded outside Newgate Prison on 1 May 1820 – one of the last public decapitations in Britain.

Figure 13.2 Robert Wedderburn from the frontispiece of *The Horrors Of Slavery* (1824). © British Library.

Both Wedderburn and Davidson were deeply affected by slavery in Jamaica and prejudice in Britain.

Wedderburn's mother, Rosanna, was sold by his father while she was pregnant, with the stipulation that the child be freed. Robert was then brought up by his grandmother, known as 'Talkee Amy', receiving only 'paltry support' from his father. As a young man he came to London, where he worked as a tailor, became a Unitarian preacher and adopted an increasingly radical creed, which he first promoted in his pamphlet *The Axe Laid to the Root* (1817). This made common cause between disadvantaged people in Britain and the West Indies and, using his own experience to validate his views, called on enslaved Jamaicans to rise in rebellion. From his pulpit he cried, 'Repent, ye christians, for flogging my aged grandmother before my face' and in his pamphlet addressed planters like his father:

> Taking your Negro wenches to your adulterous bed . . . What do you deserve at my hands? Your crimes will be visited on your legitimate offspring.

In a later pamphlet, *The Horrors of Slavery*, he described his only visit to Inveresk:

I visited my father, who had the inhumanity to threaten to send me to gaol if I troubled him ... He did not deny me to be his son, but called me a lazy fellow and said he would do nothing for me. From his cook I had one draught of small beer, and his footman gave me a cracked sixpence.

Daniel Livesay makes the point that while earlier generations would 'simply have provided a small allowance for an illegitimate child from the colonies, many whites in the 1820s wanted no possible claims on legitimate British family fortunes'. Robert challenged his legitimate half-brother Colville Wedderburn:

Perhaps, *my dear brother* knows nothing of one Esther Trotter, a free tawny, who bore my father two children, a boy and a girl, and which children my inhuman father *transported to Scotland*.[24]

Rejection by his Scottish family was at the core of Robert Wedderburn's experience in Britain.

In London in 1812, Wedderburn met the English radical Thomas Spence (1750–1814) and would become a leading figure in the Society of Spencean Philanthropists, formed after Spence's death in 1814. Despite the rather anodyne name, their aim was to install a republican government, remove the aristocracy and nationalise land, in the belief that private landownership lay at the root of all injustice, inequality and economic exploitation. Spence, who was arrested eight times and served two long prison sentences, provided intellectual leadership and inspiration but it was the actions of his followers after his death which created what was, for the establishment, the most disturbing focus for militant radicals. After the killing of peaceful and unarmed protesters at St Peter's Field, Manchester, by volunteer and regular cavalry on 16 August 1819 – known as the 'Peterloo massacre' – the Spenceans concluded that only an act of political terrorism could overthrow the Government and usher in the revolution they sought. Their followers drilled after the services at Wedderburn's chapel in Soho and, in larger exercises at Primrose Hill, their leader declared that he depended 'more on Wedderburn's division for being armed than all the rest'. Wedderburn himself brought a 'new rhetorical flourish' to the band of conspirators who, by New Year 1820, were intent on assassinating the members of the Cabinet. The year 1820 would be unparalleled in peacetime, a year of radicalism, political dislocation and near revolution across the United Kingdom.

Had he not been arrested in December and gaoled in January pending trial on charges of blasphemous libel, Wedderburn would have been in the vanguard of this plot.[25] But another Jamaican-born Afro-Scot, William Davidson, remained at the centre of what became known as the 'Cato Street conspiracy'. The conspirators were a group of impoverished tradesmen who gathered under the leadership of a former militia officer, Arthur Thistlewood. Although they had few resources with which to procure arms, by the end of January 1820 they were agreed 'that all were ready to sacrifice their lives'. They believed their opportunity had come when it was announced in a London newspaper that the Cabinet were to dine together on 23 February at the house of Lord Harrowby, the Lord President of the Council, in Grosvenor Square. They planned to attack the house, kill the members of the Cabinet, and cut off and exhibit the heads of the hated lords Castlereagh and Sidmouth on Westminster Bridge. It was a trap.

Their organisation had been infiltrated by a government agent, George Edwards. No dinner was to take place, the newspaper announcement was a government hoax and the conspirators were arrested in their makeshift headquarters in a loft in Cato Street. One police officer was killed while apprehending the plotters. Nine were arrested, including Davidson. In his closing address to the jury at Davidson's trial, the solicitor general described the arrest:

> Davidson is apprehended, and immediately exclaims, "Let those be damned who will not die in liberty's cause;" and he sings a line of the admirable ballad of the poet Burns, "Scots wha' ha' with Wallace bled". Does not this speak for itself in terms too distinct to be misunderstood?

Who was William Davidson? He was born in Jamaica and accounts which circulated in the wake of the trials and executions described him as the second son of the Attorney General of Jamaica and a woman of colour. The problem with this is that there was no Attorney General of Jamaica called Davidson. Who then was he?

Davidson had a clear connection to Aberdeenshire. One of the few character witnesses called at his trial was an architect from Aberdeen who had known him there; and in a letter to his wife from prison he told her that he was determined to maintain both his integrity and 'that spirit maintained from my youth up', a spirit which had 'so long been in possession of the ancient name of Davidson (Aberdeen's boast)'. He described himself as 'a stranger to England by birth' whose father had been an 'Englishman' and whose grandfather had been a 'Scotchman'. His final plea to the gentlemen of the jury centred on his Englishness. He cited Magna Carta and argued from the English tradition of resistance to tyranny, '. . . with arms to stand and claim their rights as Englishmen; and if every Englishman felt as I do, they would always do that'.

I believe that Davidson was probably the son of the Kingston merchant John Davidson, who was an assistant judge and was of sufficient status in the colony to be appointed in 1795 as Captain of the 1st Troop of Horse in the colony militia. This John Davidson had a clear link to the north-east of Scotland since he sent his son to Marischal College in Aberdeen for a single year in 1797. The only other Davidson from Aberdeenshire who is known to have been in Jamaica lived a generation earlier – Charles Davidson, the second son of John Davidson in Tarland, thirty miles west of Aberdeen. A gravestone at Tarland of 1787 commemorated Charles as having died in Jamaica 'some time ago'. It is possible that the merchant John Davidson was the son of Charles Davidson – and this would be consistent with William Davidson describing his grandfather as a Scotchman but his father as an Englishman (which is how a Briton in Jamaica would commonly have regarded himself).

William Davidson was born in Jamaica in 1786/7 to a free woman of colour who was herself wealthy enough to later provide him with an allowance of two guineas a week and a gift of £1,200, both of which were paid 'regularly through her agent' in England. William was sent to school in Edinburgh at an early age, against the wishes of his mother, and later attended classes in mathematics in Aberdeen. He then became articled to a solicitor in Liverpool *c.* 1802 but abandoned this *c.* 1805, tried to travel to Jamaica but instead served six months impressed as a seaman in the Navy. He became apprenticed to a cabinetmaker in Liverpool *c.* 1805/6 and was later employed as a journeyman cabinetmaker in Lichfield (Staffordshire). After setting up in business himself and failing, he moved to London, where he became a journeyman before again setting up his own business in Walworth. In 1816 he married a widow with four

Telt Del.^t   Cooper Sculp.

WILLIAM DAVIDSON.

Figure 13.3 William Davidson (1820). © National Portrait Gallery, London.

children and the couple then had two children of their own. Davidson was an affectionate father whose main concern as he awaited trial was the welfare of his wife and all these children.

But Davidson had twice suffered in his personal relationships because he was 'a man of colour', losing both a girl he planned to marry in Liverpool (when she was spirited away by her friends) and a wealthy heiress, Miss Salt, in Lichfield (when the marriage was violently opposed by her father and she was unwilling to wait until she was twenty-one). When the second relationship ended, he had tried to poison himself. Later, after he became a Sunday school teacher in London, an approach to a young female teacher led to the claim, with no evidence, that he 'habitually indulged in attempts of a gross and indelicate nature on the persons of teachers and children'. Yet Davidson did not identify with other 'men of colour' who he would hear referred to as his 'countrymen', and during his trial he told the judge, 'I never associated with men of colour, although one myself, because I always found them very ignorant.'

Although proud to be a Davidson and singing 'Scots Wha Hae' as he was arrested, he had no apparent connection to or support from relations in Aberdeen, and he had left the town abruptly about 1801. If my identification of his family is correct, then, by the time of his trial, his uncle Duncan Davidson was a prominent advocate in Aberdeen and William would have been a dangerous relation to acknowledge – but that cannot have been true when he was a boy of fourteen.

UNCERTAIN FORTUNES AND UNCERTAIN FUTURES

For some of these children it seemed that they could make the most of their luck through emigration from Scotland. The sixty-nine Scottish-Guyanese children I have identified as coming to Britain include a few who returned to the colony, like John Noble who, with his sister Mary Ann, owned a share in plantation *Maryville* on Leguan Island in the mouth of the Essequibo River. But others ended their lives in New Zealand, Australia, Argentina, North America and in Guyana's neighbour Dutch Suriname – where slavery would not be abolished for another thirty years. In some cases, their own children made similar journeys.

And with their departure the presence of these men and women of colour faded from Scotland's sense of its own history. In 1899 correspondence began in the *Celtic Monthly*, a 'magazine for Highlanders', on the fate of the Camerons of Glen Nevis. All were agreed that the last of the family to live in Lochaber was John Cameron and that he had become a planter in Berbice. One writer believed that 'he ended his days in the Channel Islands' but added that 'if he left male off-spring I never heard of them'. Yet John Cameron, last of Glen Nevis, and the free-coloured woman Elizabeth Sharp had seven children. The three older sons married in Guyana, at least two of them to 'free coloured' women,[26] while the two unmarried younger brothers returned to Britain, perhaps with their father, and then sailed from London to Australia, arriving in 1845 to become graziers on the Darling Downs.[27] John Cameron sold his property in Scotland about 1850 and moved to St Helier (Jersey) with his two daughters.[28] Between 1850 and 1854, the three older sons and their families also left Guyana and emigrated to Australia,[29] leaving their unmarried sisters to care for their ageing father, who died in London in 1862.

Two other 'coloured' children born in the middle of the nineteenth century, who came to and remained in Britain, illustrate both the continued possibility of success and the continued vulnerability of these young men and women. Andrew Watson (1856–1921) is now recognised as the first black person to play association football at international level, representing Scotland three times between 1881 and 1882. He also attended Glasgow University and later qualified as a marine engineer. His older sister Annetta (1849–89) was less fortunate and her life story highlights the vulnerability of a young black woman in Scotland in the nineteenth century.

Annetta and Andrew were illegitimate children born in Georgetown, Demerara to Peter Miller Watson (a grandson of the Robertsons of Kiltearn) and Hannah Rose, a black or 'coloured' woman. Both were sent to be educated in England. Peter Miller Watson died in 1869, leaving £6,000 in trust to Annetta and £6,000 in trust to Andrew.[30] Andrew was boarding at Crossley Heath school in Yorkshire and Annetta went to live with her father's brother, William Robertson Watson, at Innerleithen. He had also recently returned from Demerara. When she reached the age of twenty-one in 1870, Annetta was a young black woman with a substantial inheritance living in a small Scottish town. Things went badly wrong for her in 1873 when, perhaps already pregnant, she married forty-four-year-old John Hunter Stevenson (1829–1900). The marriage was irregular – that is, it was valid but was not registered. The couple left for London and ten days after their marriage Stephenson had sex with another woman, possibly a prostitute, and infected Annetta with a venereal disease. They lived together in Brighton and at various addresses in London until, on 16 May 1874, Stevenson deserted her. He returned for one night in December and again passed on a venereal disease, after having had sex with a woman named Selina Deacon on several occasions and also with 'divers women'. At some point during this year Annetta had given birth to a child who had died. In July 1875 she petitioned for divorce but this was refused by the court, probably because she was judged to have condoned her husband's adultery by spending that final night with him.[31] Annetta moved to Glasgow, where she supported herself as a music teacher. By 1883 she had developed cirrhosis of the liver. If the cause was excessive use of alcohol, it would not be surprising given her treatment at the hands of her husband and by the laws of marriage. She made her will in the same year, leaving all her property to her doctor, Robert Stewart Pollock, who took on responsibility for the expenses of 'her sickbed and funeral' – and presumably continued to treat her.[32] She died six years later, leaving only a little more than £200.

The personal histories of some families are a fankle – lines so knotted as to be almost impossible to untie. When William Cruickshank (1813–52) died in Suriname, the *Aberdeen Press & Journal* noted that he was the 'eighth son of the same family who has died in different parts of the West Indies'.[33] He was the son of Helen Steuart and Dr John Cruickshank of Corse (Huntly). Not all their children can be identified but the sons included others who had died in Suriname, Grenada, Tobago and en route to Demerara – and at least a ninth son who was in Tobago and Grenada before his death in 1860. In Banff in 1851 there was a household headed by a young woman, twenty-year- old Ann Cruickshank, born in Grenada and attending a school in the town. The others in the household were her younger brother and three cousins, born in Grenada, Tobago and Suriname. The cousins were at school, William was articled to a solicitor, and there was another Suriname-born cousin living with relations at Forgue, near Huntly. None of these children can be traced in later censuses, although some of their Grenada-born relatives later lived in England. They appear briefly and then disappear, either remaining in Britain without revealing their colonial origins or returning to these colonies in and beyond the Victorian British Empire.

Dutch Suriname, where slaves were not freed until 1863, remained important. At emancipation, British subjects received 12 per cent of the compensation paid by the Dutch Government, with Scots receiving 9 per cent for 2,707 enslaved people.[34] Classinda Mary Macdonald (1855–1906) was the only child of Gordon Macdonald (1804–59), a native of Caithness who owned plantation *Moy* in Surinam. She was an illegitimate child, the daughter of an enslaved woman named Mary on plantation *Hamilton*, and so was herself born a slave. Gordon freed her in March 1858 and she came with him to Scotland. Her father died in Burntisland in 1859, the death being reported by his 'friend Robert Kirke', and a memorial was erected in the kirkyard at Burntisland. In 1861, at the age of four, she was living in Nairn, where one of the two trustees of her father's will was the rector of the Academy. When Classinda died in 1906, in Logierait parish (Perthshire), her name was added to the memorial to her father in Burntisland.[35] She was perhaps the last Scot to be born a slave and live in Scotland.

PART 4

Reckonings

How should we understand this history and how should we respond to it? What responsibilities do we have for the past? Should we apologise? Make reparations? And who is it who might have these responsibilities?

It would be absurd to claim that any individual living today bears a personal responsibility for the evils of British colonial slavery. But does that mean that as citizens today we have no obligations and responsibilities – no moral relationship – to this past?

And what might be the particular responsibilities of historians?

PART 2

RESOURCES

'It is always easier to remember victims than to cope with the difficult issue of perpetrators'

In *Justice: What's The Right Thing To Do?* the philosopher Michael Sandel considers what he calls the 'dilemmas of loyalty' in relation to public apologies for historic injustices. He begins with this:

> The main justifications for public apologies are to honour the memory of those who have suffered injustice at the hands (or in the name) of the political community, to recognise the persisting effects of injustice on victims and their descendants, and to atone for the wrongs committed by those who inflicted the injustice or failed to prevent it.[1]

Sandel then points out that the most thoroughgoing rejection of both apologies and reparations comes from those who believe that, in principle, you cannot apologise (or be asked to make reparations) for something you did not do. This belief is firmly rooted in the mainstream of modern Western philosophical tradition. On this view, 'the free choice of each individual is the source of the only moral obligations that constrain us'. It is not a claim that people are selfish but rather that they can only be responsible for their own, freely chosen acts and commitments. It is a view with a long and respectable intellectual tradition and was an important strand in the thought of the Enlightenment, an intellectual movement to which Scotland made an important contribution and which figures prominently in current discussions of Scottish identity. But it is also a view which gives force to claims, such as that of the American congressman Henry Hyde, quoted by Sandel:

> I never owned a slave. I never oppressed anybody. I don't know that I should have to pay for someone who did [own slaves] generations before I was born.

Or the former Australian Prime Minister John Howard, who rejected making an official apology to the Aboriginal peoples:

> I do not believe that the current generation of Australians should formally apologise and accept responsibility for the deeds of an earlier generation.

In December 2020 the Free Church of Scotland took a similar stance in response to questions about donations received in the 1840s from churches in the southern United States, whose members supported slavery:

> The question over whether the Free Church today 'regrets' receiving money from slave owners is meaningless. We cannot be held accountable for the deeds of former generations.[2]

Critics of apologies rightly grasp what is at stake here – because if it is appropriate to apologise on behalf of a community then it is appropriate to be asked to atone for the wrongs committed at its hand or in its name. This was recognised in a more recent comment by Thomas Devine in relation to Scotland and its involvement with slavery:

> Sir Tom Devine has warned that Scotland apologising for its role in the slave trade 'could form the basis for reparation claims'. Scotland's leading historian, who in 2015 edited *Recovering Scotland's Slavery Past*, instead called for 'a detailed public acknowledgement of the great extent of Scottish involvement in the transatlantic slave system'.[3]

There is, then, much at stake and it is unsurprising that 'acknowledge but do not apologise' is a commonly held position. However, those who reject the appropriateness of a communal apology for slavery – and some form of atonement – risk inconsistency if they simultaneously wish to take pride in their community's past and in its achievements. These achievements are, after all, also 'the deeds of an earlier generation'. Pride and shame are bound together as moral sentiments.

> You can't really take pride in your country and its past if you're unwilling to acknowledge any responsibility for carrying its story into the present, and discharging the moral burdens that may come with it.[4]

Pride often has official encouragement. Before writing this chapter I tried a sample British citizenship test – which I am pleased to report I passed. Whoever set the questions thought it was important that, as a British citizen, I knew that Sir Frank Whittle invented the jet engine and William Wordsworth wrote 'Daffodils', presumably so that I could, as a British citizen, take pride in these British achievements. But shared identities give rise not only to pride but also to shame, and the British citizenship test has been widely condemned by historians for its 'on-going misrepresentation of slavery and Empire' and its failure to address those aspects of Britain's past of which we should, as citizens, be ashamed.[5]

The same inconsistencies can be found in the promotion of Scottish pride and Scottish identity. Alexander Herman's infectiously enthusiastic *Scottish Enlightenment: The Scots' Invention of the Modern World* (2002) was often quoted by Scotland's First Minister Alex Salmond in the run-up to the 2014 referendum on Scottish independence. In this example, he was addressing an audience in New York:

> The key to the international reputation of Scots is . . . our hard-won reputation for invention which generated prosperity – for example James Watt's condensing steam engine, the bicycle, the television, the telephone, the fax machine, the MRI scanner, penicillin – inventions which defined modernity – all the way up to Dolly the Sheep! The list of inventions is so long that an American historian, Arthur Herman, went so far as to assert that Scotland had invented the modern world.[6]

Herman has been rightly criticised and in an earlier chapter I quoted Irvine Welsh's assessment of his book:

> [Herman] almost seems to claim . . . that the 'good' things in the empire – education, social reform and engineering – were solely the Scots' doing. The bad bits – racism, slavery, religious indoctrination – were down to others (the English).[7]

A similar criticism can be directed at Scotland's civic institutions and government. The moral burdens of the past include responsibility for how that past is understood, presented and articulated in the present. At the beginning of this book I noted the absence of the word 'slavery' in the Museum of Scotland, which set out in 1998 'to tell Scotland's story over the centuries and thus position it as an independent nation within the Union'. The Museum was, in this respect, a failure – politically, culturally, psychologically and morally. It is a failure repeated elsewhere.

In 2007 the Heritage Lottery Fund offered support for projects which marked the 200th anniversary of the abolition of the African slave trade. In response there were hundreds of projects in England but only seven in Scotland – and none from Scotland's national institutions.[8] Two years later, the Government-backed Year of Homecoming (2009) was marketed to affluent 'ancestry Scots' in Canada, the USA, Australia and New Zealand, while other parts of the Commonwealth, including the Caribbean, with deep historical connections to Scotland were ignored. Stephen Mullen described this at the time in trenchant terms:

> The Scottish government has severed itself from the complexity of the nation's past and shown how it is keen to adapt a romantic Disney-style parade based upon the denial of historical evidence . . . For a country with a long imperial past, a peculiarly white vision has been authorised and published.[9]

Yet the failure of the Museum of Scotland in 1998, the silence in 2007 on Scottish involvement in the African slave trade and in slavery, the white-washed history presented in the Year of Homecoming and the failures and silences since then have attracted little criticism. It is too early to tell if the Black Lives Matter campaign of 2020 will change that. Instead the dominant narrative in Scottish public life – particularly in discussions of Scottish identity and of Scotland's constitutional future – is of Scotland as tolerant, welcoming and inclusive.

For many this is embodied in the idea of 'civic nationalism', which is presented as consisting of commitment to ideals of equality and social justice, in the belief that an independent, democratic nation-state is the means to achieve these ends, and in an expressed inclusiveness such that anyone – 'regardless of where they come from' – can share in being Scottish. The case for independence is thus argued on the basis of fairness (social justice), of democracy ('decisions about Scotland are taken by the people who care most abut Scotland') and of inclusiveness. Despite the tone-deafness of events such as the Year of Homecoming, civic nationalism is often contrasted with 'ethnic nationalism', which promotes ancestry, heritage and a sense of belonging which excludes others. Modern Scottish identity has been said to be 'much more rooted in a sense of place rather than a sense of tribe'.[10]

Yet this civic nationalism is rooted in history and in a selective reading of that history. The Scottish Enlightenment figures prominently not only in the pride taken in Scottish science, inventiveness and business acumen but in the idea that a Scottish nation-state would be based on a set of shared values – 'the values of our people'. Thus, Minna Liinpää, in her analysis of arguments used during the Scottish referendum, found that key nationalist politicians 'repeatedly drew on historical events and people – especially the Enlightenment and Adam Smith – to argue that fairness, egalitarianism and democracy are indeed "Scottish values" that "[run] through Scotland like a vein"'.[11]

Liinpää found that the Enlightenment was evoked on multiple occasions during the referendum campaign and it was repeatedly argued that there exist certain 'Scottish values' which have been apparent throughout Scotland's history. These values are presented as either in some sense inherent – in the blood – or much more commonly as the outcome of a history in which, over time, the 'Scottish people' has committed itself to these values. This is a view of the nation and state which – in the Enlightenment tradition – relies on the fiction of a contract. It is as if we had all, as rational beings, agreed to be bound together in a nation which can impose taxes, make laws, act in our name and support these values.

Civic nationalism thus seems bound to regard Scotland's involvement in slavery – and in colonialism – as lying outside that shared core of values which it is claimed constitute Scottishness. This will be of concern to all those who are disturbed by Scotland's history of involvement with slavery.

BEYOND CIVIC NATIONALISM

Michael Sandel argues that we have three kinds of moral obligation. Two of these are easy to accept and articulate – and sit well in the Enlightenment tradition. There are obligations which are universal and which we owe to all people regardless of their origins, beliefs or allegiances. And there are personal obligations which arise because we have entered into agreements with others – by making promises, concluding contracts and making commitments. But Sandel argues that there is a third kind of obligation – duties which arise from our membership of a particular community. We owe something to our fellow citizens (as they do to us) – a commitment which goes beyond our universal obligations to all people. It is also more than arises from our freely entered into commitments to others. For most, it is by accident of birth that we have duties as a citizen.

Our moral experience tells us that these are real obligations. We should, for example, pay taxes to support what is done by the government of our country because we have a special set of obligations towards the limited number of people who are our fellow citizens. This is not a universal duty we owe for the benefit of all peoples. Nor is this an agreement we have entered into and to which we can be held – although much ink has been used in attempts to construe citizenship as if it were the result of a contract to which we have, in some sense, subscribed our name. Sandel argues that our moral sensibilities tell us that we have such obligations and yet they cannot be accounted for on the model that we are the freely choosing individuals of Enlightenment thought.

Sandel suggests that a powerful alternative to the idea that only individual consent can generate moral obligations lies in the 'narrative conception' of human beings – who are essentially 'storytelling beings':

> I can only answer the question 'What am I to do?' if I can answer the prior question 'Of what story or stories do I find myself a part?'.[12]

One of the most powerful contemporary exponents of this philosophical tradition is Alasdair Macintyre, who argues against the 'individualism ... expressed by those modern Americans who deny any responsibility for the effects of slavery ... saying, "I never owned any slaves"'. Macintyre gives as a further example 'the young German who believes that being born after 1945 means that what the Nazis did to Jews has no moral relevance to his relationship to his Jewish contemporaries'. Macintyre sees this as a moral shallowness stemming from the individualist believe that 'the self is detachable from its social and historical roles and statuses'. Instead Macintyre asks us to reflect on the fact that 'we all approach our own circumstances as bearers of a particular social identity':

> I am someone's son or daughter, someone's cousin or uncle; I am a citizen of this or that city, a member of this or that guild or profession; I belong to this clan, that tribe, this nation ... As such, I inherit ... a variety of debts, inheritances, rightful expectations and obligations.

These stories of which we are part are the stories of communities, including our political communities – the states to which we belong and the nations and communities they contain. And they are stories which we do not choose but in which we find ourselves. This is true in two senses. First, we find ourselves to be part of a story because we are born into a particular state and community, unless through some injustice we are born or made stateless. And second, we find ourselves – in the sense of becoming ourselves – within that state and nation, which we have in no way chosen. Here we are born, bred and grown, and through this come to know our obligations and our rights. We thus find ourselves to be a citizen of a particular state and we mature as moral beings – we find ourselves and our identity – in a particular time, place and culture. This is who we are – the starting point from which we make choices (which may, of course, include taking leave of that state or community). But none of us begins as a disembodied individual able to ask, 'Of what story or stories do I choose to be a part?'

We are, then, like it or no, part of some story – a history – and consequently we have special responsibility for the welfare of our fellow citizens who share our history. This is an 'obligation of solidarity or membership' which cannot be reduced to an act of consent. We have, of course, wider obligations beyond the bounds of our particular citizenship. And if the story of which we are a part includes our nation's past contributions – either to our shared common good as citizens or for wider benefit beyond its boundaries – then it is natural to take pride in this. This is patriotism in a simple, unobjectionable and commendable sense.

Many people, because their sense of identity and the vitality of their life rooted in a community, accept this in principle but still feel a 'dilemma of loyalty'. We all have a strong inclination to deny or avoid the 'moral burdens' while still taking pride in our shared past. Most attempts to do this involve some form of 'distancing' – making a distinction between the community to which we owe loyalty on the one hand and some 'other' group who must shoulder the moral burdens of shame and responsibility. Historians have a special responsibility here:

> The job of the historian is to make it clear that a certain event happened. We do this as effectively as we can, for the purpose of conveying what it was like for something to have happened to those

people when it did, where it did and with what consequences . . . It's our job to get it right, again and again and again.[13]

But all citizens – and historians as citizens – also have an obligation to strive for clear-sightedness about their own country's history and to oppose the distortion of that history for political ends, however worthy. If we accept the view that we have obligations of solidarity and membership because we are part of the community in which we find ourselves, then loyalty to this community might be expressed not as the jingoistic 'my country right or wrong' but as the challenge of 'my country right and wrong'. Both pride and shame are part of our inheritance.

Given Scotland's extensive involvement with slavery, it appears to me to be impossible to hold that the values of democracy, equality and social justice are in some sense at the core of Scottish identity – part of the essence of the nation and inherent in Scottish-ness. This has rightly been described as an attempt to claim an ethnic identity that 'comes in through the back door'.[14] But widespread commitment to these values is nonetheless real and for many this creates a tension as they strive to construct a continuing sense of shared identity – carrying the story forward – in a way which accepts the moral burdens but which does not diminish either their pride or their sense of common worth. The risk is that in our response to our history we become like many who have been complicit in the crimes of oppression.

COMPLICITY

The study of complicity in historical wrongdoing is a vital task. The novelist Marilynne Robinson has suggested one reason why this is so important.

> Words such as 'sympathy' and 'compassion' encourage identification with the victim. But moral rigor and a meaningful concern for the future of humankind would require that we identify instead with the villain, while villainy is still only potential, while we can still try to ensure that we would not, actively or passively, have a part in it.[15]

The operation of all slave-worked plantations – and especially the operation of large integrated sugar plantations – relied on what can be accurately described as an 'apparatus of terror'. That apparatus was not always and everywhere physically in action, except in the important sense that it was there as a con-

stant and effective threat. Policies of amelioration brought some
constraints to its operation. Nevertheless, no one who worked
on a plantation, or lived in a Caribbean colony whose economy
was based on enslaved labour, could be unaware of its existence.
In particular, any enslaved person who rebelled against their
status as a slave knew they would feel its full force.

There were undoubtedly a number of sadists, psychopaths
and predators – men like the notorious Thomas Thistlewood in
Jamaica – who acted with impunity within the system of slavery
and who showed little or no compunction or remorse for their
actions. And it can be argued that men like Thistlewood were,
if not essential, then at least useful as unmitigated instruments
of terror.[16] But many others in the free community found themselves, both during and after the era of colonial slavery, in what
can be called 'discomfort zones'. While perhaps not directly
involved in physical acts of terror, or at least not involved in
the worst excesses, they knew what happened and were often,
at least in some way, part of the system which maintained the
'apparatus'. They also benefited, along with millions of others
in the home countries, from the products and profits of the
plantations.

I have taken the terms 'apparatus of terror' and 'discomfort
zones' from Mary Fulbrook's magisterial book *Reckonings*, an
account both of the scale and the legacies of Nazi persecution
and of the subsequent quest – mostly in vain – for justice. The
quotation at the head of the chapter is from her book.[17] Central
to her work is an exploration of the 'myriad ways in which
individuals from the early 1930s became tangled up on the side
of the perpetrators' and in ubiquitous state-sponsored violence
– state terror. Millions of people had in some way or another
supported and sustained this regime. In the same way, millions
of people in some way or another supported and sustained the
regimes of slavery.

In the post-war period, most of those who had been on the
side of the perpetrators sought to construct a view of themselves
which did not diminish their sense of self-worth and which
achieved what oral historians call 'composure', bridging the
gap – sometimes a chasm – between what they had done, or
failed to do, and the values which they believed defined them as
individuals. There is a parallel with the many individuals who
supported and sustained the 'apparatus of terror' of colonial

slavery – or who benefited from it – and yet who, both before and after emancipation, sought to present themselves to others and, more importantly, to themselves as untainted by its evils.

Fulbrook details the strategies used by those who found themselves in these 'discomfort zones', strategies which most commonly consist of some form of 'self-distancing'. Consistently, even the smallest of geographical distances from what it can be suggested was the 'real' evil was psychologically important:

> For most Germans, Auschwitz – embodiment of the 'it' about which they claimed to know nothing – remains in their minds far from the heart of Germany, despite being located on a major railway line in an industrial area that was within the Greater German Reich, rather than tucked away in Eastern Poland like the Operation Reinhard camps. Even so, 'it' can conveniently be reduced to the gas chambers here, behind the barbed wire and watch towers, rather than including the killing sites that moved with the army and the Einsatzgruppen along the Eastern Front, or the euthanasia institutions spread across Germany and Austria, or the factories and building sites and farms in which slave labourers were exploited. Auschwitz, the heart of all evil, was far away and had nothing to do with those who professed to have known nothing.

The same strategies of self-distancing – locating the evil on the 'other side of the wire' – can be seen again and again from those entangled with slavery's apparatus of terror. The real cruelties were frequently presented as in the past or elsewhere, in another time and in another place. In Chapter 2 we saw how Major General Thomas Staunton St Clair recalled the horror of boarding a slave ship in Berbice in 1806. But, from the vantage point of his account published in 1834, he claimed to have persuaded himself at the time that, since slavery existed in Africa, the trade did not therefore 'add to the number of slaves already in the world, but merely transplant them from a land of ignorance and superstition to one of civilization and improvement'. The greater evil was in Africa. Moreover, he had believed that this would over time lead to better treatment of slaves in British colonies – a position which he and his readers in 1834 could regard as justified by Britain's abolition of slavery in its colonies. And he comforted himself with the reflection that the treatment of slaves, however bad, had been better than it had been under Dutch control of these colonies.[18]

For others, the atrocities were on another plantation or under an especially cruel manager or overseer – and not on their watch. In Chapter 4 we saw how William Macintosh in Grenada held slaves who were branded with his silver branding iron, while he condemned the greater evil of the torture of slaves to extract evidence. As Governor of Barbados, Lord Seaforth incurred the wrath of planters by enforcing changes which allowed the testimony of slaves to be heard in court, while he invested in plantations in Guyana. In Jamaica, Alexander Innes condemned the inhuman and cruel actions of the manager who ordered the whipping of a heavily pregnant woman – and welcomed his dismissal a few days later – while learning the trade of a sugar planter.

It was remarkable just how quickly many were able to create distance between the horrors of slavery – the 'real' evil – and their own actions. Scots were involved in all stages of the slave trade – in the slave castles on the African coast, in the dehumanising voyages on the 'Middle Passage', and especially in the many 'Final Passages' of their victims – and Scots were disproportionately present in the development of large, integrated plantations, which relied on inflicting terror. Yet a narrow view of the slave trade emerged as a process which ended when slave ships – conveniently sailing from English ports – had completed the 'Middle Passage' and disembarked their human cargo. The many 'Final Passages' as described in Chapter 2 could be ignored. The abolition of the African trade in 1807, which is still often misleadingly referred to as the abolition of 'the slave trade', became a convenient aperture through which to view the wider crimes of slavery.

Orkney-born Dr Thomas Stewart Traill (1781–1861), who practised medicine in Liverpool, wrote the first account of the life of his friend and patron, the abolitionist William Roscoe, shortly after Roscoe's death in 1831. Traill referred to Roscoe's 'generous sympathy with the suffering sons of Africa' expressed in his poem *Mount Pleasant* (1777), noting 'how early Roscoe denounced the traffic in human flesh' and how 'this required no inconsiderable share of moral courage . . . in the chief seat of the odious traffic'. Yet, when he wrote this, four of Traill's five stepsons were working in Demerara, one of them as an overseer on a plantation. Moreover, his friends and relations in Liverpool, including the powerful Sandbach family, had made their first money as slave factors and were now prominent slave owners and traders in sugar and cotton.

In Glasgow the very limited involvement of Scottish ships in transporting enslaved Africans across the Atlantic made it even simpler for the city to distance itself from its past. Half a century after the 1833 Act, the *Glasgow Herald* newspaper summarised the history of the city's West India Association which it claimed had, from its formation in 1807, embodied the 'trading instinct of Glasgow' as successors to the 'tobacco lords' of the previous century. The writer proudly proclaimed that, despite its role as a leading sugar port, it was 'to Glasgow's lasting honour that while Liverpool and Bristol were up to their elbows in the slave trade Glasgow kept out if it'. Indeed, as the *Glasgow Herald* also pointed out, in 1845 the Glasgow West India Association had contributed £20 to the Anti-Slavery Society of Glasgow and had campaigned against the equalisation of duties on 'slave grown and free grown sugar'.[19] This all contrasted, according the writer, with Liverpool, where 'there was no stone in her streets that was not cemented with the blood of a slave'.[20]

The disassociation of Scotland from the African slave trade was made easier by the very nature of the long campaign against slavery, which 'was carefully targeting the [African] slave trade in the 1790s and was anxious not to be seen to advocate emancipation'. It had its first success in the 1807 Act, which made illegal the transporting of slaves from Africa in British ships. It did not end slavery, nor did it end the trade in slaves in the wider sense – for wherever there were slaves they were, in one way or another, traded – and focusing the campaign on this objective had involved compromises for those who were strongly committed to the wider vision of the abolition of slavery itself. Once the Glasgow West India Association came to terms with the 1807 Act, it could concentrate its resources on defending its members against accusations of ill treatment of slaves on the plantations. So, in a petition to the House of Commons presented in May 1826, it rejected 'the most odious allegations ... of cruelty, neglect, and injury to the people under their control'. Its position was, in a sense, in line with the views of some anti-slavery campaigners, such as the London-based Scot James Ramsay, who Eric Williams later described as 'one of the earliest, ablest, and most diligent of abolitionists'. Ramsay skilfully avoided a blanket condemnation of the institution of slavery in campaigning against the slave trade and, rather naively, believed that 'the simple abolition of the trade, operating as a kind of necessity on the interests and discretion of the planter, will do everything at present for the slave that humanity requires'. The Glasgow Association was claiming that everything that humanity required had and was being done.[21]

The same spin can be seen in *Old Country Houses of the Old Glasgow Gentry*. Published in 1870, its description of Possil House included the following:

> Whatever faults our West Indians had (and they had their share), it must always be remembered to their credit that they kept aloof from the slave trade. Glasgow, alone of the four great sugar ports – London, Bristol, Liverpool, and Glasgow – was clean handed in this matter.

All this was a comfortable narrative for the city – and for Scotland.

And once emancipation was enacted, the British colonies too could promote themselves as beacons of freedom. For example, late on a Monday evening in July 1841 a rowing boat, with the name 'Colin Campbell' chalked on its side, drew alongside one of the wharves at Georgetown, on the east side of the Demerara River in British Guiana. The eight men on board, exhausted and hungry, quietly surrendered themselves to the local police. They had made a dangerous, two-week journey by river and sea from the lower Saramacca in the neighbouring Dutch colony of Suriname, rowing by night and hiding in the bush by day, and with no food at all for the last two days. But they had now completed the journey from slavery to freedom – from Dutch plantations to a British colony. Both local newspapers celebrated their escape. 'They touched our shores, and their shackles fell: so free, and freedom giving, is the soil on which the British Standard is unfurled,' proclaimed the *Guiana Chronicle*; while the *Guiana Times* declared that 'Liberty is a glorious prize worth periling life and limb for'. In this way the evil was distanced. It lay in Dutch Suriname – albeit under a Highland Scot – not in freedom-loving British Guiana.[22]

COMPETITIVE VICTIMISATION

There is a further lesson to be taken from studies of the Holocaust. As the last surviving victims die and their first-hand testimonies can no longer be called on, some forms of distancing and denial become easier. Among these is what has been called competitive or comparative victimisation, an approach which was promoted in Austria in the post-war years and by means of which the country portrayed itself not as a perpetrator but as the 'first victim' of the Nazis. In 2019 a survey of twenty EU countries found that a number of European governments were even now 'rehabilitating World War II collaborators and war criminals while minimising their own [country's] guilt'.[23] The worst case is Poland:

> Poland's historic understanding of itself as the 'Jesus of the Nations,' a deeply religious country which has suffered for too long under the might of its powerful neighbours, renders its status as a country of victims, rather than oppressors, core to its self-understanding. Thus, attempts to nuance the role of Poles in the war by suggesting that they may have been at once victims and perpetrators threatens many Poles' understanding of their national identity.

Michael Morris suggests that something similar happened in Scotland from the 1920s as views of the British Empire changed and there were challenges to the prevalent sanitised version of Britain's imperial history. The moral burden of the imperial past thus became more apparent, but in some circles in Scotland the crimes of empire were commonly depicted as English, while 'the Scots were reluctant, sympathetic, benevolent: the angel on the shoulder of the imperial enterprise'.[24] That error continues to be compounded by the widely held – and entirely unfounded – view that Scotland was a colony of the British Empire (or of England). In 2014 the historian Linda Colley, who has written widely on British imperial history, expressed her surprise at just how many people believed this – whatever the 'nuances of history'.[25] Morris points out a further area of confusion in 'false equivalences' of enslaved Africans and oppressed groups in Scotland:

> [F]or example indentured servants, cleared Highlanders, or Glasgow slum-dwellers [are] held to be much the same as enslaved chattel on the plantations. Nowadays social media is cluttered with claims that 'Scots were slaves too'.

Among that clutter is the claim that Scottish colliers and salters were slaves, a view comprehensively undermined by Christopher Whatley in the 1990s and more recently by Morris. Together they show that colliers received relatively high wages, were able to transfer between collieries, and – at least in the Burgh of Paisley – could be elected as magistrates.[26] 'It should', as Morris points out elsewhere, 'be possible to explore overlaps and differences between oppressed and exploited groups ... without unhelpful conflations which are themselves a timeworn form of denial.'[27] A similar conflation persists in the claim that Highlanders were enslaved.

HIGHLAND SLAVES?

Many Scots, including many Highland Scots, found themselves labouring on Caribbean and North American plantations in brutal, sometimes deadly, conditions under cruel masters who were bent on extracting as much profit from their work as possible. Most had sold their labour for a specified number of years in order to pay for their passage to the colonies, in the hope of a better future, but were meantime bound by their signature, or mark if they could not write, on a legal document called an indenture. Others went against their will, some sentenced as criminals to a period as an 'indentured servant' abroad – sometimes for life and sometimes coerced by threats and violence. Others were banished for their religious beliefs. But they were not slaves.

They were not slaves – and the difference is not a matter of academic quibbling over language. The masters of indentured servants 'owned' their labour but the indentured servants remained persons under the law, they had legal rights, they would be free at the end of their period of indenture and their children would be born free. Slaves were 'chattel' – mere property, to be used or mis-used as their owners thought fit – and both they and their children were enslaved in perpetuity.

Among the many indentured servants in the Caribbean, the Irish and their descendants were the most despised and, in the words of Hilary Beckles, suffered 'the most intense day-to-day discrimination and humiliation' in the English West Indies. Beckles thought that their condition was 'nearer slavery than freedom' but he did not confuse the two states.[28] However, a body of writing appeared which promoted the idea of 'the Irish-as-slaves, or as proto-slaves, as black men in white skins'. No serious research supports this view, which was thoroughly debunked in the 1990s by historians of the Irish Caribbean, notably Donald Akenson, but the idea gained traction in some circles and a similar misconception infected some accounts of Scotland's involvement with slavery.[29] Thus the condition of crofters in Skye has been described as similar to – or even worse than – enslaved Africans:

> From the point of view of Lord Macdonald and his fellow land-owners, then, the crofting system was a beautiful efficient form of exploitation. By limiting the amount of land at the family's disposal, by charging a high rent for that land and by paying extremely low prices for kelp, island lairds provided themselves with a workforce which was as much at their mercy, and as firmly under their control, as any set of slaves own a colonial plantation. The slaves indeed may have been rather better off. Compared to the condition of the average crofter, wrote one early nineteenth-century traveller in the Highlands and Islands, 'the state of our negroes is paradise'.[30]

The most influential case of the alleged enslavement of Highland Scots is an incident known as *Soitheach nan Daoine* (the Ship of the People). This involved the abduction in 1739 of around a hundred men, women and children, who were forced onto a ship in Skye and were to be sold as indentured servants in America. They were saved from this fate when storms drove the ship into Donaghadeee, on the west coast of Ireland, where some of the captives escaped and raised the alarm. The local magistrates began an investigation. The resulting report and case documents in Dublin Castle, which include the evidence of the victims, have been studied by James Hunter, who confirms that this was a case of brutal kidnap and that they were to be sold as 'indentured labourers ... just one step up from black slaves in the colonial pecking order'.[31]

In earlier writing, however, Hunter had described indentured labourers as 'people whose status was virtually indistinguishable from slaves'.[32] This view was central to *The Skye Story*, presented in the Aros Centre in Portree, Skye, from 1993. The exhibition challenged conventional and romantic accounts of the island's history and of the role of clan chiefs – and its designers claimed that they were very careful as to the facts:

> It was very important to us that we were factually correct. We did a lot of research. And we were very careful. If we were in doubt about anything we didn't use it.[33]

Yet part of *The Skye Story* was a model of part of the *William,* the vessel which took away the kidnapped tenants, with explicit references to it as a 'slave ship' and to 'Highland slavery'. Both of the landowners involved, MacDonald of Sleat and MacLeod of Dunvegan, had already been described in the 1930s as having made 'an experiment in slave trafficking from Skye', a description which was uncritically reproduced in 2001 by Murray Pittock in his *Scottish Nationality*.[34] In 2007 – the year which marked two hundred years since the abolition of the African slave trade – the contribution from Gaelic-language television was 'Soitheach nan Daoine', a forty-five-minute documentary described as 'a tale of slavery from the Highlands and Islands of Scotland'. The myth continues and the entry for MacLeod of Dunvegan in the ODNB still claims that the people were 'forcibly abducted to be sold into slavery in American plantations'.[35] Competitive victimhood seems to lie behind all these comparisons.

PROFESSIONALS

In *Reckonings*, Mary Fulbrook notes another form of self-defence among perpetrators in the ability to compartmentalise, to separate 'professional interests from the inhumanity of the situation', even allowing the 'authentic' professional self to find satisfaction in a job well done. This was most notably found in Nazi Germany among members of the medical professions, whose 'professional skills could be used, but for purposes at odds with the previously ethical standards of that profession'.

The role of surgeons and doctors in the slave trade and on the slave plantations is well documented, as is the prominent role of Scots in this profession. One example is Colin Chisholm (1754/5–1825) from Inverness, who flourished as a doctor, plantation owner and slave holder in Grenada and Guyana, made a significant contribution to the study of yellow fever, and at his death was one of the oldest fellows of the Royal Society and a member of learned societies in Edinburgh, Philadelphia, New York and Geneva. His last book, *A Manual of the Climate and Diseases of the Tropical Countries*, published in London in 1822, was aimed at 'the young tropical practitioner on his first resorting to those countries'. Chisholm not only profited from and supported slavery but helped to train a new generation of colonial doctors and sponsored the training of Bristol students at Aberdeen University. Yet the entry for Chisholm in the ODNB does not use the word 'slave' or 'slavery' and merely describes Chisholm as owning a plantation.[36]

Despite the extensive role of Scottish doctors in supporting the slave trade and plantation slavery, the £4.4 million refurbishment of the Surgeons' Hall Museums in Edinburgh, completed in 2015 under the auspices of the Royal College of Surgeons of Edinburgh, makes no references to this part of the profession's history. The College thus compartmentalise their own 'professional history', separating it from the unpalatable history of the involvement of many individual surgeons with slavery. This is despite the fact that, in addition to the many doctors who worked in plantations, some 40 per cent of the surgeons who sailed on Liverpool slave ships were Scots.[37]

Another subject is avoided at Surgeons' Hall. The museum promises visitors they 'will learn about murderers and body-snatchers Burke and Hare' and see 'a pocketbook said to be made out of the skin of William Burke' – and there is a re-creation of the study of the surgeon Robert Knox, the museum's first curator who received corpses from Burke and Hare. However, there is no mention of Knox's later role in the promotion of pseudo-scientific racism which led to him being described as 'the real founder of British racism'.

MODELS

Fortunately there are better examples to follow. Glasgow-born Neil MacGregor, former director of the British Museum, memorably said on taking up his position with Berlin's Humboldt Forum in 2015, 'The great thing a museum can do is allow us to look at the world as if through other eyes.' This is a significant challenge:

> If you look at western European civilisation they are all societies where very high levels of culture have been accompanied by astounding levels of brutality. The French culture is unthinkable without the Terror; Britain: Shakespeare and the slave trade. All of our cultures had this absolutely murderous shadow side.[38]

This presents 'a curatorial challenge but also a political, cultural and psychological one'. For MacGregor there is a stark contrast in how Britain – and we might add, how Scotland – forgets or distorts its past while Germany confronts it:

> If you compare the way we remember, the perfect example was the opening ceremony of the Olympics, that selective national memory: all true but not looking at any of the difficult bits.

Scotland is awash with similar presentations of history 'not looking at the difficult bits' – especially if the difficult bits might contradict the story told to tourists.

Earlier in this chapter I quoted the philosopher Michael Sandel on the three reasons why a public apology for the historical crimes of slavery might be required: to honour the memory of those who have suffered injustice, to recognise the persisting effects of injustice on victims and their descendants, and to atone for the wrongs committed. There are some historical crimes which are now generally consigned to history because, while it is important to recognise and record the horror of what took place, there are few if any persisting effects of the injustice. This is not the case with slavery, not least because slavery involved the kidnapping and transportation of over twelve million Africans – five and a half million in the southern Atlantic trade and seven million in the northern Atlantic trade.[39] Slavery and the plantation system it supported also uprooted and destroyed indigenous peoples and cultures in the Caribbean, sometimes through acts of ethnic cleansing. And slavery – even in its abolition – bred systematic and endemic racism, the effects of which undoubtedly persist.

But something can be done. In our civic institutions, in our public policy and in our approach to our shared histories.

Afterword
Ghosts in our Blood

I began this book with an account of an incident in my home town of Cromarty in which, more than two hundred years ago, a white teenager named Hugh Miller fought with and stabbed an older black student outside the local school. While they fought here in 1818, a number of men from Cromarty were engaged in – or were recently returned from – the oppression of thousands of Africans and their descendants on the coast of Guyana. These enslaved people had been forced to engage in one of the largest engineering feats of the early nineteenth century. According to the Venn Commission on the sugar industry in British Guiana, which reported in 1949, the creation of the coastal plantations of Guyana had involved digging more than 2.5 million miles of drainage canals and the building of 2,176 miles of sea and river defences – in the course of which some 100 million tons of mud had been moved by the labour of enslaved Africans and their descendants. Scotland's longest inland waterway, the Caledonian Canal, was then being completed and would open in 1822. Its construction involved moving about 300,000 tonnes of earth and stone, with the assistance of a steam dredger. The works of civil engineering which created the coastal plantations of Guyana were thus the equivalent of about three hundred Caledonian Canals.[1]

There was another Cromarty – a plantation created on the coast between the Berbice and Corentyne rivers – which was but one part of that vast enterprise. In 1818 it held in bondage seventy-four enslaved men, women and children. Fifty-two of them had endured the Middle Passage from Africa. They were but fifty-two among more than seven million who survived that horror. And twenty of those enslaved on plantation *Cromarty* had been born in slavery in Berbice, the oldest a sixteen-year-old girl named Soucky who worked in the cotton fields. She was the same age as Hugh Miller in Cromarty.

Just as the Caledonian Canal is dwarfed by the scale of the works which engineered the landscape of Guyana – and just as plantation *Cromarty* was but a tiny part of the plantation systems of the Caribbean and North America – so the magnitude of human suffering and death in the regimes of chattel slavery exceed any of the sorrows of Highland history. It is important to remember this, not least because slavery stole the identities and the voices of its victims and consigned them to a great silence. Only occasionally and often with difficulty can we hear these voices.

This book is largely about the white Scottish Highlanders who engaged in or benefited from these crimes against humanity, some reluctantly but most with enthusiasm and without remorse. Their voices can be clearly heard in the documents in many public and private archives, in Scotland and beyond, while in the same sources their victims are reduced to numbers and lists of chattel – property to be recorded along with cattle, goats, bales of cotton and hogsheads of sugar. Yet we know that there is what the poet and novelist Mary Ann Evans, writing under her pen name George Eliot, called 'that roar which lies on the other side of silence':

> If we had a keen vision and feeling of all ordinary human life, it would be like hearing the grass grow and the squirrel's heart beat, and we should die of that roar which lies on the other side of silence. As it is, the quickest of us walk about well wadded with stupidity.[2]

If we had 'a keen vision and feeling' for all the ordinary human lives destroyed or marred by slavery it would indeed shake the frames of our being. In writing this book I have tried to hear something from beyond the silence. Something not merely from the white northern Scots but from the enslaved Africans and their descendants, from those who reclaimed their freedom, from free women of colour, from the Black Caribs of St Vincent, from house servants, and from children of mixed race who found themselves in the increasingly racist society of Britain in the mid-1800s. But these voices remain a whisper. And yet even that whisper is difficult for us to bear. We are indeed 'well wadded with stupidity' and are inclined too readily to wrap ourselves in comfortable narratives of Scottish and Highland victimhood. We will only correct this by hearing voices other than our own.

Near to plantation *Cromarty* on the Corentyne coast of Berbice was plantation *Kiltearn*. It was created by George Rainy – who would later clear the island of Raasay of its people – along with his younger brother Gilbert and their cousin Gilbert Robertson, the son of the parish minister of Kiltearn on the Cromarty Firth. The leading Caribbean writer and political thinker, Jan Carew, who died in 2012 at the age of ninety-two, was a descendant of both slaves and slave owners at *Kiltearn* and Carew's mother was a Robertson. He remembered that his great-grandmother had said this:

> There are ghosts in our blood and we're lucky because the lowliest, the ones who suffer most in the world of the living, are always top dogs in the spirit world . . . We're blessed with the blood of the most persecuted folks on earth – Africans, Caribs, Portuguese Jews, French convicts from Devil's Island, Highland Scots and the Lord alone knows what else.[3]

This was a generous comment on the Highland Scots who, like the Robertsons and the Rainys, had come to Guyana to exploit others. His great-grandmother's magnanimity had a profound influence on Carew, who used her words in his conversations with Malcolm X to summarise his own political creed:

> Whenever we cut ourselves, we can see ghosts of those others peeping out from the African and Amerindian blood. The ghosts are always there talking their conflicting talk until there's a Tower of Babel inside your head. So you've got to listen well and search out the kindest, the strongest, the most human of these voices and make them your own.

If we acknowledge the truths of our history and listen to what is on the other side of silence, I believe we too may hear the most human of these voices. And then we may be able to bear the roar which lies there.

Notes

Chapter 1

1. Hugh Miller (ed. Michael Shortland), *Hugh Miller's Memoir: From Stonemason to Geologist* (Edinburgh, 1995), 107. Compare this with his account in Hugh Miller, *My Schools and Schoolmasters* (Edinburgh, 1993), 134, first published in 1854.
2. Hugh Miller, *Testimony of the Rocks* (Edinburgh, 1857), 443–4.
3. Miller, *My Schools and Schoolmasters*, 43; Hugh Miller (ed. Lydia Miller), *Sketchbook of Popular Geology* (Edinburgh, 1859), 304.
4. David Alston, 'A Forgotten Diaspora: The Children of Enslaved and "Free Coloured" Women and Highland Scots in Guyana Before Emancipation', in *Northern Scotland*, 6:1 (Edinburgh, 2015), 49–69.
5. UK Parliamentary Papers, *Journal of the House of Commons*, 26 May and 10 June 1824.
6. Alan L. Karras, *Sojourners in the Sun: Scottish Migrants in Jamaica and the Chesapeake, 1740–1800* (London, 1992); Michel Lynch, *Scotland: A New History* (London, 1991); Anthony Cooke, Ian Donnachie, Ann MacSween and Christopher A. Whatley (eds), *Modern Scottish History, 1707 to the Present*, 5 vols (East Linton, 1998); Thomas M. Devine, *The Scottish Nation: 1700–2000* (London, 1999) and *The Tobacco Lords: A Study of the Tobacco Merchants of Glasgow and Their Trading Activities, c. 1740–90* (Edinburgh, 1975); John Butt and Kenneth Ponting (eds), *Scottish Textile History* (Edinburgh, 1987).
7. Christopher Harvie, *Scotland: A Short History* (Oxford, 2002), 125.
8. Michael Fry, 'A Commercial Empire: Scotland and British Expansion in the Eighteenth Century', in Thomas M. Devine and John Young (eds), *Eighteenth Century Scotland: New Perspectives*

(East Linton, 1999) and *The Scottish Empire* (East Linton, 2001); James Hunter, *Last of the Free: A History of the Highlands and Islands of Scotland* (Edinburgh, 1999); Allan I. Macinnes, *Clanship, Commerce and the House of Stuart, 1603–1788* (East Linton, 1996).

9. Sheila Watson, 'National Museums in Scotland', conference paper delivered at European National Museums: Identity Politics, the Uses of the Past and the European Citizen, Bologna 28–30 April 2011 online at http://www.ep.liu.se/ecp_home/index. en.aspx?issue=064.

10. Thomas M. Devine (ed.), *Recovering Scotland's Slavery Past: The Caribbean Connection* (Edinburgh, 2015), 26–7.

11. Arthur Herman, *How the Scots Invented the Modern World: The True Story of How Western Europe's Poorest Nation Created Our World & Everything in It* (2001), published in the UK as *Scottish Enlightenment: The Scots' Invention of the Modern World* (Edinburgh, 2002); Irvine Welsh, review article in the *Guardian*, 19 January 2002.

12. James Robertson, *Joseph Knight* (Edinburgh, 2003); Ali Smith, review article in the *Guardian*, 7 June 2003.

13. Douglas Hamilton, 'Patronage and Profit: Scottish Networks in the British West Indies, *c.* 1763–1807', PhD Thesis (Aberdeen, 1999) and *Scotland, the Caribbean and the Atlantic World, 1750–1820* (Manchester, 2005); Thomas M. Devine, *Scotland's Empire, 1600–1815* (London, 2004).

14. Iain Whyte, *Scotland and the Abolition of Black Slavery, 1756–1838* (Edinburgh, 2006).

15. Kevin McKenna, 'We Scots must face up to our slave trading past', *Observer* (London), 22 November 2015.

16. Cait Gillespie, 'The end of amnesia? Scotland's response to the 2007 bicentenary of the abolition of the slave trade and the quest for social justice' (Leiden, 2017), 5. Online at Leiden University Repository https://openaccess.leidenuniv.nl/handle/1887/51507.

17. Thomas M. Devine, *Scotland's Empire: The Origins of the Global Diaspora* (London, 2012); Nicholas Draper, *The Price of Emancipation: Slave-Ownership, Compensation and British Society at the End of Slavery* (Cambridge, 2013).

18. Colin Kidd and Gregg McClymont, 'Scottish independence essay: Say No to colony myth', *Scotsman*, 6 August 2014.

19. Michael Fry in the *National*, 25 August 2020.

20. Iain MacKinnon and Andrew Mackillop, 'Plantation slavery and landownership in the west Highlands and Islands: legacies and lessons' (Community Land Scotland, 2020) online at https://www.communitylandscotland.org.uk/wp-content/uploads/2020/

11/Plantation-slavery-and-landownership-in-the-west-Highlands-and-Islands-legacies-and-lessons.pdf.

21. Douglas J. Hamilton, '"Defending the Colonies against Malicious Attacks of Philanthropy": Scottish Campaigns Against the Abolitions of the Slave Trade and Slavery', in Allan I. Macinnes and Douglas J Hamilton (eds), *Jacobitism, Enlightenment and Empire, 1680–1820* (Abingdon, 2014), 193.

Chapter 2

1. Louis P. Nelson, *Architecture and Empire in Jamaica* (Yale, 2016), 10–35.
2. Anthony Tibbles, *Liverpool and the Slave Trade* (Liverpool, 2018), 2–3.
3. Edward Tufte, *Beautiful Evidence* (Connecticut, 2016), 22, describing the 'terrible grid' in the illustration of the French slave ship *La Vigilante* captured off the African coast in 1823.
4. Gregory E. O'Malley, *Final Passages: The Intercolonial Slave Trade of British America, 1619–1807* (Williamsburg, 2014).
5. Trevor Burnard, *Planters, Merchants, and Slaves* (Chicago, 2015), 1–7.
6. Burnard, *Planters, Merchants, and Slaves*, 27.
7. Nelson, *Architecture and Empire in Jamaica*, 105.
8. Burnard, *Planters, Merchants, and Slaves*, 27.
9. Alexander Falconbridge, *Account of the Slave Trade on the Coast of Africa* (London, 1788); Simon Schama, *Rough Crossings* (London, 2015), 215.
10. UK Parliamentary Papers, *House of Commons Papers: Minutes* vol. 72, 'Minutes, &c. Reported To The House, Veneris, 19° die Martii 1790', 581; *Trans-Atlantic Slave Trade Database* online at https://www.slavevoyages.org.
11. TNA, PROB 11/1314: Walpole, Quire Numbers 662–710 (1798), Will of James Fraser, Master of the Pilgrim.
12. Fraser was also able to provide evidence on the Kingdom of Bonny from which the *Emelia* loaded slaves. Paul E. Lovejoy and David Richardson, '"This horrid hole": Royal authority, commerce and credit at Bonny, 1690–1840', in *Journal of African History*, 45 (Cambridge, 2004), 363–92 online at https://www.researchgate.net/publication/231786220_%27This_horrid_hole%27_Royal_authority_commerce_and_credit_at_Bonny_1690-1840.
13. Anthony Tibbles, *Liverpool and the Slave Trade*, 24–5.
14. Stephen D. Behrendt, 'The captains in the British slave trade from 1785 to 1807', in *The Historic Society of Lancashire & Cheshire*, 140 (1990), 79–140.

15. Obituary, *Inverness Courier*, 29 July 1835; George Anderson, *Guide to the Highlands and Islands of Scotland* (Inverness, 1842), 740; and for further background, Douglas Hamilton, *Scotland, the Caribbean and the Atlantic World 1750–1820* (Manchester, 2005).

16. Historic Environment Record, GDL00137 online at http://portal. historicenvironment.scot/designation/GDL00137.

17. Raymond D. Viechweg, *Grenada Uncovered: An Uncommon View of the Island's Geocultural Beauty* (Grenada, 2010), 33.

18. HCA D456, Baillie of Dunain papers, Alexander Baillie to Alexander Baillie, 18 March 1752 quoted by Hamilton, *Scotland, the Caribbean and the Atlantic World*, 195.

19. In 1772 James Baillie married Colleen or Colina Campbell, daughter of Colin Campbell of Glenure (the 'Red Fox' who was the victim of the notorious 'Appin murder' in 1752) and Janet Mackay of Bighouse in Sutherland (a merchant family to whom the Baillies were already distantly related).

20. Christine Eickelmann, *The Mountravers Plantation Community, 1734 to 1834* online at http://eis.bris.ac.uk/~emceee/mountraver splantationcommunity.html Part II, Chapter 4, 349 using Elizabeth Donnan, *Documents Illustrative of the History of the Slave Trade to America*, Vol. 4 (New York: reprint 1965), 389, 409, 421.

21. UK Parliamentary Papers, *House of Commons*, 'Minutes of Evidence on the Slave Trade' Part 1 (1790), 188.

22. David Richardson, *Bristol, Africa and the Eighteenth-century Slave Trade to America* (Bristol, 1966), 163.

23. Dr Bancroft in *The Edinburgh Medical and Surgical Journal* (1815), 421.

24. Nicholas Draper, 'The British State and Slavery: George Baillie, merchant of London and St Vincent, and the Exchequer loans of the 1790s' online at www.ehs.org.uk/dotAsset/de55e1a1-c7f6-450b-9a1a-831601ae46d9.docx.

25. Nicholas Radburn, 'Guinea Factors, Slave Sales, and the Profits of the Transatlantic Slave Trade in Late Eighteenth-Century Jamaica: The Case of John Tailyour', in *The William and Mary Quarterly*, 72:2 (April 2015), 243–86.

26. Ibid., 285.

27. 'Port Cities Bristol' online at http://www.discoveringbristol.org. uk/slavery/routes/bristol-to-africa/shipping/four-ships-fortunes.

28. Madge Dresser, *Slavery Obscured: The Social History of the Slave Trade in an English Port* (London, 2016), 153.

29. George Baillie, *Interesting Letters addressed to Evan Baillie, Esq., of Bristol merchant and Member of Parliament for that*

Great City and Colonel of the Bristol Volunteers (London, 1809), 23–4.

30. Draper, 'The British State and Slavery'.
31. George Baillie, *Narrative of the Mercantile Transactions of the concerns of George Baillie & Co.'s Houses from the year 1793 to 1805 inclusive* (London, 1805); George Baillie, *Interesting Letters addressed to Evan Baillie, Esq., of Bristol merchant and Member of Parliament for that Great City and Colonel of the Bristol Volunteers* (London, 1809); George Baillie, *Interesting Letters addressed to James Baillie of Bedford Square partner in the House of Baillie, Thornton & Campbell* (London, 1809); George Baillie, *Interesting Letters addressed to John Bolton Esq. of Liverpool, merchant, and Colonel of a regiment of volunteers* (London, 1809).
32. *London Courier and Evening Gazette*, 23 July 1805.
33. George Baillie, *Some Interesting Letters, Addressed to Mr Baillie* (London, 1807), 46.
34. Baillie, *Interesting Letters*.
35. R. Thorne (ed.), *The History of Parliament: the House of Commons 1790–1820* (London, 1986); 'Jaffray, John (d. 1832), of 87 Queen Anne Street, Westminster' online at https://www.historyofparlia mentonline.org/volume/1790-1820/member/jaffray-john-1832.
36. NRS GD46/17/20, Peter Fairbairn to Lord Seaforth, 16 October 1801.
37. Bolton had 'gone penniless to the Caribbean in the 1770s and returned to Liverpool . . . [where] he established himself as a large-scale . . . slave-trader who shipped thousands of captive Africans in the last years of the British slave-trade'. 'John Bolton' in *Legacies of British Slave-ownership* database online at http://wwwdepts-live.ucl.ac.uk/lbs/person/view/7760/.
38. NRS GD46/17/21, Peter Fairbairn to Lord Seaforth from Demerara, 23 April 1802; GD46/17/27, 2 November 1805.
39. NRS GD23/6/391, Letters of Donald Mackay.
40. NRS GD23/6/391/7, Donald Mackay, Demerary, to James Grant, Inverness, 30 October 1806.
41. NRS GD23/6/391/17, Donald Mackay to James Grant, from Ryde, Isle of Wight, 29 August 1833.
42. NAG, *Berbice Gazette*, 20 February 1813 online at http://proxy.handle.net/10648/733ba8ba-2135-0098-6ffa-d3dfb06227f5.

Chapter 3

1. Sheila M. Kidd, 'Gaelic books as cultural icons: the maintenance of cultural links between the Highlands and the West Indies',

in Theo van Heijnbergen and Carla Sassi (eds), *Within and Without Empire: Scotland Across the (Post)colonial Borderline* (Cambridge, 2013), 46–60.

2. Scottish Poetry Library, biography of Robb Donn Mackay online at http://www.scottishpoetrylibrary.org.uk/poetry/poets/rob-donn-mackay.

3. Donald Sage, *Memorabilia Domestica: or, Parish life in the North of Scotland* (Wick, 1889), 208.

4. Andrew Wright, *Present State of Husbandry in Scotland*, vol. iv (Edinburgh, 1784), 308.

5. For Robert Sutherland's friendship with Simón Bolívar and his support for Bolívar's campaigns, see https://www.davidalston.info/documents/forgotten-scots/robert-sutherland-of-midgarty-and-the-liberation-of-latin-america.pdf.

6. NRS SC9/36/1, Will of Robert Pope Esq of Gartymore, at Navidale, 1810.

7. Sage, *Memorabilia Domestica*, 173, 192.

8. Kidd, 'Gaelic books', 46–60; Ellen L. Beard, 'Robb Donn Mackay: Finding the Music in the Songs', doctoral thesis (University of Edinburgh, 2015) online at https://www.era.lib.ed.ac.uk/bitstream/handle/1842/20991/Beard2016.pdf.

9. Beard, 'Robb Donn Mackay', 164.

10. Ibid., 144.

11. Ibid., 231.

12. James Hunter, *A Dance Called America* (Edinburgh, 1994), 53.

13. Angus Mackay, *The Book of Mackay* (Edinburgh, 1906), 250.

14. William R. Wood, *Past Years in Pickering* (Toronto, 1911), 261; *Inverness Journal*, 16 December 1831.

15. Hunter, *Set Adrift upon the World: The Sutherland Clearances* (Edinburgh, 2015), 443.

16. TNA CO 48/4.

17. Edward Long, *History of Jamaica*, 2 vols (London, 1774), ii, 286–93.

18. PE01585: Scottish Jamaican Relations online at http://www.parliament.scot/gettinginvolved/petitions/PE01500-PE01599/PE01585_BackgroundInfo.aspx.

19. Trevor Burnard, *Planters, Merchants, and Slaves* (Chicago, 2015), 27.

20. Ibid., 26.

21. Text available online at http://www.clanmacfarlanegenealogy.info/genealogy/TNGWebsite/getperson.php?personID=I45336&tree=CC.

22. Alexander Murdoch, *Scotland and America, c. 1600–c. 1800* (Edinburgh, 2009).

23. Eric J. Graham, 'The Scots Penetration of the Jamaican Plantation Business', in Thomas M. Devine (ed.), *Recovering Scotland's Slavery Past: The Caribbean Connection* (Edinburgh, 2015), 82–98.
24. Robert Mackenzie Holden, 'The First Highland Regiment: The Argyllshire Highlanders', in *The Scottish Historical Review*, 3:9 (October 1905), 27–40.
25. David Armitage, *The Ideological Origins of the British Empire* (New York, 2000).
26. Louis P. Nelson, *Architecture and Empire in Jamaica* (Yale, 2018), 132.
27. Ibid., 105.
28. Ibid., 8–9.
29. National Archives of Jamaica, 1B/11/4/2 67.
30. Nelson, *Architecture and Empire in Jamaica*, 150–6.
31. James Boswell, *The Journal of a Tour to the Hebrides* (London, 1785), 197.
32. Nelson, *Architecture and Empire in Jamaica*, 154–6 using National Archives of Jamaica, 1B/11/3. vol. 56, fos 72–81, probate inventory of John MacLeod of St Dorothy, 1 August 1775.
33. John Williamson, *Medical and Miscellaneous Observations Relative to the West India Islands*, 2 vols (Edinburgh, 1817), i, 40: 25 August 1798.
34. *Colonial Magazine* (1842).
35. NLS MS 17956 Diary of Alexander Innes. Transcript online at http://www.jamaicanfamilysearch.com/Members/JournalAlexanderInnes.htm.
36. Iain Whyte, *Zachary Macaulay 1768–1838: The Steadfast Scot in the British Anti-slavery Movement* (Liverpool, 2011), 16. Whyte wrongly identifies the wife of John MacLeod I as a daughter of Lord Bannatyne – in fact his sister.
37. Justin Roberts, *Slavery and the Enlightenment in the British Atlantic, 1750–1807* (Cambridge, 2017), 23.
38. George Otto Trevelyan, *The Life and Letters of Lord Macaulay* (London, 1876), 10.

Chapter 4

1. For what follows, see Quobna Ottobah Cugoano, *Thoughts and Sentiments on the Evil of Slavery* (London, 1787), Penguin Edition 1999 with introduction and notes by Vincent Carretta; Walter C. Ruckner, *Gold Coast Diasporas: Identity, Culture, and Power* (Indiana, 2015), 66–8.
2. Louis P. Nelson, *Architecture and Empire in Jamaica* (Yale, 2016), 16–23.

3. Vincent Carretta, in the introduction to Cugoano, *Thoughts and Sentiments*, argues for this identification. It is confirmed by Campbell's evidence to Parliament in 1790, in which he stated that he visited other islands during every year he had resided in the West Indies (as Cugoano's owner did); and by the fact that Campbell wound up his partnership in Grenada in 1772 and was in London from 1773 (as was Cugoano's owner). Mark Quintanilla, 'The World of Alexander Campbell: An Eighteenth-Century Grenadian Planter', in *Albion: A Quarterly Journal Concerned with British Studies*, 35:2 (2003), 241.

4. Quintanilla, 'Alexander Campbell', 250.

5. On Cugoano's faith, see Martha Th. Frederiks, 'Ottobah Cugoano, Son of Africa: An Angry Abolitionist Voice', in Judith Becker and Brian Stanley (eds), *Europe as the Other: External Perspectives on European Christianity* (Göttingen, 2014), 219–42.

6. The first account was by Ukawsaw Gronniosaw (*c.* 1705–75), also known as James Albert, whose *A Narrative of the Most Remarkable Particulars in the Life of James Albert Ukawsaw Gronniosaw, an African Prince, as Related by Himself* was published in 1772.

7. Brycchan Carey, *British Abolitionism and the Rhetoric of Sensibility: Writing, Sentiment, and Slavery, 1760–1807* (London, 2015), 138.

8. NPG D34151, Richard Cosway (1742–1821), *A self-portrait with Maria Cosway and Ottobah Cugoano* 1784 online at https://www.npg.org.uk/collections/search/portrait/mw148292/Richard-Cosway-Maria-Louisa-Catherine-Cecilia-Cosway-ne-Hadfield-probably-Ottobah-Cugoano?LinkID=mp01040&role=art&rNo=19.

9. Kit Candlin, 'The role of the enslaved in the "Fédon Rebellion" of 1795', in *Slavery & Abolition*, 39:4 (2018), 685–707.

10. Tessa Murphy, 'The Creole Archipelago: Colonization, Experimentation and Community in the Southern Caribbean, *c.* 1700–1796', PhD Thesis (University of Chicago, 2016), 291.

11. Andrew Jackson O'Shaughnessy, *An Empire Divided: The American Revolution and the British Caribbean* (Pennsylvania, 2000).

12. Trevor Burnard, *Planters, Merchants, and Slaves* (Chicago, 2015), 120.

13. Richard Grove, *Green Imperialism: Colonial Expansion, Tropical Island Edens, and the Origins of Environmentalism, 1600–1800* (Cambridge, 1995), 264–308.

14. Sarah Thomas, 'Envisaging a Future for Slavery: Agostino Brunias and the Imperial Politics of Labour and Reproduction',

in *Eighteenth-Century Studies*, 52:1 (Baltimore, 2018), 115–33.

15. Kay Dian Kriz, *Slavery, Sugar, and the Culture of Refinement: Picturing the British West Indies, 1700–1840* (New Haven, 2008), 36.

16. Mia L. Bagneris, *Colouring the Caribbean: Race and the Art of Agostino Brunias* (Manchester, 2018).

17. William Young, *Considerations which may tend to promote the settlement of our new West-India colonies, by encouraging individuals to embark in the undertaking* (London, 1764).

18. Douglas Hamilton, 'Transatlantic ties: Scottish migrant networks in the Caribbean, 1750–1800', in Angela Macarthy (ed.), *A Global Clan: Scottish Migrant Networks and Identities since the Eighteenth Century* (New York, 2006), 52.

19. TNA PROB 11/964/136, Will of John Harvey of Grenada. See also entries in LBS under names of these individuals. I am grateful to Alison McCall for further detail and for drawing my attention to this family.

20. Donald Polson, 'The tolerated, the indulged and the contented: ethnic alliances and rivalries in Grenadian plantation society 1763–1800', PhD Thesis (University of Warwick, 2011), 25. Online at http://webcat.warwick.ac.uk:80/record=b2580744~S1.

21. BL, Add. MS 38416, Papers of Lord Liverpool, fo. 374, 'A description of the island of Grenada, 1763'. Beverley Steele, *Grenada: A History of its People* (Oxford, 2003), 73, 80.

22. Aaron Willis, 'The Standing of New Subjects: Grenada and the Protestant Constitution after the Treaty of Paris (1763)', in *The Journal of Imperial and Commonwealth History*, 42:1 (Abingdon, 2014).

23. Quintanilla, 'Alexander Campbell', 229–56; 'Mercantile Communities in the Ceded Islands: The Alexander Bartlet & George Campbell Company', in *International Social Science Review*, 79:1/2 (2004), 14–26.

24. UK Parliamentary Papers, *House of Commons Minutes*, Vol. 71, 'Minutes of Evidence on the Slave Trade 1790', Part 1, 147.

25. Caitlin Rosenthal, *Accounting for Slavery* (Harvard, 2018), 42–6.

26. Polson, 'The tolerated, the indulged and the contented', 122.

27. Douglas Hamilton, *Scotland, the Caribbean and the Atlantic World 1750–1820* (Manchester, 2005), 147 on Melvill's acquisition of land; *Audi Alteram Partem* (London, 1770), 79 on Melvill's sexual tastes.

28. Polson, 'The tolerated, the indulged and the contented', 42.

29. Tessa Murphy, 'The Creole Archipelago: Colonization,

Experimentation and Community in the Southern Caribbean, *c.* 1700–1796', PhD Thesis (University of Chicago, 2016).
30. *Audi Alteram Partem*, 14.
31. NRS GD267/5/6, Membership of the Masonic Lodge Brotherhood, Beggars Bennison & Maryland.
32. Quintanilla, 'Alexander Campbell', 248, 250.
33. Hamilton, *Scotland, the Caribbean and the Atlantic World*, 157.
34. *A narrative of the proceedings upon the complaint against Governor Melvill* (London, 1770), 96.
35. Emma Rothschild, *The Inner Life of Empires: An Eighteenth-Century History* (Princeton, 2011).
36. Polson, 'The tolerated, the indulged and the contented', 73 wrongly identifies Macintosh as a supporter of Melvill.
37. George's son, Charles Macintosh (1766–1843), was the inventor of the eponymous raincoat.
38. Innes M. Keighren, 'Circulating Seditious Knowledge: The "Daring Absurdities, Studied Misrepresentations, and Abominable Falsehoods" of William Macintosh', in Heike Jöns, Peter Meusburger and Michael Heffernan (eds), *Mobilities of Knowledge* (Springer open access publication, 2017) online at https://link.springer.com/book/10.1007/978-3-319-44654-7. Innes Keighren's blog details his continued research into the life and writings of Macintosh online at http://inneskeighren.com/williammacintosh and I am also grateful for personal communications from Dr Keighren.
39. Murphy, 'The Creole Archipelago', 139.
40. *Audi Alteram Partem*, 29, 53–4. Macintosh is probably the author of this anonymous work.
41. See 'Colbert de Castlehill en son temps: Recherches et débats sur la vie de l'évêque de Rodez Seignelay Colbert de Castlehill' online at https://colbertdecastlehill.com/.
42. Olaudah Equiano, *The Interesting Narrative of the Life of Olaudah Equiano, Or Gustavus Vassa, The African*, vol. 2 (London, 1789), 95–8.
43. *Edinburgh Evening Courant*, 22 June 1771.
44. Joseph Price, *Some observations and remarks on a late publication, intitled, Travels in Europe, Asia, and Africa* (London, 1782), 13, 153.
45. Price, *Some Observations*, 6.
46. George Mackintosh, *Biographical memoir of the late Charles Macintosh* (Glasgow, 1847), 159–64.
47. Rothschild, *Inner Life of Empires*, 356.
48. *Political Register* (1770), review of *A narrative of the Proceeding upon a Complaint against Governor Melvill*, 282.

49. http://inneskeighren.com/williammacintosh/?p=212 quoting US Vice President Aaron Burr (1756–1836).

50. Bibliothèque Ceccano Ms. 1297 from a letter dated 15 February 1772 online at http://inneskeighren.com/williammacintosh/?p=538.

51. *Audi Alteram Partem*, 85–6.

52. Chris Taylor, *The Black Carib Wars: Freedom, Survival, and the Making of the Garifuna* (Oxford, 2012), 65–6.

53. BL MS. Liverpool Papers, ADD MSS 38718, Macartney – Letters to Germain, 10 January and 25 October 1778.

54. The Registry, Grenada Supreme Court, 'Presentation on the propriety of permitting the French Inhabitants to remain in Grenada (1784)' quoted in Jacobs below.

55. Curtis Jacobs, 'The Fédons of Grenada, 1763–1814', conference paper January 2002 online at http://www.open.uwi.edu/sites/default/files/bnccde/grenada/conference/papers/Jacobsc.html.

56. John Barrow, *The Public Life of the Earl of Macartney*, 2 vols (London, 1807), i, 6.

57. David Richardson, 'The Slave Trade, Sugar, and British Economic Growth, 1748–1775', in Barbara Lewis Solow and Stanley L. Engerman (eds), *British Capitalism and Caribbean Slavery: The Legacy of Eric Williams* (Cambridge, 1987), 114.

58. David Beck Ryden, 'Does Decline Make Sense? The West Indian Economy and the Abolition of the Slave Trade', in *The Journal of Interdisciplinary History*, 31:3 (MIT, 2001), 347–74; and 'Eric Williams' Three Faces of West India Decline', in *Review (Fernand Braudel Center)*, 35:2 (New York, 2012), 117–33.

59. BL Add. MS 38228, Papers of Lord Liverpool, fo. 325, 331.

60. Gregory E. O'Malley, *Final Passages: The Intercolonial Slave Trade of British America, 1619–1807* (Williamsburg, 2014), 30, 370; Kit Candlin and Cassandra Pybus, *Enterprising Women: Gender, Race and Power in the Revolutionary Atlantic* (Georgia, 2015), 109.

61. Eliga H. Gould and Peter S. Onuf (eds), *Empire and Nation: The American Revolution in the Atlantic World* (Baltimore, 2015).

62. *An almanac, calculated for the island of Grenada and the Grenadines, for the year of Our Lord M,DCC,LXXXVII* (Grenada, 1787).

63. Candlin, 'The role of the enslaved in the "Fédon Rebellion" of 1795', 685.

64. Stephen Mullen, 'The Great Glasgow West India House of John Campbell, senior, & Co.', in Thomas M. Devine (ed.), *Recovering Scotland's Slavery Past: The Caribbean Connection* (Edinburgh, 2015), 124–44.

65. Isabel Harriet G. Anderson, *Inverness before Railways* (Inverness, 1885).
66. BL Liverpool Papers, ADD MSS 38718, Macartney – Letter to Germain, 25 October 1778.

Chapter 5

1. HCA D456, Baillie of Dunain papers, Alexander Baillie to Alexander Baillie, 18 March 1752, quoted by Douglas Hamilton, *Scotland, the Caribbean and the Atlantic World* (Manchester, 2005), 195.
2. Thomas (elder) writes in 1771: 'be pleased to let me know about my Sister in Main. Hugh is in very good health and is very mindful of his wife and family', suggesting that Hugh is his sister's husband. D238/D/1/17/6 (5), Thomas Fraser to Simon Fraser, from Grenada, 9 June 1771.
3. HCA D238/D/1/17/6 (4), Thomas Fraser to Simon Fraser, from Granada [sic], 3 August 1771; D238/D/1/17/6 (3), from Tobago, 31 May 1778; D238/D/1/17/6 (14), from St Vincent, 12 November 1786.
4. HCA D238/D/1/17/6 (17), Thomas Fraser to Simon Fraser, from St Vincent, 8 April 1791.
5. HCA D238/D/1/17/6 (2), Thomas Fraser to Simon Fraser, from St Vincent, 20 September 1777.
6. HCA D238/D/1/17/6 (17), Thomas Fraser to Simon Fraser, from St Vincent, 8 April 1791.
7. HCA D238/D/1/17/5, Thomas Fraser to Simon Fraser, from St Vincent, 10 July 1798.
8. HCA D238/D/1/17/6 (7), Thomas Fraser to Simon Fraser, from St Vincent, 28 July 1784.
9. TNA. CO 106/9. Letter to the Lords of the Treasury from the Commissioners for the sale and disposal of lands in the islands of Grenada, the Grenadines, Tobago, St Vincent and Dominica in Record of the Sales of the lands in the Ceded Islands, 1764–8. Entry for 12 May 1765, Tobago.
10. *The Scots Magazine*, 28 (Edinburgh, 1766), 443.
11. Douglas Hamilton, 'Scottish Trading in the Caribbean', in Ned C. Landsman, *Nation and Province in the First British Empire: Scotland and the Americas, 1600–1800* (London, 2001), 106.
12. Hamilton, *Scotland, the Caribbean and the Atlantic World*, 63.
13. Andrew Jackson O'Shaughnessy, *An Empire Divided: The American Revolution and the British Caribbean* (Pennsylvania, 2000), 60.

14. K. O. Laurence, *Tobago in Wartime 1793–1815* (UWI, 1997), 5.
15. Mark Quintanilla, 'Mercantile Communities in the Ceded Islands: The Alexander Bartlet & George Campbell Company', in *International Social Science Review* (2004), 17.
16. Jonathan M. Yeager, *Early Evangelicalism: A Reader* (Oxford, 2013), 146–52.
17. For details of Walter Kennedy extracted from Dutch Colonial records by Joyce Hand and Richard Ellis, see family tree of Helen J. Weldon online at http://www.genealogy.com/ftm/w/e/l/Helen-J-Weldon/WEBSITE-0001/UHP-0792.html (accessed 4 January 2016).
18. Hamilton, *Scotland, the Caribbean and the Atlantic World*, 64.
19. John Malcolm Bulloch, *The Gordons of Cluny* (privately printed, 1911).
20. John Malcolm Bulloch (ed.), *The House of Gordon*, 2 vols (Aberdeen, 1907), ii, 479–88.
21. National Archives of Trinidad, blog available online at https://nationalarchivestt.wordpress.com/2016/07/15/colonial-planter-christopher-irvine-part-1/.
22. NLS MS 19331 fo. 119, Mrs Anne Robertson (Forbes), Kiltearn, to her daughter Christian (Mrs Watson), Crantit, Orkney, 16 August 1806.
23. John Malcolm Bulloch, *The Gordons as Colonists* (privately printed, 1911), 37.
24. Laurence, *Tobago*, 2.
25. HCA D238/D/1/17/6 (3), Thomas Fraser to Simon Fraser, from Tobago, 31 May 1778.
26. Julie Chun Kim, 'The Caribs of St Vincent and Indigenous Resistance during the Age of Revolutions', in *Early American Studies*, 11:1, Special Issue: Forming Nations, Reforming Empires: Atlantic Polities in the *Long Eighteenth Century* (Pennsylvania, 2013), 117–32.
27. James Gordon was one of the absentee proprietors consulted by the British Government on the Caribs in 1770. Bernard Marshall, 'The Black Caribs – Native Resistance to British Penetration into the Windward Side of St Vincent 1763–1773', in *Caribbean Quarterly*, 19:4 (1973), 4–19 online at www.jstor.org/stable/23050239. Citing TNA CO. 101/14; Memorial of Sundry proprietors now in London to Hillsborough, 22 January 1770.
28. Charles Shephard, *An Historical Account of the Island of Saint Vincent* (London, 1831, reprinted 2013).
29. Ibid., 64 n4.

30. HCA D238/D/1/17/6, Thomas Fraser to Simon Fraser, from St Vincent, 21 October 1795.
31. For history of Stracathro, see https://www.parksandgardens.org/places/stracathro-house.
32. HCA D238/D/1/17/6 (2), Thomas Fraser to Simon Fraser, from St Vincent, 20 September 1777.
33. Thomas wrote in May 1794 that the marriage was in 1793 but this cannot be correct given that his daughter Kate was born eleven months after the marriage and another child was expected at the end of the year.
34. HCA D238/D/1/17/6 (21), Thomas Fraser to Simon Fraser, from St Vincent, 21 October 1795.
35. HCA D238/D/1/17/6 (26), Thomas Fraser to Simon Fraser, from Chateaubelair, St Vincent, 25 February 1797.
36. Christoper Taylor, *The Black Carib Wars: Freedom, Survival and the Making of the Garifuna* (Oxford, 2012), 160–4.
37. Tessa Murphy, 'The Creole Archipelago: Colonization, Experimentation and Community in the Southern Caribbean, *c.* 1700–1796', PhD Thesis (University of Chicago, 2016), 291 online at https://knowledge.uchicago.edu/record/727.
38. English heritage, 'Black prisoners of war at Porchester Castle' online at https://www.english-heritage.org.uk/visit/places/portchester-castle/history-and-stories/black-prisoners-at-portchester/.
39. Shephard, *Historical Account of the Island of Saint Vincent*, Appendix 20, 57, 62.
40. HCA D238/D/1/17/6 (41), Thomas Fraser to Simon Fraser, from St Vincent, 3 September 1802.
41. Portrait in oil of Lieutenant Colonel George Etherington, attributed to John Trotter, The Royal Green Jackets (Rifles) Museum, Winchester. Image online at https://artuk.org/discover/artworks/lieutenant-colonel-george-etherington-25498.
42. C. J. M. R. Gullick, 'The changing Vincentian Carib population', in Michael Crawford (ed.), *Current Developments in Anthropological Genetics: Volume 3 Black Caribs A Case Study in Biocultural Adaption* (New York, 1984), 38–9.
43. Liverpool University's Victoria Gallery: *The Eruption of the Soufrière Mountains in the Island of St Vincent, 30 April 1812.*
44. Select Committee on Petition of Proprietors of Estates in Island of St Vincent, Report (Eruption of Mount Souffrier), House of Commons Papers, permalink https://parlipapers-proquest-com.nls.idm.oclc.org/parlipapers/docview/t70.d75.1812-003246?accountid=12801; Shephard, *Historical Account of the Island of Saint Vincent*, Appendix 42.

45. S. D. Smith, 'Volcanic hazard in a slave society: the 1812 eruption of Mount Soufrière in St Vincent', in *Journal of Historical Geography*, 37:1 (2011), 55–67.

46. See map reproduced in David M. Pylea, Jenni Barclay and Maria Teresa Armijos, 'The 1902–3 eruptions of the Soufrière, St Vincent: Impacts, relief and response', in *Journal of Volcanology and Geothermal Research* (March 2018) online at https://doi.org/10.1016/j.jvolgeores.2018.03.005.

47. Trelawny Wentworth, *The West India Sketchbook*, 2 vols (London, 1834), ii, 335 online at https://archive.org/details/westindiasketch03wentgoog/page/n350.

48. Shephard, *Historical Account of the Island of Saint Vincent*, Appendix No. VI:

49. HCA D238/D/1/17/6 (17), Thomas Fraser to Simon Fraser, from St Vincent, 8 April 1791.

50. B. W. Higman, *Slave Populations of the British Caribbean* (Kingston, 1995), 155.

51. HCA D238/D/1/17/6 (5), Thomas Fraser to Simon Fraser, from Grenada, 9 June 1771.

52. HCA D238/D/1/17/6 (4), Thomas Fraser to Simon Fraser, from Grenada, 5 August 1771.

53. HCA D238/D/1/17/6 (3), Thomas Fraser to Simon Fraser, from Tobago, 31 May 1778.

54. HCA D238/D/1/17/6 (14), Thomas Fraser to Simon Fraser, from St Vincent, 12 November 1786.

55. HCA D238/D/1/17/6 (12), Thomas Fraser to Simon Fraser, from St Vincent, 20 June 1786.

56. HCA D238/D/1/17/6 (3), Thomas Fraser to Simon Fraser, from Tobago, 31 May 1778; D238/D/1/17/5, Thomas Fraser to Hugh Fraser, from St Vincent, 10 July 1798.

57. HCA D238/D/1/17/6 (13), Thomas Fraser to Simon Fraser, from St Vincent, 26 December 1787.

58. HCA D238/D/1/17/6 (20), Thomas Fraser to Simon Fraser, from St Lucia, 9 August 1794.

59. HCA D238/D/1/17/6 (5), Thomas Fraser to Simon Fraser, from Grenada, 9 June 1771.

60. HCA D238/D/1/17/5, Thomas Fraser to Simon Fraser, from St Vincent, 26 November 1793.

61. HCA D238/D/1/17/6 (34), Thomas Fraser to Simon Fraser, from St Vincent, 22 April 1800.

62. HCA D238/D/1/17/6 (37), Thomas Fraser to Simon Fraser, from St Vincent, 24 April 1801.

63. HCA D238/D/1/17/6 (32), Thomas Fraser to Simon Fraser, from St Vincent, 20 June 1798.

64. HCA D238/D/1/17/6 (21), Thomas Fraser to Simon Fraser, from St Vincent, 21 October 1795.
65. HCA D238/D/1/17/6 (5), Thomas Fraser to Simon Fraser, from Grenada, 9 June 1771.
66. HCA D238/D/1/17/6 (13), Thomas Fraser to Simon Fraser, from St Vincent, 26 December 1787; D238/D/1/17/6 (23), from St Vincent, 5 June 1796.
67. HCA D238/D/1/17/6 (16), Thomas Fraser to Simon Fraser, from St Vincent, 4 January 1790.
68. HCA D238/D/1/17/6 (26), Thomas Fraser to Simon Fraser, from St Vincent, 25 February 1797.
69. HCA D238/D/1/17/6 (37), Thomas Fraser to Simon Fraser, from St Vincent, 24 April 1801.
70. Ibid.
71. David Alston, '"You have only seen the fortunate few and drawn your conclusion accordingly": Behavioural economics and the paradox of Scottish emigration', in Angela McCarthy and John Mackenzie (eds), *Global Migrations: The Scottish Diaspora since 1600* (Edinburgh, 2016), 46–62.
72. HCA D238/D/1/17/6 (37), Thomas Fraser to Simon Fraser, from St Vincent, 24 April 1801.

Chapter 6

1. André de Cuming may have been the author of *Some account of the early years of Buonaparte, at the Military School of Brienne; and of his conduct at the commencement of the French Revolution* (London, 1797). For discussion of the authorship, see Guy Godlewski and Peter Hicks, 'Late 18th-century and very early 19th-century British writings on Napoleon: myth and history', in *Napoleonica La Revue*, 9 (2010), 105–17, but note that the putative author cannot be Thomas de Cuming but his older brother, André, as correctly stated in Frederich M. Kircheisen, *Bibliographie des Napoleonischen Zeitalters: einschliesslich der Vereinigten Staaten von Nordamerika* (Berlin, 1908).
2. NRS GD23/6/364, Thomas Cuming to Thomas Mewburn, Demerary, 11 September 1799.
3. *Essequebo & Demerary Royal Gazette*, 18 April 1812.
4. Memorial in Dallas Parish Church, Moray.
5. TNA PROB 11/941, Will of Jean Gordon; Douglas Hamilton, *Scotland, the Caribbean and the Atlantic World* (Manchester, 2005), 50; Simon David Smith, *Slavery, Family, and Gentry Capitalism in the British Atlantic* (Cambridge, 2006), 117.
6. Esther Mijers, 'Scotland, the Dutch Republic and Union:

Commerce and cosmopolitanism', in Allan I. Macinnes and Douglas J. Hamilton (eds), *Jacobitism, Enlightenment and Empire, 1680–1820* (Abingdon, 2015), 93–108; Esther Mijers, 'Between Empires and Cultures: Scots in New Netherlands and New York', in *Journal of Scottish Historical Studies*, 33:2 (2013), 165–95; Alison Games, 'A Dutch moment in Atlantic historiography', in Gert Oostindie and Jessica V. Roitman (eds), *Dutch Atlantic Connections, 1680–1800: Linking Empires, Bridging Borders* (Leiden, 2014), 362.

7. Stephen Conway, 'The Scots Brigade in the Eighteenth Century', in *Northern Scotland 1* (Edinburgh, 2010), 30–41; Joachim Miggelbrink, 'The End of the Scots-Dutch Brigade', in Steve Murdoch and Andrew MacKillop (eds), *Fighting for Identity: Scottish Military Experience c. 1550–1900* (Leiden, 2002), 83–104.

8. Smith, *Slavery, Family, and Gentry Capitalism*, 117; P. M. Netscher, *History of the Colonies of Essequebo, Demerara & Berbice* (Utrecht, 1888).

9. NRS CC8/8/128, Testament dative of Alexander Cuming of Craigmiln, who died in London in 1746.

10. Edward Bancroft, *An Essay on the Natural History of Guiana, in South America* (London, 1769), 366; Thomas J. Schaeper, *Edward Bancroft: Scientist, Author, Spy* (Yale, 2011).

11. Het Utrecht Archif online at https://www.archieven.nl/nl/ zoeken?miadt=39&mizig=100&miview=tbl&milang=nl&mic ols=1&mires=0&mizk_alle=cuming; University of Amsterdam Library, *Caerte van de rivier Demerary*, 1759 online at http://dpc. uba.uva.nl/cgi/i/image/image-idx?view=entry;subview=detail;e ntryid=x-166;viewid=SURI01_KAARTENZL-105-10-05.SID; sid=dc83faf3b87ea0535efc86c2f2e7816f;c=surinamica;cc=sur inamica;corig=surinamica;lasttype=boolean;lastview=thumbfull; np=next.

12. Henrietta Tayler, *Domestic Papers of the Rose Family* (Aberdeen, 1926), 15.

13. George Pinckard, *Notes on the West Indies Written During the Expedition Under the Command of the Late General Sir Ralph Abercromby*, 3 vols (London, 1806), i, 358–403.

14. NRS GD/46/17/14, fo. 337. The 'Mr Elliott of Demerary' referred to was another early Scots planter in the colony, probably William Elliot whose brother David was a merchant in Glasgow and a partner in the tobacco house of Robert Bogle and Company.

15. HCA D238/D/1/17/6, Thomas Fraser, St Vincent, to Simon Fraser, baker, Inverness, 4 January 1790.

16. Inverness Museum, Inglis papers.

17. Eileen Curran, 'Biographies of Some Obscure Contributors to 19th-century Periodicals', entry for Charles Kenneth Mackenzie online at http://victorianresearch.org/Obscure_contributors.html# mackenzie.

18. NRS GD/46/17/14, fos 337–64.

19. NRAS 2696, Papers of Fraser family of Reelig, Edward Fraser to his mother, 17 February 1805.

20. Marjoleine Kars, *Blood on the River: A Chronicle of Mutiny and Freedom on the Wild Coast* (London, 2020); National Archives of the Netherlands, Johannes van Keulen, *Nieuwe ez zeer accuraate generaale caart van de twee rievieren Berbice en Canja* [1771] online at https://www.nationaalarchief.nl/en/research/archive/ 4.VEL/invnr/1572/file/NL-HaNA_4.VEL_1572_Deelopname-02.

21. Donald Wood, 'Berbice and the Unification of British Guiana, 1831', in Michael Twaddle (ed.), *Imperialism and the State in the Third World* (London, 1992).

22. *Naamlyst der bestierders, officieren en bediendens en plantag-ien op de Colonie der Berbice, 1794* transcribed by Paul Koulen available at http://sites.rootsweb.com/~nyggbs/Transcriptions/ BerbiceColonists1794.pdf.

23. NRS GD/46/17/14, fo. 337, Lord Seaforth's draft memorandum to the Duke of Portland.

24. NRS GD/46/17/14, fo. 386, Edward Satchwell Fraser to Lord Seaforth.

25. NRS GD/46/17/14, fo. 337, Lord Seaforth's draft memorandum to the Duke of Portland.

26. John Shaw, *Water Power in Scotland, 1550–1870* (John Donald, 1984), 238.

27. HCA D456/A/10/49.

28. NRS GD/46/17/14, fo. 386, Edward Satchwell Fraser to Lord Seaforth, late 1800.

29. Storm van 's Gravesande, *The Rise of British Guiana* (republished and translated by the Hakluyt Society (London, 1911).

30. NRS GD46/17/20, Edward Satchwell Fraser to Lord Seaforth, 10 April 1801.

31. NRS GD46/17/20, Edward Satchwell Fraser to Lord Seaforth, 18 June 1801.

32. NRS GD/46/17/14, fo. 337.

33. David Alston, 'Scottish Slave-owners in Suriname: 1651–1863', in *Northern Scotland*, 9:1 (Edinburgh, 2018), 17–43.

34. NRS GD46/17/36, James Baillie Fraser to Lord Seaforth, 14 February 1814.

35. NRS GD46/17/35, fo. 332, Edward Satchwell Fraser to Lord Seaforth, 30 November 1810.

Chapter 7

1. Randy M. Browne, *Surviving Slavery in the British Caribbean* (Philadelphia, 2017), 5–7.
2. For Brutus' complaint, see TNA CO 116/138/app.12–13.
3. NRS GD23/6/427.
4. 'Als Sklave aus der Karibik 1822 zur Taufe nach Lindau gebracht' online at http://www.edition-inseltor-lindau.de/Sklave.pdf. It is possible that Rader was resident attorney rather than owner of *Belair*.
5. TNA CO 116/138/39–40.
6. TNA CO 116/138/137–8.
7. Caitlin Rosenthal, *Accounting for Slavery* (Harvard, 2018), 37.
8. NAG Minutes of Court of Policy and Criminal Justice, 11 July 1808 online at http://proxy.handle.net/10648/bc86ab1f-07c7-f0ed-70e5-76c56e3c9eae.
9. Parliamentary Papers, *Minutes of evidence before the Privy Council*, 2 vols (1828), i, 26.
10. Alexander Macrae, *A Manual of Plantation Management in British Guiana* (London, 1856), and Farquhar Macrae, various articles in *Farmer's Register* (Virginia, 1835).
11. TNA CO48/46 transcribed online at https://www.eggsa.org/1820-settlers/index.php/pre-1820-letters/t-menu/1209-sp-1941371150.
12. Kathy Fraser, *For the Love of a Highland Home: The Fraser Brothers' Indian Quest* (St Kilda, Australia, 2016).
13. Thomas Staunton St Clair, *A Residence in the West Indies*, 2 vols (London, 1834), i, 208.
14. NAG Court of Policy and Criminal Justice, 2 January 1812 online at http://proxy.handle.net/10648/20c7b7d2-3989-bf46-5057-2ef595893322.
15. NAG Court of Policy and Criminal Justice, 12–15 November 1810 online at http://proxy.handle.net/10648/b5d8a3f4-9d58-8e73-25b2-d2140d4c873e.
16. Steven Mullen, review of *Lord Seaforth* in the *Innes Review*, 71(2), 286–93.
17. Bram Hoonhout, *Borderless Empire: Dutch Guiana in the Atlantic World, 1750–1800* (Georgia, 2020).
18. Hoonhout, *Borderless Empire*, 92.
19. For example, the case of the laundress Antoinette described in Thomas Rain, *Life and Labours of John Wray* (London, 1892), 132–3, 245, 269.
20. NAG Court of Policy and Criminal Justice, 6 May 1811 online at http://proxy.handle.net/10648/2b5141d9-9bc7-2fed-c952-3e198f

0e92d8 and 5 February 1811 http://proxy.handle.net/10648/fd82 446a-6a6b-74bc-1127-95c05ccb274a. Both these sentences were imposed when Fairbairn was a member of the Court.

21. *Essequebo & Demerary Royal Gazette*, 9 January 1810.
22. NAG Court of Policy and Criminal Justice, 6 May 1811 online at http://proxy.handle.net/10648/2b5141d9-9bc7-2fed-c952-3e19 8f0e92d8.
23. NAG Court of Policy and Criminal Justice, 1 April 1811 online at http://proxy.handle.net/10648/9a8d7fad-bca1-5805-7471-344 0590c1a55.
24. NAG Court of Policy and Criminal Justice, 7 July 1811 online at http://proxy.handle.net/10648/a6737048-0a27-7d3d-8681-b17 e4321d04f.
25. Fraser, *Highland Home*, 136.
26. Alvin O. Thompson, *Unprofitable Servants: Crown Slaves in Berbice, Guyana, 1803–1831* (UWI, 2002), 155, 221–2.
27. Browne, *Surviving Slavery*, 158.
28. Marjoleine Kars, 'Dodging Rebellion: Politics and Gender in the Berbice Slave Uprising of 1763', in *The American Historical Review*, 121:1 (2016), 39–69; *Blood on the River: A Chronicle of Mutiny and Freedom on the Wild Coast* (London, 2020).
29. St Clair, *A Residence in the West Indies*, ii, 142–8.
30. TNA CO 111/8, Nicholson to Castlereagh, 6 June 1808, quoted in Eric Williams, 'The Historical Background of British Guiana's Problems', in *The Journal of Negro History*, 30:4 (Chicago, 1945), 357–81.
31. Rain, *John Wray*, 122.
32. NAG Court of Policy and Criminal Justice, 7 July 1814 online at http://proxy.handle.net/10648/23aa37c2-035a-6f0e-fa8c-ff96 3cfd14b6.
33. NLS Papers of Thomas Stewart Traill, MS 19332, fo. 102, Hugh Munro Robertson to Dr Traill, 17 April 1814.
34. Rain, *John Wray*, 122.
35. NAG Court of Policy and Criminal Justice, 7 July 1814 online at http://proxy.handle.net/10648/2ab249a2-f6a1-012d-a3bf-ca7d 7169520a.
36. These estates, which had been the property of the Berbice Association of Amsterdam, were run by Commissioners from 1811, returned to the Association under the Peace Treaty of 1815, and sold to Davidson & Barkly, John Cameron and Donald Charles Cameron in 1818. See Thompson, *Unprofitable Servants*.
37. Rain, *John Wray*, 121.
38. UK Parliamentary Papers, *House of Commons Reports*, Vol. 17,

'Further Papers relating to the Treatment of Slaves in the Colonies' (1818), 278–303.

39. Donald Wood, typescript of *British Berbice*. I am grateful to Peter Fraser for the opportunity to see this unpublished work.

40. NAG Minutes of Court of Policy and Criminal Justice online at http://proxy.handle.net/10648/dfeefcb3-80ac-22ad-2159-554a63 e131ac.

41. NRAS 2696, Papers of Fraser family of Reelig, Bundle 108, fo. 4a^r, William Munro to Edward Satchwell Fraser, 17 June 1804.

42. *Catalogue of the Library of the Royal Medical and Chirurgical Society of London* (London, 1856), 456; *List of the Graduates in Medicine in the University of Edinburgh* (Edinburgh, 1867), 16; William Smellie, *Account of the Institution and Progress of the Society of the Antiquaries of Scotland* (Edinburgh, 1882), 40, 106; Colin Chisholm, *An Essay on the Malignant Pestilential Fever introduced into the West Indian Islands from Boullam, on the Coast of Guinea, as it appeared in 1793 and 1794* (1795).

43. 1851 Census (England), Class: HO107; Piece: 1555; Fo. 26; Page: 18; GSU roll: 174787; TNA PROB 11/1803, Will of William Munro of Berbice.

44. NLS Ms 19331, fo. 65, Anne Robertson, Kiltearn, to her daughter Christian (Mrs Watson), Crantit, Orkney, 23 November 1801.

45. TNA CO 116/138.

46. *Chester Chronicle*, 22 May 1818 and many others.

47. George Pinckard, *Notes on the West Indies, Written during the Expedition under the Command of the Late General Sir Ralph Abercromby*, 3 vols (London 1816), i, 371–9.

48. Emilia Viotti da Costa, *Crowns of Glory, Tears of Blood: The Demerara Slave Rebellion of 1823* (Oxford, 1994); Janet Mills, *'Quamina, do you hear this?' Revisiting the Demerara Slave Rebellion, 1823*, Master's Thesis (Dalhousie University Halifax, Nova Scotia, November 2018) online at https://dalspace.library.dal.ca/bitstream/handle/10222/75038/Mills-Janet-MA-HIST-December-2018.pdf.

49. Mills, *Quamina*, 2.

Chapter 8

1. Kit Candlin and Cassandra Pybus, *Enterprising Women: Gender, Race and Power in the Revolutionary Atlantic* (Georgia, 2015), 15–31.

2. TNA CO 111/95, Petition of white planters and merchants to Lord Bathhurst, 18 December 1822.

3. TNA CO 111/94, Bear to Bathhurst, December 1822.

4. Christopher C. Thornburn, *No Messing: The Story of an Essex Man: The Autobiography of John Castelfranc Cheveley I, 1795–1870*, 2 vols (Privately published, 2001 and 2012), ii, 62.

5. Thornburn, *No Messing*, ii, 84.

6. Thornburn, *No Messing*, ii, 76.

7. Thornburn, *No Messing*, ii, 72.

8. Henry Bolingbroke, *A Voyage to the Demerary, Containing a Statistical Account of the Settlements There, and of Those on the Essequebo, the Berbice, and Other Contiguous Rivers of Guyana* (London, 1809), 51.

9. Thornburn, *No Messing*, ii, 66, 77, 113.

10. TNA T71/391–6.

11. Sixty-five of the women who made their mark can be matched with free coloured women who paid tax as recorded in the *Essequebo & Demerary Royal Gazette*, 25 September 1810.

12. *Essequebo & Demerary Royal Gazette*, 18 March 1815.

13. William Lloyd MD, *Letters from the West Indies, during a visit in the autumn of 1836, and the spring of 1837* (London, 1839), 49.

14. Thornburn, *No Messing*, ii, 76.

15. Matthew Henry Barker, *The Victory; or the Ward Room Mess* (London, 1844), 191. Barker left the West Indies, where he had edited a newspaper, about 1827.

16. NLS MS 19332, fo. 17. Gilbert Robertson, London, to Thomas Stewart Traill, Liverpool, 30 January 1824.

17. James Rodway, 'Other Times. Other Manners', in *Timehri: Journal of the Royal Agricultural and Commercial Society of British Guiana* (1889), 240 online at https://archive.org/details/nstimehri10roya/page/240.

18. Thornburn, *No Messing*, ii, 113.

19. Thornburn, *No Messing*, ii, 76.

20. Candlin and Pybus, *Enterprising Women*, 126–46, using NRS CS271/66510 Dorothea Christina Gordon & others v Major John Gordon.

21. The Gordon family had remained a force in their native Sutherland and in 1817 one of John's younger brothers, Adam, who had returned from army service, proposed leading an emigration of evicted Kildonan tenants to settle on the South African veldt. Although be claimed in the following April that 'more than one half of the inhabitants of [the Strath of] Kildonan [had] expressed their determination to accompany him', the plan came to nothing. See James Hunter, *Set Adrift Upon the World* (Edinburgh, 2015), 443.

22. Candlin and Pybus, *Enterprising Women*, 131–7.

23. John Malcolm Bulloch, *The Family of Gordon in Griamachary* (Dingwall, 1907).

24. Nicholas Draper, *The Price of Emancipation: Slave-Ownership, Compensation and British Society at the End of Slavery* (Cambridge, 2013), 236.

25. John Adams, *Old Square-Toes and His Lady* (British Columbia, 2001). For the Douglas connections to the north of Scotland, see http://www.spanglefish.com/slavesandhighlanders/index.asp? pageid=230027.

26. Adams, *Old Square-Toes*, 189.

27. TNA T391/510 Entry 550.

28. NRS SC70/1/25, Will of John Fraser died Findhorn, May 1818; for Alexander and John Fraser, see https://www.spanglefish.com/ slavesandhighlanders/index.asp?pageid=441886.

29. Candlin and Pybus, *Enterprising Women*, 97.

30. *Essequebo & Demerara Gazette* and *Royal Gazette*, 17 December 1808, 1 September 1810, 12 February 1811, 31 August 1811, 4 January 1812, 1 August 1812, 27 October 1812, 19 January 1813, 24 June 1815, 11 May 1805, 28 November 1807, 29 October 1808; *Demerary & Essequebo Royal Gazette*, 18 November 1817.

31. James Rodway, *Timehri: Journal of the Royal Agricultural and Commercial Society of British Guiana*, x (Georgetown, 1886), 236 online at https://archive.org/details/nstimehri10roya.

32. James Rodway, *Timehri*, x, 232 online at https://archive.org/ details/nstimehri10roya, quoted in Candlin and Pybus, *Enterprising Women*, 100.

33. Candlin and Pybus, *Enterprising Women*, 179.

34. George Augustus Sala, 'Travels in the County of Middlesex', in *Temple Bar* (London, 1887), i, 246.

35. Records accessed by Jeff van Aalst.

36. GROS Old Parish Registers 061/00 0010 0156; TNA CO 111/96, Petition from William Fraser, formerly of Berbice, then residing in the city of London, 19 October 1823.

37. TNA PROB 11/1780/160, Will of William Fraser; Pedro L. V. Welch, 'What's in a name?: From Slavery to Freedom in Barbados', Barbados Association of Retired Persons' Lecture, 23 September 2003 at www.h-net.org/~slavery under Discussion logs, March 2005. Dates of birth are from TNA CO 111/96 and, for Jane, from census returns. For Elizabeth, details are from TNA T71, Slave Registers, Berbice.

38. R. C. Downer had children born in Marseilles from 1821, see http://www.british-genealogy.com/forums/archive/index.php/ t-37757.html; NAS CS96/2131, William Fraser, plantation

owner, Berbice, journal 1819–29; TNA T71, Slave Registers, Berbice.

39. TNA T71, Slave Registers, Berbice.

40. TNA CO 116/143/235-36.

41. Robert Brown, *The History of Paisley Grammar School* (1875), 523; will of Elizabeth Swayne Bannister cited in Pedro L. V. Welch, 'Madams and Mariners', paper presented at Annual Conference of the Association of Caribbean Historians, April 7–12, 1997 at http://www.reocities.com/Athens/Ithaca/1834/document3.htm. Also referred to in Welch, 'What's in a name?', where the date of the will is given as 1823.

42. Pedro L. V. Welch, *'Unhappy and Afflicted Women?': Free Colored Women in Barbados: 1780–1834* (1999) online at http://cai.sg.inter.edu/revista-ciscla/volume29/welch.pdf but confusingly listed in the contents under a different title.

43. TNA PROB 11/1780; NRS CS96 2151; *London Gazette*, 5 February 1861.

44. Douwe Martens Teenstra, *De Negerslaven in de Kolonie Suriname* (Dordrecht, 1842).

45. David Alston, 'Scottish Slave-owners in Suriname: 1651–1863', in *Northern Scotland*, 9:1 (Edinburgh, 2018), 17–43.

46. David Alston, 'A Forgotten Diaspora: The Children of Enslaved and "Free Coloured" Women and Highland Scots in Guyana Before Emancipation', in *Northern Scotland*, 6:1 (Edinburgh, 2015), 49–69. Note that I incorrectly state that Elizabeth Munro, William Fraser's wife, was born in 1811. She was in fact born in 1787 and was forty-three when they married.

47. Rawle Farley, 'The Shadow and the Substance', in *Caribbean Quarterly* (December 1955), 132–53.

48. Henry G. Dalton, *The History of British Guiana*, 2 vols (London, 1855), i, 310–11.

49. Evidence of Henry Barkly in UK Parliamentary Papers, *House of Commons*, 'Select Committee on West India Colonies' (1842), 189.

50. NAG AL2.1A Census of Georgetown, 1838. The ward analysed covered Werk en Rust, Freeburg and Newburg.

Chapter 9

1. Nicholas Draper, *The Price of Emancipation: Slave-Ownership, Compensation and British Society at the End of Slavery* (Cambridge, 2013), 103.

2. Michael Taylor, *The Interest: How the British Establishment Resisted the Abolition of Slavery* (London, 2020).

3. Draper, *Price of Emancipation*, 273.
4. Philippe Chalmin, *Tate and Lyle: Géant du Sucre* (Paris, 1983), translated by Erica Long-Michalke, *The Making of a Sugar Giant: Tate and Lyle, 1859–1989* (1990).
5. Draper, *Price of Emancipation*, 236.
6. Mona Macmillan, *Sir Henry Barkly: Mediator & Moderator, 1815–1898* (Cape Town, 1970), 6.
7. Draper, *Price of Emancipation*, 236, 342.
8. Hugh Miller, *Scenes and Legends of the North of Scotland: Or, The Traditional History of Cromarty* (Edinburgh, 1st edn, 1835; 2nd edn, 1850; new edn ed. James Robertson, 1994), 392. References are to 1994 edn.
9. Gordon E. Bannerman, *Merchants and the Military in Eighteenth-Century Britain* (London, 2008), 117–18; John Finlay, *Legal Practice in Eighteenth-Century Scotland* (Leiden, 2015), 128.
10. *London Magazine: Or, Gentleman's Monthly Intelligencer*, 19 (1750).
11. The Davidson brothers also had their attachments to the Highlands but it was their older brother Duncan (1800–81) who in 1827 inherited the estate of Tulloch in Dingwall – along with £30,000, property in Dublin, shares in the Forth and Clyde Navigation Company, the Union Canal, the Dingwall Canal, the British Herring Companies, and a plantation in Grenada named *Mount Gay*, for which he received compensation of £5,000 for the emancipation of its slaves.
12. LRO 920 PAR/II/14/28, Patrick Parker (Liverpool) to his mother, 18 November 1835.
13. Under a wadset the lender gained possession but not absolute ownership of a property.
14. Bram Hoonhout, *Borderless Empire: Dutch Guiana in the Atlantic World, 1750–1800* (Georgia, 2020), 53–73, 190.
15. Edwin R. Purple, *Contributions to the history of ancient families of New Amsterdam and New York* (New York, 1881).
16. Eliga H. Gould and Peter S. Onuf (eds), *Empire and Nation: The American Revolution in the Atlantic World* (Baltimore, 2015), 250.
17. Hoonhout, *Borderless Empire*, 182.
18. NLS MS 19331, fo. 96, Mrs Anne Robertson, Kiltearn, to her daughter Christian (Mrs Watson), Crantit, Orkney, 14 February 1805. LRO Parker papers, letter of May 1792 quoted by David Hollett, *Passage from India to El Dorado* (London, 1999), 38.
19. NLS MS 19331, fo. 109, Mrs Anne Robertson, Kiltearn, to her daughter Christian (Mrs Watson), Crantit, Orkney, 9 October 1805.

20. Based on information in the Traill papers (NLS) and Parker papers (LRO).
21. LRO PAR 6/1, Gilbert Robertson to Charles Parker, 24 March 1799.
22. LRO PAR 1/53, C. S. Parker to E. Parker, 28 June 1810.
23. Thornburn, *No Messing*, i, 124. For George Buchanan (1782–1832), see https://www.spanglefish.com/slavesandhighlanders/index.asp?pageid=605729.
24. Mona Macmillan, *Sir Henry Barkly: Mediator and Moderator, 1815–1898* (Cape Town, 1970), 8.
25. *Timehri: Journal of the Royal Agricultural and Commercial Society of British Guiana*, ii (Georgetown, 1883), 272 online at https://archive.org/details/timehri02guiagoog/page/n3/mode/2up.
26. Stephen Mullen, 'The Great Glasgow West India House of John Campbell, senior, & Co.', in Thomas M. Devine (ed.), *Recovering Scotland's Slavery Past* (Edinburgh, 2015), 124–44.
27. NRS CS96/972–83.
28. *Timehri*, ii, 273.
29. Caitlin Rosenthal, *Accounting for Slavery* (Harvard, 2019), 54.
30. ODNB, 'Barkly, Sir Henry (1815–1898)' online at https://doi-org.nls.idm.oclc.org/10.1093/ref:odnb/1424.
31. UK Parliamentary Papers, *House of Commons*, 'Report on West India Colonies' (1842). Henry Barkly gave evidence on 23, 26 and 30 May 1842.
32. Trevor Burnard, *Hearing Slaves Speak* (Guyana, 2010), 5, 10.
33. UK Parliamentary Papers, *House of Lords*, 'Papers Relative to the Abolition of Slavery' (1835), Enclosure No. 108.
34. Liverpool Maritime Museum, D/EARLE/5/6/1. In 1830 *Highbury* produced 303 tonnes of sugar, 117,707 litres of rum and 48,034 litres of molasses.
35. Burnard, *Hearing Slaves Speak*, 1.
36. 'Report on West India Colonies', 187.
37. John Scoble, *Hill coolies: a brief exposure of the deplorable condition of the hill coolies in British Guiana and Mauritius, and of the nefarious means by which they were induced to resort to these colonies* (London, 1840), 20.
38. *Report of Messrs. Peck and Price* (Baltimore, 1840), 9.
39. Ramesh Gampal, *Guyana: from Slavery to the Present, Vol. 1 Health System* (Bloomington, 2015), 148.
40. Institute of Commonwealth Studies Library, ICS 70/197. McInroy Sandbach & Co. wrote to Sandbach Tinné & Co., 30 August 1834.
41. NLS MS 19330, fo. 6, Mrs Traill (Christian Robertson) to Mrs Yule, Kirkwall, 8 December 1834.

42. ICS 70/226, 21 January 1837.
43. Pat Hudson, 'Slavery, the slave trade and economic growth: a contribution to the debate', in Catherine Hall, Nicholas Draper and Keith McClelland (eds), *Emancipation and the Remaking of the British Imperial World* (Manchester, 2014), 50–1.

Introduction to Part 3

1. David Worthington, 'Sugar, Slave-Owning, Suriname and the Dutch Imperial Entanglement of the Scottish Highlands before 1707', in *Dutch Crossing: Journal of Low Countries Studies*, 44:1 (2019), 3–20; David Alston, 'Scottish slave-owners in Suriname, 1651–1863', in *Northern Scotland* 9:1 (Edinburgh, 2018), 17–43.

Chapter 10

1. Thomas M. Devine, 'Did Slavery make Scotia great?', in *Britain and the World*, 4:1 (Edinburgh, 2011), 40–64, 11.
2. Eric Williams, *British Historians and the West Indies* (Trinidad, 1964). The title of Carlyle's book was in fact more offensive but is now rendered thus.
3. Pat Hudson, 'Slavery, the slave trade and economic growth: a contribution to the debate', in Catherine Hall, Nicholas Draper and Keith McClelland (eds), *Emancipation and the Remaking of the British Imperial World* (Manchester, 2014), 44–7.
4. Hudson, 'Slavery, the slave trade and economic growth', 37.
5. Andrew Wight, *Present state of husbandry in Scotland*, vol. iv (Edinburgh, 1784), 81.
6. David Alston, 'Social and economic change in the old shire of Cromarty: 1650–1850', PhD Thesis (Dundee, 1999).
7. James Donaldson, *General View of the Agriculture of the County of Elgin or Moray* (London, 1794); ODNB, 'Duff, James, second Earl Fife (1729–1809), landowner' online at https://doi-org.nls.idm.oclc.org/10.1093/ref:odnb/8168; TNA T71/915, 48 *Grange* sugar estate, Hanover, Jamaica.
8. Alston, 'The old shire of Cromarty'.
9. James Robertson, *General View of the Agriculture of the County of Inverness* (London, 1813), 393–400.
10. Gordon E. Bannerman, *Merchants and the Military in Eighteenth-Century Britain* (London, 2008), 64.
11. Alexander Fraser, *The Frasers of Philorth* (Edinburgh, 1879), 210. In 1761 Fraser married a Margaret Wilson, in Gibraltar, and the couple had two children, Simon (1752–93) and Marjory (1754–1851). Simon junior was said to have had 'an ineptitude

for business' and objected to his father's plan that he should begin his career as a clerk in the merchant house. In 1790 it was agreed that he should go to Dominica to take charge of the firm's interests there but he died not long after his arrival. The daughter Marjory Fraser married Alexander Fraser, Lord Saltoun (1758–93) and it was their son William who entered the West India merchant house.

12. Bannerman, *Merchants and the Military*, 150.
13. Thomas Pennant, *A Tour in Wales* (London, 1778), ii, 351; Chris Evans, *Slave Wales: The Welsh and Atlantic Slavery 1660–1850* (Cardiff, 2010) and *From Sheep to Sugar: Welsh Wool and Slavery/ O Wlân I Siwgr:Brethym Cymreig a Chaethwasiaeth* online at http://www.spanglefish.com/welshplainsresearch.
14. C. Gulvin, 'The Union and the Scottish Woollen Industry, 1707–1760', *The Scottish Historical Review* (Edinburgh, 1971), 121–37.
15. Glasgow City Archives, T-SK22/2, original online at https://www. glasgowlife.org.uk/media/2925/tsk-22-2-new.pdf.
16. Beinecke Lesser Antilles Collection, M182 Calculation of the Annual Expenses on the Estates of Montrose. 'Cotton' was used to refer to other cloth, in this case woollen.
17. Pat Hudson, 'The Limits of Wool and the Potential of Cotton in the Eighteenth and Nineteenth Centuries', in Giorgio Riello and Prasannan Parthasarathi (eds), *The Spinning World: A Global History of Cotton Textiles, 1200–1850* (Oxford, 2009), 327–50.
18. United States Congressional Serial Set, Volume 6081, 'Customs Tariffs of 1842', 113.
19. John Evans, *The Gentleman Usher: The Life and Times of George Dempster*, 1732–1818 (Barnsley, 2005), 232 quoting Dempster to Sir Adam Ferguson, 27 November 1794.
20. NRS E726/28/1; NAS E787/24; David Loch, *A tour through most of the trading towns and villages of Scotland* (Edinburgh, 1778), 54–5 (Loch's visit to Cromarty was in 1776); Andrew Wight, *State of Husbandry* (Wight's first visit to Cromarty in 1781 is recorded in Vol. III and his return visit in 1784 in Vol. IV); NAS E726/28/ 1.
21. Hugh Miller, *My Schools and Schoolmasters* (Edinburgh, 1993), 455.
22. Ray P. Fereday (ed.), *The Autobiography of Samuel Laing of Papdale 1780–1868* (Kirkwall, 2000), 206–8.
23. UK Parliamentary Papers, 'Reports from Commissioners Vol. 22: Irish Fisheries' (1837), 53; evidence gathered from merchants in Wick by James Loch MP.
24. UK Parliamentary Papers, *House of Commons*, Hansard, 8 June 1836.

25. Jan Penrose and Craig Cumming, 'Money talks: banknote iconography and symbolic constructions of Scotland', in *Nations and Nationalism*, 17:4 (2011), 821–42.

26. *Inverness Courier*, 18 November 1840.

27. Justin Roberts, *Slavery and the Enlightenment in the British Atlantic, 1750–1807* (Cambridge, 2013), 57–8; Alistair Mutch, 'Religion and accounting texts in eighteenth century Scotland: organizational practices and a culture of accountability' (n.d.) online at http://irep.ntu.ac.uk/id/eprint/28360/1/5889_Mutch.pdf.

28. David Alston, *My Little Town of Cromarty* (Edinburgh, 2005), 173–8 and 'The old shire of Cromarty', Chapter 3.

29. Thomas M. Devine, *The Scottish Clearances: A history of the dispossessed 1600–1900* (London, 2018).

30. James Robertson, *A General View of the Agriculture in the County of Inverness* (London, 1808), 81.

31. Alston, 'The old shire of Cromarty'.

32. Devine, *The Scottish Clearances* 141–2.

33. Ibid., 318.

34. Ibid., 228.

35. As examples, Alastair McIntosh, *Decolonising Land and Soul: A Quaker Testimony* (Ottowa, 2015) online at http://www.alastairmcintosh.com/articles/2015-CYM-McIntosh-Decolonising-Quaker-Testimony.pdf and Dòmhnall Iain Dòmhnallach in *The Oxford Left Review* (2014) online at https://oxfordleftreview.com/whose-land-is-it-anyway/.

36. Iain MacKinnon, 'Colonialism and the Highland Clearances', in *Northern Scotland*, 8 (Edinburgh, 2017), 22–48.

37. Eric Richards, *The Highland Clearances* (Edinburgh, 2000), 217; Eric Richards, 'The prospect of economic growth in Sutherland at the time of the clearances 1809 to 1813', in *Scottish Historical Review*, 49:2 (1970), 154–70 at 164.

38. Allan I. Macinnes, 'Commercial Landlordism and Clearance in the Scottish Highlands: The Case of Arichonan', in Juan Pan-Montojo and Frederik Pedersen (eds), *Communities in European History: Representations, Jurisdictions, Conflicts* (Pisa, 2007), 49, 58.

39. Allan Macinnes, *Clanship, Commerce and the House of Stuart, 1603–1788* (East Linton, 1996), 223–4.

40. Jurgen Osterhammel, *Colonialism: A Theoretical Overview* (Princeton, 2005).

41. Devine, *The Scottish Clearances*, 319.

42. Catherine Hall, *Civilizing Subjects: Metropole and Colony in the English Imagination* (Chicago, 2002), 48–9.

43. Colin Kidd, 'Race, Empire, and the Limits of Nineteenth-Century

Scottish Nationhood', in *The Historical Journal*, 46:4 (Cambridge, 2003), 873–92.

44. Philip D. Curtin, *The Image of Africa: British Ideas and Action, 1780–1850*, 2 vols (Wisconsin, 1964), ii, 337.

45. Thomas Douglas, *Observations on the present state of the Highlands of Scotland, with a view of the causes and probable consequences of emigration* (London, 1805).

46. Robertson, *General View (Inverness)*, 451–8.

47. For a summary, see https://louisstott.com/tag/rev-james-robertson-dd/.

48. Kate Louise McCullough, *Building the Highland Empire: The Highland Society of London and the Formation of Charitable Networks in Great Britain and Canada, 1778–1857*, Doctoral Thesis (Guelph, 2014). For her conclusion, see 397–407.

49. McCullough describes the Society's network, which she dubs their 'Highland Empire', as extending through Great Britain, India and British North America. But there were also members in the Caribbean and South America. In 1810 Adam Cameron (*c.* 1771–1841), an illegitimate son of Cameron of Eracht (Lochaber), led fund-raising among the inhabitants of Paramaribo (Suriname) to support the establishment of a Gaelic Chapel in London for the benefit of their 'Christian brothers the Highlanders of Scotland'. He became a member of the HSL in 1816, referred to as 'Adam Cameron Esquire of Surinam' after his holdings of land and slaves in the colony, which had now been returned to Dutch control. In much the same vein, Revd James Robertson, although he decried Selkirk's promotion of emigration, found no difficulty in his eldest son Henry becoming a doctor in the East India Company nor in his third son, Duncan Robertson (1781–1850), becoming a significant slave holder in Jamaica, where he later led the suppression of an uprising of enslaved people in 1831.

50. Eric Richards, 'Scotland and the Uses of the Atlantic Empire', in Bernard Bailyn and Philip D. Morgan (eds), *Strangers Within the Realm: Cultural Margins of the First British Empire* (North Carolina, 1991), 67–114.

51. Trevor Burnard, *Planters, Merchants, and Slaves* (Chicago, 2015), 264–5.

Chapter 11

1. Iain MacKinnon and Andrew Mackillop, 'Plantation slavery and landownership in the west Highlands and Islands: legacies and lessons' – a Report for Community Land Scotland (November 2020) online at https://www.communitylandscotland.org.uk/

2020/11/new-research-reveals-extent-of-historical-links-between-plantation-slavery-and-landownership-in-the-west-highlands-and-islands.

2. Finlay McKichan, *Lord Seaforth: Highland Landowner, Caribbean Governor* (Edinburgh, 2018).

3. Steven Mullen, review of McKichan, *Lord Seaforth* in *The Innes Review*, 71:2 (Edinburgh, 2020), 286–93.

4. The Highlanders Museum, 'Francis Humberston (1754–1815), Lord Seaforth, MP for Ross-shire (1784–1790), Governor of Barbados (after Thomas Lawrence)' by William Dyce online at https://artuk.org/discover/artworks/francis-humberston-17541 815-lord-seaforth-mp-for-ross-shire-17841790-governor-of-barb ados-167121; Figge Art Museum, 'Portrait of Lord Seaforth' by Thomas Lawrence online at https://figgeartmuseum.org/art/collec tions/item/portrait-of-lord-seaforth-250170/990; NGS, Benjamin West, 'Alexander III of Scotland Rescued from the Fury of a Stag by the Intrepidity of Colin Fitzgerald' online at https://www. nationalgalleries.org/art-and-artists/5702/alexander-iii-scotland-rescued-fury-stag-intrepidity-colin-fitzgerald-death-stag.

5. Alexander Macrae, *The History of Clan Macrae* (Dingwall, 1899), 104; *The Late Lieutenant-Colonel F. Macrae, of the Demerary Militia, and Arthur Blair, Esq. Major-Commandant of the Royal Volunteer Cavalry Raised by Him* (London, 1806).

6. Allan I. Macinnes, 'Commercial Landlordism and Clearance in the Scottish Highlands: The Case of Arichonan', in Juan Pan-Montojo and Frederik Pedersen (eds), *Communities in European History: Representations, Jurisdictions, Conflicts* (Pisa, 2007), 47–64.

7. Ned C. Lansman, *Nation and Province in the First British Empire: Scotland and the Americas, 1600–1800* (London, 2001), 97–8.

8. ODNB, 'Malcolm of Poltalloch, Neill (iii) (1797–1857)' online at https://doi-org.nls.idm.oclc.org/10.1093/ref:odnb/110207.

9. S. Karly Kehoe, 'From the Caribbean to the Scottish Highlands: Charitable Enterprise in the Age of Improvement, *c.* 1750 to *c.* 1820', in *Rural History 27*, 37–59.

10. Macinnes, 'Commercial Landlordism', 55.

11. *Aberdeen Evening Express*, 1 June 1893.

12. *Cheltenham Chronicle*, 5 July 1810.

13. *London Courier and Evening Gazette*, 14 January 1809; *Morning Post*, 5 November 1802; Robert Huish, *Memoirs of George IV*, 2 vols (London, 1830), ii, 280.

14. NLS MS 17956, 'Journal of —— —— of Loanhead near Rathven, Banffshire'. Partial transcription online at http://www.jamaican familysearch.com/Members/JournalAlexanderInnes.htm.

15. Richard Sheridan, 'The rise of a colonial gentry: A case study of Antigua, 1730–1775', in *Economic History Review*, 13:3 (1961), 349.
16. Arthur S. Marks, 'Hogarth's "Mackinen Children"', in *The British Art Journal*, 9:1 (2008), 38–56. The portrait is online at http://onlinecollection.nationalgallery.ie/objects/11120/portrait-of-the-mackinen-children?ctx=d8a2bf2e-d586-4ac5-b53c-67cd 5144b961&idx=10.
17. Sheridan, 'The rise of a colonial gentry', 356.
18. Douglas Hamilton, *Scotland, the Caribbean and the Atlantic World* (Manchester, 2005), 114.
19. Sir Walter Scott to Miss Joanna Baillie, 19 July 1810 in *The Complete Works of Sir Walter Scott: With a Biography*, 7 vols (New York, 1833), vii, 155.
20. Slave Register online at https://www.ancestry.co.uk/interactive/ 1129/CSUK1812_133684-00000?backurl=https%3a%2f%2fse arch.ancestry.co.uk%2fsearch%2fdb.aspx%3fdbid%3d1129% 26path%3d&ssrc=&backlabel=ReturnBrowsing#?imageId=CS UK1812_133684-00460; Legacies of British Slave-Ownership online at https://www.ucl.ac.uk/lbs/claim/view/189.
21. Brian Harrison, *Peaceable Kingdom: Stability and Change in Modern Britain* (Oxford, 1982), 85.
22. *Scotsman*, 15 March 2016. Picture offered for sale by auction by 25 Blythe Road, auctioneers, catalogue 17 March 2016. *Oxford Dictionary of Art and Artists* (Oxford, 2009). The portrait is online at https://commons.wikimedia.org/wiki/File:William_ Alexander_Mackinnon_attributed_to_George_Hayter.jpg.
23. Online at https://www.themackinnon.com/history.html.
24. Eric Richards, *The Highland Clearances* (Edinburgh, 2000), 207–25.
25. Ian Shepherd, *Aberdeenshire: Donside and Strathbogie: An Illustrated Architectural Guide* (Edinburgh, 2006).
26. *History of Parliament*, 'GORDON, John (*c*. 1776–1858), of Cluny' by Stephen Farrell, online at http://www.historyofparliamenton line.org/volume/1820-1832/member/gordon-john-1776-1858.
27. Thomas M. Devine, *Clanship to Crofters' War: The social transformation of the Scottish Highlands* (Manchester, 1994), 77.
28. James A. Stewart Jr, 'The Jaws of Sheep: The 1851 Hebridean Clearances of Gordon of Cluny', in *Proceedings of the Harvard Celtic Colloquium*, 18/19 (Harvard, 1998/9), 205–26.
29. John N. MacLeod, *Memorials of the Rev. Norman MacLeod* (Edinburgh, 1898), 231–2.
30. Alexander Mackenzie, *The History of the Highland Clearances* (Inverness, 1883), 259.

31. *History of Parliament*, 'GORDON, John, of Cluny' online at https://www.historyofparliamentonline.org/volume/1820-1832/member/gordon-john-1776-1858.
32. Obituary in *Banffshire Journal*, 1 July 1858.
33. Evidence to the Napier Commission online at http://napier-skye.blogspot.com/2010/09/torran-raasay-22-may-1883-donald-mcleod.html.
34. John Macinnes (ed. Michael Newton), *Selected Essays of John Macinnes* (Edinburgh, 2006), 418; James Hunter, *Scottish Exodus: Travels Among a Worldwide Clan* (Edinburgh, 2007); Roger Hutchison, *Calum's Road* (Edinburgh, 2011).
35. Christopher C. Thornburn, *No Messing: The Story of an Essex Man: The Autobiography of John Castelfranc Cheveley I, 1795–1870*, 2 vols (Privately published, 2001), ii, 124.
36. *London Courier and Evening Gazette*, 14 January 1809.
37. Eric Richards, *Leviathan of Wealth: The Sutherland Fortune in the Industrial Revolution* (London, 1973).
38. Court of Session, 'Elizabeth Maxwell, alias Hairstones *v* the nearest of kin of her children (11 February 1747)' online at https://www.casemine.com/judgement/uk/5a8ff80a60d03e7f57eb86e8.

Chapter 12

1. James Allardyce, *Historical papers relating to the Jacobite period, 1699–1750* (Aberdeen, 1895), 562.
2. Angus Stewart, 'The Last Chief: Dougal Stewart of Appin (Died 1764)', in *The Scottish Historical Review*, 76:202, Part 2 (October 1997), 203–21.
3. Quoted in Peter Fryer, *Staying Power: The History of Black People in Britain* (London, 1984), 25.
4. David Bindman, 'The Black presence in British Art: Sixteenth and Seventeenth Centuries', in David Bindman and Henry Louis Gates, *The Image of the Black in Western Art* III, Part 1 (Harvard, 2010), 235–70.
5. Scottish National Portrait Gallery (SNPG) portrait online at https://www.nationalgalleries.org/art-and-artists/3473/james-drummond-2nd-titular-duke-perth-1673-1720-jacobite; ODNB, 'Drummond, James, styled fifth earl of Perth and Jacobite second duke of Perth' online at https://doi-org.nls.idm.oclc.org/10.1093/ref:odnb/8071.
6. ODNB, 'Kennedy [known as Douglas], Scipio [Sipio] (1693x7–1774), freed slave and weaver' online at https://doi-org.nls.idm.oclc.org/10.1093/ref:odnb/107129.

7. NPG, 'George Keith, earl Marischal' online at https://www.npg. org.uk/collections/search/portrait/mw04205/George-Keith-10th-Earl-Marischal.

8. Iain Whyte, *Scotland and the Abolition of Black Slavery: 1756–1838* (Edinburgh, 2006), 13.

9. Channel 4 documentary *Britain's Slave Trade* (1999) and accompanying book, Steve Martin, *Britain and the Slave Trade* (1999).

10. Kathy Fraser, *For the Love of a Highland Home: The Fraser Brothers' Indian Quest* (St Kilda, Australia, 2016), 3–5; GROS OPR Births 103/0010 0125 Kirkhill.

11. NPG, 'Sir Hector Munro' online at https://www.npg.org.uk/coll ections/search/portrait/mw04577/Sir-Hector-Munro?LinkID= mp03219&role=sit&rNo=0.

12. Emma Rothschild, *The Inner Life of Empires* (Princeton, 2011), 87–91; Gwenda Morgan and Peter Rushton, *Banishment in the Early Atlantic World: Convicts, Rebels and Slaves* (London, 2013), 29–42. Also discussed by Michael Morris in his *Scotland and the Caribbean, c. 1740–1833: Atlantic Archipelagos* (Abingdon, 2014), 203–4 but Morris wrongly locates the incident and muddles John Johnstone's relationship to John Wedderburn.

13. John W. Cairns, 'The definition of slavery in eighteenth-century thinking', in Jean Allen (ed.), *The Legal Understanding of Slavery: From the Historical to the Contemporary* (Oxford, 2012), 61–84. Dolly MacKinnon gives a detailed account of the case in '"Good God Mrs Nicholson!": slaves and domestic disquiet in eighteenth-century Scotland', in David Ellison and Andrew Leach (eds), *On Discomfort: Moments in a Modern History of Architectural Culture* (Abingdon, 2017), 8–23. MacKinnon gives the servant's name as 'Lauchen'.

14. *Caledonian Mercury*, 17 January 1778.

15. *Runaway Slaves in Britain: bondage, freedom and race in the eighteenth century* online at https://runaways.gla.ac.uk/. For analysis, see Stephen Mullen, Nelson Mundell and Simon P. Newman, 'Black Runaways in Eighteenth-Century Britain', in Gretchen H. Gerzina (ed.), *Britain's Black Past* (Liverpool, 2020), 81–98.

16. Donald Polson, 'The tolerated, the indulged and the contented: ethnic alliances and rivalries in Grenadian plantation society 1763–1800', PhD Thesis (University of Warwick, 2011), 292–3. Online at http://webcat.warwick.ac.uk:80/record=b2580744~S1.

17. Glasgow City Archives, TD301/6/3/1.

18. SOAS, CWM/LMS/12/05/03/West Indies and British Guiana/ Journals. Box 4: Diary of Rev. John Smith. Transcript online at https://www.vc.id.au/fh/jsmith.html.

19. *Derby Mercury*, 22 June 1753.
20. Whyte, *Scotland and the Abolition of Black Slavery*, 13.
21. Gretchen Gerzina, *Black England: Life before Emancipation* (London, 1995), published in the USA as *Black London: Life before Emancipation* (New Jersey, 1995), 136.
22. Royal Museums Greenwich, image online at https://collections.rmg.co.uk/collections/objects/14194.html.
23. Glasgow Museums online article at https://glasgowmuseumsslavery.co.uk/2018/08/14/john-glassfords-family-portrait/.
24. Analysis of notices in the *Demerara and Essequibo Royal Gazette*. The total included seven references to 'and family'. If each of these include a spouse and at least two children, then the total is at least 443. I have excluded second notices in the same year for the same individual (who might not have left as planned or might be making a second voyage). I have also excluded thirty slaves sent to Berbice and a 'troop of rope dancers'.
25. NLS MS 19332 fos 67–72, Hugh M. Robertson to Thomas Traill, physician, 21 Islington, Liverpool from Kensington, Demerary, 17 August 1806 and 9 September 1806.
26. Matthew Henry Barker, *The Victory; or the Ward Room Mess* (London, 1844), 207.
27. August Kappler, *Six Years in Surinam* (Stuttgart, 1854).
28. Manumission records online from Netherlands National Archives. This entry at http://www.gahetna.nl/collectie/index/nt00340/29eb7337-0571-43f5-938e-5e1f4049a552/view/NT00340_manumissies/sort_column/prs_achternaam/sort_type/asc/q/zoekterm/balfour/q/comments/1.
29. Manumission record online at http://www.gahetna.nl/collectie/index/nt00340/06f261e8-3410-47d2-a966-be8cc5559b2e/view/NT00340_manumissies/sort_column/prs_achternaam/sort_type/asc/q/zoekterm/kirke/q/comments/1/f/ove_tekst_eigenaar/Pl%20Hazard%20%28Nickerie%29%20en%20vrijdom%20verzocht%20door%20W.E.%20Ruhmann%20qq. There is a discrepancy between the age given on her death certificate and the year of birth (1832) given at manumission and also between the surname Hendrick and the surname Vaak given at manumission. However, it seems certain this is the same woman.
30. Lachlan Shaw and James Frederick Skinner Gordon, *History of the Province of Moray* (Glasgow, 1882), 352.

Chapter 13

1. NLS, Trail papers MS 19331, fo. 83, Anne Robertson, Kiltearn, to her daughter Christian (Mrs Watson), Crantit, Orkney, 20 April

1804. The term 'brigand' was sometimes used for free women of colour.

2. NLS, Traill papers, MS 19331, fo. 59, Mrs Anne Robertson, from Aberdeen, to her daughter Christian (Mrs Watson), Crantit, Orkney, 7 November 1800.

3. Abraham Rynier van Nest, *Memoir of Rev. George W. Bethune* (New York, 1867).

4. Daniel Livesay, 'Children of Uncertain Fortune: Mixed Race Migration from the West Indies to Britain, 1750–1820', PhD Thesis (University of Michigan, 2010) and *Children of Uncertain Fortune: Mixed-race Jamaicans in Britain and the Atlantic Family, 1733–1833* (North Carolina, 2018).

5. Kathy Fraser, *For the Love of a Highland Home: The Fraser Brothers' Indian Quest* (St Kilda, Australia, 2016), 312.

6. NRAS 2696, Papers of Fraser family of Reelig, James Baillie Fraser to his mother, 13 July 1828, quoted in Fraser, *For the Love of a Highland Home*, 318.

7. Donald Sage, *Memorabilia Domestica* (Edinburgh, 1889), 149–60. Sage does not say that the Hay brothers were from Jamaica but it is a reasonable assumption for Livesay to make.

8. HCA D238/D/1/17/6 (32), Thomas Fraser to Simon Fraser, from St Vincent, 20 June 1798.

9. NRS GD23/6/527; *Inverness Courier*, 31 December 1818.

10. *Inverness Courier*, 9 July 1818.

11. HCA D238/D/1/17/6 (37), Thomas Fraser to Simon Fraser of Boblainy, Inverness, from St Vincent, 24 April 1801.

12. University of Aberdeen, Rolls of Graduates online at https://www.abdn.ac.uk/special-collections/rolls-of-graduates-212.php#panel403.

13. Livesay, PhD Thesis, 127–32. Unfortunately Livesay provides only percentages for each decade and not the actual numbers.

14. Livesay, *Children of Uncertain Fortune*, 361.

15. HCA D766/5/6/1/2 Inventory. Grant's plantation was in the parish of St Thomas in the East. There was another *Airy Castle* in the parish of St Andrew.

16. David Beck Ryden, 'Manumission in Late Eighteenth-Century Jamaica', in *New West Indian Guide/Nieuwe West-Indische Gids*, 92:3/4 open access online at https://doi.org/10.1163/22134360-09203054.

17. From Revd William Leslie, *General View of the Agriculture of the Counties of Nairn and Moray* (Board of Agriculture, 1811). The Jamaican estates on whose profits this opulence was founded were *Bull Pen* and *Chatham*, both in the parish of St James. These had been owned by James Peterkin from the late 1780s, with his

older brother Alexander as overseer and then attorney. James was certainly there in person in 1795–6, when he was an assistant judge and a lieutenant in the militia during the Second Maroon War, during which Quamim, an enslaved man on Peterkin's estate who had escaped and joined the Maroons, was hunted down by 'Spanish dogs', killed while resisting capture, decapitated and his head placed on a spike at *Chatham*, and his body burnt. These bloodhounds had been brought from Cuba, along with their Spanish handlers, and the incident was described by critics in Parliament as 'an extraordinary circumstance of cruelty and barbarity'. *London Packet or New Lloyd's Evening Post*, 15 July 1796, 'From a Jamaica paper, Montego Bay, May 1796'; Gwenda Morgan and Peter Rushton, *Banishment in the Early Atlantic World: Convicts, Rebels and Slaves* (London: Bloomsbury, 2013), 118.

18. Portrait online at https://gallerix.org/storeroom/1265835004/N/ 147593580/. The date of *c.* 1800 attributed by the Louvre is at least a decade too early.

19. Sarah Harrison (ed.), *A Jamaican Master in Chancery: The Letter Books of Herbert James Jarrett, 1821–1840* (n.d.) online at https:// www.repository.cam.ac.uk/bitstream/handle/1810/254050/HJJ% 20letter%20book%20full%20numbered%20text.pdf.

20. David Alston, 'Scottish Slave-owners in Suriname: 1651–1863', in *Northern Scotland*, 9 (Edinburgh, 2018).

21. William Duguid Geddes, *Memorials of John Geddes. Being a record of life in an upland glen, 1797–1881* (Banff, 1899), 23, 37–9.

22. 'Lieutenant Jas. Fyfe, in Edinglassie, and Archibald Young, Procurator Fiscal of Banff v. Margaret Williamson, Wife of James Gordon, in Haugh of Edinglassie, and the said James Gordon, for his interest', House of Lords (1796) Paton 3, 478.

23. HCA D1038 Diary of Anne Fraser.

24. Livesay, *Children of Uncertain Fortune*, 96.

25. Malcolm Chase, *1820: Disorder and Stability in the United Kingdom* (Manchester, 2013), 50–5, 80, 208.

26. The sons were Alexander (1812–81), Evan (1817–72), John (1821–1904), Charles Matheson (1825–1907) and Donald Charles (1828–1914); the daughters were Helen (1809–84) and Isabella (1826–65).

27. Elizabeth Tarnawski, *The Camerons of Southeast Queensland* (1984).

28. Census Return, 1851.

29. For Evan Cameron, see New South Wales, Australia, Unassisted Immigrant Passenger Lists, 1826–1922 at www.records.nsw.gov. au/state-archives/research-topics/immigration/immigration; for

Alexander Cameron, see State Records Authority of New South Wales, Passengers Arriving 1855–1922, NRS13278, [X91] reel 400.

30. Leeds Probate Registry, Will of Peter Miller Watson formerly of Demerara, proved 30 April 1869.

31. TNA Divorce and Matrimonial Causes Files, J 77; Piece: 162; Item: 3927 & J 77; Piece: 155; Item: 3635A.

32. NRS SC36/51/100 Glasgow Sheriff Court Wills, Annette or Annetta Stephenson, 18 November 1889; SC36/48/127 Glasgow Sheriff Court Inventories, Annette or Annetta Stephenson, 18 November 1889.

33. *Aberdeen Press and Journal*, 2 February 1853.

34. Alston, 'Scottish Slave-owners in Suriname', 17–43.

35. *Inverness Courier*, 12 November 1909, report of Court of Session case arising from the will of Gordon Macdonald; manumission record available online at http://www.gahetna.nl/collectie/index/nt00340/446229de-1f1c-4c3a-9a72-7d33af9a0d86/view/NT00340_manumissies/sort_column/prs_achternaam/sort_type/asc/q/zoekterm/hamilton/q/comments/1/f/ove_tekst_eigenaar/M.C.%20Hamilton – surname wrongly transcribed as 'Namilton'; census returns.

Chapter 14

1. Michael J. Sandel, *Justice: What's the Right Thing to Do?* (London, 2009), 208–43.

2. Statement issued to BBC Alba, broadcast 11 December 2020.

3. 'Devine: Scotland apologising for slavery could cause problems', in *The National*, 21 July 2019.

4. Sandel, *Justice*, 235.

5. 'Historians Call for a Review of Home Office Citizenship and Settlement Test', letter by 181 historians of Britain and the British Empire and writing in protest in *History, the journal of the Historical Association* (July 2020).

6. Alex Salmond, speech in New York, April 2014 online at https://www.opendemocracy.net/en/opendemocracyuk/good-global-citizen-alex-salmonds-speech-on-scotlands-role-in-world.

7. Irvine Welsh, 'Review of *Scottish Enlightenment: The Scots' Invention of the Modern World'*, *Scotsman*, 19 January 2002.

8. Cait Gillespie, *The end of amnesia? Scotland's response to the 2007 bicentenary of the abolition of the slave trade and the quest for social justice* (Leiden, 2017), Master's Thesis online at http://hdl.handle.net/1887/51507.

9. Quoted in Minna Liinpää, 'Nationalism and Scotland's Imperial

Past', in *No Problem Here: Understanding Racism in Scotland* (Edinburgh, 2018).

10. T. C. Smout quoted in Antonia Kearton, 'Imagining the "Mongrel Nation": Political Uses of History in the Recent Scottish Nationalist Movement', in *National Identities*, 7:1 (2005), 23–50 online at https://doi.org/10.1080/14608940500072933.

11. Minna Liinpää, 'Nationalism from Above and Below: Interrogating "race", "ethnicity" and belonging in post-devolutionary Scotland', PhD Thesis (University of Glasgow, 2018) online at http://theses. gla.ac.uk/30906/1/2018liinpaaphd.pdf. The statement that 'fairness runs through Scotland like a vein' is taken from a Scottish National Party publication, *Your Scotland: Your Future* (2011).

12. Alasdair Macintyre, *After Virtue* (Notre Dame, 1981), 201, quoted in Sandel, *Justice*, 221.

13. Tony Judt with Timothy Snyder, *Thinking the Twentieth Century* (London, 2013), 268.

14. Kearton, 'Imagining the Mongrel Nation', 23–50.

15. Marilynne Robinson, *When I Was A Child I Read Books* (London, 2012), 56.

16. Trevor Burnard, *Mastery, Tyranny, and Desire: Thomas Thistlewood and His Slaves in the Anglo-Jamaican World* (North Carolina, 2004).

17. Mary Fulbrook, *Reckonings: Legacies of Nazi Persecution and the Quest for Justice* (Oxford, 2018).

18. Thomas Staunton St Clair, *A residence in the West Indies and America*, 2 vols (London, 1834), i, 189–90, 203.

19. Michael Morris, 'Multidirectional Memory, Many-Headed Hydra and Glasgow', in Katie Donington, Ryan Hanley and Jessica Moody (eds), *Britain's History and Memory of Transatlantic Slavery* (Liverpool, 2016).

20. *Glasgow Herald*, 1 June 1883.

21. Iain Whyte, *Scotland and the Abolition of Black Slavery, 1756–1838* (Edinburgh, 2006), 112–17, 145.

22. *Guiana Chronicle* and *Guiana Times*, 16 July 1841, both quoted in *Parliamentary Papers, Correspondence relative to the Slave Trade* (1841), 804.

23. William Echikson, *Holocaust Remembrance Project: How European Countries Treat Their Wartime Past* (Institute for Jewish Policy Research, 2019) online at https://archive.jpr.org.uk/object-eur216.

24. Michael Morris posting on Dundee Centre for Scottish Culture Blog, https://dundeescottishculture.org/history/confronting-the-legacy-of-slavery-in-scotland.

25. Linda Colley, 'Britain's identity: Scotland was never a colony',

interview for *The Economist* (8 January 2014). This misconception was, however, being encouraged by a rhetoric which equated Scotland with former colonies, as for example: 'An independent Scotland would be following over 50 nations that were once ruled from Westminster, like: United States, Ireland, Canada, Australia, South Africa, India, Pakistan, New Zealand, Barbados, Singapore.' The SNP, *Choice – An historic opportunity for our nation* (Perth, 2012), no longer available online but quoted in Liinpää, 'Nationalism from Above and Below', 170.

26. Christopher Whatley, 'The Dark Side of the Enlightenment: Sorting our Serfdom', in *Eighteenth Century Scotland: New Perspectives* (West Linton, 1999); Michael Morris, *Scotland and the Caribbean, c. 1740–1833: Atlantic Archipelagos* (London, 2015), 85.

27. Morris, 'Scottish Culture Blog'.

28. Hilary Beckles, 'A "riotous and unruly lot": Irish Indentured Servants and Freemen in the English West Indies, 1644–1713', in *William and Mary Quarterly*, 3:47 (1990), 511.

29. Donald Akenson, *If the Irish Ran the World: Montserrat, 1630–1730* (Montreal, 1997), 49.

30. Cailean Maclean and James Hunter, *Skye: The Island* (Edinburgh, 1996), Chapter 5 quoting James Hall, *Travels in Scotland*, Vol. 2 (London, 1807), 549, which is, in fact, a reference to the condition of landless *scallags*.

31. James Hunter, *Scottish Exodus: Travels Among a Worldwide Clan* (Edinburgh, 2005).

32. Maclean and Hunter, *Skye: The Island*.

33. Sharon Macdonald, 'A People's Story: Heritage, Identity and Authenticity', in Chris Rojek and John Urry (eds), *Touring Cultures: Transformations of Travel and Theory* (London, 1997), 155–76, 279; Sharon Macdonald, *Memorylands: Heritage and Identity in Europe Today* (Abingdon, 2013).

34. Sorley Maclean, 'The Poetry of the Clearances', *Transactions of the Gaelic Society of Inverness*, 38 (1939), 297, reprinted in William Gillies (ed.), *Ris a' Bhruthaich: The Criticism and Prose Writings of Sorley MacLean* (Stornoway, 1985); Murray Pittock, *Scottish Nationality* (Basingstoke, 2001), 91.

35. ODNB, 'MacLeod, Norman, of Dunvegan (1705–1772)' online at https://doi-org.nls.idm.oclc.org/10.1093/ref:odnb/64086.

36. Richard B. Sheridan, *Doctors and slaves: a medical and demographic history of slavery in the British West Indies, 1680–1834* (Cambridge, 1985); ODNB, 'Chisholm, Colin (1754/5–1825)' online at https://doi-org.nls.idm.oclc.org/10.1093/ref:odnb/5322; David Alston, 'Dr Colin Chisholm' online at https://www.spanglefish.com/slavesandhighlanders/index.asp?pageid=164925.

37. Susanne Schwartz, 'Scottish Surgeons in the Liverpool Slave Trade in the Late Eighteenth and Early Nineteenth Centuries', in Thomas M. Devine (ed.) *Recovering Scotland's Slavery Past: The Caribbean Connection* (Edinburgh, 2015), 145–65.
38. Neil MacGregor, 'Britain forgets its past. Germany confronts it', *Guardian*, 17 April 2016.
39. Anthony Tibbles, *Liverpool and the Slave Trade* (Liverpool, 2018), 2–3.

Afterword

1. Statistics from TNA CO 946 Papers of British Guiana Sugar Industry Commission (Venn Commission, 1948 to 1949): Institution of Civil Engineers online at https://www.ice.org.uk/what-is-civil-engineering/what-do-civil-engineers-do/caledonian-canal.
2. George Eliot, *Middlemarch* (1872, ed. D. Carroll 2008, Oxford), 182.
3. Jan Carew, *Potaro Dreams: My Youth in Guyana* (Hertford, 2014), 12; and *Ghosts in Our Blood: with Malcolm X in Africa, England, and the Caribbean* (Chicago, 1994), 49–50, 62, 138–46.

Index